Krino 1986-1996

AN ANTHOLOGY OF MODERN IRISH WRITING

Gerald Dawe and Jonathan Williams
Editors

Gill & Macmillan

Gill & Macmillan Ltd
Goldenbridge
Dublin 8
with associated companies throughout the world

© Preface Gerald Dawe and Aodán Mac Póilin 1996
© Selection Gerald Dawe and Jonathan Williams 1996
Copyright in the selected writings is the property of the individual authors.
0 7171 2457 6 (hardback)
0 7171 2508 4 (paperback)

Index compiled by Denis O'Brien
Print origination by Peanntrónaic Teoranta
Printed by ColourBooks Ltd, Dublin

A catalogue record is available for this book from the
British Library.

5 4 3 2 1

CONTENTS

Preface

Krino, to pick out for oneself, to choose.
That's what the word means.

Ezra Pound

I

Krino was first published in the spring of 1986. It was simply flagged as a 'new magazine devoted to contemporary literature produced, in the main, by Irish writers'. This anthology represents a selection taken from the past eighteen issues of *Krino*. To convey the range of writing included in the magazine's ten years was not easy. As it turned out, both myself, as founder-editor, and Jonathan Williams, as associate editor, drew up lists which were checked against each other. With the consultation of the Irish-language editor, Aodán Mac Póilin, Eve Patten, who was involved in several issues, and Eveleen Coyle of Gill & Macmillan, we struck a consensus which makes up the present volume.

The first issue of *Krino* was designed by John Behan to page-specifications created by Liam Miller and printed in Galway, the magazine's base until 1991. Having established in 1980 and edited for its first five years 'Writing in the West', the literary supplement published by *The Connacht Tribune*, I thought that a new magazine, devoted to Irish writing in the English and Irish languages, could provide an important outlet for publishing both well-known and emerging talent.

With the support of the Arts Council, Ireland and (somewhat later) the Northern Ireland Arts Council, the review quickly established itself as an important literary and critical voice. The reception in Ireland and Britain was very favourable and the volume of unsolicited work which started to arrive was staggering.

Krino has engaged with many of the cultural issues of the past decade and more in relation to Ireland as a whole, inter-relationships between the islands of Britain and Ireland, continental Europe, and further afield. If there has been one unstated theme in much of what appeared in *Krino*, it was a questioning, critical reading of the present and an unwillingness to recycle literary stereotypes in new jargon.

The conviction that the most radical thing a writer can offer is a fully achieved literary art has only been strengthened throughout the years of my editing *Krino*. A few further points are worth mentioning in this regard.

Krino registered the extraordinarily rapid change which the past ten years have seen in the reception of Irish writing abroad, particularly in Britain. From the early nineteen eighties writing from Ireland — prose and plays, less so poetry — took off. Hardly a week seems to go by these days without a collection of stories or a novel coming from a leading London publisher, with the attendant, and increasingly more predictable, media attention.

By ironic comparison, what could not be foreseen was that seemingly most intractable of the problems which afflict 'little magazines' — distribution. The lifeblood of a literary culture depends upon its own inner resources and, regrettably, an independent review sinks or swims on the thinnest of commercial lines. But this is not the place to recount that story.

Finally, it was, and is, my belief that literature is its own country; the biographical angles from which various different writers come have an interest all their own. Thus the *Krino* interviews concentrated upon artistic issue and not the banal self-promotional sound-bite of so much that makes up the present-day coverage of writing.

I am most grateful to all the people who helped keep *Krino* on the road. Many friends gave of their time, and often money, during the early days, and their support, practical and otherwise, made the venture possible. In particular I would like to thank the Arts Council, Ireland and the Northern Ireland Arts Council for their support and financial assistance.

Gerald Dawe

II

There are currently two languages and two literary traditions in Ireland, engaged in a complex, problematic and occasionally enriching relationship. I use the word 'currently' because one of these languages and its literary tradition could disappear as an effective cultural force before the youngest among us are drawing our pensions.

Yes, Gaelic doomsters are boring. Yes, Irish was a drag a school. Yes, the Irish-language movement was implicated for decades in a sterile orthodoxy, compounded of nationalist essentialism and Catholic triumphalism. Yes, Irish literature in English does reflect the greater reality of the greater number of Irish people. Yes, there is enough current hypocrisy around the language issue to make a cat sick. Yes, we have all met and suffered from the tunnel-visionaries, impossibilists, messiahs, inadequates and straight loonies who infest the language movement.

But the issue is more important than its apologists. Unfortunately, the implications for Ireland's cultural vitality of a shift from a bilingual society to a monolingual one are unlikely to be noticed until the language has safely popped its clogs. At that point, Ireland's cultural pundits, currently collaborating silently in the death of the language, will be loud in their lamentations and profound in their deliberations. In the meantime, the debate expresses itself most loudly in the gentle but insistent sound of dragging feet, as cultural power-brokers react with embarrassment, distaste or guilt-induced tokenism to the excesses of the Gaeilgeoir lobby. To give them their due, language activists have found to their cost that nothing succeeds but excess.

But it is still extraordinary that, in Ireland, culturally aware anglophones of mature years appear not to have outgrown their adolescent resentments to engage with the broader issues involved. Except among those who are already committed to the language, the level of debate on the implications for this country of the death of a language, the still unwritten literature in that language, and the enormous potential for creative interaction between the two linguistic traditions, remains remarkably low.

Put bluntly, the loss of Irish will involve the total loss of a language and the unknown potential literature in that language not only from Ireland, but from the world. In terms of cultural ecology, we are looking at a calamity — the linguistic and literary equivalent of a small to medium-sized tropical rain-forest.

It will also have implications for English literature in Ireland. The exchange between the various literary traditions in the two languages, at its best, involves a genuinely creative symbiosis. This interchange is as unpredictable as it is useful — who could have foreseen the present flowering of modern poetry in Irish? No Irish-language writer rejects literature in English, beyond the intermittent perversity of personal creative strategies. Historically, Yeats's public stand for artistic freedom in the early years created the space in which writers in Irish could find their authentic voice, and some, particularly poets, have found a wider audience through the translation cottage industry. It can equally be argued that Anglo-Irish literature has been the net beneficiary: literature in Irish provides home-grown exotica, ready-made raw material, and coat-hangers for fantasy and satire. Our literati can translate the modern poetry for their dry periods, and the older literature to show they are authentically in touch with their roots. Even our critics can use their compulsory school Irish to beat overfunded Americans at their own game.

Irish may survive as a tokenistic, emblematic marker, but, as Synge noted, all art is a collaboration between the artist and the community. Literature is a collaboration between a writer and a linguistic community. While writers in

English do not have to worry about the survival of the language they are writing in, writers in Irish, whatever evasions they may use to avoid becoming language activists, write always in the context of a linguistic community which may not survive. They know that, without a community underpinning it, new literature in Irish will be, at best, no more that an opportunity for linguistically gifted show-offs producing increasingly arcane matter for a diminishing band of cognoscenti and a small army of translators. While being aware of the larger culture, they engage with their modern hang-ups for a small but passionately committed audience, and within a literary tradition which is both one of the oldest and one of the most fragile in Europe. This double or triple vision is qualitatively different to that of English-language writers in Ireland, and provides a useful alternative perspective for those writing within the tradition of a local variant of an over-large and over-confident international world literature. If literary bulk-buying on a compare-and-contrast basis is the only consideration, English is the only option. If the development and maintenance of a creative environment for generations to come is anywhere on the agenda, the loss of Irish would be a disaster.

The language movement, in that it is a movement to maintain a linguistic community, is a necessary evil. For all its faults, and its occasional folly, it is a movement to maintain a civilization. It must not be reduced to a symbol of nationality, or ghostly essence of national identity, or a Bord Fáilte tourist attraction, or atavistic root-hoking, even if that is what some of its adherents propose. At its best, it is a complex, multifaceted, self-contradictory, incomplete, evolving, non-prescriptive, wounded, but still living, civilization. In the long term the continuing tension and exchange between that civilization and English-language civilization in Ireland are as important as any other cultural issue facing the country. The debate should not be confined to the committed, and is far too important for the present benevolent neglect.

Aodán Mac Póilin

John McGahern

THE CREAMERY MANAGER

The books and files had been taken out but no one yet had stopped him from entering his office. Tired of sitting alone listening to the rain beat on the iron, he came out on the platform where he could look down on the long queue of tractors towing in the steel tanks, the wipers making furious, relentless arcs across the windscreens as they waited. He knew all the men sitting behind the glass of the cabs by name. That he had made his first business when he came to manage the creamery years before. Often on a wet summer's day, when there could be no rush at hay, many of them would pull in below the platform to sit and talk. The rough, childish faces would look up in a glow of pleasure at the recognition when he shouted out their names. Some would flash their lights.

Today no one looked up, but he could see them observing him in their mirrors after they had passed. They probably already knew more precisely than he what awaited him. Even with that knowledge he would have preferred if they looked up. All his life he had the weakness of wanting to please and give pleasure.

When the angelus bell rang from Cootehall, he began to think that they might have put off coming for him for another day, but soon after the last stroke he heard heavy boots crossing the cement. A low knock came on the door. Guard Casey was in the doorway but there was no sign of the sergeant. Guard Guider was the other guard.

'You know why we're here, Jim,' Guard Casey said.

'I know, Ned.' Quickly the guard read out the statement of arrest.

'You'll come with us, then?'

'Sure I'll come.'

'I'm sorry to have to do this but they're the rules.' He brought out a pair of bright handcuffs with a small green ribbon on the linking bar. Guider quickly handcuffed him to Casey and withdrew the key. The bar with the green ribbon kept the wrists apart but the hands and elbows touched. This caused them to walk stiffly and hesitantly and in step. The cement had been hosed clean but the people who worked for him were out of sight. The electric hum of the separators drowned their footsteps as they crossed to the squad car.

In the barracks the sergeant was waiting for him with a peace commissioner, a teacher from the other end of the parish, and they began committal proceedings at once. The sergeant was grim-faced and inscrutable.

'I'm sorry for that Sunday in Clones,' the creamery manager blurted out in nervousness. 'I only meant it as a day out together.'

The grimness of the sergeant's face did not relent; it was as if he had never spoken. He was asked if he had a solicitor. He had none. Did he want to be represented? Did he need to be? he responded. It was not necessary at this stage, he was told. In that case, they could begin. Anything he said, he was warned, could be used against him. He would say nothing. Though it directly concerned him, it seemed to be hardly about him at all, and it did not take long. Tonight he'd spend in the barracks. The cell was already prepared for him. Tomorrow he'd be transferred to Mountjoy to await his trial. The proceedings for the present were at an end. There was a mild air of relief. He felt like a railway carriage that had been pushed by hand down rails into some siding. It suited him well enough. He had never been assertive and he had no hope of being acquitted.

Less than a month before, he had bought stand tickets for the Ulster Final and had taken the sergeant and Guard Casey to Clones. He already knew then that the end couldn't be far off. It must have been cowardice and an old need to ingratiate. Now it was the only part of the whole business that made him really cringe.

They set off in the sergeant's small Ford. Guard Casey sat with the sergeant in the front. They were both big men, Casey running to flesh, but the sergeant retained some of an athlete's spareness of feature. He had played three or four times for Cavan and had been on the fringe of the team for a few seasons several years before.

'You were a terrible man to go and buy those stand tickets, Jim,' Casey had said for the fifth time as the car travelled over the dusty white roads.

'What's terrible about it? Aren't we all Ulster men even if we are stranded in the west? It's a day out, a day out of all our lives. And the sergeant here even played for Cavan.'

'Once or twice. Once or twice. Trial runs. You could hardly call it *played*. I just wasn't good enough.'

'You were more than good enough by all accounts. There was a clique.'

'You're blaming the selectors now. The selectors had a job to do. They couldn't pick everybody.'

'More than me has said they were a clique. They had their favourites. You weren't called "the boiler" for nothing.'

A car parked round a corner forced the sergeant to swerve out into the road. Nothing was coming.

'You'd think the car was specially parked there to deliver an accident.'

'They're all driving around in cars,' Casey said, 'but the mentality is still of the jennet and cart.'

It had been a sort of suffering to keep the talk going, but silence was even worse. There were many small flowers in the grass margins of the roadside.

They took their seats in the stand halfway through the minor game. There was one grace: though he came from close to Clones, there wasn't a single person he knew sitting in any of the nearby seats. The minor game ended. Once the seniors came on the field he started at the sudden power and speed with which the ball was driven about. The game was never close. Cavan drew gradually ahead to win easily. Such was the air of unreality he felt, of three men watching themselves watch a game, that he was glad to buy oranges from a seller moving between the seats, to hand the fruit around, to peel the skin away, to taste the bitter juice. Only once did he start and stir uncomfortably, when Guard Casey remarked about the powerful Cavan fullback who was roughing up the Tyrone forwards: 'The Gunner is taking no prisoners today.'

He was not to be so lucky on leaving the game. In the packed streets of the town a voice called out, 'Is it not Jimmy McCarron?' And at once the whole street seemed to know him. They stood in his path, put arms around him, drew him to the bars. 'An Ulster Final, look at the evening we'll have, and it's only starting.'

'Another time, Mick. Another time, Joe. Great to see you but we have to get back.' He had pushed desperately on, not introducing his two companions.

'You seem to be the most popular man in town,' the sergeant said sarcastically once they were clear.

'I'm from round here.'

'It's better to be popular anyhow than buried away out of sight,' Casey came to his defence.

'Up to a point. Up to a point,' the sergeant said. 'Everything has its point.'

They stopped for tea at the Lawn Hotel in Belturbet. By slipping out to the reception desk while they were eating he managed to pay for the meal. Except for the sergeant's petrol he had paid for the entire day. This was brought up as they parted outside the barracks in the early evening.

'It was a great day. We'll have to make an annual day of the Ulster Final. But next year will be our day. Next year you'll not be allowed spend a penny,' the sergeant said, but still he could see their satisfaction that the whole outing had cost them nothing.

Now that the committal proceedings were at an end an air of uncertainty crept into the dayroom. Did they feel compromised by the day? He did not look at their faces. The door on the river had to be unlocked in order to allow the peace commissioner to leave and was again locked after he left. He caught the sergeant and Guard Casey looking at one another.

'You better show him his place,' the sergeant said.

To the right of the door on the river was a big, heavy red door. It was not locked. Casey opened it slowly to show him his cell for the night.

'It's not great, Jimmy, but it's as good as we could get it.'

The cement floor was still damp from being washed. Above the cement was a mattress on a low platform of boards. There was a pillow and several heavy grey blankets on the mattress. High in the wall a narrow window was cut, a single steel bar in its centre.

'It's fine. It couldn't be better.'

'If you want anything at all, just bang or shout, Jim,' and the heavy door was closed and locked. He heard bolts being drawn.

Casually he felt the pillow, the coarse blankets, moved the mattress, and with his palm tested the solidity of the wooden platform; its boards were of white deal and they too had been freshly scrubbed. There was an old oil can beside a steel bucket in the corner. Carefully he moved it under the window, and by climbing on the can and gripping the iron bar he could see out on either side: a sort of lawn, a circular flowerbed, netting-wire, a bole of the sycamore tree, sallies, a strip of river. He tried to get down as silently as possible, but as soon as he took his weight off the oil can it rattled.

'Are you all right there, Jimmy?' Casey was at once asking anxiously from the other side of the door.

'I'm fine. I was just surveying the surroundings. Soon I'll lie down for a while.'

He heard Casey hesitate for a moment, but then his feet sounded on the hollow boards of the dayroom, going towards the table and chairs. As much as to reassure Casey as from any need, he covered the mattress with one of the grey blankets and lay down, loosening his collar and tie. The bed was hard but not uncomfortable. He lay there, sometimes thinking, more of the time with his mind as blank as the white ceiling, and occasionally he drifted in and out of sleep.

There were things he was grateful for . . . that his parents were dead . . . that he did not have to face his mother's uncomprehending distress. He felt little guilt. The shareholders would write him off as a loss against other profits. The old creamery would not cry out with the hurt. People he had always been afraid of hurting, and even when he disliked them he felt that he partly understood them, could put himself in their place, and that was almost the end of dislike. Sure, he had seen evil and around it a stupid, heartless laughing that echoed darkness; and yet, and yet he had wanted to love. He felt that more than ever now, even seeing where he was, to what he had come.

That other darkness, all that surrounded life, used to trouble him once, but he had long given up making anything out of it, like a poor talent, and he no longer cared. Coming into the world, he was sure now, was not unlike getting into this poor cell. There was constant daylight above his head, split by the single bar, and beyond the sycamore leaves a radio aerial disappeared into a high branch. He could make jokes about it, but to make jokes alone was madness. He'd need a crowd for that, a blazing fire, rounds of drinks, and the whole long night awaiting.

There was another fact that struck him now like coldness. In the long juggling act he'd engaged in for years that eventually got him to this cell — four years before only the sudden windfall of a legacy had lifted him clear — whenever he was known to be flush all loans he's out would flow back as soon as he called; but when he was seen to be in desperate need, nothing worthwhile was given back. It was not a pretty picture, but in this cell he was too far out to care much about it now.

He'd had escapes too, enough of them to want no more. The first had been the roman collar, to hand the pain and the joy of his own life into the keeping of an idea, and to will the idea true. It had been a near thing, especially because his mother had the vocation for him as well; but the pull of sex had been too strong, a dream of one girl in a silken dress among gardens disguising healthy animality. All his life he had moved among disguises, was moving among them still. He had even escaped marriage. The girl he'd loved, with the black head of hair thrown back and the sideways laugh, had been too wise to marry him: no framework could have withstood that second passion for immolation. There was the woman he didn't love that he was resigned to marry when she told him she was pregnant. The weekend she discovered she wasn't they'd gone to the Metropole and danced and drank the whole night away, he celebrating his escape out to where there were lungfuls of air, she celebrating that they were now free to choose to marry and have many children: 'It will be no Protestant family.' 'It will be no family at all.' Among so many disguises there was no lack of ironies.

The monies he had given out, the sums that were given back, the larger sums that would never be returned, the rounds of drinks he'd paid for, the names he'd called out, the glow of recognition, his own name shouted to the sky, the day Moon Dancer had won at the Phoenix Park, other days and horses that had lost — all dwindling down to the small, ingratiating act of taking the sergeant and Guard Casey to the Ulster Final.

The bolts were being drawn. Casey was standing in the doorway. 'There's something for you to eat, Jimmy.' He hadn't realized how dark the cell had been until he came out into the dayroom, and he had to shade his eyes against the light. He thought he'd be eating at the dayroom table, but he was brought up a long hallway to the sergeant's living quarters. At the end of the hallway was a huge kitchen, and one place was set on a big table in its centre. The sergeant wasn't there but his wife was and several children. No one spoke. In the big sideboard mirror he could see most of the room and Casey standing directly behind him with his arms folded. A lovely, strong girl of fourteen or fifteen placed a plate of sausages, black pudding, bacon and a small piece of liver between his knife and fork and poured him a steaming mug of tea. There was brown bread on the table, sugar, milk, salt, pepper. At first no one spoke and his knife and fork were loud on the plate as the children watched him covertly but with intense curiosity. Then Casey began to tease the children about their day in school.

'Thanks,' he said after he'd signed a docket at the end of the meal which stated that he had been provided with food.

'For nothing at all,' the sergeant's wife answered quietly, but it was little above a whisper, and he had to fight back a wave of gratitude. With Casey he went back down the long hallway to the dayroom. He was moving across the hollow boards to the cell door when Casey stopped him.

'There's no need to go in there yet, Jimmy. You can sit here for a while in front of the fire.'

They sat on the yellow chairs in front of the fire. Casey spent a long time arranging turf around the blazing centre of the fire with tongs. There were heavy ledgers on the table at their back. A row of baton cases and the gleaming handcuffs with the green ribbons hung from hooks on the wall. A stripped, narrow bed stood along the wall of the cell, its head beneath the phone on the wall. Only the cell wall stood between Casey's bed and his own plain boards.

'When do you think they'll come?' he asked when the Guard seemed to have arranged the sods of turf to his satisfaction.

'They'll come sometime in the morning. Do you know I feel badly about all this? It's a pity it had to happen at all,' Casey said out of a long silence.

'It's done now anyhow.'

'Do you know what I think? There were too many spongers around. They took advantage. It's them that should by rights be in your place.'

'I don't know . . . I don't think so . . . It was me that allowed it . . . even abetted it.'

'You don't mind me asking this? How did it start? Don't answer if you don't want.'

'As far as I know it began in small things. "He that contemneth small things . . ." '

'Shall fall little by little into grievous error,' Casey finished the quotation in a low, meditative voice as he started to arrange the fire again. 'No. I wouldn't go as far as that. That's too hard. You'd think it was God Almighty we were offending. What's an old creamery anyhow? It'll still go on taking in milk, turning out butter. No. Only in law is it anything at all.'

'There were a few times I thought I might get out of it,' he said slowly. 'But the fact is that I didn't. I don't think people can change. They like to imagine they can, that is all.'

'Maybe they can if they try hard enough — or they have to,' Casey said without much confidence.

'Then it's nearly always too late,' he said. 'The one thing I feel really badly about is taking the sergeant and yourself to the Ulster Final those few Sundays back. That was dragging the pair of you into the business. That wasn't right.'

'The sergeant takes that personally. In my opinion he's wrong. What was personal about it? You gave us a great day out, a day out of all our lives,' Casey said. 'And everything was normal then.'

That was the trouble, everything was not normal then, he was about to say, but decided not to speak. Everything was normal now. He had been afraid of his own fear and was spreading the taint everywhere. Now that what he had feared most had happened he was no longer afraid. His own life seemed to be happening as satisfactorily as if he were free again among people.

Do you think people can change, Ned? he felt like asking Casey. Do you think people can change or are they given a set star at birth that they have to follow. What part does luck play in the whole shemozzle?

Casey had taken to arranging the fire again and would plainly welcome any conversation, but he found that he did not want to continue. He felt that he knew already as much as he'd ever come to know about these matters. Discussing them further could only be a form of idleness or Clones in some other light. He liked the guard, but he did not want to draw any closer.

Soon he'd have to ask him for leave to go back to his cell.

Eve Patten

WOMEN AND FICTION 1985-1990

I t often seems as though women's fiction in Ireland is undergoing an
abnormally long adolescence. In 1985 Nuala O'Faolain addressed the
subject with some frank admissions. 'There is no feminist Irish writer using
the imaginative modes, or rather more the philosophic range that would make
her indispensable.' Why, she enquired, is women's writing so bad? In an Irish
tradition which has consistently ventured beyond the boundaries of realism,
women have lost out in clinging to realist and autobiographical modes. Their
need to express a sense of identity has been met, but at the expense of artistic
merit: 'the real hunger of women readers for confessional women writers has
made quality unimportant' (in *Irish Women: Image and Achievement*, ed. Ní
Chuilleanáin, 1985).

It is typical of O'Faolain to touch such a nerve. In poetry, McGuckian and
Ní Dhomhnaill have broken the ice of form and image and language. Prose
writers, other than an occasional fling with a murky surrealism if a repressed
female character becomes psychotic, tend to stick not only to telling the story
straight, but telling very much the same story: that of the individual struggling
against domestic and economic hardship, against sexual repression, against
patriarchy. Ireland's constitution remains unchanged; so then does the urgent
need experienced by women to put it all down in writing. To find a voice, as
black and Caribbean women writers have done. To establish, politically and
sexually, an identity. 'There is too much suffering, violence and anger still to
be written over and through. Our troubles are too raw to be denied and there
is so much personal history still to be recorded' (Ailbhe Smyth, *Wildish Things*,
1989). Confessional realism is a necessity, not a choice.

Five years on, however, O'Faolain's comments still have a ring of
uncomfortable truth. There is a sense of stasis in Irish women's fiction, and
responsibility for it is shared by market forces *and* political ego. I make this
statement well aware that numerous women have produced stories and novels
completely independently of any overt political axis and without prioritizing in
their pages some pursuit of the female self, but aware also that in a survey of
the Irish shelves in a Dublin bookseller's, the following blurbs leap off recent
covers with a depressing familiarity: '. . . the pain of a woman coming to terms
with her own sexuality while at the same time making sense of the bigotry and

death of her Northern Ireland adolescence', or 'experiences of adolescent turmoil and uncertainty, of friendships and relationships, of love, sex and motherhood . . .', or '. . . a lonely woman's voyage of self-discovery', or '[her] stories concern individuals, usually women, who are seeking personal identity and happiness in a society which is confused, changing, and often downright hostile.' And these are books which, quite simply, I no longer want to read.

If feminism in Ireland lags behind its Continental counterpart by as much as sixty years, as one commentator has suggested, how long will its powerful grip on writing continue to define, and to fossilize, the fiction which frequently becomes its vehicle? How long can the need for a distinctive 'woman's voice' hold priority over stylistic and imaginative development? These are not new questions, but they continue to be crucial ones, and the relationship which operates between political reality and fictional narrative cries out to be interrogated.

In 1985, Virago Press published Frances Molloy's *No Mate for the Magpie*, a pseudo-autobiographical novel which worked its way through various standard themes — the poor Irish upbringing, the convent, internment and the civil rights movement, Dublin corruption and condoms and a litany of eradicable social ills from which the heroine finally takes Stephen Dedalus-style flight. Molloy followed the realist conventions of the genre but did so ironically. She offered major breakthroughs, in her use of dialect, her satire, and her development of a perspective which never stopped short of implicating *women* — the Reverend Mother or the Dublin landlady — within and frequently responsible for the malaise of Irish society. Women, such as the heroine's factory co-workers, are seen to be capable of power and victimization:

Wan of them said, are you a catholic or a protestant? A said nothin'. Another of them took a cigarette lighter outa her pocket an' lit it an' hel the flame close te me face an' said, we only allow catholics to sit at this table. A got up an' walked away an' set at another table. They all follied me an' kept askin was a catholic or protestant? In the en' a said a was a christian. Then the wan way the cigarette lighter said, we know, you're a prod. A said, if ye know so much, why de ye waste yer breath askin' questions? She lit the lighter again te the side of me hair.

The strength of Molloy's writing derives from its self-consciousness: it is a 'social' novel, but in its tendency towards caricature and its parodying of Joyce's *Portrait* it also recognizes its own ficticiousness. Molloy thus offered a challenge to domestic realism — an opportunity for departure which was not taken up by subsequent writers from the North.

Mary Beckett's first collection of short stories sought the 'identity' criterion even in its title, *A Belfast Woman*. Her recent and well-received novel, *Give Them Stones* (Bloomsbury, 1987) consolidates even further upon the 'reality' of its central character, to the extent that it was praised in reviews as 'a tale of ordinary life in Belfast that's believable and memorable, as if you'd met the narrator and knew her'. The narrative exudes historical authenticity, and likewise the credible identity of the protagonist is paramount. Her progression from war-torn childhood through marriage and family to the 'troubles' is encased in contemporary events, and the style is never more than one step away from reportage:

> I had heard on the radio about Catholics beginning to look for civil rights — houses that they were entitled to and local government votes for all . . . . I heard about the Protestant girl in County Tyrone being given a house for herself instead of a Catholic family, but it was no great wonder. It was the way of life we were used to.

The documenting of recent history (or one side of it at least) which permeates *Give Them Stones* is a legitimate fictional mode, but additionally it legitimizes the experience of 'struggling woman' which is its core. The identity of the stoical female becomes archetypal via the experience of the individual, and Beckett's book becomes a sociological tract in a way in which Molloy's does not.

This is not, in itself, a problem, but it points to a dangerous trend; namely, that a fictional autobiography of a woman, intertwined with the political history by which it is determined, is somehow sacrosanct and above imaginative distortion. Beckett's novel confers authenticity on one kind of woman's experience in the north of Ireland, to the exclusion, we must assume, of other experiences — 'the Rhonda Paisley kind', to borrow a recent phrase from Edna Longley — which inevitably lack the necessary street-credibility. One distinct identity is promoted as valid. Others are not.

South of the border, as might be expected, the emphasis shifts from political discrimination and territorial violence to sexual discrimination and oppression — not, fortunately, without humour — but with a similar tendency towards the 'representative' plight of the individual woman. Rose, the protagonist of Evelyn Conlon's *Stars in the Daytime* (Attic, 1989), plods the well-trodden route from inspired childhood to disillusioned maturity, via the traumas of menstruation, bad marriage and motherhood, with the enduring cul-de-sac of the Irish woman's lot frequently interrupting the happy scenes in dogmatic asides:

Their grandmothers before them had been starved in the famine, their mothers before them had been thankful for minor improvements after that, all the time they had become pregnant and become pregnant without choice. Choice and babies couldn't go together. Choice and marriage were natural enemies. No-one had ever heard about an orgasm, not even men and they had them . . . . But Rose wouldn't know that for some years to come.

Rose does indeed have some troubled waters ahead, and at the risk of spoiling the story I will mention that after many trials she finds freedom, identity and independence. Likewise the eponymous heroine of Catherine Brophy's *The Liberation of Margaret McCabe* (Wolfhound, 1985/Fontana, 1987). Margaret also has a tough time, having made the mistake of allying herself rather late in the day to a Man Who Does Not Listen. There are a few skirmishes along the route to the union — the brush-up with the church, the repressive parents, the lesbian friend — and a witty little adventure trying to buy Durex from a Sligo chemist ('Oh, Mr Maher deals with the veterinary things') — all of which serve to consolidate Margaret's quest for self in relation to her sexual conditioning and relationships:

> Then a thought came to me. Maybe I'm a lesbian and I never knew it. A latent lesbian, isn't that what they call it? Perhaps that's why I'm still a virgin. Maybe it is nothing to do with my upbringing and the fear of getting pregnant and the lack of suitable men. Well, there is only way to find out. I'll just have to find a man I like and go to bed with him.

Margaret eventually comes to a point of self-assertion and packs her suitcase, leaving her partner with his male chauvinist piggery and the reader with the sinking feeling that Irish sexual repression has now become comic fodder for an English readership. But the point remains that it is the individual's personal/sexual development which provides the moral heart of the book. As with Mary Beckett's novel, the resort to confessional realism and the 'biographical' structure are troubling in that they establish and confirm a representative norm — the struggling woman — contextualized by the particular social and political conditions by which she is determined, and exclusive of anything else.

In 1980 critic Rosaline Coward, in an article recently revised under the title 'The True Story of How I Became My Own Person', suggested the production of novels which foreground 'women's experience to be ironically self-limiting. Women-centred novels represent a fictionalized version of our culture's contemporary obsession with autobiography and with intimate revelations.' Fiction which concentrates on releasing aspects of the woman's lot serves, perversely, to contain it, by 'reproducing the ideology where (albeit disillusioned) women are viewed in relation to their sexual history. Women again defined through their sexuality are the sex to be interrogated and understood. "Becoming my own person or woman" is in the grain of the sexual; it is how a woman deals with her sexuality.'

Is the female protagonist, then, no more than a sociological projection of her sexual and political environment? If Coward's insights are accepted, in conjunction with the above arguments which located in Mary Beckett's novel and its reception the promotion of a 'definitive' womanhood, it can be seen that the search for 'identity' operates as a fictional straitjacket. Confessional realism offers women a voice, but frequently that voice seems to add up to no more than a metaphorical 'bodice-ripping'. Eavan Boland rejoices that women have at last 'moved from being the subjects and objects of Irish poems to being the authors of them' (*LIP*, 1989). In prose fiction, also, that transition has been achieved, but in the process of becoming 'author'; in the need to 'authorize', women writers have reinforced their sex as 'object', constructed according to ideological requirements. Is there any real gain in exchanging a masculine-made myth for the 'struggling woman' — stoical, angry, victimized — of a new iconography?

While there are still political and economic axes to grind, the *tendenzroman* will remain a phenomenon in women's prose in Ireland. In recent years, the conscious juxtaposition of social needs with literary product has been perpetuated by the existence of a separatist publishing movement — a factor which Katie Donovan challenged in her 1988 pamphlet *Irish Women Writers*: 'Self-proclaimed feminist publishing houses today place their protegées in a custom-made pool where they hover, maternal lifeguards, ready to buoy up their charges. Such books will be bought by other feminists — a converted audience — and will not reach the audience amongst whom they might affect the attitude-changes they desire.' Donovan's claim is premature, I think, given the successful range of activities carried out by women's presses in the UK, and her point obscures the fact that it is not a separatist press *per se* which is a limitation, but rather the constraints imposed or the perceptions encouraged by editorial policy.

It is difficult to judge the extent to which a discreet (or perhaps not so discreet) processes of editing — the creation of a standard, the elicitation of a formula, the suppression of difference — goes on behind the scenes. As always, it is the anthology which reveals the hidden agenda. Rosaline Coward observes that in women's fiction 'it has become a standing joke that we are to expect the first period, first kiss, first (tumbled) intercourse, first (disastrous)

marriage, lesbian affair and usually lonely resolution.' But this biographical
Bildungsroman structure may be significantly reinforced in an editorial
arrangement. In *The Female Line*, the anthology published by the Northern
Ireland Women's Right Movement in 1985, editor Ruth Hooley's
introduction innocently sanctions a conventional linear progression:

> Finding the predominant themes to relate to family and personal life, the
> pieces are arranged in an informal sequence which moves through
> childhood, adolescence, growing awareness, personal relationships at various
> stages, marriage, motherhood, disillusionment, independence and old age.

Hooley's arrangement is logical, I agree, but predictable. Not half as
predictable, however, as the editorial introduction provided by Ailbhe Smyth
to the anthology *Wildish Things* (Attic, 1989): 'I looked for writing which,
without conforming to a pre-determined agenda, was unashamedly rooted in
the experiences and politics of women's lives diversely lived'. The feminist
intention is acknowledged, and the political memorandum provided is blatant:
'Divorce no, abortion no, a job no, no-go, no. Head down, feet together,
mouth shut and whatever you say, say nothing.' As a result, looking for
feminist capital in the anthology is, as Nabokov would say, like looking for
images of large mammals in *Moby-Dick*. From the prose contributions alone, it
becomes apparent — transparent — that women have 'diversely lived' more or
less exactly the same experience. Of twelve pieces, two-thirds are primarily
concerned with a woman in a bad relationship with a man; often it is marriage,
usually it is in some state of breakdown. Of this figure, in half again, the male
element resorts to physical violence.

Given this quota (and momentarily forgiving this kind of callous
calculation), it is strange that Smyth needed to provide any comment, let alone
over nine pages of soap-box polemicism. Though included in the book, Sara
Berkeley objected to the editorial's 'his-boot-on-my-back' stance (*Stet*, spring
1990), and certainly much of it reads like a parody of 1970s' evangelical feminist
piety. It does, of course, deconstruct itself within seconds, largely as a result of
Smyth's curious (subversive?) decision to use the rhetoric both of the pulpit ('As
women we have been denied the right to speak by the patriarchs who have
appropriated unto themselves exclusive rights of public utterance') and of the
kind of military address given to would-be marines in Vietnam movies:

> Living and creating on the margin makes you sharp, tough, sometimes
> wise, but it's still a hard, lonely, dangerous place to be. There is little room
> for compassion and none for the comfort of illusion. Purism, ideological or
> aesthetic, has no place in the world of those who struggle simply to survive.

Once again the stress on what is 'real' comes to the fore. These contributors have written in blood. More troubling than this, however, is the built-in time-warp; the fact that Ailbhe Smyth writes as though the whole project has initiated some pioneering spark in a vacuum. The reductive emphasis on 'new' and 'raw' and 'real' attempts to carve out a virgin canon — purist and ideological — as though Jennifer Johnston and Mary Lavin and Edna O'Brien had never existed, and as though Binchy's blockbuster romances and Dillon's historical sagas were not rattling with other numerous skeletons in the cupboard.

The overwhelming need is to homogenize, and to validate, and thus the military overtones are apt. Deserters from the cause are rapped sharply over the knuckles in Evelyn Conlon's article on 'Women and Irish Literary Culture' (*Graph*, autumn 1988). Books by women, as Conlon rightly observes, are frequently reviewed in groups rather than on individual merit, but, she continues:

> Other times the book by a women which is not dangerous — slightly provocative but not dangerous — the book where a woman is playing at being a baby male; or the book where she is being daring about the acts that lead to orgasm, but again never dangerous, that is the book which gets most approval.

The terminology employed here is suspect, to say the least: Conlon, like Smyth, chooses the word 'dangerous' to suggest that fiction — as thinly veiled truth — can mount a challenge to a repressive political system, but there is no attempt to query the 'repressive' content of her own literary policy. Don't fictionalize your orgasms, girls. (But it's all right to write about not having them.) Meanwhile the ranks close on an assimilable and biologically determined 'identity' as the ideal basis for creativity, and critique descends into bathos:

> The lack of mothers writing has surely been one of the most dangerous silences in the world. If our consciences had been informed by a little more of that individual but *collective* view that comes firstly when the baby's head comes out and secondly on the morning after as you perceive the cot and a little less of macho-man goose-stepping to the sound of a war-drum, the world would be in a healthier state. [my italics]

Circumscription, the need to establish a corporate and facilitating identity, the suppression of difference, are features of any political body seeking voice. That literature is infected by this is an inevitability, but it is not one which must be left unquestioned because of the sensitivity of the subject matter concerned. Again, women poets in Ireland have met the challenge. Eavan Boland suggests that 'the gradual emphasis on the appropriate subject matter and the correct feelings has become as constricting and corrupt within Feminism as within Romanticism' (*Krino*, spring 1986). This is a dangerous position for the female writer; it 'promises to ease her technical problems with the solvent of polemic', but it fails to penetrate the true depths of the artist's imagination.

In addition to its dubious role in producing a collective identity, the effectiveness of confessional realism as part of a political lobby is questionable. The reality of (most) women's subjection is evident. Men smash bottles. Wives get hit. Relationships fail. Women are lonely and victimized and denied. Channelling this material into fiction may be considered an important aspect of a consciousness-raising incentive, but only up to a finite point at which it becomes reflexive and counter-productive. In a recent *New Statesman* interview the German novelist Christa Wolf, while admitting a place for subjectivity in writing, stated that 'I often find women's emotional outbursts frightful . . . those unadulterated, unreflective and unformed explosions of speech.' If this is how a certain kind of creativity is being perceived, then it is without doubt time to move on, bearing in mind the words of Carlos Fuentes: 'There are so many novels in Latin America about the plight of the Bolivian tin-miner that do not change the life of the tin-miner and do not add anything to literature.'

The historical attachment of female writers to confessional and autobiographical realism is a tradition, but not a necessity. Economic and sexual constraints on women still exist in Ireland, but meeting them head-on with literary restraints and conventions is essentially negative. In Ireland, there is a vested interest in producing women's writing which is stylistically transparent, reactionary, anti-intellectual, anti-philosophical, and realist to the point at which it slips easily into journalism or polemic. But the flip-side to this coin is a sad lack of encouragement for experiment in the kind of futurist fantasy or magic realism with which Angela Carter and Margaret Atwood have created rigorously critical social visions, or for any exploration, subversive or otherwise, of the romance and crime-thriller genres which continue to provide the staple commercial diet of women writers and readers.

The past five years have not been without promise. Many independent women writers have proved themselves in control of their content, rather than controlled by it. I would include Deirdre Madden's elegant *Birds of the Innocent Wood* (Faber, 1988) and Clare Boylan's riotously inventive and acerbic *Black Baby* (Hamish Hamilton, 1988). Frances Molloy's *No Mate for the Magpie* will, finally, remain a classic. But confessional realism has made its point. I hope that the next five years will witness the end of the distracting 'identity' quest, the exhaustion of the tendentious, biographical, monotone trend which dominated women's fiction in the ninteen eighties, and perhaps even the emergence, for Nuala O'Faolain, of recognizably 'indispensable' women's writing.

Jennifer Johnston

LAURA

From a work-in-progress

I stand by the window and watch the woman running.
Is it Laura?
I wonder that as I watch her flickering like blown leaves through the trees.
I am Laura.
Sometimes I run so fast that my legs buckle under me, ungainly, painful.
This woman runs with dignity.
I have to say that for her.
Sometimes it is dark and I find it difficult to see her as she passes below the trees, running.
Her clothes are dark colours, the colours of weariness.
It is hard to tell from where or what she is running.
Perhaps, I think to myself, she is running towards something.
I think that on good days.
On the other days I know she is running away.
That makes me laugh.
What's the point in that?
I ask the question aloud and the words spring back at me from the four walls of the room.
She always wears dark clothes.
Sometime, someone must have said to her . . . black suits you, Laura.
No, I am Laura.
I must remember that, but I seem to remember a voice saying that . . . black suits you, Laura. Maurice perhaps.
I do wear black from time to time.
I also like bright colours, pinks and yellows, flame colours and purple. I have always thought purple to be a noble colour, a colour worn by courageous people, by people longing to be noticed.
The running woman never wears purple.
If she were to wear brighter colours it would be easier for me to see her; perhaps it would be of some comfort to me, if I could see her more easily.
Perhaps not.

Perhaps, perhaps not.

I don't suppose it matters much.

'Laura!'

When she passes into the darkness of my unseeing I still stare out through the panes at the fields and beyond these fields there are more fields; sand-coloured fields at this time of the year, with patches of grass growing up through the dead winter stubble. Beyond the fields are the hills and then the sea.

Sand, stones, waves, shells, birds, pebbles, ripples, waves breathing waves heaving, rolling, spume, spray, pools, wrack, weed, glitter tiny torn claws, glitter . . . diamonds, pearls . . .

All this I see through these panes of glass with my X-ray eyes.

'Laura!'

I love lists.

I spend a lot of time making lists; lists of the things I love; lists also of the things I hate. Sometimes I write them down on coloured pieces of paper, but most times I say them inside my head.

Incantations.

'What is this?'

Maurice said it to me once, handing me a yellow rag of paper. I took it from him and held it between my thumb and forefinger.

Tree, branch, twig, bark, leaf, sap, bud, flower, wood, ivy, trunk, smooth trunk, knots, coruscations, axe, cracking, splitting, raging death.

'It's a list.'

'A list of what, for God's sake?'

'A tree list.'

He snatched the paper from me and threw it into the fire.

It was consumed.

'Sometimes I think you're mad.'

I watched the flames consume my tree.

Mad.

'What is mad?' I asked Maurice.

It must have been winter. The fire consumed my tree.

'The way you carry on.'

That's right, it was winter. It was coming up to Christmas time; ivy trailed from the pictures and red ribbons held holly branches above the doors and windows: another tree, or was it the same one, I can't remember, laced with silver and glitter, stood in the corner of the room.

Maurice's family always come here for Christmas, old Mrs Quinlan, that's Maurice's mother, Doreen and her husband Bill, Seán and his wife Madge and

Brigid who isn't married. They bring their children and we all have a very good time.

It's nice to have the house full.

All the rooms full of sound and movement.

This is my house.

It's strange really, for three generations it has descended through the female line.

I inherited it from my mother and she inherited it from hers.

I did try to have a daughter.

I believe in continuity; the handing down of secrets; I want someone else to hear the whispers, the breaths from the past, as I have always done; someone else to be stirred by the tremors of memory.

Some of the tremors of memory.

I did try.

All those seeds were rejected.

'Laura!'

'Yes.'

'Are you ready?'

'Ready?'

'That's what I said.'

'I have my black gloves and my black bag and a scarf to cover my head.'

'You're ready then.'

'I suppose so.'

Maurice comes across the room towards me and takes my arm.

He bends and kisses my cheek. He smells faintly of Eau Sauvage. I bought him that for his birthday.

I continue to look out through the window. The leaves are acid green, uncurling; the wind lifts them and makes them tremble.

'Don't worry,' he says, in his kind voice. 'Everything will be all right.'

'Spring', I say, for no reason.

He takes my elbow and walks me towards the door.

Such scenes stay with me.

The feel of Maurice's fingers pressing through my coat and my black woolly will stay with me for ever . . . not of course in the front region of my mind, but I will be able to recall when I need to, the feel of those fingers, the faint smell of Eau Sauvage, the sound of his steps, confident on the polished parquet as we cross the hall.

Such scenes reverberate and conjure up other similar scenes in the past: my father's soft white fingers imprinting their marks on my arms, as he shook me and my feet clattered on the floor and a dog barked at nothing outside in the sunshine. The sound of my own voice screaming tears suddenly at the soft corners of my brain.

Some memories are so joyful that you could bask forever in them; others you long to shove back, away, back into the darkness out of which they have sprung uninvited.

I try to exorcise that picture of my father and myself in the hall, as we drive in the car towards the church, by calling into my mind happier, more tranquil recollections.

Maurice talks, but I don't hear him; his words patter around me like a summer shower.

The streets around the church are lined with cars; the car park is full; women with nothing better to do stand round the church gate waiting to catch a glimpse of something or someone out of the ordinary, a Cabinet Minister, a Bishop, the diminished red-rimmed eyes of the bereaved.

I will not be crying.

It is a huge, ornate church.

We walk past the waiting hearse and the watching women.

Maurice holds my arm tight. Maybe he thinks that I might escape, fly away like a balloon escaping from the fingers of a child; I don't suppose he does, he is not the sort of person who indulges in such flights of fancy.

My mother never put her foot inside this church.

I wonder to myself, if, had she lived, she would have been with us now, walking beside us with immaculate dignity.

'A vulgarity', she once said to me. 'Built on the backs and out of the pockets of people who could hardly afford to feed their children. They paid more towards it than your father ever did, or any of his like, because they felt what they gave, those few pounds impinged on their lives.'

My father always hoped that she would turn.

I remember her laughing at him once.

'Divil a bit of it,' she said. 'Haven't you got my house and my land and my beautiful body? What makes you think you should have my soul as well?'

He hated such irony.

She was the only person in my world who didn't jump when he snapped his fingers; who didn't succumb to his enormous charm: perhaps I shouldn't say that, perhaps she had indeed succumbed and thereafter had to protect herself from it.

The organ is playing; something sonorous but unrecognizable.

Our feet clatter on the tiles as we walk to the front of the church.

The tall windows, alive for a moment as the sun comes from behind the clouds, glow into patterned life, heads, hands, haloes, wings make patterns rich with jewel colours, and cast their muted patterns on the tiles and on the congregation: the brightness passes and the church is dark again.

Of course we have to sit in the front.

I do not look to left or right as I follow the little fellow who leads us along the aisle. I don't recognize him, dressed in sober black: black tie, sombre face . . . a professional I would think. His walk is that of a professional, unobtrusive, almost obsequious, adapted to my pace, consoling in its smoothness.

He turns and inclines his head slightly towards me as we reach the front pew.

I move past him and kneel down.

Our Father which art in Heaven . . .

The only prayer that trips from my tongue.

Hallowed by Thy name.

A poem.

Thy Kingdom come,

Thy will be done on earth.

Maurice settles to his knees beside me, dipping his head down towards his hands.

As it is in heaven.

Give us this day our daily bread.

My mother's voice is still in my ears.

and forgive us our trespasses

as we forgive them that . . .

'Laura!'

Trespass against us.

I can't.

I cannot forgive.

Forget it God.

Forget I ever said those words.

No point in speaking lies to You.

'Laura.'

His elbow nudges me.

'Laura.'

I get up from my knees, angry with myself, that even at such a moment I am unable to overcome hatred.

'What?'

'The President's ADC has just arrived.'

Across the aisle from us he is being settled into the front pew with all due obsequiousness.

My flowers are the only ones on the coffin. I notice this. Maurice must have organized that gesture.

Spring flowers, yellow and green and white; a laugh almost escapes through my lips. Green, white and yellow.

I never intended such a statement, but I'm sure that the President's ADC had made a pleasant mental note; that the Ministers and other dignitaries present will commend me in their hearts.

Along the aisle the flowers are heaped, wreaths, crosses, cushions, sprays; a great sheaf of waxlike lilies lies to the right of the coffin.

There is a rustling at the back of the church; the sound of the organ swells.

We stand up.

The ceremony will take its course.

Oration, peroration, homily, sermon, valediction, obsequy, exequy, benediction.

If I got up and spoke the words I have inside me, what a shock they'd get.

The hole that they dig for you won't be deep enough, dear father.

How petty to think such a thought in the middle of all this formality.

They dance: the words like music punctuate the movements.

With each amen the tempo changes.

They dance to the glory of whatever God may be: advance retreat turn, bow.

Candles dance, men dance, boys dance.

They dance in celebration of my father's life.

I feel cold. It is as if a wind has penetrated the stone walls and is numbing my body, or perhaps the cold is spreading out from me, maybe it will embrace the whole church, the whole town, the whole island; I will infect this race with my hatred.

Maurice is praying, his hands placed together like some saint in an Italian painting. His eyes are closed. His face still is tinted with brown from his two weeks in January spent in Mustique.

'Will you come, dote?'

'How can I come? Isn't my father dying?'

'There's nothing you can do about that.'

'I must be here.'

'Suit yourself.'

He'd have got a rare shock if I'd said yes; if I'd rushed up to town and bought the bikinis, the silk shirts, the Ambre Solaire.

That would not have been playing the game at all.

Requiem aeternam dona eis, Domine, et lux perpetua luceat eis.

'Forgive me,' he had said.

I had to stoop towards him to catch the words, so frail was his voice.

He pulled at the sheet that seemed to weigh him down into the bed with his anguished fingers.

'Laura?'

Exaudi orationem meam, ad te omnis caro veniet.

'Will you?'

The nurse read a magazine in a chair by the window.

That was last week, only last week.

The spring sun, weak and all as it was, hurt his eyes and we had to keep the blinds half drawn.

I put my hand on his: for a moment his fingers were still, then as I lifted my hand, the restless tearing and plucking started again.

'Child?'

Agnus Dei, qui tollis peccata mundi

'Yes.'

dona eis requiem.

I whispered yes.

'That's all now,' said the nurse, putting her book on the table and getting up from the basket chair that crackled as she moved and her starched apron crackled as she came over to the bed.

Agnus Dei, qui tollis peccata mundi . . .

'He's tired. Aren't you tired, pet?'

She took his restless hand in hers and bent smiling towards him.

dona eis requiem sempiternam.

'Laura.'

The procession is forming. The dancers moving slowly from the altar down into the aisle; without much grace the coffin is lifted onto the shoulders of my four cousins, my father's nephews, their feet clatter as they move slowly down the church. Maurice takes my arm and together we walk between the watching people as we had done on the day of our wedding.

Geraldine Mulgrew

LOS OLVIDADOS

Teacher's coat trails through the door.
Maud slides out of the desk, primps down the aisle to where
Winnie sits plaiting marla into ponies' tails. Prancing she pipes . . .
— Icky ocky kippers, Winnie's got no knickers . . .
A weasel rises in Winnie's look.
Humped on the high stool, Regina croups . . .
— I see London, I see France, Winnie's got no underpants . . .

Winnie balls her patchwork skirt. Down her gullet the wind plays musical bottles.
Maud floats to the front of the class . . .
— Mine's is strawberry . . .
She flips up her skirt, twirls, sleepy fish-eyes.
— Polka dot. Regina's dots flash purple, milky warts on her knee.
Tucking her skirt inside the strawberries — ya could eat mine — Maud glides into a strut, fingers clicking time. On the window-sill a star-fish catches her eye, she claps it on her head, basks — star of the sea.
She circles the teacher's table.
Winnie's eyes coming through her glib.
A goose-feather flies to Maud, she pops it into her pants, blows a pink bubble . . .
— Yum, yum bubble-gum. Stick it up a ghost's bum . . .
By the blackboard, Regina, her back to the class, counts the polka dots. She gathers them in threes. At twenty-seven she turns.
— Maud . . .
From behind the frog-screen Maud pops out in a yellow hula-hoop. It bobs on her hips, she jigs . . .
— You put your backside in, you put your backside out. In, out, in out. Shake it all about . . .
Chafing a lump of chewing gum on the underside of the desk, Winnie watches.
Maud hops out of the hoop, flings it at Regina, misses. On the second go she lassoes her, pulls her into the jig. Maud's rowdy voice, Regina's crackly under it. In the centre of the floor they shimmy . . .

— Oh okey kokey kokey . . . Knees bent, arms stretched . . .
. . . Ra, ra, ra . . .

Winnie slips from the desk, hugs the wall as she makes her way to the top of the room. On the teacher's table a row of ink bottles taking her in. She puts her hand to one, shakes it up — a green colour settles. Checks another. Rosydendron.

Skipping-hoop-skip, the two chant . . .

— Tinker, tailor, soldier, sailor . . .

Bottle in each hand, Winnie ducks under the teacher's table. Holding herself like a secret. Dollops from one on to her leg, dollops from the other. Has a lick. Sooty taste. She claps the mess on her wind-burned cheeks.

A curse out of Maud, tussling with the vacuum cleaner. Regina flicks it on. Maud raises the hose to her head, lets her long honey hair into the suck. It plays her scalp. Ooooh, she feels . . . she feels . . . she feels like pissing.

Bilberry. Winnie's pelt comes up bilberry. Her eyes scout the space. Teacher's black shawl draped across the chair. She whips it over her shoulders. Big as a tent.

Smiles to herself, steps up on the chair.

Regina sees the bat-shape rise, falls still. And onto the table, Winnie high-steps, the black shawl wheels.

Maud clutches the hose. Rump up, tripping in the shawl, Winnie jiggles *The Siege of Ennis*. Her feet pound the table. The roll-book falls to the floor.

The shawl takes wing, balloons over their heads. Winnie swells as she purrs, centres them. She hikes her skirt, splays her thighs, shoots them an eyeful, how's that. Apple-shape mark on her inside thigh. Way up there. Maud is struck on the mouth, a famished cry crosses her breath. Regina bows her head, fingers her warts like worry beads. Draft from an open window lifts the shawl off the map of Asia.

Winnie shrugs. Maud shoots out a hand, locks Winnie's in a badger's grip, tugs her onto the floor. They ram Regina, pin her between them. Someone gives her an ass's bite. Winnie raises her arm, rattles the polka dots. They fix the panties on Regina's head.

From the corridor the bell bursts on their ree-raw.

Maud stirs, gathers herself, tosses the satchel to Regina. Panties on again.

— Come on snagglepuss.

Maud. Regina. Winnie follows. Single file they join the traffic.

Behind them the vacuum cleaner pulses summer comin' an' wait for the honey-flow.

Ivy Bannister

THE DANCING CHICKEN OF CHINATOWN

There is a case full of chicken embryos in jars of formaldehyde somewhere in Dublin's Natural History Museum. I remember them from years ago, the time that my mother brought me to the museum. It was a couple of weeks after my Dad had beetled off to England without a return ticket in his back pocket, and I was still in short pants. The outing was intended to distract me — and maybe my mother — from fretting about my departed Dad. It wasn't meant to awaken my conscience, but as it happened, those pickled chicks are the only thing about that museum that stayed in my head.

The jars were arranged in a tidy row, and I can picture the victims inside quite clearly, from the tiniest reddish blob, the size of a pinhead, to the translucent feathery birdshape, arrested forever on the brink of birth. To think of it! Generations of Irish kids, noses pressed against the glass, inspecting that row of tiny corpses. I never wanted any child of mine to endure such official ghoulishness.

Not that I'll ever have a kid now. But I've been thinking about those chicks of late, even though I'm living a world away, right in the guts of New York City. There's a lively arcade over on Mott Street in nearby Chinatown, a place jumping with video games, one-armed bandits and pinball machines. However, the star attraction is no glitzy machine. No. It's a wee simple cage that looks empty at first glance, only there's a velvet banner above it that reads, THE DANCING CHICKEN OF CHINATOWN. Feed 75 cents into the slot, a partition clatters up, and the bird herself appears, a little brown hen, stretching her wings. With a blast of rock music, the floor of the cage begins to spin, and the hen bops and flaps and jumps like a feathery disco queen. This dancing bird is a hit with Chinese and tourists alike, and shrieks of laughter melt in with the rock music, the racket of the machines and the roaring traffic outside.

Marlene. Even her name is beautiful. Silver and mysterious, a name too exotic for Ireland.

A bit of dirty cardboard has been tied onto the cage like an afterthought. Chinese characters are scrawled in black ink, with what I take to be the English translation underneath: 'This bird is happy in her work.' Well, who am I to say that she isn't? She has an appreciative audience, at least. Her feathers are sleek. Her eyes have a bright glitter to them, which I would describe as defiant, if I knew anything about chickens, which I don't. Besides, isn't the little hen better off dancing on cue, than she would be roasting in an oven, or pickled on a shelf in a museum?

Not so very long ago, defying cleaver or even imprisonment, I would have forced open the door of that bird's cage, to watch her flutter free: out from the noisy arcade and up into the night sky. But I've changed. Now I can see that life is neither black nor white, but endless shades of grey, all melting into one another, just like this incredible city. If I set that hen free, there might be nothing for her but roosting alone in a scraggy plane tree, until she starved to death. Besides, so long as she dances in her cage, that birdie is a gold mine. These are the figures as I've calculated them: 75 cents a dance, a hundred times a day, makes 75 bucks, 500 a week or 25 grand a year. And that's a wage that most of the lads back home wouldn't turn up their noses at.

Marlene. I can see her now, climbing the hill in Killiney, her full white skirt rising in the breeze. Marlene. I can hear her calling me, 'Billy boy!' As I lie on my back, I can see the leafy branches lacing over our heads like the vaulting of a cathedral.

I walk for miles in New York City, uptown and back each day, more than I ever walked in Dublin. I walk until my feet feel like lead weights, but I keep my eyes open wide, and let the whole scene soak in. Believe me, this crazy metropolis makes Dublin look clean and wholesome. Garbage cans overflow on every corner, and men and women root for sustenance among the pickings. There are so many people here, endless faces flashing past, faces that I'll never see again. It embraces me, this bustling anonymity. I am only in my twenties, and already I've ruined my life.

I've written to Marlene, dozens of letters, amusing letters. I've told her about the dancing chicken, but not about the sick feeling that watching her gives me, and not about the fact that the cage floor is wired, and that it's electrical jolts that make her dance. Instead, I've joked about setting up a similar business in Ireland. 'I know that there's no Chinatown in Dublin,' I've written, 'but I'm going to start one up. I'll plaster my eyelids down with tape and gabble like Fu Manchu. It'll make us rich, and our kids will live like gods.'

Keep it light, I tell myself, as I scribble. Make it sound like a dream, like paradise. Make her want to be with you, like that day that we went out in the boat from Dun Laoghaire pier. We sat in the back, kissing, as the boat chugged round Dalkey Island, and the wind blew Marlene's hair against my cheek. I wrapped my arm around her shoulders, curling my fingers under her breast. She sucked on my lip, whispering that she'd gone damp between her thighs.

I write to Marlene, page after page, from the dark squalid room where I sleep. As I write, I can hear the roaches scratching inside the walls. I don't tell

Marlene the truth. I don't tell her lies either, but I embroider, I invent. I pretend that it's not too late to rebuild bridges. If only she'd answer just one of my letters, I'd catch the next plane home.

What happened between us was my fault. I went over the top. I lashed out at her, as if she were the enemy. My own rage shocked me. I still don't understand it, not even now. How can you suddenly hate somebody so much, when the truth is that you love them? Why couldn't I listen, wait, hold on to what we had?

The sidewalks are cracked in this place. As I walk, the rubbish swills around my ankles. Night and day, sirens scream: fire engines, police cars, ambulances. Once, at the corner of 23rd and Lexington, I saw a body stretched out along the curb. It was covered in a white sheet, blood seeping like red wine. A beefy New York cop stood guard, champing on gum, his revolver bulging on his hip. But nobody else was paying much attention. It's not like Dublin, where crowds gather at the hint of disaster to speculate in hushed tones. The taste buds for disaster have grown jaded here.

From the time that I first laid eyes on Marlene, I pictured her with a baby. Two babies, if you want to know the truth. Twins to start out, and then some. No way was I going to be the louser that my Da was. I was going to rush home every night to my wife and kids, to look after them and love them, happily ever after. Talk about romantic. That's the kind I was, really wet behind the ears. It was inevitable that, sooner or later, reality would creep in. And when it happened, I blew it. It never even occurred to me what it must have cost her to do what she did.

As I walk, I can see her in my head. I'm lying in her bed, the duvet clean against my body. She has slipped out from my arms to dress. The sun lights her back with a pearly glow. Near the window, the table is laid for breakfast, the crusty loaf waiting on the bread board.

In the place where I sleep now, the light struggles through windows encrusted with grease and soot. I share with a transient crowd. A long apartment of airless rooms off a stinking corridor. My fellow tenants are illegals like myself: a Romanian, an Estonian Jew, but mostly Hispanics, coming and going, always looking over their shoulders for fear of deportation. They keep on the move, out to Jersey to pick fruit, down to Florida, to Chicago, Detroit and points further west. Nobody stays long. Nobody, that is, except me. At nine months, I have become the senior occupant. Unlike the others, my interest in my own fate has faded.

The letterbox is in the hallway below. The flap springs open, if you tap the lock sharply. I often wonder if a letter from Marlene has been stolen. It's a fantasy that engages my imagination, but I don't really believe in it. Nobody would bother to nick a personal letter, not even in New York. Besides, I get regular post from my mother. She writes out the football results, and snippets of political scandal. But I sift through her words in vain for reference to Marlene. Occasionally, by return, I send my mother a twenty dollar bill wrapped in a sheet of newspaper.

Miles uptown is the apartment block where I work as a doorman. It's a massive building with a marble portico, high ceilings, thick carpet everywhere. Each apartment has an entire floor to itself. I got the position, no questions asked, because my skin is the right colour, and my English is fluent. My job is to keep the undesirables out. You'd think they'd pay me in gold nuggets, but the fact is that the dancing chicken makes out better than I do. The rich don't get rich by being sentimental. In Dublin I worked with computers, but I can't fool with that here, not with only a phony social security number, I can't.

'It's a free country.' That's what they say all the time here. That, and 'Have a nice day.'

I often think of the sea, and what it looked like, those last minutes that I spent with Marlene. We were strolling in Sandymount, well out on the flats, the wet sand cool under out feet. She nuzzled her warm lips against my hand. I asked her how she'd got on, down in the country, where she'd been to see her folks. She stared out at the water, glittering in the distance, brilliant as diamonds. I looked with her; it was so pretty. It was then that she told me that she hadn't gone down to the country after all. 'I went across the water,' she said. 'To London.' I looked at her strange, cold eyes, but I still didn't understand, I was that innocent.

So she stood there, tapping herself on the belly, her head halfcocked sideways, a nervous twist to her lips. Tapping herself on the belly, until the penny finally dropped. 'I didn't want to spoil it all, Billy boy,' she said. 'We're too young. We need to grow up ourselves first.'

I looked at her beautiful mouth, and I hit her. A great belt on the face. I can still hear the sound of flesh meeting flesh, the crushing of cartilage. I can see the blood streaming from her nose, the hurt look in her eyes. But I turned my back on her and ran away. Later, when I tried to call her, again and again, she wouldn't speak to me.

New York is an old people's city. It's not like Dublin, with young mothers everywhere, pushing buggies. There are more geriatrics than babies on the streets of New York, out with their nurses and minders, in wheelchairs and walkers, their shaky old hands covered in loose skin.

Sometimes when I'm walking, I just stop, dead in the centre of the sidewalk. I close my eyes and stick out my elbows. I imagine my feet on a turntable with jolts of electricity sparking up through my soles. I hear the beat of rock music, thudding out over the sirens and grunting buses. I cackle, flap my arms and dance, and around me, the crowd parts, passing me by with a wide berth.

Angela Bourke

NESTING

Are you sure you've had enough to eat? I know what that journey's like. Those last few miles are incredible. All that emptiness. Though actually the bog's interesting when you start looking at different plants and everything — Ronan could tell you all about them. I have to warn you though, he's so tired when he gets home these days you'll be lucky if he says hello.

It's amazing that you made it. I can't get over it. Remember the way everyone promised to come and see me? Well they all had great intentions till they looked at the map. You're the first one who's sat at that table. Is it like what you expected? Actually I can't stand the house. The landlord's a bit too fond of yellow. Come outside and look, the scenery's the good part.

I always come out here in the evening. I love the way the sun hits the mountains. All the little field walls stand out so clearly — that one's like lace against the sky, isn't it? And it's so still. There's even a corncrake in one of those fields. Do you know about corncrakes? They used to be all over the country, but they've got very rare. You only find them now in places like this, the west of Scotland, a few other places. The machinery's wiping them out and people are starting to get all nostalgic about them. You know the idea in the thirties, all the crossroads dances and couples courting behind haystacks? Then the priests built dance halls so they could keep an eye on them, and it all stopped? Anyway it seems the corncrake was one bird they used always hear on summer nights. But it's the weirdest call, like something wooden. Crake, crake. It's a mating call. He's somewhere down there in the hayfield. The males come first and stake out a territory, then they start up that racket, and females come and join them. He'll go on all night now, once he's started. He even kept me awake a couple of nights last week. Of course it wasn't even dark. I love the long days really. It's after eleven now, see? And it's still daylight. Sometimes I'm just waiting for it to get dark so I can go to bed. It's ridiculous. Do you remember that poem?

In winter I get up at night
And dress by yellow candlelight.
In summer, quite the other way,
I have to go to bed by day.

Is it Robert Louis Stevenson? We learned it in primary school. It's not something you notice so much in the city, but my god you notice it here. Long days in summer, long nights in winter. I couldn't believe the winter. It wasn't daylight till nine and then it got dark again at four o'clock. I mean black dark. I felt I was getting smaller and smaller. I was crouching down under all the darkness. I still feel it a bit. I don't know if you notice — am I different from the way I used to be? It did something to me. I'd better not start though — Ronan's sick and tired of me going on about it and he'll be back soon.

We could walk down as far as the road if you like. D'you see that there? That's a scarlet pimpernel. I never knew it was the name of a flower, did you? A lot of them grow among the carrots. And that's silverweed, with the yellow flower. See the silvery backing on the leaves? It's a bit hard to see in this light. They used to eat that during the Famine. The root maybe. I'll have to dig one up sometime and see.

You still hear stories about the Famine here; there's ruins of houses all over the place. There must have been an awful lot more people living around here then. You can even see marks way up on the hillsides, really rough land where they used to have fields. I think that's why people here buy so many tins and packets. It drives Ronan crazy, but I think they remember too much about poverty.

Those are our vegetables. Carrots and leeks and beetroot and lettuce and then the spuds and cabbage and onions. That's dill down there — see the tall feathery stuff beside the elder tree? I'd no idea what it'd look like when I put the seeds in. Ronan kept laughing at me, but I was so sick of outside leaves of cabbage. Would you believe that's the only green thing we had all winter?

The one with the heads of white flowers, that's the elder. Ronan wants to make elderflower wine, but I can't work up much enthusiasm. It's supposed to be an unlucky tree. The wood's no good for anything except making whistles. They say it was used for the crucifixion and it's cursed ever since, so you're not even supposed to cut a stick from it to drive cattle.

You end up believing that sort of thing. 'Elders and nettles and corncrakes: three signs of an abandoned house', there's an Irish saying for you: *trom, traonach is neantóg*. There are nettles in there too, see? They grow wherever people pissed. Wherever they emptied their chamberpots, I suppose. They like nitrogen.

That house over there — the two chimneys in the trees — the woman in that house just had twins. But wait till I tell you — she already had fourteen kids. She's a nice woman. I talk to her sometimes when I walk over that way. I think that was part of the problem. Ronan started here last May, but I didn't come till September and then it was really wet, so I didn't get to know any of the women before the winter set in. They hardly ever go out you know. You meet only them if you go to their houses, and the men don't really talk to strange women at all.

We're unusual too, that we're not related to anyone. Mary Dick's one though. I went to see her in hospital. And she has a sister, back the other way, that talks to me as well. Can you imagine though? Sixteen kids. The big ones are all gone, of course. They're in England and Boston and places. But imagine being pregnant that many times? I suppose a lot of people were. Bach had twenty-two kids, didn't he? But were they all by the same wife? I can't remember. Mary Dick's a lovely woman. A great sense of humour, but I'd have sworn she was way over fifty till I saw her pregnant. She has hardly any teeth. It's a great name, isn't it? Mary Dick. Her father was Dick. I thought first it was her husband. That'd be just too much. And he's the most inoffensive-looking little man.

I walk down this way a lot. If you go left at the bottom you come to a pier. It's good that you're with me — if I walk on my own I get the feeling people think I'm weird. It's okay if you're a visitor, you can go anywhere you like, but if you live here it's different. Married women are supposed to have things to do. They all work really hard here. But then they all have kids. It's funny, the way people talk, I feel I'm supposed to be up in the house all the time, getting pregnant. But you'd think the way to get pregnant was staying inside by yourself all day, washing clothes and cooking.

Maybe that's the idea. Maybe you're so glad to see him at the end of the day that you jump on him when he comes in and tear the clothes off him? That's not the effect it has on me though. It must be my spoilt city upbringing — I'm not tough enough. When I was on my own all day in the beginning I just used to turn into this tight little lump of misery. Poor Ronan had a lot to put up with.

Crake crake. There he goes again. Crake crake. All the way from Africa. I can't imagine how they get here. I mean obviously they fly, but they're not like swallows. They're big. You never see them flying. As soon as they get here they flop down into the long grass and that's that. They just stay there.

Crake crake. Crake crake. I did a terrible thing the other night. I was up there on my own in the house when he started up with his craking, letting the world know he was there. I couldn't see him, of course. You hardly ever see a corncrake, but he got on my nerves, with his god-given right to be so stupid out there, saying the same thing, over and over. I don't know what got into me. I came flying out the door down the path, straight into the hayfield over the wall — I never knew I could run that fast. He was in there in the long grass, craking away, and I went crashing and flailing in through it, just to make him show himself. God knows what I did to the grass. I hope no one saw me, but in the end he flew up right in front of me. He's a little brown lump, like a young hen, a pullet. You'd never think something that apologetic-looking could make so much noise. I'm relieved he's still there though — I was afraid I'd chased him away, and Ronan'd kill me. Don't say anything to him, will you?

It just seems so stupid. What happens is the birds come from Africa and make nests in the hayfield or the cornfield or whatever, but now instead of men coming with scythes late in the summer to cut whatever it is, they either cut early for silage, or they bring in these big heavy machines, and the birds haven't a chance. The nest and the eggs get crushed to bits. You'd see egg yolk smeared all around, and baby birds dead. But the worst thing is sometimes the hen bird won't leave the nest. They cut right through her legs while she's sitting there. I've seen pictures of them. They're still alive, but their feet are chopped off.

It's just the thought of that. Imagine coming all the way from Africa and then hunkering down in a hayfield until they come to cut your feet off?

Lucille Redmond

FISH

In the tank which held the fish for passengers to eat during the journey anxious trout swam to and fro. The water moved with the ship's movement.

They could see — if fish can see beyond the water — on one side a compartment of smoking men, and one of writing women, on one side the metal-sheeted wall of the ship, on one side the dining-room with its linen damask cloths, the band's red wood instruments still strewn on the bandstand, a waiter gathering broken bread, on one side Mrs Ormsby stepping through the flights of birds in her silver-buckled slippers.

Mrs Ormsby was in an aviary as full of birdsong as a miner's dream, but she was straining to hear her husband's voice, coming through the glass-bead curtains with wisps of cigar smoke.

With one nail she tapped a bangle on her white arm. She tapped it down towards her elbow, then brought it back up to the soft lace that fell across her shoulder.

The birdsong was mixing with bad news: her husband, a man of forty-five, would not will all his money to his bride.

She knew she looked a flower in her silk-panelled cream and white gown, her glorious hair piled above her sweet face with its rosy lips.

With a decided gesture Mrs Ormsby walked through the beads into a corridor and reappeared in the correspondence room. She was not afraid of being snubbed. But two women glanced at each other as she entered.

The fish could not have seen Mrs Ormsby pick up a newspaper dated for the day the ship left Ireland. They swam from end to end of the tank, however.

If they thought, their urgent concern was with the chef and his net, with which he periodically scooped the bodies of some fishes on to a wooden slab, to eviscerate them and immediately plunge them on to an iron pan cooking over one of the roaring ranges that heated the kitchen air so that the chefs' faces teemed with sweat.

Mrs Ormsby sat and crossed her ankles, laying the newspaper on the knee of her skirt: oyster silk brocaded with a pattern of lilies, overlaid with a cream-coloured silk lace in a whimsical Irish crochet design of wild roses.

A letter stated: 'On principle I never allow any of my children to wear machine-washed linen, for their sake and that of the linen. But though I am anxious and willing to pay well for hand-done laundry, I find it impossible to get any of these starving women to undertake to wash even the simplest garments, though I hear that many starving creatures, unable to find work, surround me.'

The two watching women were murmuring together, their high-coiffed hair buckled with silver combs. Faintly, Mrs Ormsby heard an andante of birdsong, but she returned her attention to the newspaper: to the presumed loss of the steamer *Koombana*, gone down with all hands in a typhoon, to the advertisement which said: 'A Satisfied Expression marks the rider of the Record-Breaking Rudge', to the hunting-down of the anarchist Motor Bandits, to floods in north Ontario, to the police notice for a missing child. 'On Monday evening she is stated to have been seen dancing to the music of a barrel-organ outside a church in Sandymount; and she is also said to have been seen in that district on Tuesday. The child has a rosy face, deep blue eyes, and fair hair, and is rather robust for her years. When she left home she was wearing a brown velvet dress, and has a new pair of black laced boots, and her hair was tied with a blue ribbon. She is unable to speak plainly, and is extremely shy in the presence of strangers.'

Mrs Ormsby's beauty lived in movement, but its seat of residence was in her lips; a pucker turned up the corners, giving her a look of freedom.

She saw her husband pass the door, and flung the paper aside and ran to him with little steps, holding the train away from her hobble skirt.

'Dearest,' she said, and she looked up into his face. The smell of brandy came from his sweat as she drew close.

The money was bequeathed to his elder son, a man five years older than herself. He must have made his conscience easy so. It could, on the other hand, have been care for his business interests.

'Don't bother your little head with that,' he was laughing, as she brushed his waistcoat over his watch chain, where a stub of undissolved cigar ash had lodged.

'But what would I do only take care of my husband,' she said, and saw him flinch.

'My dear, it is time to dress for dinner.' He turned to go, but paused to look at the trout which swam at the wall of the correspondence room. 'That one, I think,' he said, and strode away, hands clasped behind his back. That rose-bellied trout swam upwards, flicked into a circle and dived. She swam under a bigger fish, flicking him with her dorsal fin and tail. He followed her.

Mrs Ormsby and her tall husband went down the steps and along the hall to their staterooms, where he turned and closed the door, resting one hot hand on her neck. He leaned down and kissed her. Here came his thick tongue, poking into her mouth and fishing around.

When he stepped back for a breath she went behind him and drew his jacket over his shoulders. He took out one cuff-link, then the other. Soon they were on the bed and he was thumping his hard penis deep into her, as her hairpins and combs flew out and her hair fell across the pillow. She tried not to bite her lip but to keep a smile, gagging as the penis hit her at the neck of her womb. Streams of perspiration ran down his face to drop on hers and stung the grazed skin where his cheek had rasped her. He moved his arm and his elbow tangled in her hair, giving it a wrenching pull. Her eyes watered.

'I have done you great wrong,' he cried, and she felt his penis throb as he gasped and fell on her with a moan.

The salt of his sweat covered her body. After a few moments she slid out and rose to pour water from the ewer and wash in the adjacent dressing-room.

'In the course of the night the police ascertained that Bonnot, the murderer of Chief Detective Jouin, and the perpetrator of numerous other crimes, had taken refuge in an isolated new building, used as a garage, at Choisy-le-Roi, a suburb on the Seine, a few miles out of Paris,' said the newspaper she propped against the basin.

'The garage, which was a jerry-built structure, was riddled with bullets. It belonged to a rich anarchist named Fromentin, who let it to Dubois, who is a Russian subject and a notorious anarchist. It is believed that the garage had been a regular resort of the motor bandits who for months past have terrorized Paris.'

Mr and Mrs Ormsby passed the fish-tank again as they walked towards the dining room, he holding her elbow cupped in his hand. She was dressed again in creamy white, in evening dress, as lovely as a mermaid.

She thought of her father as she had seen him one morning, standing, his face crimson. He was yawning and holding an egg in his hand, while his fob watch boiled in the long-handled pot over the fire.

The chef's net was hunting after the fish and they stopped to watch. Twice he almost caught the rose-bellied trout, but he was obstructed by two fish that flashed in front of her.

'Wouldn't you think they were doing it on purpose?' said Mrs Ormsby, and laughed.

'I'll have you again,' he told the fish, and pointed his finger.

Everyone at the captain's table was watching the chef's exciting battle with the shoals of fish swooping around the tank that covered the length of the salon, passing thirty damask-clad, crystal-covered, plump-millionaire-surrounded tables. He picked his fish, or the guest laughingly picked it for him, and then he stalked the trout from the warm water beside the kitchen to the icy end by the ship wall. There, where the fish was stunned and soporific with cold, he swept it up with one skilful nip of his net. But the little pink-bellied trout and her brown-backed companion eluded him still, and some guests started to cheer them on until the chef was red with temper.

The captain and Mr Ormsby were talking quietly about the business; the building of ships, the running of fleets, the engulfing of companies.

'Stocks are falling,' said the captain, and Mr Ormsby seriously concurred, nodding with a heavy gesture.

His wife considered him, the crease that ran beside his mouth to his jaw and the way his thumb caressed it in thought.

'Maybe it's that people are coming to the end of their harvest food,' she said, and her husband's eyes flickered up to her, then dropped again. He made no acknowledgment, but turned to the captain and said: 'We must calculate on a continued fall in our financial plans.'

'You know, they call it the hungry gap,' she tried again, 'living on beans and oats till the summer crops begin: it makes people a bit cautious.'

Her husband's eyes flicked up to her again and he turned away to the captain.

Food began to arrive, the chickens, trout hopping with freshness, turbot, a soufflé, vegetables glazed and swimming with butter.

'Excuse me,' said Mrs Ormsby, and drew back her chair.

Her husband caught her at the door. 'I feel a little fatigued, my dear,' she said. 'I think I'll just take a turn on the deck,' and he went back to his discussion with the captain. She looked at the salon of seven hundred people, the darts of the fish flying from the chef's net, and the orchestra jigging away at Chopin.

It was cold on deck, the air stung her arms under the fringed silk shawl, spindrift flying even this high, and at the side she could feel the movement of the ship.

She felt a jarring crash, tottered and recovered, and ran to the side to see the iceberg roaring leisurely along the side.

Mrs Ormsby ran in again to the dining salon, and people turned smiling to see the girl scarcely old enough to put her hair up running in her satin slippers. She sat by her husband and looked into his face, again admiring the soft lips in their bed of muscle, the firm gaze of his dark eye, his flat nails and straight fingers.

'My dear,' he murmured, and began, to the waiter's consternation, to fill a plate with food for her, making a picture of trout and glazed beans on the china.

The room jarred again and settled, and the orchestra hesitated in the syncopation of the jazztime tune. 'Good, more ice!' called a man, saluting the berg with a raised glass as it passed the door. 'Time to sleep,' said his friend, stumbling for the companionway, already in his drunkenness undoing the stud of his collar.

The crowd continued to eat and the orchestra to play while the ship's gait grew heavier on one side, like a stranger who has had a stroke as he walks in the street.

If the fish conversed, it may have been some talk about the people who watched them.

'Fish are variously coloured.'

'I have seen men whose skins are black.'

'But none are here.'

One passenger at Walter Ormsby's table left to go to sleep in his cabin. Another went on deck to watch the workingmen testing the lashings on the boats and their gantries.

Mr Ormsby said nothing to his wife. His eyes followed her movements as she brought food to her mouth and ate it. He saw a freckle on her knuckle: oval, elliptoid.

Later, as the ship's electric lights continued to burn below the sea, the fish swam away. They could not hear the roar like the sound of a football crowd which rose from the people in the water, or see the half-empty lifeboats hovering not far away with their remorseful load.

Scattering ice-shards tumbled down through the green sea, lit by the electric lights which still shone for a while.

Fog was heavy on the sea that night, and sound travelled far.

Riana O'Dwyer

NORA OR MOLLY/MAKER OR MUSE:
JAMES JOYCE AND NORA BARNACLE

Brenda Maddox, *Nora: A Biography of Nora Joyce*.
London: Hamish Hamilton, 1988
Brenda Maddox, *Nora: The Real Life of Molly Bloom*.
Boston: Houghton Mifflin Co., 1988

In many ways, Nora Joyce is a fictional character. She exists in the writings of her husband, his letters and those of others, in Stanislaus's *Diaries*, in reminiscences by friends, and now also in her biography. Indeed, the subtitle of the American edition of Brenda Maddox's *Nora: The Real Life of Molly Bloom* allows no distinction between fiction and life. The scattered material relating to Nora, which takes four closely printed pages of acknowledgments to list, is an appropriate metaphor for the shards of her existence which have been reconstructed by Brenda Maddox through what she describes as 'a work of excavation'. The volume of material is enormous, and has been explored with the purpose of creating a journalistic account of Nora Joyce, a woman in her own right. Brenda Maddox adopts at the outset the stance of reporter, illuminating 'an unexplored corner of the Joyce story'. The expected journalistic realism does not materialize, however, and what emerges is an image more reminiscent of Picasso's 'Nude descending a staircase' than of a Sunday newspaper's 'Lifestyle' article.

Nora's refracted image is distorted by a multiplicity of subtexts, since she was rarely the central focus of the documents through which she has been reconstructed, except, of course, in photographs themselves. She kept no diaries, and few of her letters have survived. Central to this book is her role as Muse, beginning with the epigraph taken from *A Portrait*: 'Her image had passed into his soul for ever . . .' The biography is divided into sections based on James Joyce's fictional women: Lily, Bertha, Molly, Anna Livia. Nora's importance is seen as a voice which Joyce transmuted creatively: 'She talked and talked. Joyce listened and listened, and put her voice into all his major female characters.' Brenda Maddox concludes her biography, as she began it, with Nora's voice: 'Joyce gave his country, and his century, the voice of female desire. It was Nora's voice.' It follows that it is also Joyce who had given us Nora. The voice is no longer Nora's, but Joyce's. She was his Muse, and survives as his creation.

The women in Joyce's fictions express a man's version of female desire. Joyce did this convincingly, but it is what he did. Not just Nora but Marthe Fleischmann, Amalia Popper, Lillian Wallace, and others contributed to Molly Bloom, fuelled by his own powerful sexual fantasies. He also gave the world the voice of male desire: the complicated combination of physical need, unfulfilled past impulses, unformed future wishes, affection and withdrawal that constitute sexuality. The interaction of Nora and Joyce as sexual and marital partners is the motor that powered these fictions.

The creative relationship of James and Nora Joyce, like their domestic arrangements, is disconcertingly conventional. For centuries the Muse or source of inspiration has been depicted as female, and the artist or godlike originator has been male. The Muse is passive, archetypal, static, a model. The artist is active, individualistic, in motion, a creator. The Muse is unable to reveal herself, but must wait for revelation through the artist. Some Muses, it is clear, are never revealed at all, just as in the past the domestic lives of women were less likely to attract the attention of historians than the public lives of men. The cliché that behind every successful man is a supportive woman is also true of this conventional Muse/Artist relationship. Creativity is more highly prized than being an inspiration, and it is also more demanding, and more rewarding for the individual. Nora's role as Muse is by implication a supportive one, played in relation to Joyce, the hero and protagonist, who initiates the action, determines the pace, and takes the decisions, as if, in his own words, 'he wanted the soul of his beloved to be entirely a slow and painful creation of his own (Joyce, writing about William Blake's wife Catherine in 1912, see *Critical Writings*, pp. 217-18). Brenda Maddox seems to suggest that he succeeded, concluding her account of Nora's aborted trip to Ireland in 1922 with the statement: 'The episode marked the end of Nora's most determined break for freedom. She surrendered to the truth: she had no existence except as Mrs James Joyce.'

In spite of all this, and indeed because of it, it is pertinent to ask: why should not this Wife's Tale be written? Why should not the real Nora be revealed to the world? I believe that she cannot now be revealed because she chose not to reveal herself. She did not weave fictions out of her life or leave any account of it in any medium, except perhaps in conversation, could that now be recaptured. Women's experience needs an independent witness, separate from the reflections of it in the privileged texts of the literary canon.

Ulysses delves deeply into the question of gender stereotypes, and confounds them, depicting Bloom as a womanly man, and Molly imagining the world controlled by women. This is, perhaps, the way in which the female Muse has expressed herself: submitting to the creative power of the artist, but also forcing him to recognize alternative experiences to his own.

Creativity is not confined to the male artist, but is also an essential component of the female muse. Female creativity however, when not expressed conventionally in music, art, painting or writing, is not yet easily recognized and applauded. We can assume that Nora Joyce experienced fulfilment from creative achievements of her own in the course of her life with Joyce and afterwards, but we do not know what those achievements were. Did she derive satisfaction from cookery, from dressing well, from rearing her children, from sex, from conversation, from friendships, from music? Women who keep journals, write letters, songs, poems, stories and plays have given expression to their creativity. In the nineteenth century, painting and sketching were acceptable pursuits for middle-class women, and the talent that developed is now recognized by high prices for their work in sales rooms. All too often, however, women's creativity was not recognized because it had no commercial value. The limitation of this biography is set by the conventional nature of the creative relationship between Nora and Joyce and the impossibility of escaping from it in the unavoidable absence of Nora herself. As Brenda Maddox admits, revealingly: 'I could have done with five minutes conversation with Nora herself'.

The dependence of this biography on Joyce is revealed also in its focus on his children. Though Giorgio was closest to his mother, and remained her companion after his father's death, he is almost as absent from this biography as he was from *Ulysses*. His affairs did not provoke extensive correspondence, nor penetrate to the centre of Joyce's fictional world. Lucia, on the other hand, by falling ill, became an obsessive concern of Joyce's, discussed endlessly in letters, and absorbing the emotional and financial resources of the entire family throughout the thirties. Though this must have affected Nora as much as it did Joyce, we do not have access to her response to the crisis, and so Lucia's illness is presented to us by Brenda Maddox as Joyce experienced it. There are three chapters on 'Madness in Progress' and Nora is peripheral to all of them. We do get a clearer focus in this biography than in Ellmann's on the women who befriended the family, on Sylvia Beach, Harriet Weaver, Maria Jolas and Carola Giedion-Welcker, but except for Kathleen Bailly they were Joyce's friends, rather than Nora's. Brenda Maddox is perceptive on the waxing and waning of these relationships, which are vital supports to the Joyces throughout the twenties and thirties. While Paul Leon, Eugene Jolas, Samuel Beckett and others assisted Joyce with his writing, the women friends helped with money, typing, train tickets, hotel reservations, finding doctors and nursing Lucia. Some of these wrote about their relationships with the Joyces. Nora, unfortunately for her biographer, did not record how she felt about them. In this respect, as in so many others, the account is refracted and incomplete. When Nora is finally left to herself, after Joyce's death, the sources dwindle to legal documents regarding his complicated estate and a couple of written accounts by visitors to her in Zurich. The reality that Nora survives as a creation of James Joyce is nowhere more evident than in the scanty tale of her life after his death.

I do not mean to suggest that Nora did not live a full, courageous, fulfilled and interesting life: on the contrary. The barest outline of her biographical data suggests that she was an outstanding woman of great gifts, who put them at the disposal of her husband as wife and Muse. The difficulty of trying to separate her biography from that of James Joyce is that it cannot be done because she did not do it herself. A biography of Nora is a biography of Joyce from a different angle — one which permits their joint lives to be considered with only passing references to the fiction, which was in many ways their joint creation. Nora was aware herself of the dividing line between fiction and life, and devoted herself to living life while her husband devoted himself to fictionalizing it. She was able to cope with the stress of this in a way that their children were not, but she did not leave us a record of how she was able to survive, or what her personal sources of strength were. Since Nora did not write her autobiography, the real story of the achievements will never be known, and she remains a private person, forever exclusive, forever tantalizing, forever protected by her role of Muse.

Susan Schreibman

THOMAS MacGREEVY: KEEPING THE FAITH

And with our contemporaries, we oughtn't to be so busy
enquiring whether they are great or not; we ought to
stick to the question: 'Are they genuine?' and leave
the question whether they are great to the only tribunal
which can decide: time. T. S. Eliot

Time has not been kind to Thomas MacGreevy's work. His poetry is routinely left out of anthologies of Irish poetry, and all but unheard of in the greater sphere of Anglo-American literature. MacGreevy might have disappeared from posterity altogether except for the fact that his name frequently appears in the indices and footnotes of biographies of people more famous than himself, including those of Samuel Beckett, James Joyce, Wallace Stevens and W. B. Yeats. And although clearly an integral part of the Joyce family life for many years, MacGreevy serves only as an addendum, even in the new biography of Nora Joyce. It is perhaps time, twenty-two years after Thomas MacGreevy's death, to look again at his work and re-evaluate it within the modernist framework in which he wrote and lived.

As early as 1922, MacGreevy wholeheartedly embraced modernism in all its many manifestations, from the creation of his own poetry to his collaboration with, and support of, some of the greatest writers of the period, including T. S. Eliot and James Joyce. MacGreevy was a tireless defender of James Joyce's genius, and many of his articles about Joyce's work were aimed at an Irish readership which was, by and large, hostile to Joyce's writing. MacGreevy met Joyce in 1924 on a visit to Paris, but it was not until 1928 when MacGreevy moved there that their personal and professional relationship deepened. Thus in 1929 when Joyce was putting together his twelve 'apostles' for his apologia for *Work in Progress, Our Exagmination round His Factification for Incamination of Work in Progress*, he turned to MacGreevy to write a defence from a Catholic point of view. At that time, MacGreevy was thirty-six and at the height of his creative powers. He was living in Paris, the assistant secretary of *Formes* (a journal of fine arts), at the centre of James Joyce's inner circle, and a regular contributor to T.S. Eliot's *The Criterion*. And it is obvious from the ease with which MacGreevy writes about *Work in Progress* that he was one of the few people who understood what Joyce was trying to achieve. Unlike many, MacGreevy saw no inconsistency whatsoever with Joyce's work and the keeping of the Catholic Faith.

Perhaps one of the reasons MacGreevy understood Joyce so well was that many of Joyce's preoccupations were so similar to his own. As early as 1929 he realized that *Work in Progress* was an attempt to create a linguistic order, not unlike that of God Given, or Universal Order. In his essay 'The Catholic Element in *Work in Progress*', MacGreevy compared St Thomas's conception of 'the splendour of order' to Joyce's literary technique, a splendour which previously 'had not been the dominating characteristic of modern English prose'. MacGreevy believed that the success of *Ulysses* marked a 'literary revolution . . . in spite of [Joyce's] difficulty of having to invent a new language as he writes' which combines a 'flawless sense of the significance of words with a power to construct on a scale scarcely equalled in English Literature since the Renaissance' (120). MacGreevy, a profoundly religious man, saw nothing obscene or sacrilegious, as many did at home, in Joyce's work. He saw Joyce's work as being essential to his time, an epic in the great tradition of epics, and thus necessitating a journey through some of the more 'unsavoury' elements of the modern world: 'Catholicism in literature has never been merely ladylike and that when a really great Catholic writer sets out to create an inferno it will be an inferno.' And just as Homer sent Ulysses through the inferno of Greek mythology, and Dante himself voyaged through the 'inferno of the medieval Christian imagination', Joyce sent 'his hero through the inferno of modern subjectivity' (123). Thus when Seán O'Faoláin, one of the chief critics of *Work in Progress*, wrote a letter to the editor of the *Irish Statesman* accusing it of being (among other things) 'one of the most interesting and pathetic literary adventures I know', MacGreevy wrote a letter back immediately defending Joyce, and then wrote the following:

For an Irish Book, 1929

A rich fig tree
The large leaves lovely to see
The fruits delicious to taste
It was manured with a dung of English literature
And a slag of Catholic theology
But these have been tried elsewhere
Here the earth was fertile

The root strong
The gardener knew how to entrap the sun
And to anticipate the listing
Of even the gentlest wind.

Although the composition and public response to *Finnegans Wake* provided the theme for MacGreevy's poem, much of its imagery is from the Gospels. MacGreevy alludes to several passages in the Gospels, particularly those dealing with the fig tree, a recurrent of fruitfulness. The unusual image of a 'dung of English literature' comes from the parable in Luke 13:6-9 in which a lord, after seeing a barren fig tree in his orchard, told his gardener to fell it. The gardener pleaded with him to let it remain one year more until he 'dig about it and dung it'. For MacGreevy, as for the Gospel writers, the fruitful tree represents the faithful, the members of Christ's church, and the test of Joyce's work is its fruitfulness: 'By their fruits you shall know them. Do men gather grapes from thorns, or figs from thistles? Even so every good tree bringeth forth good fruit' (Matthew 7:16-17). MacGreevy, however, is not content to simply borrow from the Bible. His poem creates its own parable — here the fig tree becomes Joyce's work growing out of the twin roots of English literature and Catholic theology: an argument previously advanced in the article on *Work in Progress*. It is also worthwhile to note here how fully and early on in the modernist movement MacGreevy had internalized the principles of modernist poetry. The poem employs enough poetic form, such as rhyme (tree/see), imperfect rhymes (listing/wind), and alliteration (large leaves lovely to see) to know that MacGreevy was not simply writing *vers libre*, but was a very conscious manipulator of sound and phrase.

MacGreevy also had a long working relationship, as well as a personal friendship, with T. S. Eliot. When MacGreevy moved from Dublin to London in 1925, he called on Eliot with a letter of introduction from W.B. Yeats. Eliot warmed to MacGreevy immediately, and soon MacGreevy was a regular contributor to *The Criterion*, and guest-edited at least one issue. In 1931 Chatto and Windus published two of MacGreevy's monographs on contemporary writers, one on T.S. Eliot, and the other on Richard Aldington. Both books represent early criticism (and in the case of Aldington, the only study of his work until well into the nineteen fifties) of the writers' work. MacGreevy's insightful and very often penetrating commentary should not be underestimated, especially when one considers that he put himself in the very vulnerable position of evaluating a living, and still very much changing, author's work. Some of his assumptions would be proven wrong by the passing of time, but many would hold true. And as with Joyce's work,

MacGreevy intuitively understood Eliot's method of fragmentation and allusion long before most people would even regard it as poetry. He, for example, linked Eliot's 'apparently arbitrary association of . . . a typist of present-day London with Queen Elizabeth', realizing that Eliot's personages were often 'less important than the truths they exemplify, [and that] they may be used, not independently so much as interdependently. They are bound to each other by the Thames and by what they do' (56). MacGreevy also successfully illuminated Eliot's references to the Church (not included in his notes) a good ten years before the literary establishment would. For example, MacGreevy interpreted 'The Son of Man' passage in 'The Waste Land' to be 'the broken images [of] . . . the weakened churches today, the dead tree to be dead faith, and the cricket to represent the inadequacy of mere natural companionship . . .' (42). MacGreevy fully embraced the unwritten modernist doctrine that it was the role of the artist to synthesize the fragments of modern life into art, and as he states in his monograph on Jack B. Yeats: 'with men of genius influences are things to use, not things to be used by.' MacGreevy also made a further connection between Eliot's and Joyce's genius as early as 1931 when he wrote: 'Both writers are . . . preoccupied with the death and resurrection of the spirit.'

MacGreevy, however, wrote on many other topics besides his contemporaries. The breadth and depth of his interests is impressive; his expertise ranged from art to opera, from history to literature, and his critical work, spanning a fifty-year period, always highlighted the human aspect rather than the technical. MacGreevy's humanistic approach to criticism is no more evident than in his books *Jack B. Yeats* and *Nicolas Poussin* (published in 1945 and 1960 respectively). Both books stand today as critical surveys of the artists' work, particularly *Jack B. Yeats*, which is an excellent introduction to the environment which shaped Yeats as an artist by presenting him in the context of his time. MacGreevy paints a portrait of Jack Yeats in words: Jack Yeats the humanist, the painter with the ability to depict 'the Ireland that matters' by capturing the people of Ireland with a 'passionate directness'. Like his essay about Yeats, MacGreevy's book on the great French painter Nicolas Poussin (1594-1665) is a meandering, very human view of the artist's life and work. MacGreevy does not discuss the virtuosity of one painting's colours, or the brush strokes of another, but rather sheds light on the artist's genius through reflection on the artist's life and environment. And, as with the book on Yeats, those looking for technical explication of Poussin's work will have to go elsewhere.

MacGreevy himself was aware that his monographs on painters did not neatly fit into one literary genre or another, and seemed to be anticipating a critical onslaught when he wrote in the introduction to *Poussin* that the study might 'fail to satisfy either the art historian or the man of letters, straying, as it probably does, too far away from art history for the one, and too far towards it for the other . . .' He thus hoped that if, for the academy, the book 'prove[d] to be neither fish nor flesh, that it may nevertheless pass, with the general reader . . . for a tolerable red herring.' MacGreevy's monographs, however, were much more than 'tolerable red herrings': they were (and are) interassociative and interdisciplinary portraits of the artists' life and work. He was one of a dying breed of nineteenth-century men of letters whose idea of critical analysis was to interweave, rather than to compartmentalize.

Indeed, MacGreevy's work can provide us with an intelligent and lively account of the way in which modernist literature was perceived during the time it was being written: perceived by an intellectual versed in both modern and ancient literatures as well as the plastic arts, and a member of the innermost sanctums of the new aesthetic.

II

Although a pacifist, MacGreevy was caught in the crossfire of two wars: World War I, for which he enlisted (believing the threat of Irish conscription would transpire), serving as a second lieutenant in the Royal Field Artillery for twenty-two months, and the Irish Civil War which took place around him when MacGreevy returned to study in 1919 at Trinity College, Dublin. MacGreevy records his experiences during World War I in two poems: the widely anthologized 'De Civitate Hominum', and the lesser known 'Nocturne'. 'Nocturne' is a simply stated four-line epitaph which captures the disillusionment, sense of futility and confusion in which the men of MacGreevy's generation found themselves in the muddied trenches of World War I. And try as he might to take the narrator of the poem into the dark oblivion of space, he cannot help but return to the horror being enacted on the earth: a horror captured in the last line of the poem which fuses the voices of the dying and wounded scattered over the ground with the earth itself, until the voices become part of a surreal, disembodied landscape of cries emanating from the darkness below:

I labour in a barren place,
Alone, self-conscious, frightened, blundering;
Far away, stars wheeling in space,
About my feet, earth voices whispering.

Although MacGreevy did not fight in either the Rising or the Civil War, no one could live in Dublin during those years without being a participant. He witnessed the destruction of Dublin at first hand while a student at Trinity College, and the image of bombed shells of buildings, the grief he witnessed, and the loss of thousands of lives, haunts his verse. The impetus to much of MacGreevy's poetry came from a specific scene that he witnessed or some event that he himself experienced. His poem 'The Six Who Were Hanged' combines both these experiences in recounting the hanging on 14 March 1921 of six Republican prisoners. Over 20,000 people came to witness the executions, which were held at six, seven and eight p.m. Dorothy MacArdle, in her book *The Irish Republic*, relates that 'March 14th was a day of public mourning in Dublin, all business was suspended until 11 a.m. Before dawn crowds began to assemble outside Mountjoy Jail; sacred pictures and candles were set up in the streets and around these about twenty thousand people stood, praying and singing hymns' (424). For MacGreevy, a recent graduate of Trinity College, and living in Dublin for the first time since 1913, the situation in Ireland was almost a personal affront. Irish soldiers in the British Army had been told that one of the reasons for World War I was to guarantee the sovereignty of small nations. Yet, nearly three years after the end of the war, Ireland was still 'paying dearly' for its right to self-determination.

MacGreevy, always aware of 'visuality' in his writing, evokes the flag of Ireland in the first lines by interweaving green, white and gold (rather than orange) into the imagery of the poem. The poem, with its recurring religious motif, is a meditation on the scenes he witnessed that morning, punctuated by the responses of the crowd ('Hail Mary' and 'Pray for us') as the Rosary and the Litany of the Blessed Virgin are recited over and over again.

The Six Who Were Hanged

The sky turns limpid green.
The stars go silver white.
They must be stirring in their cells now —

Unspeaking likely!
Waiting for an attack
With death uncertain
One said little

For these there is no uncertainty.

The sun will come soon,
All gold.

'Tis you shall have the golden throne —

It will come ere its time.
It will not be time,
Oh, it will not be time,
Not for silver and gold,
Not with green,
Till they all have dropped home,
Till gaol bells have clanged,
Till all six have been hanged.

And after?
Will it be time?

There are two to be hanged at six o'clock,
Two others at seven,
And the others,
The epilogue two,
At eight.
The sun will have risen
And two will be hanging
In green, white and gold,
In a premature Easter.

The white-faced stars are silent,
Silent the pale sky;
Up on his iron car
The small conqueror's robot
Sits quiet.
But *Hail Mary! Hail Mary!*
They say it and say it,
These hundreds of lamenting women and girls
Holding Crucified Christs.

Daughters of Jerusalem . . .

Perhaps women have Easters.

There are very few men.
Why am I here?

At the hour of our death
At this hour of youth's death,
Hail Mary! Hail Mary!
Now young bodies swing up
Then
Young souls
Slip after the stars.
Hail Mary! Hail Mary!

Alas! I am not their Saint John —

Tired of sorrow,
My sorrow, their sorrow, all sorrow,
I go from the hanged,
From the women,
I go from the hanging;
Scarcely moved by the thought of the two to be hanged,
I go from the epilogue.

Morning Star, Pray for us!

What, these seven hundred years,
Has Ireland had to do
With the morning star?

And still, I too say,
Pray for us . . .

Mountjoy, March 1921

MacGreevy, surrounded by women, and confronted with their overpowering grief and anger, retreats, both physically and spiritually: clearly disoriented by the experience, he does not stay to watch the last two prisoners being hanged. He retreats emotionally, distancing himself from the plot being enacted by losing himself in biblical references. And MacGreevy's concluding lines are only one of several references scattered throughout the poetry of his inability to reconcile Ireland's fate at the hands of the British with his unquestioning religious devotion. Although he concedes, if only briefly, that God may have forsaken Ireland, he allows his doubt to surface for a moment, and concludes with an affirmation of faith bordering on defeat.

Although many of MacGreevy's poems centre on Ireland, or Irish themes, one should not make the mistake of thinking him an insular poet. Some of his best poems reflect universal themes, and speak to a much wider audience. One poem in this category is 'Winter', a singularly elegant statement on grief. It is dedicated to Richard Aldington, a close friend of MacGreevy throughout the late nineteen twenties and early thirties. At first reading, one might think that the poem commemorates the death of a common friend of MacGreevy and Aldington'. But since both men served in the war, perhaps a wider reading might be considered: a reading which encompasses the feelings of those who served in the war and their disillusionment afterwards. And as he used the Gospels as a source for his poem 'For an Irish Book, 1929', MacGreevy turned to Gaelic mythology for 'Winter', evoking those legends in which swans are used as a medium of communication between the supernatural and natural worlds:

> The swans on the leaden coloured water
> Look like hostile ghosts
> Of kings
> Who resent our presence.
>
> Are they not right?
> How should we
> Whose hearts are with the dead
> Come here
> And not die?

During the nineteen twenties and early thirties, when most of the work discussed in this article was written, MacGreevy saw himself as the 'roving poor scholar of Irish tradition', and his writing has always reflected that outlook. MacGreevy did not write many poems which were published, thirty-seven in all. He was, however, among Ireland's first modernists, and a catalyst to a younger generation of Irish poets who went to Paris in the late nineteen twenties and early thirties, including Samuel Beckett, Brian Coffey and Denis Devlin. He was very much a modernist and internationalist, and in the nineteen forties his poetry appealed to the Harvard-bound Wallace Stevens, who read universality into MacGreevy's verse. MacGreevy is also, perhaps, one of Ireland's most overlooked nationalist poets. 'The Six Who Were Hanged' is just one among many poems (such as 'Crón Tráth Na nDéithe' and 'Homage to Hieronymus Bosch') chronicling Irish events which took place during the nineteen twenties. While much of the anger and irony of MacGreevy's poetry on Ireland may be evident, his highly coded messages against British aggression towards the Irish begs re-examination. Much of this verse is couched in such surrealistic imagery, or so heavily dependent on allusion, as to be unintelligible without some commentary. His work remains today not simply as the testament of an Irishman 'eager to be at the heart of this time', as Wallace Stevens saw it, but of an artist who was able to record the cultural politics that shaped Ireland during the first half of the twentieth century. Understanding why he failed both in achieving the recognition that he well deserves, and in his dream of bringing modernism to Ireland in the nineteen thirties, is best left for another time.

Thomas Kilroy

ANGELA FALLING FROM GRACE

Extract from a work in progress

Ahand came round the bathroom door, tossed in her clothes, toilet bag, withdrew. She looked at the heap of clothes with nostalgia. Mechanically, she began to dress. She picked out a lipstick and put two bright spots on her white cheeks. Then crudely drew an outsize cherub mouth where she believed her mouth to be. With a ho and a hum she sketched two great black arcs over her eyes with eyebrow pencil. Looked in the mirror, took her nail scissors and dug without caution into her hair, grey-black tufts drifting down onto the wash basin, fringeless, grinning monkey and, side view, untidy mane at the back. Yes, toilette completed, with ho and hum and hey nonny-no, out to face the day, as they say.

'Jesus, Mary and Joseph, Miss Kirwan, what have you gone and done to yourself?'

'I might, nurse', Angela attempted to weave past like a dancer, 'I might, might I not, have mutilated some essential part. I might have performed a do-it-yourself mastectomy, might I not? You've no idea how fortunate we all are.'

'Grab her, Josie. You've seen the last of your scissors and make-up so you have. Take the things off her.'

'No. No,' sobbed Angela. 'Leave me alone, you harpies, cows!'

'You've been reckless, Angela.' He spoke sorrowfully, as if she had let down his side by her behaviour. As he sat her down in the chair his hands hurt her, like clamps.

'Oh,' she flopped, 'saving your presence, doctor, your honour.'

'I would not, normally,' joining his episcopal hands over his desk, 'speak to a patient in this way.'

'What way, Herr Doktor?'

'You see, Angela, you're not really as sick as you would wish to be.'

'Oh, really? Fancy that now. Oh my goodness, gracious me!'

'What I am saying, Angela, is that you may have your freedom.'

'To hell with freedom!' she cried, gaily, springing both her feet up on his desk, his photos of loved ones, dossiers of lunatics, everything. Then, minutely observing something distasteful on her shoes, she took them down again. 'Answer me this! Ever heard of R.D. Laing? Course not. You're pre-historic. Where?' waving her arms, her beautiful Isadora Duncan arms above her head, 'where is my straight-jacket?'

'Freedom', he repeated, with deep-browed meaning.

'Freedom?' Which of several kinds? For Heaven's sake! The concept is illusory without specifics.'

'Whatever it is you wish to make of it.'

'You're threatening me, Doctor O!'

'Nonsense. See how rational you are, Angela.'

'Huh!'

'You see, Angela, for the fully rounded person, to be free is to be in harmony with a responsible structure.'

'Right! Structure! You're trying to frighten me! To beat me down. You alchemist, you!'

'Hm. You're being melodramatic.'

'Would you say female, Doctor? Doesn't that explain everything, Doctor O?'

A dull strain of irritation spread across his face.

'I will be blunt with you. You understand perfectly what I say. You are indulging yourself. At the expense of everyone around you. It must stop. The whole place is disturbed by your antics which are quite within your control. You know this.'

'For Heaven's sake 'tisn't an orchestra you're conducting!'

He said nothing, looking at his hands.

'What about me?' she screamed at him. 'Just me!'

He was still silent. She looked closely at him as if seeing him for the first time. Something in the coldness with which he studied his hands stopped her short.

'You're a man, oh, you're a man, right enough,' she murmured.

Still he did not bother to look up. She felt like clouting him over the head with something.

'Tell me, doc', she asked spitefully, 'how did you ever get into this game, the gonad syndrome? I bet you're a great believer in women's inner space and everything. I bet your notion is getting the old female engine back on the road, again. Reconditioned. Half-price. I bet . . .'

'You are free to leave St Gabriel's, Angela. Now. You may simply indicate to sister that you wish to go.'

Something suddenly opened inside her head and she slid off the chair, weeping hysterically.

'Oh, why do you say such a thing? You know very well I couldn't do that! Why? You know I'm . . . you know how frightened I am. Why do you say . . .'.

'Stand up, Angela.'

'No. No. No. Don't. Don't send me out, Doctor. No.'

'But of course not, Angela. Here, let me help you up. You don't have to go anywhere if you don't wish to. You know that.'

'Oh, but where? To where?'

'Come along now, Angela. Look! It's time for our evening session with the staff and other patients.'

'Evening! What do you mean, evening? It's only morning.'

'Give me your hand, Angela. Let's get down to the assembly hall. The others are waiting.'

'What do you mean?'

'For our group-therapy together. You can't have forgotten?'

'You're trying to trap me! It's not that time! It couldn't be that time!'

'But of course it is, Angela. It's after five o'clock.'

'No. No. No.'

'Now, Angela! There you are, now!'

'I look a fright.'

'You look fine. Come along, Angela. It's vitally important that you be part, participate. You see, this is very much part of your problem.'

She looked at him in utter amazement. He let her into the bathroom. I've just walked out of here and now I'm back again. Her good blue dress hung loose and all down one side. When she caught the material in one hand she felt herself away inside it at some centre. She brushed her cardigan with a bit of toilet tissue but, as she could not bring herself to look at her face in the mirror, she left, more or less, as she came in.

All assembled, smiling, nodding heads, happy chatter, nurses playful, nuns indulgent at the rear and all facing forward to the podium with the deceptive promise of its old upright piano. Doctor O took his place at the back and, at once, bowed his head. As Angela staggered towards a seat, Mrs M had already been persuaded to go forward and address the expectant audience on her subject of the vegetable garden.

For several minutes she clearly had difficulty in remembering what she had to say, pausing after every other word to interject. 'We will take up that point tomorrow, my dear.' A small, porcelain woman with white cropped hair, she suddenly began to give her credentials: numerous prizes at the Bray Horticultural Show, twenty years of asparagus and artichokes, demonstrations to the Irish Countrywomen's Association, and correspondents in Kent and Surrey. Finally, the chatter had to be quieted and Mrs M was followed by Miss

G in a brief, sporadic account of her work in the bank, Mrs A with a talk on her Papal Audience in 1967, Mrs O'B with crochet patterns, Mrs L, who was unable to speak about potted plants, Miss P, who spoke coherently, and all too briefly, about social work during the Biafran War, Mrs J on interior decoration which went on too long and eventually too aggressively, with several ferocious asides on former friends in the trade, Mrs L again, who was still unable to speak about potted plants, Miss O'K, who spoke about Equal Opportunity for All, irrespective of Creed, Class or Sex.

Throughout this, cries of varying tempi and distinctiveness rose and fell from the audience. Angela heard herself cry out at one point. 'This is preposterous. We are all women, women,' but this had no effect whatsoever.

Seizing her chance after Miss O'K, she rose up and yelled, stopping several aspirant speakers in their tracks: 'Halt!' They tried to shout her down. 'It's mine! No, it's mine! Mine!' She went on and climbed awkwardly on to the platform and turned to face them.

A moment of panic in space, hung free of objects, nowhere to place a shaking hand. Smile. She tried to smile again but the muscles of her face became twisted. All looked at her in disbelief and even he, at the back, raised his head. I have entered the final stage of becoming, she wanted to cry out. I cannot be reached except by way of what I have to offer. Someone tittered and stopped.

'I bring the fruits of my journey,' she called out and the shock of this made them all silent.

'Girls! Girls! I am a teacher. A moulder of minds. I had wished to speak, today, briefly, of Giovanni Boccaccio. An Italian writer, girls, of the fourteenth century. Check the dates, girls, in the library.' Uproar. Stamping of feet. All of which she blithely ignored. 'But why choose an old story? Why choose a misfortunate male who failed in his expectations, an unhappy diabetic in Certaldo pining for his beloved Naples, his beloved Fiammeta, when I can recount such tales myself? Silence, girls. You there at the back. *Studium fuit alma poesis.* That's Latin, girls. I shall translate in a moment.'

'Shall we have reality?' she demanded in a new voice. She saw their fright, a curtain of unknowing riding across before her eyes. 'Do forgive my appearance.' All the buttons were missing on her cardigan and she snatched it about her. 'And that's another matter we might consider: the dreadful state of the bathrooms in this institution. Another time, perhaps. We women', she struggled, 'we women . . .'

At this, the room erupted once more and one hot-faced woman was scarcely restrained from making her way up to the platform. Angela watched and listened with a grim confidence.

'Sit down, you brazen hussey!' shouted the elderly creature from the middle of the room. There was applause at this, hand-clapping. It is just like a school concert, thought Angela. Good heavens!

'I've reached and passed my meridian,' explained Angela.

'What has that got to do with it?' the woman, still on her feet, a kind of spokeswoman in a chorus of yeses.

'Bear with me!' Angela appealed. 'Am I a teacher, now? Certainly not. Am I a visitor to the unfortunate Pope? No! A debater of inanities? A cultivator of potted plants? No! No! I am woman. All woman!' She embraced their jeers and cat-calls with open arms, eyes closed, impervious to the racket.

'Come down out of there or I'll pull the hair off your head!' The woman was now wielding something in her hand but Angela dismissed her and took a fresh stance in the centre of her little stage. She saw the room arching away above her head and began to leave them all behind. The ladies walked in the Tuscan garden, weaving their garlands and dancing. The hour of nones. Oh, Filomena! Such tales could I tell you were I Neifile! Her head was expanding like a balloon and she had to struggle to reduce it.

'Girls! Girls! Girls!' another conversation creeping out of the past. 'Girls, the truth is painful.' She blinked her eyes, finally focusing upon an island of the present. 'Here,' she called, 'here in this sanctuary we are safe. Do not be afraid. Am I not showing you finality? Be of good heart, children. Consider what I myself was able to accomplish with inadequately developed breasts!'

She paused again, bewildered. A thin, emaciated figure, the hair standing about her head. She squinted through the hall but of him she could see nothing. Oh, Doctor O! How I've disappointed you! You hollow bastard! Why were they leaving it all to her? Did they know that she alone could speak to these women, these poor broken women? She saw herself at the centre, having journeyed along a series of lines across a white space to a luminescence, a blinding spot that only the few could stand in. Here, she wanted to shout out: here, this is it! This is an ending!

She had created a hush before her, a pause outside her own pause but still hers because she could feel it well up out of her anticipation. And while she waited, the stillness appeared to empty the world about her. Then slowly, like a drum-beat, a moaning sound rose up from her audience of faces; they appeared to rock back and forth in the front of the hall; she was even aware of their joining hands from seat to seat, as they swayed. Then she saw them no more. And her voice dropped, intimately addressing a single, perfect confidante. Oh, the arched vault of the room, a cathedral of hollow space that phoned her voice so that she heard it speak to herself as she spoke, this other, warm, fulfilled and over-flowing person.

'You', she whispered, 'you may feel, in view of conversations recently enacted, that I'm a whore.' She waited for it, eyes closed, but it never came, the screech of outrage, nothing but again that steady drum-beat, moan on moan. Surrendering, she lifted and sank on the rhythm. 'Girls. Nothing could be further from the truth. My sister, my poor sister, Rita. Hardly a responsible witness, do you think? Oh, beware the incomprehension of blood-relations! We women are much maligned. Let me tell you (you're the first person I've ever spoken to like this), let me tell you I've only had, in all, all, but what an all, I've only had but three lovers. No, correct that, girls, but two and a half lovers.' She laughed cheerily at the joke, springing her arms above her head.

'Shall I begin with him, lover number one, the half him, that little con-man in Switzerland (I was young then) who once affrighted the continent with his exploits, my first, perhaps my only love, my half love? A brief review of certain areas of European history may be necessary. A reading list will be handed out at the end of class. No, my dears, ignore pedantry. The personal is all, girls, his undeniable style, his charm. He had his personal tailor in the West End of London. A connoisseur of sauces, carrying his deceptions in monogrammed pigskin bags across the Alps, a latter-day Hannibal but without his elephants. He had such chic, my dears, and I, I, oh, I was a lost creature, gauche and gangling (never, never gangle, girls), a virgin Miss abroad, avid for Life, scarcely knowing what it was that moved me! But which of us has not experienced that first tremulous motion towards the sun? When we begin to live, my dears, we begin to die. His name, by the way, may, or may not, have been Butler. Note my doubt, girls, a veritable mystery. How precious is that imminence, not to say immanence of eighteen, before we begin to live! Anyway, to cut a long story short, I met my fate on Mont Lachette, at the foot of the Col de Rochers. These are place-names *en Suisse*, girls, consult your atlas. Ignore the directive, girls. This is not a geography lesson. The point is, that in my encounter with my amanuensis (a Greek word, girls) or, if you wish my balding *hochstapler* with his alpenstock, I failed to lose you know what. That was to be later in a flat on Leeson Street. Good Heavens, my neurosis may well be due to successive efforts to lose my maidenhead! Consult the doctor at the back of the room.

'Passing quickly on, how shall I describe, Good Heavens, I've forgotten his name! I mean the one who actually did it with me or to me on Leeson Street. At any rate, lover number two. Or rather lover number three since, oddly enough, one other intervened before him but he, too, I mean the intervener, like my alpine one, failed, if you will excuse a dreadful pun, to rise to the occasion, at least until lover number three (as we shall now call him) had shown the way (what on earth was the fellow's name?), so you see, lover

number three should really be lover number two by right of performance and
lover number two demoted to lovership of the third order, by default. Good
Heavens, I complicate what is obviously a simple tale to while away a showery
afternoon (is it raining outside, anyone?). I remember his name, easily, out of
the mists of time etcetera, I mean lover number two now relegated to
lovership third class, for who could ever forget Tom? Poor Tom, old Tom,
lumbering Tom with the wife and kids in Stillorgan. Yes, girls, adultery raises
its ugly head! But Tom was no mercurial lover in a Jaguar, not Tom,
woebegone Tom. Pity him, girls! He believed, perhaps still believes now that
he's back in the bosom of his family, he believed that life had passed him by. To
love him was to love the pathetic effort of humans to be what they are not. I
weep for him, girls! I weep, don't be embarrassed by my tears. And there was I,
girls, palpitating for experience, with a lover who didn't wish to be a lover until
I was loved by someone else, lover number two awaiting lover number three
who became lover number two, leaving lover number two to become three, if
you follow me. Oh, Christ, the cowardice of some men! Poor cowardly Tom,
who had to have me travelled by another before he could undertake the
journey with his diseased conscience. We must blame our educational system,
girls! Since there are religious present I will refrain, restrain myself.

'I wish, girls, I could remember his name. I mean my seducer. But was I
not, girls, in view of my self-portrait, a willing victim? Let us proclaim our
needs, girls, if necessary from the proverbial roof-tops. Michael? No. John,
Paul, Cosmas and Damian? Such names! Richard! Yes! Yes, because I
remember, quite clearly now, his irritation when I called him Dick. Never
underestimate the absurdity of male vanity. Oh, girls, beware of the man who
has given himself to commerce. The pin-striped gigolo. The hunter of older
or younger women. The true seducer, my dears, is ill-at-ease with a
contemporary. Oh, la, such experiences I could recount to you if the times
were auspicious! I digress! I will simply content myself by saying it wasn't all
it was cracked up to be. It never is. The body needs habit, girls, in this as in
other exercises before it becomes subtle, I mean supple, I mean sublime. But
to get back to Dick, daring Dick, an auctioneer, for Heaven's sake, would you
believe it! An up and coming junior in the firm of Jones, O'Brien and Kiely,
Valuers and Estate Agents near St Stephen's Green. A lecher, girls, but which
of us doesn't need a lecher from time to time? Who can know what hordes of
females fell at the feet, so to speak, of lively Dick, expert squash player, ancient
hard body at age twenty-eight, typists of all types, widows with empty houses,
women with family heirlooms for the dreadful hammer of the auction room,
prospective purchasers of properties in furs, pink girls at parties, brown girls in

bars just back from Tenerife. He had, or still has, perhaps, back at his desk, recharging for the nocturnal prowl, he had the eye of a hunter. Oh, Christ, but I loved that bastard! Girls! Girls! They describe us, our lovers. They are our different signatures. When we have passed on, we have left with them something of ourselves. I weep, girls. Don't be embarrassed by my tears! It's not regret. Good Heavens, no! I have had, to use that dreadful word, my fling. Consider what I achieved with minute breasts and rather bony knees! Be of good heart as ye go forth! Open wide the portals of your hearts! The plague has ended. The road is safe, down from Fiesole! I've given you the fruits of my journey. I bring you a sense of finality. Tempus Fugit! (A Latin phrase, girls) . . .'

She threw her arms wide, hearing a crescendo of distant acclamation. But the room appeared empty. Chairs and tables vacated. A falling, evening light was over all, a window-sash rattling. She became extremely frightened and made a clumsy effort to leap from the platform. Then she saw them, two or three nurses at the very back of the room and he, he, he, standing, observing her without emotion. 'Why has everything stopped?' she screamed at them, 'why has everything stopped?' They made no movement, no answer of any kind. She shrank back on the small stage and cowered near the piano. And already, although they hadn't moved, she saw them begin to advance, captors with their bonds of words, their manacles of blankets and pills.

SWITZERLAND, 1956

Extract from a work in progress

So many attempts by her to twist facts!

If you were to include everything (first shy meeting to final heebie-jeebies) her total acquaintance with the impotent if dexterous Butler extended only over a couple of weeks. Her much vaunted 'year-in-Switzerland' can have lasted only six months. Let's get the dates right. She arrived in early September 1956. Butler finally returned in his desperate attempt to stave off the bankruptcy of the school, sometime before Christmas. The hegira to Happelstadt (half flight, one quarter holiday, one quarter ambush, children snatched by hysterical parents at each station up the mountain, vengeful Italian cooks waving demands for their money while she, flushed, rode with Butler in the Porsche) in January. Her battered encounter with M. Weissen in Geneva (Do I look as abused as I feel? Are my eyelids still blue and puffy?) sometime in February. Weissen was the spectral investigator from the Inter Banking Union into the collapse of the bank (grey, tailored eminence behind the long table, rimless spectacles, concentric circles of heavy glass diminishing to fluid iris germ, flicker of pink tongue, judicious touch of velvet fingers on table-top, instant impression of fingerprints as instantly fading away). The police wouldn't hear of her leaving the country until she had given her bits of evidence (Sure he never even spoke to me about money — not quite true, that — so how could I know anything about this bank or that bank? Can I go home now? Please?). It was old Weissen who suggested that Butler might have fled to Brazil.

'I may have been fucked, doctor, or at least attempted to, by a possible Nazi.'

To which her ever-reliable Doctor O had not answered directly except to remark upon her use of a triple indefinite, citing this as something she should try to avoid at all costs, imprecision. Odd that, since she thought that that was his own major drawback as a psychiatrist, a certain vagueness, a tailing-off of opinions and judgments which always made her furious in her sessions with him in the clinic. And she told him so.

That time with old Weissen she could only think: Is this to be the final judge of everything that has happened to me? This old fellow, old as the hills?

In February, then. Six months in Switzerland. No more. Let us settle for six months.

But she hadn't opened her mouth to her notebook-wielding medico about other incidents in the school before she even met Butler. Incidents which she herself came to recognize as possibly having some bearing upon her state, upon her extravagant reaction to what, in retrospect, she could laugh at as a virginal fumble in the dark with yet another oldie. Laugh, that is, until everything went haywire again twenty years later in Dublin and she did her disappearing act.

'I think something must have been already, you know, giving way inside my head, you know, before I even met him.'

'In what way?' asked Doctor O. Pencil poised. In so far as he could ever spring, he sprang. She was convinced he hadn't been listening to a word she said before. Irritably, she changed the subject completely.

So, Doctor O never heard about her brush with the esurient Hersch, the big ski instructor (how she hated the way that man ate in the *salle á manger*, great gobbets of fondue, grease all down the mountainy chin) on her very first day in Heisel. Nor did he hear about her fear of the treacherous couple John and Doris (they of the Mussolini story) who ran the girls' chalet. They seemed to know more about Butler's past than anyone else and that was why she often wondered what had happened to them in the end. As for Wendy Jane, the

American girl, all she said to Doctor O was that, yes, there was one girl in the school whom she liked but that she was expelled. Nothing about the disgrace with Hersch. Nothing about the last dance. Even at that late stage of the day in the clinic with Doctor O she was trying to draw lines.

What she had meant about things giving way inside her head was that for all those early weeks in the school at Heisel layers in her brain seemed to be shifting, likes plates. Every other day she had a little sickness. Not much, just cramps or dizziness or runs but sickness all the same. It was enough to do just to keep going. She did ask herself if it was something in her background, maybe, that made her unfit to cope with the strangeness of Switzerland or, maybe, it was something inside herself like a fault or a weakness in her body.

'I was a bit sick at first,' she said to no one in particular that first day in the bureau of La Prairie.

'Ah,' M. Raymond Gedolet, the school manager, grasped at this in a kind of relief, nodding to Hersch in the doorway, who nodded back, both men nodding, nodding, superior to her problem, 'it is the automobile.'

As instructed by Butler's letter she had left the Lausanne train at Asile just before it took that sharp left-hand turn into Valais. Then the spiral hedgeless drive up over the Rhone to Heisel. But, no, she corrected them, it wasn't the car at all, it was the plane. Falling away from its suspension in the bright metallic sunlight, winter blue, her fist grinding a paper napkin to a damp mess, the great wing sucked down sideways at her elbow, clouds breaking over it like boiling water. She found herself pushing at the ledge beside her with one hand. Floor opening. And before the familiar earth colours, grey and green and brown, rose to meet her again like an old coverlet, she had her last view of the peaks, old faces pocked with snow, malevolent knuckles against the serenity above.

'You should have taken the sickness pills,' was what Maurice Gedolet said, comfortably. Hersch made some additional comment behind her and both men laughed, sharp bark of the ski-instructor, Gedolet's fat soft sound. She was mad at them. Her body drummed with tiredness and there was this burnt taste in her mouth. Typical of men to drag a body into an office like this for an interview without asking her if she needed a cup of tea or anything after her trip.

'But I think Switzerland is very nice,' she blurted out, angrily.

'Ah,' whispered Gedolet, 'but you must see the snow.' Then in a different tone, 'In the absence of Monsieur Butler, le directeur — ' and stopped as if he didn't know what to do with the rustling papers in front of him.

At the magic word of directeur, Hersch (white ski-jacket emblazoned with red crest) gave an appreciative growl over her shoulder and made a horse-like shift from one foot to the other. The salon smelled of heavy polish. A table crouched in the centre on clumsy knotted legs, surrounded by straight-backed chairs. She had a crazy impression of awkward people standing around at a party. A wireless in the corner with winking black knobs, the only mechanical object in this polished room of wood. When Hersch moved his feet again his heels rapped the slabbed floor. In the wide naked fireplace between her and Gedolet a fat rust-coloured log lay as if for years, untouched. Why was there always such emptiness in the front rooms of buildings? If this were the convent in Donnybrook, now, there would be a statue of St Joseph beyond in that corner there carrying sprigs of long-stemmed flowers, a frozen white carpenter's rule plastered to his side, hand transfixed in benediction, a dead how-do-you-do.

Oh please God don't let him read out my references, don't, not here, I'd die with mortification! And, indeed, Gedolet was holding the bits of paper aloft with pudgy fingers. Reverend Mother's famous epigrams. 'Angela has proven herself both before and on the rostrum.' Everyone hooted at that. 'There y'are, Angela, you'll never be stuck with that in your pocket.'

Anyway why wasn't he here to receive her, the great Mr Butler, after all his old talk in his letters about how much her coming meant to him, also the school, how certain he was from what she said in her letters that she was the blessed answer to his needs also the school, the stern principles evidenced in her application, this great adventure of ours to educate towards a New Age, rebuilding our battered continent, *erudition et eloquentia*, also her quite delightful style of expression etcetera plus his own never completely explained but clearly stated connection with Ireland adding to the general warmth. Her mother had seized on this last point saying several times how relieved she was he was Irish and that the school would be all right so, even if it was in a foreign country. Poor Mammy! She hadn't an earthly notion.

Some of Mr Butler's remarks in his letters had been overbearing and Angela couldn't stand people who lorded it over others. 'Allow me to interpolate at this point.' 'Actually, I simply must explain.' 'I should say, by the way.' The voice was kind of high-pitched. When she tried to put a face on it, it came out as long and pointy with sunken cheeks. It came as a shock to her when she actually met him later and first saw the round, pink face, the balding head, the chubby body.

In the bureau she suddenly had the hot and cold feeling of being stared at behind her back. That big brute at the door. With a rush she was flooded in perspiration and with a skill which she had long since perfected for such moments she began to count herself back to composure, counting the chairs, counting the bars on the firescreen, counting the buttons on Monsieur

Gedolet's suede waistcoat, hand grasping hand in her lap. But still big Hersch loomed over her head. Doesn't he understand a word of English?

Meanwhile M. Gedolet in front of her had begun what sounded like an address of welcome to her. He had a milky face with wrinkles which were not of age or any other impressive experience. They were effortless creases that appeared and disappeared on his forehead, leaving the pale infant skin unruffled. She had once been in a creamery and seen the thin milk separated from its butter-cream come streaming from a spout into the farmers' churns. When she had tried to explain her disgust at the sight to her sister Rita she was told she was morbid. Still she couldn't taste milk for weeks afterwards. Raymond Gedolet raised his milk-white face to her and spoke about the healthy climate.

'This International Pensionat is situated in the centre of the Alps in the canton of Vaud in the sunniest corner of Switzerland.'

The same sun shone on Donnybrook and on the long walk of loose gravel, through the trees, to the convent steps.

'Your daughters will be well looked after here, Mrs Kirwan,' Reverend Mother had said. 'We have a fine convent with fine grounds and the children are always in the shadow of Our Lord and His Blessed Mother.' The tall woman in black towering over herself and Rita, the restless thumb of the masculine hand lifting the black beads at the waist, the roughness of the skin when the nun touched her forehead on that first day in the school. And now Reverend Mother had promised her a job teaching there 'after your sojourn in Switzerland'. Reverend Mother had grinned at her with those yellow teeth. Some of the teachers in the school openly said that the old nun was going off her rocker. In the bureau of La Prairie Angela felt a chill. A bubble of rebellion against the nun and everything she stood for, rose in her throat but she quickly swallowed it. She should be grateful for what was offered to her. Not many had the security.

'Our pupils from many different countries are preparing themselves for their future lives under the careful guidance of highly qualified professors. The aesthetic, calm beauty which surrounds La Prairie in winter and summer contributes to this —'

Her tiredness was like wiring through her body, the two images of school, convent and alpine, drifting together like the last thoughts before sleep. She suddenly snapped upright. It was the odd sing-song of Gedolet's voice. When she looked questioningly at him his eyes fluttered away from her like birds trying to escape out of the room. He blushed bright pink. There he was, secretly reading from the school brochure in English, would you believe, a copy of which she already had herself in her blue suitcase. She was immediately sorry for his embarrassment and tried to look indifferent. If there was one thing she hated it was to catch someone else out in embarrassment or shame or just foolishness because she knew only too well how she'd feel herself if the tables were turned.

'In winter,' Gedolet struggled with the words, his forehead glistening, 'the slopes are covered in rich snow with marvellous ski-pistes — '

How could these green pastures be buried under snow? It seemed indecent in such lovely twilight. She looked outside the window to where the mountain dropped into the darkness of the Rhône valley, a thousand feet below. She had never thought before of how mountains would hold a little daylight after darkness had covered the valleys. The big black cows which she had already seen from the car had been moving up and down the mountain now for some time, each coming home to the village of Heisel. As they moved their solemn heads from side to side the bells swung from their necks, now nearby just outside the window like church bells, now distant further down the valley, a sound impending. She had the sense of sound gathering itself out of the gut of the earth.

'I beg your pardon. I didn't hear what you said.'

'I was announcing your duties, mademoiselle.'

'Oh yes.'

'There is *surveillance* three evenings each week.'

'I see.'

'Pardon?'

'I mean I understand. Of course.'

Hersch said something in French from the doorway. He deflected the words away from her by rubbing fingers down the side of his nose. She thought he was a horror and no mistake. Then he excused himself and went out.

'You will eat in your room,' said Raymond Gedolet. It sounded like a question.

'Thank you. *Merci.*'

They stood up and approached the door together. At one point they were both obstructed by the same chair and Gedolet said, '*Pardon*'. She felt like sitting down on the floor in front of him with his suede jacket and all and refusing to go an inch further.

In fact she followed him hypnotically. She found herself on a narrow wooden staircase boxed in on all sides with the same brown timber. Grimm's fairy tales. Woodmen and witches. Creatures of a forest where no real leaves could ever grow, false huts of spliced and sapless logs.

Gedolet left her alone in a little room off the top of the stairs and for a moment she stood there in the tiny cell, her body ticking with weariness, dried perspiration. She looked down at her plaintive suitcases huddled together on the floor. She even counted them. Then she staggered over them to the little window with the ceiling sloping down so that she could touch it with her forehead. Why do people automatically go and look out a window as soon as they enter a strange room? They just walk over to the first window they see, like sheep. Is it that they want to check out the quickest way to escape?

First she just saw her own reflection in the dark pool. No matter what was to happen to her now she believed she could do nothing to change it. If the whole place were to go up in smoke she wouldn't be able to stir to safety. It was like a weight encasing her body.

Two small boys came into sight running, pushing one another down the mountain road. They appeared so unexpectedly that she thought she might be dreaming. They were quite breathless and before entering the door beneath her she could see their brown, perspiring faces and the wrist of one raised in an exhausted gesture to the side of his head. There followed a violent shouting in the hallway below, a man's voice which rose to a single piercing syllable and then there was the hushed silence as before, muffled sounds in the distance, so that again she wondered if she had merely dreamt of the boys. Or who were they? Or what had they been doing out so late at night?

Suddenly there was someone in the room behind her. She turned quickly, frightened, and compared to the weak light outside she was shocked by the darkness within. Hersch, a tray in his hand, was already halfway across the room. He appeared to be smiling and by some odd association she was reminded of his coarse laughter earlier in the bureau below. He said nothing placing the tray on a chair but then moved silently quickly to her side at the window.

'You speak English.'

Angela heard herself laugh, once, at this idiocy. A queer choking laugh of derision and fear. He reached out and touched the side of her face and all the tension drained from her. She became weightless and couldn't care less about a thing. It was a moment of exquisite indifference.

'Hersch!' someone roared from below.

His hand had formed a huge cup at the back of her neck and from this cradle she saw his face begin to recede. Later she remembered how she had understood with amazing clarity, given her circumstances, that if he were to let her go quickly she could still support herself on the windowsill at her back.

'Hersch!' from downstairs. 'Hersch!' The third time, more insistently.

He had left her for some minutes before she realized he had gone. Then, as if in the beginning of life, each nerve in her body seemed to start up again, finding out pains all over her, like signals. And the shivers. God Almighty, how was she going to manage! It was like looking at someone she didn't know. What had come over her? She had stood there throughout it all like a zombie. Maybe it was the long distance she had travelled? And the funny thing was, although she knew she should be frightened by her behaviour, she was more curious about it than anything else. It wasn't that she wasn't terrified of that big ape but more than that she couldn't get over herself and she remained there in the dark for she didn't know how long in a kind of amazement at the way she was possessed by such indifference at such a moment of danger. What did it all mean?

Suddenly the lights in the room went on. Just like that. Click. If they could turn on her lights down below what else could they do? Maybe she should barricade the door? Maybe with that table over there? Also find the light switches, heart thumping. But again she was overtaken by something strange. The more she looked, the more beautiful was the lighting. She had never seen anything like it in all her life. It was so modern. Such a contrast to the wooden room with its homely bed and patchwork quilt. An intricate series of honey-coloured plastic covers set into alcoves and shelves, black metal rods pointing thin light into corners, a lovely tracing around the carvings on the clothes–closets, while in the centre of the room, like some curious modern sculpture, a large inverted iron plate, pressing down upon some glowing source which flowed out across the floor like a mysterious spill.

Gerry Dukes

HAND TO MOUTH:
'TRANSLATING' BECKETT'S TRILOGY
FOR THE STAGE

T he project began for me on a wet Sunday morning in the Monaghan village of Inniskeen. The occasion was the concluding session of the 1984 Patrick Kavanagh weekend. A group of Abbey Theatre players had just staged a semi-dramatic reading of some of Kavanagh's poetry and prose in the local hall and the audience had dispersed, some to visit the grave down the road, others to an adjacent bar for insulation against the creeping dampness and cold. I was among the latter. It was in the bar that I met the actor Barry McGovern who had taken part in the reading and, during the course of conversation, I learnt that Michael Colgan of the Gate Theatre had suggested to Barry that the time was right for a one-man Beckett show. I had not known until then of Barry's enthusiasm for the work of Samuel Beckett though I had seen his Vladimir in the Irish Theatre Company's *Godot* which had toured the country some years before. The final outcome of our conversation was that we agreed to reread the canon of Beckett's English-language work with a view to assembling an actable script from the wealth of material therein.

Such a script already existed, mined from the work by Beckett himself for the actor Jack MacGowran. Both Barry and I had seen that show, *Beginning to End* (a typical Beckettian pun), when it had toured to the Gaiety in Dublin. The rights to this script were available to the Gate but Barry, understandably, had a certain reluctance to take it on. MacGowran had scored a critical triumph with his performance and had become widely recognized as the leading theatrical interpreter of Beckett's work. For an actor with a cognate name to attempt the same script seemed to us a project with little to recommend it.

Appropriately enough, nothing happened regarding a script for a considerable time. Barry and I were reading assiduously and independently and when we met briefly in late January 1985 we had reached a similar conviction. The territory to explore minutely was the trilogy of novels, *Molloy*, *Malone Dies* and *The Unnamable*. We were both fully aware that the task of condensing nearly four hundred pages of text into a viable script for a one-man theatrical piece was going to be fraught with challenges, not to speak of difficulties. Not the least of these was the basic theatrical requirement laid down by the producer, Michael Colgan: the first act should not exceed a playing time of fifty-five minutes and the second should have not more than forty-five. There we were then, the sea before us and a thimble in our hands.

It was April before anything practical happened. In the latter half of the month the producer called a meeting at which it was finally decided that the trilogy was to be the source for the script: Colm Ó Briain was to direct, Robert Ballagh to design and Rupert Murray to do the lighting design. All that was needed in order to get the show on the boards was the script, which for the moment did not have even a title. That was not to come until the final days of the work despite the fact that Barry kept a special notebook in which he inscribed a large number of possibilities culled from the text. What we eventually settled on, *I'll go on*, that last phrase of the trilogy and the last words spoken in the show, has a resonance to which I shall return below. Before we left the meeting Barry and I agreed two binding rules of procedure: firstly, that the integrity of the narrative pattern of the novels was to be respected and, secondly, that only Beckett's words would be allowed in the script.

It is necessary at this point to offer a rationale for selecting the trilogy as the raw material from which to compose the script. The fact that the novels were originally written in French should not be regarded as in any way devaluing their significance in English. The translingual phenomenon that is Beckett is a special case. The case of *Company* (1980) is instructive. The novel was first written in English and then translated into French and published in Paris. The original English version was then revised in the light of the French version and published in London later the same year. The question of the priority of a Beckett text resides almost exclusively in the realms of scholarship and bibliography and is of little direct concern to either the reader or the theatre-goer. When Beckett autotranslates his work, the result is not so much a translation as a re-imagining within the contours specific to the target language. A brief example will demonstrate the point. Here is a fragment of Lucky's speech:

> . . . Je reprends l'aviation le golf tant à neuf qu'à dix-huit trous le tennis sur glace bref on ne sait pourquoi en Seine Seine-et-Oise Seine-et-Marne Marne-et-Oise assavoir en même temps parallèlement on ne sait pourquoi de maigrir rétrécir je reprends Oise Marne bref la perte sèche par tête de pipe depuis la mort de Voltaire étant de l'ordre de deux doigts cent grammes par tête de pipe environ en moyenne à peu près chiffres ronds

bon poids déshabillé en Normandie . . .
(*En Attendant Godot*, Les Editions de Minuit, Paris, 1952, pp. 60-61)

Beckett's first translation gives the following:

> . . . I resume flying gliding golf over nine and eighteen holes tennis of all sorts in a word for reasons unknown in Feckham Peckham Fulham Clapham namely concurrently simultaneously what is more for reasons unknown but time will tell fades away I resume Fulham Clapham in a word the dead loss per head since the death of Bishop Berkeley being to the tune of one inch four ounce per head approximately by end large more or less to the nearest decimal good measure round figures stark naked in the stockinged feet in Connemara . . .
> (*Waiting for Godot*, Grove Press, New York, 1954. p. 29)

The second English-language (1955) version runs thus (quoted from the unreliable *The Complete Dramatic Works*, Faber and Faber, London, 1986, pp. 41-42):

> . . . I resume flying gliding golf over nine and eighteen holes tennis of all sorts in a word for reasons unknown in Feckham Peckham Fulham Clapham namely concurrently simultaneously what is more for reasons unknown but time will tell to dwindle dwindle I resume Fulham Clapham in a word the dead loss per capita since the death of Samuel Johnson being to the tune of one inch four ounce per capita approximately by and large more or less to the nearest decimal good measure round figures stark naked in the stockinged feet in Connemara . . .

Beckett's most recently published English version exhibits even further changes:

> . . . I resume flying gliding golf over nine and eighteen holes tennis of all sorts in a word for reasons unknown in Feckham Peckham Fulham Clapham namely concurrently simultaneously what is more for reasons unknown but time will tell to shrink and dwindle I resume Fulham Clapham in a word the dead loss per caput since the death of Bishop Berkeley being to the tune of one inch four ounce per caput approximately by and large more or less to the nearest decimal good measure round figures stark naked in the stockinged feet in Connemara . . .

> (*Waiting for Godot*, Faber and Faber, London, 1965, p. 44)

Beckett's process of re-imagining is apparent in the parallel passages quoted. The translation of 'l'aviation' to 'flying gliding' responds to the bias of English towards more strict denotation. The oddity 'le tennis sur glace' in the original French text is keyed to earlier reference to 'le tennis sur gazon sur sapin et sur terre battue' which is immediately followed by 'le hockey sur terre sur mer': it is probable that the 'sur glace' has become detached from 'le hockey' in a breathless elision produced by Lucky's rising panic and consternation. In all the English versions tennis and hockey are modified by the phrase 'of all sorts'. Some readers may feel that the English is inferior to the French on this point but it should be noted that Lucky is concerned with large definitions and ought not to be diverted (dramatically speaking) by details or risk being exhausted by enumeration. The translation of the list of place-names is, to my ears, nothing short of superb, given the expansion of the suggestive possibilities. The change from Voltaire to Berkeley to Samuel Johnson and back to Berkeley is worthy of note. It is obvious that Lucky's subtext is mainly scholarly/philosophical, hence Voltaire and Berkeley. The inclusion of Johnson is an aberration but justified in a text addressed to a London audience in 1955. The revision of 'per head' to 'per capita' and finally to 'per caput' highlights the re-imagining process very clearly. The first English version is literal, the second pedantic but the third is a radical improvement over the original in that the Latin 'head' is retained with the audible German 'kaput' drawing into the text notions of the head being broken or finished. 'Stark naked in the stockinged feet in Connemara' is doubtless a more extreme and primitive condition than being merely undressed in Normandy but then I am not party to the attitude of Parisians to those living to the north of them.

Much more could be said of this short fragment but my digression has gone on long enough. Before returning to the main theme, however, I would like to make a plea for a dual-language, multi-column annotated edition of *Waiting for Godot* with a full critical apparatus concentrating exclusively on textual matters. When I suggested the project to Beckett some time ago he was quite supportive, saying that it was 'amply justified by my deplorable neglect of successive editions both in French and English' (in a letter dated 19/12/86).

I resume the main theme having 'established beyond all doubt all other doubt than that which clings to the labours of men' that Beckettian translation constitutes a special case of the art. Such a conviction informed my commitment to the trilogy in its English version. The problem of turning written fictions into spoken text was not particularly inhibiting because each of the novels takes the form of an extended soliloquy or monologue (two monologues in the case of *Molloy*). In a sense the novels are already scored for voice, and the task of the stage adaptor is merely to animate or orchestrate it for the theatre. The tasks associated with staging the script could be safely left to the director, always bearing in mind that the actor must be provided with words, action and character of a sufficient coherence to inform the deployment of his expressive skills.

It was in May finally that the key decision to shape the script as four linked monologues was taken. This meant that the actor would be enabled to pitch his playing through four separate characters, namely Molloy, Moran, Malone and the Unnamable. Theoretically, this would yield an appropriately symmetrical structure with two characters in each of the two acts and would reflect the bi-partite structure of the first novel, *Molloy*, and the 'univocality' of the other two. Barry and I felt that there was adequate sanction in Beckett's post-trilogy work for the theatre to validate this arrangement. Of the two dozen or so pieces for theatre from *Krapp's Last Tape* onwards, over half of them feature the use of the monologue in a variety of arresting and innovative ways. Beckett's writing for the theatre manifests a development which closely parallels his fiction writing. The early fiction both in English and in French furnishes itself with multiple persons and the semblances of plot, however experimentally treated. In this context *More Pricks than Kicks*, *Murphy*, *Watt* and *Mercier et Camier* spring to mind. From the early French novellas onwards the fictions tend increasingly towards 'univocal' forms such as the monologue or the meditative retrospect. Much the same can be said of the theatre writing which follows on from *Fin de partie* (1957). It is curious to note in passing that the dramatic writings since then have more frequently been originated in English than in French, thus reversing the trend discernible in the fictions as to the language of initial composition but confirming it with regard to formal considerations.

Barry and I met throughout May and into June for sessions which often lasted an entire day and well into the night. Our basic equipment consisted of multiple copies of the Picador paperback edition of the trilogy, colouring pencils and a stopwatch. By this time both of us had almost eidetic recall of much of the text and could call up apposite tracts at will. As we had long ago given up the notion of condensing the text, we were free to exercise a ruthless selectivity, cutting away large areas in which the unrelenting accretion of detail would have impeded dramatic presentation had it been incorporated into the script. There were losses which we both regretted, the principal one being the exit of Moran from the script. An outline of the basis on which we decided to cut Moran reveals, as much as anything, the nature of the editorial procedures.

Molloy is the first character we encounter. He is a richly complex and grotesquely comic figure. The key manifestation of his character is given in the celebrated 'sucking stones' episode where the mismatch between the intractable world and the intransigent self is most witheringly displayed. Molloy without his sucking stones could not be entertained. The episode, cut to the bone, occupies twelve minutes of stage time. Our best efforts with Moran cut him back to a mere seventeen minutes but some five minutes too long. Moran or the stones had to go, so Moran went. We were then reduced to three rather than four monologues and our theoretical structure was in tatters. But suddenly it began to sing within us, 'like a verse of Isaiah, or of Jeremiah', that what we had lost in theory we had gained in theatrical practice. The first monologue would feature a decrepit but essentially mobile man telling of his absurd transactions with his mother, various policemen, his bicycle, a rheumatic mistress and so on. As he moved about the playing area he could conjure up the scenes with the assistance of the lighting plot. In the second monologue, motion would be reduced to a minimum, as would befit a dying man communing with an audience but increasingly with himself alone. The third monologue could then be brought downstage as far as possible and the actor lit by intense spotlights suggesting the glare of ineradicable but tightly circumscribed selfhood.

That was the structure we finally adopted, 'inelegant assuredly, but sound, sound'. Its soundness was liberally attested to by critics throughout Europe and the United States. At the centre of the whole enterprise, of course, was Barry McGovern's extraordinary performance. Night after night, wrung out and used up by the imperious demands of the script, his final words are 'I'll go on'. In a one-person show one has no choice. C'est la vie.

Thomas Murphy

LULLABY

Where are the angry mountains
the winds that whispered with revengeful solace
long ago in Catholic childhood
when I could quench my pain in
the burning fires of hell
when fear was food to my existence
was mystery and was meaning to my soul
now to quench this dark monotonous despair
I shut my eyes
and the poor evaporated God
that was a frowning mountain
is but a sad slow moving mist
in the vacuum of space
Now in the darkness
to recharge my soul with wonder power astonishment
and awe
I explore the possibilities of murder
and of love
Or
further in perversity
try to warm my vapid senses with induced insanity
But fail
and find in all
incredulity
or
mundane response

*The piece was a 'doodle' I found in an old diary, written during one of those so-called periods of
inactivity: now I realize that it was part of an unconscious incubation period for a play I was to
write later: it contains images I developed upon in* The Sanctuary Lamp. *Emasculated man,
emasculated God — that sort of thing. So I dickied-up my doodle in, this time, conscious
attempt at — a poem? T. M.*

Des Hogan

QUIET WATERS: A JOURNEY HOME

A work in progress

'Four country roads winding to a town in Galway. Four country roads leading to the friends I left behind'. Pascal met Daniel in the Fox and Firkin for a cider before he left for Prague. Daniel knew about it all. An art teacher and an artist once, his mind had gone. It had come, his malady, his inability before total breakdown, to not having been able to confront a class without vodka on the brain, at the end a whole bottle of vodka. Daniel had gotten a job with a firm of builders. Entering a flat the first summer during his new job, to renovate it, he'd been confronted by one of the paintings he'd done in his youth, a prize-winning painting of final exhibition at art school. Suddenly the mind, the imagination which has pulverised, is called into focus again, is miraculously neatened again — if only for seconds. The painting had many lemon colours in it, a triangular dash of vermilion stuck in the bottom right-hand corner of it. 'The world did not love me,' Daniel said. 'It let me die'. Daniel still worked as a labourer and he, all paradoxically renewed brawniness of him, effulgently muscled arms when he wore sleeveless T-shirts, Samson-head with its long, greasy black hair, attended gospel study meetings in a dirty-façaded terracotta building among the uniform and often rain-sodden precincts of South Sydenham.

Pascal's mind too had gone early in the year; there'd been a sojourn in a mental hospital, a corridor which had come to seem like an unremoveable, an eradicable bit of furniture of the mind. Now he was going to Prague. Some money his mother had left him the previous November, some of his own savings — the thing was made possible by both.

'I'll see you in September,' Pascal said at the end of the meeting, out on Lewisham High Street, Daniel about to drive off on his motor cycle. And a sentence came back from the town in which he grew up, a tinker's common farewell. 'See you in Claremorris.' One of the first bits of his mind's memory which had come back since January when the world around him had begun to eddy. As Daniel's face beamed at him, those heavy black brows puckering acrobatically, Pascal divined something else of the town in which he grew up. Trees at the end of one street, oak trees in blossom. Time he was there for his mother's funeral those trees were gone but there were trees like them in a sign outside a pub. The Oak Tree Pub. Disappeared heritage had been conjured up again — a talisman on what was in fact the main street.

Since he'd come out of the mental hospital Daniel had visited him faithfully. They'd worked together in the school. Pascal had taught art and English literature. A polytechnic in South-East London. Geraldine, Pascal's sometimes girlfriend, taught there too. He hadn't seen her much in the previous few months but he was going to move into her flat on the sixth floor of a high rise building in September, about to give up the place he'd lived in for six years now. A cottage, a pastoral enclave among 1930s' two-storey, South Circular flanking buildings. The old lady, his landlady, had recently gone to an old people's home and he had had to move out. It was here Daniel had visited him. They'd both stoop over a gas fire under a mosaic of postcards. Goya's 'The Forge'. Eugene Boudin's 'Approaching Storm'. A picture of a family outside a hopping hut in Kent in 1909. Geraldine was taking a year off, going to teach English in France. During their last meeting by the cottage gas fire Pascal and Daniel had been aware of ending, of apocalypse even; this cottage, which had snowdrops strung outside it promptly in late January, had not just been an anchor for Pascal but one for Daniel — a place he'd been drawn towards at the worst of times. The lady had lived in the poky quarters upstairs. Otherwise Pascal had had the run of the place. Outside it a little Isis figure stood over the pond and very often you saw a grey squirrel hopping on to the Isis' head and then off, hurrying off on a Mercury-like mission.

'See you in Claremorris.' Night before he left for Prague Pascal handled a letter of rejection from a local building firm. J.M. Tiernan. Anyway it didn't matter. He was getting his job back in September, teaching. It was June now. Pascal saw himself reflected in the glass over the postcard mosaic. His face against two teddyboys. A small English town in the late fifties, council houses, a dark figure — a man — being ushered into the runny darkness of the council houses behind the boys. Smiles on the boys' faces. And trees somewhere at the end of the street. There'd been trees outside the mental hospital. Someone — a boy he'd met while he'd been swimming in Highgate Pond once — had brought him an iced almond cake from a Jewish bakery one day. The cake had stood between them, bartering something, the insanity of one for the common sense and totality of the other. But these states are interchangeable. Pascal had once, in similar circumstances, been Daniel's foil, the same commonsensical one confronting — in a grey Victorian mental hospital more to the verdant South-West of London — the one who'd tried to leap off the top of Lewisham fire station. A circus had come to the green of the park outside the building

Daniel had been in during his time there and Pascal hadn't gone home immediately after leaving Daniel one night but had lingered among the circus caravans until he'd met a boy, a circus boy, and had stared at him and touched his shoulder, a quick, almost unacknowledged interchange, and then gone home, wondering if there'd been a tattoo just below that shoulder. Someone had told him that day of a tattoo shop in Earlsfield where a man, tattooed all over as a dalmatian, slept on the floor at night. He'd been a mercenary in South Africa once.

'No more will we go harvesting together in the golden corn'. The voice of a song came back the night before he left for Prague. Who was singing that song? Someone of his childhood. A man's voice. In his dreams that night a man wandered, stooped, braces over his white shirt, bold, claret braces, walking stick picking the way, ashen hair in a poet's tail at the back of his head. The man was heading towards oak trees in blossom and suddenly the trees ignited and became a burning bush, a blaze which in its colours revealed, constructed, the mosaic of a village in Czechoslovakia. Pascal saw a white horse dip his head over a well in the middle of a street. Then the dream, its confusion, its panic even, faded into a shop window of an Irish country town, Laskowska's — wedding and engagement rings, gold and silver jewellery, trophies, Waterford crystal, Belleek China, a sign promising all these things and a further poster advertising a recital by a soprano from Kenya who lived in Dublin, her small photograph on the poster like that of someone who'd passed away, blurred, slightly inchoate as if from grief, from sundering with the world but a rosette still to be distinguished at her breast.

There was no sign of the grey squirrel in the morning when he got up; no sign of his cat Eamon. It was a quiet June morning in the grove. The milkman had come. An old lady, she was ninety-three, swept along the path, her wartime jewels strung around her neck, a black crepe dress on, it reached well below her gangly knees. If Pascal didn't avoid her she'd start talking about her husband who'd died in 1953.

His favourite song. 'To think that I should have to wear a nest of robins in my hair. I'm a tree'. He'd sung that in Saint George's Hall on Carholme Road the night before he'd died.

'O you're a Christmas cracker, Marion,' he'd always say. 'A Christmas cracker'. And she still looked like a Christmas cracker, vermilion cheeks of her, lean length, the sudden phosphorescence of colour, around eyes, on hands.

'To think that I should have to wear a nest of robins in my hair. I'm a tree. I'm a tree.'

A bus brought him in from the airport in Prague. People had sipped coffee at the airport, around tall circular tables, they made conversation, they gossiped at these vantage points. There'd been tanks around the tarmac. The morning was as yet grey. But a woman on the bus carried a bunch of yellow ochre marigolds.

There'd been marigolds outside the courthouse when he was a child, a bed of marigolds he'd often tried to persuade his mother to look at as they'd passed it. She had no time for marigolds. Two years ago he'd driven her to Kerry in his mini in a last attempt to win her over from her pall, her perpetually cultivated despondency. He wanted to show her the first view of the Blaskets around a bend of the Dingle Peninsula, a precipitous bend, the Blaskets out there, marooned, peaceful, beatific even. She'd strolled swiftly from the sight to fixate on the tall crucifix on the other side of the road, the Virgin Mary distraught under the cross and a stream lapping the Virgin's feet before meandering across the road and plunging into the vista where the sun was a pale spider-chrysanthemum now, the tendrils of the Atlantic sunset staying with them until they reached Dun Caoin, Paul Masson bottles with flowers in them lit up in a graveyard on their right-hand side before they swerved down towards the village.

Nicholas Grene

JOHN McGAHERN'S THE POWER OF DARKNESS

When in 1895 Tolstoy's *The Power of Darkness* was produced in St Petersburg, he recorded his reaction in his diary: '*The Power of Darkness* is a success. Thank God, it doesn't make me glad.' One suspects that John McGahern wouldn't have minded having to feel glad, when his version of the play opened in Dublin. As it was, there was a violently critical reaction, with headline after damning headline in the press: 'Sadly risible drama debut for author'; 'No good points in the murk'; 'McGahern's Darkness a tad grey'; 'Power cut'. There were those that blamed the Abbey for exposing a fine novelist to the humiliation of having such a totally inadequate play staged; there were those who thought that Garry Hynes's production went some way to salvaging what was obviously a disastrous text. But the majority view on the play was overwhelmingly negative. That was the majority view. However, there were other views expressed, notably by Michael Billington in *The Guardian*, who acclaimed it as 'an impressive theatrical debut', and Michael Coveney in *The Observer*, who spoke of it as 'a sock in the face of a play'. Since then there have been eloquent defences of the play and production by Brendan Kennelly, Colm Tóibín and others.

Those who attacked it criticized its lack of plausibility, its unreality: 'melodramatic' was a word often used as a term of abuse. Gerry Colgan, in the especially destructive *Irish Times* review, complained that the play wasted 'no time on plot or character development'. When English reviewers were impressed by the vision of Irish experience in McGahern, it was implied that they, being English, didn't know what they were talking about. Thus Paddy Woodworth, again in *The Irish Times*: 'The Observer's Michael Coveney may be right in praising the production, but it may also be that some British critics feel comfortable with a view of Ireland which seems embarrassingly stereotyped, if not altogether incoherent, to most of us'. A letter to the paper then took issue with this, suggesting that Irish critics were rejecting the play precisely because of its uncomfortable truth to the realities of Irish social life. It didn't help that this letter came from someone who was English and wrote from Northern Ireland. It began to sound like the controversies over Synge's plays all over again. 'The Shadow of the Glen is a travesty of Irish womanhood; no it's not, it reveals the horrors of Irish loveless marriages. It is true; it isn't; 'tis, 'tisn't, 'tis, 'tisn't.'

Underlying this argument appeared to be a series of mistaken assumptions that people brought to the play. The assumptions were that this was an original play by John McGahern, and given that it was by John McGahern, it could be expected to be an anti-clerical humanist's anatomy of the social/psychological realities of rural Catholic Ireland. John McGahern, in his programme note on the play, and the Abbey in their marketing of it, may have contributed to these assumptions. Whatever their origins, though, they were mistaken on at least three counts:

1. McGahern's The Power of Darkness is not a fully original play, but a version, and at times a remarkably faithful and literal version, of Tolstoy.
2. It is written in the theatrical idiom of melodrama, not of realism.
3. Differences between Russia and Ireland, the late nineteenth and late twentieth centuries, Tolstoy and McGahern, make for a complex rather than a homogeneous texture in the play.

II

Much that is puzzling in McGahern's play at first glance, becomes clearer when one realizes how closely he is sticking to Tolstoy. For instance, there is the figure of Oliver, the pious father and the tongue-tied spokesman for God and goodness. This sort of devoutness has not, traditionally, been a man's role in Irish Catholicism, or indeed in Catholicism generally. Though Irish men may well be devout, it is most often women who voice their devotion, who speak for the religious principles of the family. McGahern, though, is faithfully following his original in the contrast between the inarticulate but right-minded peasant Akim, and his fluent, materialist, unprincipled wife, Matryona. Again, Irish audiences might be surprised by Paul's fear of opposing the wishes of his father: 'I'd hate to go against my father. There was a fellow from Cloone who went against his father like that a few years back and he came to a terrible pass.' Goodness knows, any number of Irish sons have gone in fear of their fathers, but not religious fear. The positive reverence for the authority of the father comes over from the Russian text. So too does Paul's action in removing his shoes and socks in the final scene as he confesses to his father. Paul goes barefoot because his Tolstoyan counterpart, Nikita, does so in the climactic public confession, which he makes to the whole community assembled for the wedding in the play's last scene. In incident after incident, character after character, detail after detail, McGahern holds tenaciously to the givens of his source text, however little they correspond to the Irish milieu.

What McGahern inherited from Tolstoy was a black peasant melodrama which moves relentlessly from crisis to crisis. It is melodrama without the usual let-up of popular sentiment or light relieving humour. The characterization has the bold simplicity of melodrama, the situations its starkness. The basic shape of the story, with its five acts of strong theatrical scenes, is carried over from Tolstoy to McGahern. Thus, in the first act we start straight into the tension of the young wife married to the sick older husband, in love with the farmworker, tempted towards murder by the farmworker's grasping mother. The second act presents the murder itself, committed by the wife under the urgent threat of the husband's death which may deprive her of his money, but engineered by the mother to ensure her son gets both money and widow. In the third act we see the bad marriage that results with the now married and dissipated son in an affair with his wife's step-daughter's. The fourth act brings infantacide, the step-daughter's baby killed by its own father, once again at the instigation of the evil, conniving mother to make possible a marriage covering up the step-daughter's affair. In the fifth act, finally, there is Nikita/Paul's attempted suicide, frustrated in Tolstoy as in McGahern by the drunken ex-soldier who refuses to yield up the rope, followed by his spontaneous public confession of guilt. To *accuse* such a play of being melodramatic, of lacking subtly shaded characterization, is like accusing *King Lear* of tasteless violence, or *The Importance of Being Earnest* of farcial triviality.

III

McGahern took the substance of the melodrama over from Tolstoy. But he stripped it down, cutting out the usual nineteenth-century clutter of supporting characters, and he turned it towards black comedy and satire. Baby, for instance, in McGahern's version becomes a brilliantly knowing counterpart to Tolstoy's sinister Matryona. Baby is one of the most splendid creations of McGahern's play, stunningly well acted by Marie Mullen in the Abbey production, as even some of the more hostile reviewers had to admit. She presides over the action with an odious mixture of pseudo-motherly concern and a specious worldly wisdom, as she eases Eileen towards murdering her ailing husband: 'Maybe if the man was blooming it'd be different. As it is, he's betwixt and between, neither in this world or the next. Sure, it's an everyday occurrence nowadays. Doctors give it as a kindness every day of the week, though they can't say that they do.' She is mellifluous in her management of cliché, whether pious consolation to the dying Peter (whom she is helping to murder) . . . 'everything is well taken care of. You've had the priest. You're leaving a fine family behind; or grim-faced realism — 'Women are able for a lot more than the men. They have to be.' One speech which McGahern derives from Tolstoy illustrates the sort of poised irony he achieves with Baby and how he tunes it towards the comic. When Matryona has finally persuaded Anisya to take the poison from her, she adds some reassurance:

> And now, my jewel, keep it as close as you can, so that no one should find it out. Heaven defend that it should happen, but *if* any one notices it, tell 'em it's for the black-beetles. . . . It's also used for beetles.

In McGahern this becomes a definite laugh-line:

BABY: Now, love, don't let them out of your sight.

EILEEN: Nobody will look in there, but later I'll put them in a safer place.

BABY: That's the kind of talk I like to hear, But if by any misfortune they saw the light, all you have to say is that they're for dogs that go around killing sheep. Actually they work very well on dogs.

Shaw called Tolstoy a 'tragi-comedian', and there is a black comic vein even in his *Power of Darkness*. McGahern works this up deliberately into a comedy of the grotesque, particularly in the scene where Paul, bent on suicide, has to fight it out with the outrageously drunk Paddy, who won't let go of the rope.

PAUL: (*Anxiously*) Give me the rope. I'm in a hurry.

PADDY: I'm giving nobody the rope. I might be fluthered but the one thing I'm not giving up is the rope. (*Falls down.*) The drink got the better of me that time but the next time I'll do for it. (*From the straw.*) Maybe you're thinking of doing away with yourself? (*Finds this wildly funny.*)

PAUL: (*Petulantly, but anxiously*) What's so funny about that?

This is in the vein of modern black theatre of the absurd with its derisive comic perspective which won't allow to the protagonist the luxury of a tragic end in all its dignity. The play is written in an intentionally flat style, which contributes to the effect of deflationary satire. If Joyce's keynote in *Dubliners* was that of 'scrupulous meanness', then McGahern's self-imposed discipline is a style of studied vulgarity, of nicely judged crudeness. This is especially true of the language of sexuality in the play. Baby condones Eileen's affair with Paul in a tone of nonchalant coarseness: 'Isn't it only natural? There was never much jizz left in poor Peter the best day ever he was.' Especially offensive is Paul's attitude towards women, a mixture of traditional male triumphalism and a sort of harassed fear: 'God, when these women come abulling you'd think there wasn't a fence up anywhere in the country.' This is repellent, yet it rings true — true to a gross language which has no way of dealing with sex but in the terms of a reductive agricultural animality. Brendan Kennelly perceptively identifies this sort of style in McGahern as a conscious resistance to Synge and his highly coloured peasant speech: 'McGahern's stubborn integrity as a writer is closely linked to what is almost a terror of colour or any kind of strongly amplifying eloquence from a character about his or her plight'. Instead, the characters in the play expose themselves through their speech to a fierce satiric scrutiny.

We don't understand McGahern's *The Power of Darkness* unless we understand what he drew from Tolstoy and how he adapted it — not only adapted but fundamentally reinterpreted. Because the two playwrights are talking about different forms of darkness. For Tolstoy, the power of darkness is the power of evil. This is post-conversion Tolstoy, writing explicitly didactic Christian drama: Nikita sins when he seduces Marina, the innocent peasant girl, and then perjures himself before his father to avoid marrying her. All that follows is the result of this sin, as Nikita acknowledges in his final confession to his father:

> Father, dear father, forgive me . . . — fiend that I am! You told me from the first, when I took to bad ways, you said then, 'If a claw is caught, the bird is lost!' I would not listen to your words, dog that I was, and it has turned out as you said! Forgive me, for Christ's sake!

This was the Tolstoy of the period of *The Kreutzer Sonata*, that great and terrible novella which so dramatically embodies his conviction that sexuality is a primary source of human sinfulness, and the same darkness overspreads his play. For McGahern the darkness is the darkness of ignorance and of poverty. There is no one step into sin but a sequence of situations, each ordinary and understandable enough in terms of the human conditions prevailing. When Paul looks back in horror at all that has gone so desperately wrong with his life, he remembers his rejection of Rosie (the Irish counterpart of Marina) as the path not taken:

If I'd gone with my father that time and married Rosie we wouldn't have much but we'd be happy. There'd be none of this on our minds. We'd have our own lives. Rosie, oh Rosie, why didn't you keep me? It was my one chance. You should never have let me go. Why didn't I know it was my one chance?

This is a self-pitying retrospect on what might have been, not as in Tolstoy, the recognition of the entry into sin. McGahern cannot regard sexuality itself with the same disgust as Tolstoy. After all, if the man who wrote the original *Power of Darkness* was the author of *The Kreutzer Sonata*, the adaptation is by the author of *The Leavetaking*, someone committed to the view that sex is at least potentially liberating and life-enhancing. Sexuality in McGahern's play is seen as something destructive rather because it has been deformed and perverted by the twin forces of social repression and material need. In this it represents a secular humanist rewriting of Tolstoy's Christian moralist drama.

IV

Essential to Tolstoy's vision was the gift of repentance which comes to Nikita and which makes possible the uplifted ending voiced by the father, Akim:

AKIM: (*Rapturously*) God will forgive you, my own son! (*Embraces him.*) You have had no mercy on yourself, He will show mercy on you! God — God! It is he!

Akim is within the Russian tradition of the saintly fool: Tolstoy told an actor who was to play the part that he should 'exploit the contrast between his comic, incoherent babbling and the ardent, and at times solemn, delivery of the words which *issue forth* from him. 'McGahern could not manage anything quite equivalent with Oliver, his counterpart of Akim. In fact there is an uneasiness with the figure of Oliver which remains a weakness in the play. He is portrayed as an essentially decent man but too close to conventional petit bourgeois uprightness to have the full authority needed. Thus, one is inclined to expect when Paul makes his confession to Oliver that he will be scandalized out of his wits, rather than being able to act as absolving father confessor: 'These are terrible sins, terrible before God, but God will forgive you.'

It is partly because of this difficulty with the part of Oliver that Paddy, the drunken former soldier, takes on a much more important role in the play. In his account of the plot prefacing the published text, McGahern describes how 'Paddy . . . is lured into the drama, and gradually becomes its moral voice.'

The equivalent figure in Tolstoy, Mitrich, was also important as a disengaged onlooker and choric figure, but for Tolstoy his authority is necessarily damaged by his drunkenness. For McGahern, by contrast, this is just what grants him the moral force he has in the play's final scene. Because he has faced his own self-destructiveness, speaks out of the heart of his own darkness, he can provide a mortality-conscious, earthed vision which paradoxically gives Paul courage to take responsibility for himself:

PAUL: Did you say there was never a reason to fear any man?

PADDY: What reason could there be to fear? Aren't they all made of the same dirt as ourselves? They all have to die. Look at them. One is bow-legged, another has a pot-belly; someone else can run with a football half the length of a field. One is as grey as a badger, another has a shining head of hair — and how long will that last? and what difference will it all make? They all have to shite. Doesn't it melt down to the same old shit in the finish? All the young women think the sun shines out of their arses and fellas like you, Paul, run around as if you had the meaning of life in your trousers. What does it add up to? It adds up to fuck all. What should you be afraid of them for? All they can make you do is die once, and then you're with the kings and county councillors.

And it's with a reprise of this speech, rather than with Paul's confession, that McGahern's play ends. Instead of the triumphant emergence of God's grace attending on repentance and forgiveness, there is this comic-grotesque perspective in which the human horror of the action is finally set.

V

What significance, if any, has *The Power of Darkness* in terms of directions in Irish theatre? Two points might be made. First of all, the reviews suggest that we in Ireland are still very hung up on representational authenticity, truth to life. This has been a sort of bugbear of Irish drama through the century from Synge on, and it still hasn't gone away. Some of the best and most exciting work in Irish theatre over the last twenty years — plays by Brian Friel, Tom Murphy, Frank McGuinness and many more — has involved the effort to escape from the need to represent Irish life as she is lived, the whole deadening legacy of Abbey play realism, while yet writing out of the experience of Ireland. *The Power of Darkness* is another such effort. It tries to tap into the larger theatrical forms and bolder energies of melodrama, while rendering them in a style deliberately unleavened with lyricism or rhetoric. It is not therefore, as many of the reviewers seemed to think, a would-be realistic play which tumbled into a melodrama by mistake, but a disciplined and sophisticated reworking of melodramatic form.

Secondly McGahern's work can be placed in relation to other Irish adaptations of Russian texts. There have been plenty of these, going back to before 1916 and continuing with a spate in the 1980s: Thomas Kilroy's *The Seagull*, Friel and McGuinness each with a version of *The Three Sisters*, Friel's adaptation of Turgenev's *Fathers and Sons*. McGahern himself was originally commissioned to do a version of *The Power of Darkness* by the BBC, presumably on the basis of this long-standing tradition. But his play has to be seen as different in certain crucial respects. It is an adaptation of a play with a peasant setting, rather than the minor gentry/middle-class milieu beloved of Chekhov. An added dimension is that McGahern, in writing his version, is taking back to his own rural small farming background a work originally written by an aristocrat about peasants. More important, though, is the extent to which McGahern's interpretation goes against the grain of the original. On the whole, Irish versions of Chekhov have been very much in sympathy with their source texts, particularly in the case of Friel, who has a real affinity with Chekhov as a writer. But McGahern has had to struggle with a play which both imaginatively preoccupies him and, in so far as it represents a didactic Christian ascetic vision, is alien to him. A part of the impressiveness of the play is the imaginative encounter with another culture which it represents, the Irish setting to which it is adapted illuminated by finding the points of resistance, the otherness of the other text.

Quotations from McGahern's play are from the text published by Faber and Faber in 1991; those from Tolstoy's play from Leo Tolstoy, Plays, *trans. Louise and Aylmer Maude (Oxford University Press, 1923).*

Eoin Bourke

PITFALLS OF THE SOIL —
POETRY AND ATAVISM*

Recent reviewers of Paul Muldoon's *Faber Book of Contemporary Irish Poetry* have expressed their bewilderment at the editor's tactic of introducing the anthology with a dialogue between F. R. Higgins and Louis MacNeice, recorded almost fifty years ago, in lieu of an editorial comment. In fact, Muldoon's choice of this particular excerpt from a *Listener* article from 1939, entitled 'Tendencies in Modern Poetry', is apposite because it presents in an extreme way two poles of thinking that to this day characterize Irish poetry and poetics: those of atavism and rationality. I say extreme, because Higgins, a Protestant fascinated by the pagan component in Catholicism, as well as a racist who thought that the Irish were predecessors to a breed of supermen, used a jargon too close for comfort to what Viktor Klemperer called 'LTI' (*Lingua Tertii Imperii*, language of the Third Reich). In the radio discussion Higgins says that poetry, to be as good as Irish poetry, must derive from a 'belief emanating from life, from nature, from revealed religion and from the nation'. It must be 'fundamentally rooted in rural civilization', which is why urban English poetry of 'the macadamed street' and 'the cinder heap . . . so pathetically droops today'. With the brazenness born of a secure *esprit de corps*, he tries to bulldoze the more cosmopolitan Louis MacNeice into admitting that he, as an Irishman, cannot escape from his 'blood, nor from our blood-music that brings the racial character to mind'. MacNeice replies with a disarming sobriety: 'I think one may have such a thing as one's racial blood-music, but that, like one's unconscious, it may be left to take care of itself. Compared with you, I take a rather common-sense view of poetry'. The dialogue is strangely reminiscent of that fictional one between The Citizen and the 'rootless' Leopold Bloom, where the Jew, bullied into defining 'nation', says 'a nation is the same people in the same place'.

The trouble with Muldoon's Prologue is that he does not reveal where he himself stands, unless, as Derek Mahon suggests, his giving the last word to MacNeice is a signal of his own position. As Mahon says, the contents of the anthology do not fall in with one or the other: 'Would Kinsella, Montague or

* Published in *Krino* 3 (1987).

Heaney, all represented here, subscribe to a "common-sense view of poetry"? I doubt it'. But although Mahon demurs with regard to his own position, I think he (and for that matter Muldoon also) as a poet is firmly aligned with MacNeice and 'those forces which at the moment make for progress', whereas Mahon's remark about Kinsella, Montague and Heaney, arguably Ireland's other most famous poets, begs the question as to *their* position.

Irish literary theory has been revolving since Yeats around the same dichotomy. Nina Witoszek and Pat Sheeran see the Crane Baggers as the rational and demystifying, urban and therefore un-Irish, descendants of what I would see as the MacNeice lineage. But even the Cultural Debate, as it has come to be grandly called, is based on assumptions that belong more on Higgins's side of the fence: for instance, that a poet is nothing without a myth, and secondly, that it is the first and foremost task of a country's intelligentsia to establish the national identity. These two assumptions are posited over and over again with such self-evidence that one feels slightly freakish in comprehending neither. The myth, the supposed *sine qua non* of poetry, can be taken from the country's history or be set up by the poet. Heaney, having read about 'the frontier and the west as an important myth in the American consciousness', set up 'the bog as an answering Irish myth'. But myths, as Richard Kearney has pointed out, are a double-edged sword. The Cuchulainn myth, when cited in connection with 1916, was tailored to the needs of anti-colonial liberation and as such had an important but transitory political function. But as James Simmons has shown in his poem 'At Emain Macha', the same myth contains a legacy of cold-blooded brutality and deviousness. It could just as well be tapped for repressive as for emancipatory purposes. And the modern myth that inspired Heaney, that of the Western frontier, is a perfect example of one that distorts the truth in glorifying the genocide perpetrated upon the native Americans by white landgrabbers. As a myth it continues to service the hawkish elements in American society. In the same way the 'mythopoeic bog' could well serve as a holdall for dubious ideologies — to use Heaney's own metaphor, 'the wet centre is bottomless'.

As regards 'national identity', the idea of corporateness that it implies does not seem to bother anyone: in publications of all kinds we read about *the* Irish mind, *the* national psyche, *our* national soul, *our* indigenous being, as if concepts like mind, psyche, soul and being were not problematic enough when applied to individuals without using them in an all-inclusive phyletic sense. Desmond Fennell even talks of the nation as a 'collective personality' (it being made, of course, in Fennell's own likeness). The consensus seems to be that the identity is there, and that it just has to be found. The mind's eye conjures up the picture of hundreds of bespectacled and pipe-smoking intellectuals dressed in mackintoshes and wellies and equipped with spades combing the windswept bogland in search of our Irish identity. Here one catches a glimpse of Heaney digging with his squat pen looking for the severed Celtic head, there Brendan Kennelly rummaging through the entrails of a freshly slaughtered Kerry pig, somewhere else Thomas Kinsella interrogating every *cailleach* that passes by as to whether she is The Real One, Dennis O'Driscoll looking for the atavistic thread that leads to the lost centre, or Pat Sheeran levitating in the intermediate level of being. What they do not realize is that the search party can be called off, since Desmond Fennell has already unearthed our Irish identity. The one he found has only a very slight smell of putrefaction about it. It is described in the first chapter of his homily on *The State of the Nation*: 'our' collective personality is literary, Celtic, maritime, and above all Catholic. For all those non-Celts and non-Catholics in this nation who might chafe at being thus pigeonholed, Fennell has some comforting words: it is better for such individuals to belong to a nation distinguished as Catholic and well-bonded than to one which has little sense of distinct identity and a weak bonding. Why it is better, he does not feel constrained to explain, since he is speaking *ex cathedra*.

Fennell's arrogations demonstrate the folly of *The Crane Bag*'s setting out along this path in the first place, because the whole question of identity favours the organic and deterministic view of society and plays into the hands of conservatism. That is not to deny that group bondings, like myths, are essential at times of social upheaval — freedom struggles need symbols and slogans to counter the colonialist tactic of insinuating a sense of permanent dependency. But once the Free State was set up without any real *structural* revolution, complete with replica class system, Special Branch, courts and jails, then the self-assertive shibboleths of nationalism became a smokescreen for the new power structure. Brendan Behan's grandmother put it in a nutshell: 'You'll get an eviction order written in Irish with a harp, rather than one written in English with a lion and the unicorn.' As Liam O'Dowd has pointed out, 'Ireland has long been part of an international capitalist system deeply divided on class lines.' The people of Ballymun, I reckon, have more grounds for identity with those in Toxteth and Brixton and the Falls Road (and perhaps even the Shankill Road) than with the inhabitants of Dublin 4. The portrayal of society as a corporate national psyche with common 'roots', common mores and common 'destiny', instead of as a dialectically active complex, serves only to distract from the fact that this complex is linked with other such complexes on the level of power through capitalist economics. Seamus Heaney calls such matters 'agnostic', i.e. outside the spiritual sphere of poetry. But the fact that class divisions are more real than 'inherited boundaries' can very well be illumined by the poetic flash of truth, as has been demonstrated recently by Paul Durcan's 'The Anglo-Irish Agreement, 1986', a marvellously radical poem that uncovers unsuspected nexuses of power by shock juxtaposition.

Usually, when subdivisions are acknowledged and dividing lines are drawn, they are as unsatisfactory and vague as the pan-Irish 'soul', as in the case of Mark Patrick Hederman's phrase 'the psychic world of the "Southern Irish"' (as against that of the Northern Irish), Sebastian Barry's gobbledygook on the 'two sensibilities' and 'two poetries' of North and South, Heaney's woolly concept of 'community' or, worse still, in that atavistic word bandied about by so many: 'tribe'. But then atavism seems to be quite respectable, indeed something without which poetry cannot survive, according to Seamus Deane. Timothy Kearney states that without the nourishment of myth and atavism poetry loses its imaginative vitality. The cognitive, on the other hand, is presented as 'intellectual baggage', something that puts a curb on poetry, as in Heaney's strange remark that 'in the case of almost every Northern poet, the rational wins out too strong'. If I may try to distil the hotch-potch of verbiage that has seethed and burbled in the Cultural Debate, the message seems to be that in order to become the vatic spokesman of one's tribe, one must plug into the atavisms of that tribe. To be able to write racially conscious poetry, one must have contact with the soil. John Montague's dictum 'what's in the poet's blood must speak through him' has become something of an axiom of Irish aesthetics. No one seems to be disturbed by the fact that usages like 'race', 'soil', 'tribe' and 'blood' stem from the murky theories of Social Darwinists like Hippolyte Taine and Ludwig Gumplowitz, as well as proto-fascists like Count Gobineau and Houston Stewart Chamberlain. The idea of the poet as *vates* is very much more ancient, but fits in well to the anti-rational morass of the biogenic terminology. Heaney sees it as the daunting responsibility of anyone worth the name of poet, in Joyce's phrase, 'to forge . . . the uncreated conscience of [the] race'. That was an arrogance when Stephen Dedalus said it and continues to be an arrogance when Heaney quotes it. The wish to be vatic is a strange aberration that befalls poets in middle age. As Edna Longley observes, 'the fine obliqueness with which Heaney's first three books spoke "for the people" has been replaced by speaking to the people'. Moreover, it seems to be a particularly *male*, patriarchal vanity to believe that, like de Valera, one has only to look into one's own heart to gauge the state of the 'national psyche', and then to feel called upon to give forth resonant enigmas and dark, oracular sayings on the future of 'the' community. What's in the poet's blood must speak through *him*, not her. Judging by the Yeatsian motto with which Sebastian Barry introduces his anthology of seven male poets, including himself, he feels that he and the others are 'the few minds where the flame has burnt pure' and that they body forth 'the permanent character' of the race. That no woman poet good enough to be included was born in the nineteen fifties is ascribed by Barry to a 'parsimony of blood'. While it is a rather hopeless undertaking to try to analyse any of Barry's introduction — it is like looking at porridge through a magnifying glass — this particular statement has to be commented upon, because it seems to be saying that the bio-programme of the Irish race did not allow for any potential women poets in the baby production of the fifties. Such are the grotesque offshoots of Taine's cultural matrix of 'moment, milieu, race'.

All this is very heady stuff, but it gets even headier when Seamus Heaney introduces the hieratic dimension: the poetic self 'takes its spiritual pulse from the inward spiritual structure of the community to which it belongs'. Heaney's critical writing is peppered with religious terminology ('incarnation', 'sacral', 'sacramental', *religare*, 'epiphany', 'Numen') when referring to the processes of poetic creation, because he sees the poet as a 'celebrant of mysteries', a sacerdotal mediator between 'the' community and the wellsprings of eternal truth. The poet-seer makes his pilgrimage to celebrate at the pagan/Catholic navel of Irishness, Lough Derg, and to return to the world with his poetic exegesis of our inward spiritual structure, whether we lay-people feel Lough Derg is our spiritual hub or not. The poet = priest analogy is an attempt to set the poet apart as a person with the special power to lead us back to our perennial essences and away from the vulgarities and unpredictability of the market-place. 'We Irish', wrote Yeats, 'born into that ancient sect/But thrown upon this filthy modern tide/And by its formless spawning fury wrecked,/Climb to our proper dark', led, of course, by the poet's sensitive hand, or, if we do not particularly trust the dark, dragged kicking and screaming. But for all the contempt for the 'agnostic' world of capitalism that the poet = priest analogy implies, it has, in fact, a banal economic dimension. Priesthoods of most religions base their power as a caste on the fact (or fiction) that they hold the key to a certain set of mysteries. For them words such as 'rationalism', 'secularism' and 'humanism' are distinctly pejorative terms because they represent modes of thought and behaviour that set out to *demystify* reality and, by lessening people's emotional dependency on mysteries, undermine the priests' power basis (and with it their income). When Seamus Deane and Seamus Heaney use the same words 'humanism' and 'rationalism' in a similarly derogatory way, it must also be because poets have a vested interest in keeping their audience emotionally dependent on obfuscation and charisma, and that never seemed to me to be a worthy objective for intellectuals.

The mixture of atavism and mysticism is by no means peculiar to Irish poetry. In history it alternated with periods in which poetry was geared to a quest for illumination, clarification and exposure, or an atavistic school of poetry was set up simultaneously to a progressive school with the object of combatting it. I would like to make a very brief sketch of trends in Germany in order to broaden the scope of the argument and to provide a contrast to the Irish poetic scene, but also because in Germany the cult of the atavistic led to a crisis of an enormity otherwise unknown in recent history. Around the turn of the century, that is at the same time as Celtic Twilight here, right-wing German authors formed groups to cultivate *Heimatkunst*, a bardic art of the soil, and *Stammesdichtung*, tribal poetry, to counteract what they called the 'asphalt literature' of Naturalism and, by so doing, to halt and reverse the social developments connected with urbanization, industrialization and democratization. *Heimatkunst* drew from the myriad forms of pseudo-mysticism that had swept fin-de-siècle Europe as a result of the intellectual capitulation of a section of the bourgeoisie in the face of rapid social changes that they could not assimilate. The poets began to revere the Earth Mother and the native gods of Germanic legend in a stale Romantic broth spiced with Social Darwinism. Rational concepts were replaced by metaphors drawn from biology in order to describe both aesthetic and socio-political phenomena: roots, sod, soil, insemination, gestation, birth, breed, blood, race. Literature had to be autochthonous to be genuinely German. In the jingoistic build-up to World War I, the outstanding Symbolist poet Stefan George was prevailed upon by his right-wing disciples to drop the private cult of *l'art pour l'art* and to turn to soil mysticism. He began to entitle his poems *Primal Landscape* (depicting the furrowed bog where in the life-generating smell of the earth 'Forefather dug, foremother milked, nourishing the Destiny of a whole people'), *Consecration, Dream-Dark, Conception, Litany, Ravine, Man and the Druid*. Through the mediation of his disciples in the universities, he became the Poet Seer of Germany, the 'vatic spokesman of his tribe'. Borrowing copiously from Catholic liturgy, he fashioned his own myth, or as Heaney would call it, an 'indigenous territorial Numen', in the form of the young German god Maximin, who would raise his noble brow above the teeming rabble of the cities and the 'double poison' of Bolshevism and Capitalism (cf. the 'filthy modern tide' above) and would call down the cleansing cataclysm of war to rid the German soil of human parasites, crushing them with his sinewy heel. Anti-democratic authors like Alfred Bäumler exulted: German Man had again established contact with Mother Earth. 'The energies are flowing once more out of the dark depths, Man feels joined with the mysteries of life'.

George, not surprisingly, was to be asked to become the National Poet in 1933, but fled to Switzerland instead. Adolf Bartels, the main founder of the *Heimatkunst* movement, became one of Nazism's foremost ideologists, because biogenic metaphor tied in with the genocentric, subrational, undialectical and affective nature of fascism. The word 'society' was rejected as too suggestive of diversity and replaced by 'blood community' to give a mystical touch to the policy of *Gleichschaltung* and the persecution of intellectuals. History was reinterpreted in terms of blood: 'When even Goethe felt an abject reverence for Napoleon', it was because 'the voice of blood in him had atrophied'. The excellent urban poetry of Naturalism and Expressionism, condemned as the domain of the 'rootless Jew', disappeared overnight, as if there were no cities any more, and was replaced exclusively by thoroughly mendacious *Blut und Boden* verse. There was more talk than ever of 'the dark ineffability of myth' being restored to poetry, 'the voices of our landscape', 'the darkly reigning forces of the clay', 'the rootedness of the individual German soul in the German *Volksseele*'. Famous authors like Thomas Mann were accused of lacking a sense of race, breed and blood, while reactionary third-rate writers who had smarted under non-recognition during the Weimar Republic now had their heyday, and fusty professors of literature like the aptly named Hermann Pongs vied with one another to eulogize about the nationalistic poetry. 'The poet who is rooted in his people's traditions must bring forth divination. Divination is vision, not intellect, belief, not questioning skepsis, augury, not analysis' (Pongs). 'Our new German poets extract their art and energy from the German landscape and the German tribes' (Friedrich von der Leyen). 'We comprehend the creative process of poetry as a biological process, as a blood circulation of the soul and spirit, because the creative personality of the poet receives its most vital energies from the community of race, of the nation, of the tribe, and, as the Chosen and Consecrated One, bestows it, newly formed, on the community' (Heinz Kindermann). 'The soul of the nation is incarnate in great poets. In them the primal spirit weaves and swells' (Joseph Magnus Wehner). Such artistic and critical mediocrity formed a perfect symbiosis with the fascist system, writers and professors sanctifying the atavisms that were expertly channelized by the Nazi regime into war and barbarity.

The distressing thing about such wet-centred gunge is its persistence. If one were to substitute 'Irish' for 'German' in the above statements, one would come very close to what Irish poets and critics still take for granted, to Heaney's talk about 'presciences', 'poetic impulses', 'psychic energies', 'ancient

mythic shapes', 'search for a sustaining landscape'. That is not to say that
Seamus Heaney's usages betray fascist leanings. On the contrary: he and all the
other Irish poets mentioned have written the kind of warm, socially observant
poetry of which a fascist mentality would be quite incapable (one thinks
immediately of the wonderfully discerning poem 'The Other Side', or of John
Montague's witty but cordial 'Clear the Way') I would not even consider F. R.
Higgins to have been a fascist, although he made his statement about racial
blood-music right in the middle of the Hitler period and believed in a Celtic
Master Race. Despite that, his character was, by all reports, too Falstaffian to
be anywhere near a fascist personality structure. His fault probably lay in
nothing worse than wanting, in Patrick Kavanagh's words, 'to be what
mystically, or poetically, does not exist, an "*Irishman*"', and trying so
desperately hard to be it that the result was contrived. Or perhaps it was just
that blessed innocence with regard to fascism that inhabitants of the Republic
often display to this very day. Through our neutrality, most Irish (with the
exception of those incredibly courageous few who defied public opinion in the
thirties and went to fight against Franco) never had a direct confrontation with
the phenomenon of fascism and look upon it as a Continental problem. Many
Irish think of history as a diachronic continuum from the Civil War until
today, the thirties and forties being best remembered for the Eucharistic
Congress, de Valera's radio reply to Churchill, and food rationing. I think it is
a higher form of the same *insouciance* displayed by both Kavanagh in his poem
'Epic' and by Heaney in his discussion of the poem. I mean the reference to
'the Munich bother', which, the poem tells us, is poetically less significant for
the poet than the Monaghan feud between the Duffys and the McCabes.
Heaney comments approvingly: 'Munich, the European theatre, is translated
into the local speech to become bother, and once it is bother, it has become
knowable, and no more splendid than the bother at home'. There was nothing
splendid about the Munich Agreement, that spectacle of jaded European
conservatism mesmerized by what it saw as the dynamism of fascism, and even
less so about its consequences, the rape of Czechoslovakia, which in turn led to
the turning of the entire town of Theresienstadt into a concentration camp, as
well as the extinction of Lidice. For Kavanagh to use that particular event as a
backdrop for his manifesto on aesthetic parochialism showed a smugness that
has always put me off the otherwise excellent poem. Is it not the same almost
culpable *insouciance* that makes the continued acceptance of 'LTI' in the Irish
Cultural Debate possible? Ireland, they think, is somehow unique, because it
has been left aside by what Heaney distancingly and self-exoneratingly calls
'the great noisy cataclysmic and famous acts that make up history', and so Irish

thinkers and poets feel the right to indulge in crypto-Celtic race instincts free of intellectual or political accountability. And what is more, the rest of the world lets them get away with it, or even positively encourages it. It is as if some British and American critics, living as they do in polyethnic societies, want their Irish pure, as if Irish poetry gives them a clandestine opportunity to give rein to nativist feelings. H. Ernest Lewald, in *The Cry of Home — Cultural Nationalism and the Modern Writer*, expects the European artist to draw upon 'the stream of life that springs from his native land'. Robert Tracy says: 'The Vietnam years, when nationalism merged into imperialism, have made American poets a little shy of explicitly national poems', adding with apparent relief that the Irish have no such inhibitions. C. B. Cox raves in *The Spectator* about 'the soil-reek of Ireland' and 'the full-blooded energy' in Heaney's poems, while the West German poet and critic Peter Härtling, initially shocked by the trenchancy of Heaney's work ('he goes among the thin-skinned lispers and brags of his dirty skin'), finally succumbs to an earthiness that is taboo in his own country: 'He does not have to name his gods, his numina, for they inhabit the bog, the mud, the wood'. These are the expectations of Irish poetry that have established themselves, and sociologists of literature have pointed out that the recipients' expectations form aesthetics just as much as the other way around. Writing, like everything else under capitalism, is a commodity that has to seek out a market and adapt to its needs, the main outlets in the case of Irish writing being the American campus and the British publishing house. I ask myself, then, whether the 'Irish identity' syndrome is not, at least in part, just the result of a piece of instinctive *marketing* analysis and therefore something that could be put in its proper place by a piece of critical *system* analysis instead.

Post-war German poetry was forced by circumstances to go the way of system analysis. For the poets, the 'Munich bother' and all that had followed upon it was a most violent trauma, leading to a crisis in writing. It was suggested that to write poetry after the Holocaust was like decorating a slaughterhouse with geraniums. The catchphrases *tabula rasa*, *Kahlschlag* (deforestation) and Rubble Literature arose — the world of ideas was in an absolute shambles. 'Not even the language itself could be used' said Wolfdietrich Schnurre; 'the Nazi years and war had sullied it.' He said it had to be checked and counter-checked anew, word for word. The only style that could stand the test was a 'bald, tentative, stock-taking one', devoid of embellishing attributes, pathos, mythic echoes and archetypal imagery. There could be no more soil, sod, roots, clay, not because these words were *per se* offensive but because their nebulousness as concepts was eminently harnessable by fascism and because their sub-rational import had let to subhuman behaviour. Not even the word *Volk* was usable, a word that had originally meant nothing more than 'people' but had accumulated, since Fichte, so many obscure stratifications of meaning that it became one of the mainstays of the muddy fascist vocabulary. If the word 'blood' still cropped up, then it was the deeply lamented blood of atrocities, as in Hans Magnus Enzensberger's bitter apostrophe of his compatriots as a 'simmering pool of bockbeer and blood'. There could also be no vatic voice any more. As Günter Eich pointed out with sobering but indisputable logic, 'How should a poet know more than a non-poet? The sacerdotal posture has become redundant.' They reversed what Yeats, according to Heaney, had wanted to do: they wanted to elude a legendary and literary vision of race in favour of social and political interpretations of society. If they opened 'Doors into the Dark', then certainly not for any Heaney-like 'hankering for the underground side of things' but rather to throw analytical light on the mass seducibility of the previous generation. And when the West German population began to tuck into the Black Forest Gâteau of the Economic miracle in a largely successful attempt to repress the memory of the recent past, the poets became alarmed at the kind of Federal Republic that was shaping up under Adenauer's Restoration, with its Cold War rhetoric, its resurgent nationalism, its remilitarization (despite a constitutional ban on rearmament), its joining of NATO, and its new anti-trade-union Emergency Laws. Recognizing that war was not 'merely a continuation of politics with other means' (Clausewitz), but rather an essential function of supranational capitalist economics, they became sensitized to a structural crisis amidst prosperity and embarked upon a preventative and innovative *Systemkritik*, calling upon their readers to go into opposition, too. 'Be awkward, be sand, not the oil in the gears of the world' (Eich). Alfred Andersch led the way 'out of unconditional obedience into unconditional critique', and even the introverted and philosophically minded Ingeborg Bachmann called through her poetry for a sabotaging of the machine of permanent warfare by non-cooperation, promising a symbolic decoration, 'the wretched star/of hope over the heart',

> for deserting the flag,
> for bravery in the face of the friend,
> for the betrayal of unworthy secrets
> and the non-observance
> of all commands.

The former writer of delicate nature lyrics, Marie-Luise Kaschnitz, called out with anarchic humour to her sisters to defy the belligerent patriarchate that oppressed them:

> Pour milk into the telephone
> Let cats litter
> In the dishwasher
> Trample the clocks in the washing trough
> Step out of your shoes
> Spice the peach with paprika
> And the knuckle of pork with honey.

Erich Fried, as an exiled Austrian Jew living in London, lacks that 'sense of place' considered so essential by Heaney, that 'stable element, the land itself', and yet his poetry is all the more compelling for it. Untrammelled by the bribes of national pieties and mythopoeic landscapes, he constantly turns the German language over and over and inside out to put it through the acid test of integrity, to rid it of its equivocations and place the purified end-product into the service of emancipation:

> But the Lukewarm
>
> Those who stand
> for wars
> without atrocities
> for executions
> without cruelties
> for sentencing
> without executions
> for penal systems
> without beatings
> for interrogations
> without torture
> for torture
> without lasting effects
> for exploitation
> without unreasonable hardships
> should be blessed
> without a blessing
> or be cursed
> without a curse.

In the nineteen sixties and seventies poets like Peter Rühmkorf, Arnfrid Astel, Helga Novak, Wolf Biermann and many others gave the lie to those insular dogmatisms that Irish commentators sometimes allow themselves with regard to political poetry, such as Edna Longley's bland statement that poetry and politics, like Church and State, should be separated, or Brendan Kennelly's that there is no such thing as a public poem — 'a poem is private and personal or it is nothing'. The younger German poets saw what history had shown, as, for instance, in the case of George: even poetry that is intentionally apolitical can be made to function politically. Therefore they felt it imperative to clarify their own oppositional stance in their poetry so that it could not as easily be absorbed by an inimical system. This overall strategy, while proscribing the occult and the fuzzily mythic which had been found to be politically exploitable, certainly did not exclude the lyrical or even the evocative, as long as these qualities were not allowed to be used as escape routes from reality. In Ingeborg Bachmann's hymn to the Earth, 'Safe Conduct', she is not invoking clay-spawned myths but praising the wondrous metabolism of nature that has been so wantonly tampered with by Man's greed-driven nuclear physics:

> The earth wants to bear no mushroom of smoke,
> to spew no creature to the heavens
> to rid itself with rain and flashes of rage
> of the monstrous voices of doom.
>
> With us it wants to see the bright-hued brothers
> and the grey sisters awake,
> King Fish, Highness Nightingale
> and the Fire Prince Salamander.
>
> For us it plants corals in the sea.
> It commands forests to be still,
> marble to swell its lovely vein,
> the dew to spread over the ash once more.

Whether lyrical or starkly combative, modern German poetry is a cry to the public to stand up and fight against the faceless powermongers of today. Hans Magnus Enzensberger joined the battle against acquiescence in his provocatively entitled poem, 'defence of the wolves against the lambs':

> look into the mirror: craven,
> shying away from the grind of truth,
> reluctant to learn, handing

thought over to the wolves,
the nose-ring your costliest adornment,
no deception too stupid, no consolation
too cheap, every blackmail
is too lenient for you.

But to learn, you had to do more than wield a metaphorical spade, plumbing line or divining rod, and to illuminate things you had to do more than look into your heart and give forth druidic utterances on race memory. It meant learning *facts*, the kind of scientific, political and sociological facts that the powers-that-be do not want us to know. German poets had learnt the hard way that they had to invert the poetic process promulgated by fascism: their poetry had to be informed by intellect, not vision, questioning skepsis, not belief, analysis, not divination. To this end Enzensberger set up his Left Review *Kursbuch* in order to probe the mechanisms and machinations of power and provide himself with a solid cognitive basis for his writing. He edited articles on revolutionary movements in South America, futurology, repressive education, the politics of psychiatry, urban planning, the students' movement, the CIA, the causes of alienation, the uses of torture in the 'Free World', women's liberation, socialism in practice in the Eastern Bloc, computer technology and robotization, ecology, the sociology of factory work, the USA and the Third World, the structure of multinationals, the arms and atomic industry, neo-fascism, state terrorism, consciousness manipulation through the media, because he and his generation felt that poetry that blinded itself to these things was at best irrelevant and at worst potentially dangerous. And all the while, our leading poet sat contemplating his *omphalos*, and our up-and-coming *philosophes* agonized over the Irishness of Irishness.

Brendan Hamill

THE TROUBLES HE'S SEEN: FIACC AND BELFAST 1967

Belfast again, and the boat, the *Ulster Prince*, had been droning deeply for the past fifteen minutes. We felt like people who had had socks washed in our eyes. It was seven thirty a.m. on Belfast Lough. The hills were a creamy patchwork of snow jigsaws between the television masts. The little house with the trees on the Hatchet Field was lightly dusted with snow too. The boat gave a violent spasm and docked with a blank bump against the wharf. It was November 1967. A few stiff morning faces broke in verticals and horizontals when they saw their loved ones on the dockside.

Off the middle Falls Road at that time was a broad stoney lane which led to the Whiterock Road housing estate — by and large a decent, settled working-class red brick housing estate built in the late nineteen twenties. The broad lane was known as the Giant's Foot. It was about 300 metres long and was so named because it resulted in a long curving instep. About halfway up, two old pen-knifed telegraph poles held sickly yellow lights. They flickered rather than burned. At right angles to the Giant's Foot was a long dark road with a large gate at the end, which led to Our Lady's Hospice — a hospital for old people, run by nuns. It was forbidden, and screened by large thickets of laurel and tall Scots pines. It was imaginatively named, but nobody ever knew by whom. No plate endorsed its name.

Girls were afraid to walk that way at night because it was wild with tall nettles, and a bump in the slushy pebble-dashed wall was supposed to have been a nun's head. That's all we ever knew. Also, because of the depression of the nineteen fifties and official neglect, a smattering of localized crime was evident. Unemployment was always chronic and the railings turned year after year to rusted husks.

Big box-like suitcases were packed in sad silences for England, America or Canada. The squat boats made their way to Liverpool with their cargoes of human grief. They went away in the frosts and rains over the glassy seas. Those people remained alive only in conversations in dark little fortresses with small glittering fires, and soon faded from memory. An occasional photograph arrived postmarked Sydney, California or London. Few had telephones then.

It was November 1967, and brown and yellow leaves were everywhere and skirling in wind gusts now and again. They packed against the old granite walls and railings — slippery underfoot, but sweet-smelling.

After some years in London, I thought Belfast was a quiet city — full of sullen repressed raw energy and clotted with hard men who asked you with fierce eyes 'Who the fuck do you think you're lukin at?' — to which the reply was a derisory 'Not much', and then you ran for dear life.

Big melancholy constables passed by in preternatural silences. Belfast seemed to work manic shifts of feeling and mood and Dinah Washington sang 'September in the Rain' to knots of soft-eyed girls in fishnet stockings in Jim's Café on the Whiterock Road. Jim was a handsome Italian and wore a white apron. I once saw a fellow — a teddy boy with one lung and a flick knife — being kicked to death there when I was eleven years old.

The old teddy boys of the nineteen fifties had, by now, hung up their luminous pink and green socks, the studded belts and knuckle dusters, and had settled down gratefully to pints of Guinness and tough hard-voiced women. The macho princes had walked into their final sunsets or so it seemed — their lean muscular bodies clacking 78s on to turntables in maisonettes or rented rooms, in transit, maybe, to better lives. If they were pacifists, I would have been more frightened at a vicarage tea party. They were sparse and hard and favoured big raw-boned dogs named Rebel or Rover. The seagulls came like omens to the grey roofs in the smoky mornings.

People from the Shankill drank on the Falls and nobody made heavy weather of it. Mixed marriages were commonplace and worked. There were unstable Jeremiahs, though, with faintly foetid alliances. The women were largely stitchers, seamstresses, nurses or waitresses. Most of them made their own dresses — the cloth was bought, amongst other places, in a big Baghdad of a shop in Royal Avenue called the Spinning Mill. From the planes at night Belfast was laid out like a lighted necklace in a valley. People on the airport bus used to marvel at how beautiful the setting was as they ploughed into the thick scent of night hawthorn and the dark — to English cities on struggling old Viscounts.

That world of submerged violence didn't affect me in any direct way. I was young and indifferent and, besides, London was about adventure, new sounds, new people and places. The Beatles, the Rolling Stones and Frank Sinatra — that master of the pause — absorbed my interest. Also the great sprawling Metropolis was an emotional relief from the thin film of moral paranoia that was Belfast.

Life on the eighth floor of Stuart House in Soho Square was quiet. It was a law-enforcement section of the Ministry of Transport. It was cosy and urbane.

Also, I was going with a girl, Janet Hartley, a sweet girl from the genial village of Holmfirth, outside Huddersfield.

She was the first Marxist I ever met, but I liked her anyway. She liked my pink face and honest eyes, she told me in a funny, pleading accent. She lived in Jessel House at King's Cross and made lovely strawberry jam. She was a lecturer in education at Goldsmiths College in London. I was introduced to *A Sentimental Education* by Gustave Flaubert and *The Loneliness of the Long Distance Runner* by Alan Sillitoe.

My friend Gordon Winerow was from Bolton and a part-time reserve sailor on a coastal minesweeper anchored in the Thames, and when we got drunk we used to sing 'A Nightingale Sang in Berkeley Square' in a kind of tuneless farce. London was a great, exuberant city then and people were generally happy.

When I thought of Belfast, it was with some kind of confused despondency and awe. It was a place of deep pain never expressed — a place of psychic battering and secrecy. The abnormal had become the normal. The dark messengers had been waiting in the woodwork and were coming out now.

This particular night, though, I was back in my own home town and going to a poetry reading in a house in the Upper Donegall Road. It was cheek by jowl with the chapel of St John the Evangelist. A grocer's son who lived beside the Sandbanks was there with a sheaf of poems. They sounded like fizzy drinks though and, if I may say so, I was glad when he stopped. It was a tidy street which shielded a little colony of middle-class people. One side had brick, three-storied houses and an attic. A few well-placed trees set the street off. They were mainly humble civil servants, schoolteachers, insurance men and a few tradesmen. Like those in most similar areas of Belfast, they wanted their children 'to get on'. There was a faint odour of sanctity and a strong lust for respectability. They were — variously — the noblest Romans of them all. At least they were humorously thought of as such 'by the low types' with a jocular brutality. They were anonymous and discreet. The relationship between the classes on the Falls Road then was both rancid and intimate in our agreed thinly veneered antagonism — the sacred and the profane as it were, but they really said nothing twice to each other in the one day. Of course, they were all Catholic in the most elastic and highly snappable sense of that word. There is always a hiss when the waters of heaven meet the fires of hell.

Conleth Ellis, who was a schoolteacher at St Malachy's College, a Catholic grammar school for boys, led Padraic Fiacc into the room in a gauze of fluster. The door was chamfered and neatly panelled. Fiacc sat down beside a writing bureau, which was behind the door oddly enough, and he sat on a single straight-backed hearth chair. Ellis was a tall bird-like-man whose eyes looked as if they had been transplanted from a thrush. He had about twenty white-backed copies of *This Ripening Time*, which he had published at his own expense. He stood imperiously in the middle of the room, as young men do. The host, a conscientious Catholic of early middle age and mild in manner, made us welcome. I sat by the bay window, curious and too earnest.

Conleth Ellis was from Carlow, and Fiacc had lived in New York City, in Amsterdam Avenue in the garment district of Manhattan. He had been back home in Belfast since 1947 and lived in Newtownabbey. He was a gentle soul and reminded me of a man dipped in hazel varnish who had dried out unevenly. I am uncertain whether or not he read from the *Capuchin Annual* or the *Dublin Magazine*.

At that time Marshall's Newsagents in Donegall Street was the only place which stocked literary magazines or foreign newspapers like the *New York Herald Tribune*. The Lyric Theatre, though, had a very good bookshop on the Grosvenor Road, near the Ritz Cinema, and Mullan's Bookshop in Royal Avenue was a little gem of a place. But here I was, this November night, back in my own home town, at a loose end, seeing it all anew through the bright metropolitan filter of London, where everything was available.

There was a short awkward silence, then the introductions were made and I noticed that Fiacc's right hand shuddered and he looked slightly spooky. He glanced at me furtively, perhaps to see if my face was kind — the way the Hunchback of Notre Dame did, I imagined, in the Broadway Picture House years ago, when everybody clapped when the beautiful girl saw the heart of the Hunchback, and everybody clapped, but mostly us children in the cheap front-row seats — the soul of man under socialism, so to speak.

'Read "Alive Alive O",' exhorted Conleth Ellis; 'that's a lovely poem.' A short tense silence — and Fiacc's voice crackled into a kind of bland-monotone, like the hum of high cables over a cowshed on a clear country night, 'Should I — really?' There was a brief thunderstorm of nervous release which crackled around the room again, and I heard Conleth Ellis enthusing — 'I love the word bucket; bucket is a lovely word.' Fiacc wanted to be coaxed and then read — shakily.

The altar boy from a Mass for the dead
Romps through the streets of the town
Lolls on brick-studded grass
Jumps up, bolts back down

With wild pup eyes . . .
The morning at twist of winter to spring
Small hands clutched a big brass cross
Followed the stern brow of the priest
Encircle the man in the box . . .

A bell-tossed head sneezed
In a blue daze of incense on
Shrivelled bit lips, then
Just to stay awake, prayed
Too loud for the man to be at rest . . .

O now where has he got to
But climbed an apple tree!

The voice swayed like a tipsy metronome in my head. There was silence and a polite little cough. Copies of *This Ripening Time* were sold at 2s-6d a time. The host was a gracious and dignified man and we had another cup of tea. It was, too, a judicious act of recovery. My mind flooded with the soft purple mystery of Lent as I had remembered it as a schoolboy in the chapel nearby. I had begun to feel an unlocated guilt, as though London had robbed something of my soul. But I had come back to this little St Petersburg à la Dostoevsky's *The Idiot*. I was seventeen and a mixture of awe and lostness.

The year was lived season by season in Belfast, but in London the head shot forward. The heart leapt uncomprehendingly somewhere behind. I was caught between cultures, one angular and hard with a heart like a swinging brick. That was commerce. The other was poor and eschatological in its gradations of thought, feeling and mood, and blended with a city naturalism of sorts. That was Belfast specifically in time and place as I knew it, whatever the general picture might have been.

Even as young teenagers we went west — west to the Gully in the Black Mountain, west to the small town of Crumlin of the curved glen, to the airshows at Aldergrove, in the slow train — the tinny bus and corrugated grey Nissen huts, the mangled wreckages of wartime air raid shelters, and the final incongruity of rabbits and old silver Viscounts frozen into the runways. W. H. Auden's 'unimpassioned beauty of great machines'.

Immediately I sensed Fiacc's urbanity and humiliation — the poet as victim. Of what I didn't know. Although I loved Heaney's clean masculine tactile poetry in *Death of a Naturalist* and Festival Publication's *Eleven Poems*, I sensed Fiacc was closer in spirit to the fire and air world of the young Derek Mahon — though not a classicist in style or syntax. Clearly he was an original both as man and poet. His experiences of New York saw to that — the most sentimental of all American cities — the melting pot on the Hudson River. 'Give me the moon over Brooklyn', they'd say, those American visitors with baffled disdain when confronted with the vagaries of the Ancient Quarrel.

The chamfered door opened. Somebody wanted to know where Mister Dowds, the insurance man, lived. But it was a languid and proper house and nobody was ruffled. Conleth Ellis stood up and read a poem dedicated to Padraic Fiacc, entitled 'Remembering', the last verse of which read as follows:

And did the heron stand as in a dream
To watch a trout against a speckled rock,
As now he stands to bring that childhood back?

A loose rambling discussion on the poetry of Gerard Manley Hopkins followed. On the lower half of the Donegall Road, people were watching 'The Mountain' in the Windsor Picture House. It starred Spencer Tracey. Nobody ever called them cinemas. There was also popular enthusiasm for a film called 'The Invisible Man' at the time. About seventy metres on either side of the Windsor Picture House were small mission halls, a Methodist church and the Monarch Laundry. Underneath the grey bridge ran the Belfast-Dublin railway line. There were waterhens, mallard ducks and bullrushes in the Bog Meadows.

Peggy Greer lived nearby on Donegall Avenue. She worked with my sisters in The Star — a garment-making firm. With my mother, she would shake with seismic laughter, usually about Mr Grimble, who was finicky and straight-laced. It was a private joke, though, amongst the women.

The fire was getting low and people became restless. The bay windows caught our breath and became pimpled with fine droplets. The last poem was a sign maybe — certainly the only published poem on the event. Two years earlier, in the spring of 1964, I was working in Stuart House, a branch of the Ministry of Transport, in Soho Square, or the Wicked Square Mile as people sometimes called it. I was catching up on spot-checks in accordance with the 1960 Road Traffic Act and Mr Thurston, the executive officer, came into the comfortable office — eight stories up.

He was a mannered Londoner, who would smile and whistle to convey an air of nonchalance to put us at our ease. He fumbled with his umbrella and gabardine coat, before resting them in the cloakroom. The office was empty. It was 7.55 a.m. Sunlight was slipping off the tall buildings and spires of London, and shadowed angles widened.

'Brendan' he said enquiringly and quietly — aware that he might sound petty or alarmist — 'there was rioting in Belfast last night — no one hurt though, old cock.'

Something about a flag and a preacher — an Elmer Gantry style figure, the type you get at Hyde Park Corner. It was the first time in a year I'd heard Belfast mentioned by anyone in the office. It existed indifferently, north of Dublin. 'Rainy like Manchester', the women in the typing pool chorused abstractly when I first started the job.

'I was at a clear up on the minesweeper with Winerow last night. Didn't hear the news, got back late from Charing Cross — they're going to France at the weekend. Some sort of drill they do. Those minesweepers have a shallow draught, it seems. They expect bad weather', I recounted in a sleepy reply.

Thurston was a happy man and he liked Winerow and me. He felt sorry for us being away from home so young. It elicited from him a kind of prudent and avuncular interest in us which was unobtrusive.

Winerow didn't appear, and I got on with my work. Thurston straightened his tie and contemplated London through the high window beside his desk. Drunken drivers and tired lorry drivers had been causing pile ups on the M.1. motorway the previous Christmas and the control car men were coming in with resolve and cold anger. It made work for everybody, not to mention the undertakers.

Strolling down Greek Street at lunchtime I told Winerow — jaded from the previous night — that I wanted to get a copy of *The Guardian* on Shaftesbury Avenue. He had heard the news too, somehow. 'Do you do examinations in sin over there?' he teased in a superior way. 'I know what you mean, Winerow, but it's more complicated than that,' I replied absently. 'There hasn't been a shot fired in merry England since the War of the Roses', he persisted with a grin. 'Okay, Winerow, so you're the lovely people. You'll be smoking dope next and falling asleep at the wheel and the boat'll go down. No more mockers and scoffers meeting the mayors of the wee French towns.' He laughed good-naturedly and waved his hand in mock disparagement. From the back page of *The Guardian* it seemed ugly enough in its own demented way. Men were playing three card tricks on cardboard boxes in Greek Street with quiet speed. It was illegal.

Fiacc's hand shuddered the teacup and broke my reverie. I didn't know whether or not I'd see him again because I'd be going back to London soon. Conleth Ellis read the last poem. It was entitled 'Belfast 1964'.

Autumn came to Divis Street in splintered glass,
Twisted gratings, stones and hurleys; grass
Behind the railings of Saint Comgall's strewn
With shrivelled leaves: outside — because a tune,
A phrase, a flag can strangle rote-learnt grace —
Find splintered, shrivelled heart and twisted face.
Imagining green hills the ashen breezes brushed
The glazed mill race, wide-whorled, that rushed
To find its stream, I find my path down grasses,
Over brown stones where the night herd passes,
Where only coins of light fall through leaves,
And foxes hunt, buds burst, the spider weaves.

On the Heysham boat a few Belfast lads were singing a Bob Dylan song aggressively and garrulously, 'It's a haard, it's a haard, it's a haard rain that's gonna fall.' I ordered a bottle of wee Willie Dark at the bar and wondered about Belfast and the little dainty man with the hazel head and eyes. I had no answers for anything. I wearied of the loudness of the song and went up to the starry deck amongst the soldiers and the sailors. We were all sea-struck. It was quiet. Belfast was left behind in a great moonlit track of foam. I felt relieved in some sort of grave way. I was still an adolescent feeling my way between two worlds, wanting to understand what I didn't know — exactly.

Fiacc at that time in 1967 was a 'bell-tossed head'. His poetry was witty, vagrant and tough. He had a deft knack of slapping the sacred cows on the butt. The poems had the depth of sonic echoes. I knew then he would be mocked, because people didn't want their corners of the cobweb shaken, and a cobweb it was. They had a point, but the world of tight moral constraint was loosening and I knew that from my aviary in London.

Apart from a few poets and poems, I felt there was little to get excited about — apart from Derek Mahon's 'In Belfast', Louis MacNiece's 'Autumn Journal', some of W. R. Rodgers, Norman Dugdale and Heaney's 'Docker' — not world-shaking by any means.

From that little meeting came *Words* magazine. It looked like a film brochure. It contained poems by Michael Boyle, Michael Brophy, Seamus Heaney's 'Gravities', and work by John Morrow (who cut his literary teeth there) and an article by Ralph Bossence of the *Newsletter*. Michael Emmerson of the Belfast Festival was interviewed there, but it didn't see a second issue. People went to universities or lost interest.

For me Fiacc epitomized the secret spirit and atmospherics of Belfast at the time. The third eye so to speak. His poem 'First Movement' was an emotional flare.

> Low clouds, yellow in a mist wind,
> Sift on far-off Ards
> Drift hazily . . .

> I was born on such a morning
> Smelling of the Bone Yards

> The smoking chimneys over the slate roof tops
> The wayward storm birds

> And to the east where morning is, the sea
> And to the west where evening is, the sea

> Threatening with danger

> And it would always darken suddenly.

This was an Ancient Mariner poem — the sense of a great bruised swell of feeling bloating. Fiacc and the poets came to understand painfully the meaning of Shakespeare's lines at the end of 'Love's Labour's Lost' — 'The words of Mercury are harsh after the Songs of Apollo'. This was the beginning of the end of a period of fatalistic aphasia. Poetry in the North began to flourish, often with rancour and weaseling.

Fiacc was the beginning — the rascal amongst the monks, the sign and the soothsayer — from Hell's Kitchen to the Dark Country — to Dante's 'Inferno', and . . . finally to life lived in the shadow of the gun. He shares with Sir John Betjeman and the dogs of Belfast a love of lamp-posts and dark corners. When his autobiography comes out it will be like a Belfast version of Robert Graves's great autobiography *Goodbye To All That*. Meanwhile, I'll not take the third light. I believe in luck and the words of William Blake: 'the tigers of wrath are wiser than the horses of instruction'. Imagination can create a new world — where the old one failed. Fiacc's poetry talks the language of wrath.

Perhaps the horses of instruction should take off the blinkers and listen.

Nuala Ní Dhomhnaill

TRADUCTIO AD ABSURDUM

When the publication of Irish-language poetry in dual-language format (i.e. with English translations across the page) was first adopted in the late nineteen eighties, it was an important and decisive step. An important pulse was touched, and signs on, starting with the Raven anthology, *An Tonn Gheal*, many of the books were in the bestseller lists, sometimes for weeks on end. A whole population, it seemed, rushed to buy them. These were often people who had had reasonably good Irish at school but who had subsequently been to all intents and purposes linguistically disenfranchised because of the lack of a functional context where they could use the language without embarrassment or fear of correction. This had the effect of opening up the gates of the language ghetto. Irish language literature, hitherto relegated to Bantustan status by linguistic apartheid, became visible again in its own country. The translation policy also effectively cut the ground from under the middlemen, a shower of pundits who had taken upon themselves the monopoly for Irish, pontificating upon it to the great unwashed. From now on poetry in Irish was accessible to many, with the help of good translations in English. All this was undoubtably to the good — of the poetry, of Irish-language poets, of English-language poets, of the reading public and of the general wider culture.

Nevertheless, this policy is not without some serious problems, one of which struck me most forcibly recently in a review in *The Irish Times* by Catherine Foley of my book *The Astrakhan Cloak* (trans. Paul Muldoon) and Liam Ó Muirthile's (Irish only) *Dialann Bóthair*. In it she says: 'It's an added bonus that Nuala Ní Dhomhnaill's work in *The Astrakhan Cloak* is accompanied by English versions by the poet Paul Muldoon. The translations shed light on the work and add new dimensions and meanings to many of the poems . . . *What a pity Gallery Press did not follow the same plan with Ó Muirthile's collection.*' (my italics). I don't think this was written with any malice or ill-will, but it is symptomatic of an attitude that is gaining ground. An even more glaring example was a critique in *The Irish Times* by Katie Donovan of an Irish-Scottish night held at Cúirt International in Galway last April at which Johnny Chóil Mhaidhc and myself read for the Irish and Anne Frater and Iain Crichton Smith read for the Scots. The Scots, as is their wont, had English translations, and even though I don't particularly like reading in English, especially in Galway, I gave a dual-language reading. Katie Donovan wrote: 'Johnny Chóil Mhaidhc did not read any English translation, however, so that half of the audience missed out. This was a cogent illustration of the fact that, like it or not, the colonizer's language is here to stay, and only poets who write in English or who translate, can enjoy a wide audience for their work.' I have no argument with the facts of this statement, as such, but it is the attitude behind it that gives me room for pause. There is no cognizance of the need for poetry in Irish to exist *in its own right*, and if you don't understand it, well, tough. The translations are really never more than a secondary consideration, and should not be taken to stand for, or to stand in for, the originals. It also puts me in the invidious position of being a stick in the hands of the 'monolingual meatheads' (Aodán Mac Póilin, *Krino* 11, 1991) with which to beat Johnny Chóil Mhaidhc and other Irish language poets over the head. I find this intolerable and not what was envisaged in any way by the adoption of a translation policy.

It seems to me that this extension of the majority language *herrenvolk* mentality must be resisted at all costs and that we need to take another step in our cultural strategy. Some poets in Irish have already declared their unwillingness to be translated into English in Ireland. This is the stand taken by Biddy Jenkinson (who doesn't mind being translated into French) and by Louis de Paor, who, living in Australia, has taken his cue from Aboriginal culture. These are undoubtably very brave and worthwhile gestures, but where do they leave us? Do we return to the status quo of the fifties and sixties, when every literary or academic rag worth the name contained an example of Irish-language poetry, untranslated, as a token piece of exotica. These so-called 'poems' were usually completely devoid of any literary value, gave a thoroughly misleading picture of contemporary literature in Irish, and functioned as a tedious knee-jerk ritual of appeasement towards that great sacred cow, the shibbolethic language policy of the Irish Republic. Do we want to return to this, and if not, what is the alternative? Translation, but with a mandatory health warning — *caveat lector*?

Michael Davitt

AN DÍBEARTACH

Tháinig is d'imigh fir an bhrúscair.
Táim im luí ar thaobh sráide
Faoin mbáisteach ag bogadh sall is anall
Ar mo bholg plaisteach sa ghaoith.
Tá máilín cruinn súchaite tae
Greamaithe dem chléibh,
Cárta poist de thráigh aislingiúil dem thóin.
Dá bhféadfainn breith ar mo hata
Atá caite i mbéal geata
Ní bheifeá ag sá do shúl
Chomh sotalach síos im anam dorcha
Tusa a bhfuil do hata geal miotail
Fáiscthe anuas go dlúth ar do cheann.

THE OUTCAST

The rubbish men came and went.
I'm lying in the gutter
In the rain rolling back and forth
On my plastic stomach in the wind.
There's a round clapped-out tea-bag
Stuck to my side,
To my bottom a postcard of some idyllic strand.
If I could just grab hold of my hat
Thrown in the gateway
You wouldn't be gawking so snottily
Down into my dark soul,
You with your bright metal lid
Fixed firmly on your head.

(translated by the author)

AN FOCAL

Cianta cairbreacha ár n-aontís
Ní rabhais riamh chun caighdeáin:
Rómhór mar seo, ró-mhar siúd.

Is an focal úd nach bhfuaimneofá ceart
Dhein neascóid de, neascóid fhoirfe
Mar a mbíodh cluas liom.

Le linn ár scarúna
Is sa chneasú a lean
Chneasaigh an neascóid, tharla athrú —

Ní i bhfuaimniú an fhocail úd agat
Ach sa tslí a chloisim anois tú,
Díreach mar a ceapadh duit labhairt

Ag an Té a cheap cluas is canúint.

Cathal Ó Searcaigh

SNEACHTA

D'éalaínn amach le teacht an lae
ar na maidneacha geala geimhridh adaí
is an sneachta ag titim mar chlúmh gé.

Bhíodh ar tír chomh coimhthíoch le fásach;
na harda uilig ina ndumhcha is na bóithigh
cuachta go cruiteach, camaill chodlatacha.

Ba mhór an tógáil croí ar maidin go luath
an bhalbh-bháine adaí a bheith i mo thimpeall
is an saol á shamhlú agam ansiúd as an nua.

Tá an leathanach bán seo dálta thír an tsneachta
ag mealladh an pháiste atá istigh amach
lena chuma féin a chur ar lom na cruthaitheachta.

SNOW

I used slip out at daybreak
those bright winter mornings;
snow falling like goose-down.

The land strange as a desert;
the hills all sand-dunes, and the byres
humped, huddled, sleepy camels.

Those early mornings filled me with exhilaration —
dumb whiteness all around
and the world imagined anew.

This white page, like the snow-land
tempts the child within
to put his own stamp on blank creation.

MUIRBHÉ

Cérbh as í murarbh ón tsáile í? Caidé
eile a réiteodh
le feamainn rua na ndual, le glas na súl,
le suathadh síoraí
an bhrollaigh, le cáitheadh cúrach
na hanála adaí.

Is mar thiontódh trá i Machaire Rabhartaigh
chas sí uaim i dtobainne
is ina diaidh níl fágtha ach raic na gcuimhní
ar chladaí m'intinne;
carraig chreimthe an chroí agus och,
na deora goirte.

SEA-WOMAN

Where was she from if not the sea? What
else explains
that seaweed-auburn hair, those grey-green eyes,
the ceaseless agitation
of her breast, the foaming spume
of her breath.

And as the tide turns in Machaire Rabhartaigh
she turned from me suddenly
leaving only the wrack of memories
on the shore of my mind;
the abraded rock of the heart, and O,
the salt tears.

AON SÉASÚR DEN BHLIAIN

Inár seomra suí leapa
seargann na plandaí tí
fiú i dtús an tSamhraidh.

Titeann duilleoga feoite
i measc deora taisligh
dusta agus proinn dhóite.

Ní ghlaonn an ghrian
isteach trí fhuinneog an dín
aon séasúr den bhliain.

Is anseo i saol seargtha
an bhrocsholais, tá sé ina Shamhain
ag plandaí is ag leannáin.

ANY SEASON OF THE YEAR

In our bed-sitting room
the house-plants wither
even in early summer.

Leaves shrivel and fall
amid the dampness
the dust and the burnt meals.

No sun visits us here
nor calls through the skylight
any season of the year.

And here in the withered world
of this foul light, it is November
for plants and lovers.

(*translated by Aodán Mac Póilin with Cathal Ó Searcaigh*)

Paul Celan

SEVEN POEMS

OUT OF FISTS, whitened
by Truth hammered
free from the word-face,
a new brain blooms for you.

Beautiful, veilable by nothing,
it casts them, the
thought-shadows.
Therein, unshiftable,
they fold, today now,
twelve mountains, twelve foreheads.

The she-vagrant Melancholia,
star-eyed by you too,
learns this.

MUSSELSHELL-MIDDEN: with
the stone-club I burst into it,
following the rivers up to the
melting ice —
homeland,
towards the fireflint —
to be etched after whose sign? —
in the breath of the dwarf-birch.

Lemmings burrowed.

No Later.

No
shallow-urn, no
openwork-disc,
no starfoot-
fibula.

Unappeased,
unattached, art-less,
the All-transforming ascended, slowly
scraping,
after me.

JOTTINGS-PAIN,
snowed on, snowed under:

in the calendar-blank
it's cradled, cradled
by the new-born
Nothing.

DREAM-POWERED in your orbit,
charred,

two masks instead of one,
planet-dust in your hollowed
eyes,

night-blind, day-blind,
world-blind,

the poppy-capsule in you
goes down somewhere,
ensilences with
a fellowstar,

the floating domain of sorrow
registers one more shadow,

they're all helping you.

the heart-stone pierces its fan,
no coolness,
none at all,

they're all helping you,

you sail, glow down, gleam away,
eye-swarms pass through the straits,
a blood-clot enters your orbit,

earth-swarms speak kindly to you.

the weather in space
is reaping.

CLOWN-FACED BY NOW,
in the mirror of naught.

Truth, your make-up, frozen blue
in the angled mouth.

Frostpollen powder on the polished superskull,
around thin Black, the question-curl.

The eyebrows, eyebrows: waxing,
two giant feeler-combs, two,
— you combed, you probed, you
tall, tall haunt-night Foreverever — ,
swung away already from the snowflake World,
not to, not fro.

BARGE-DRAGGING TIME,
the half-transformed are hauling
one of the worlds,

the brought-low, inwarded,
he speaks among the foreheads on the bank:

Death — quits, God —
quits.

YOU BE AS YOU, always.

*Stand up, Jerusalem, and
arise*

Even who cut the bond with you,

and shine

tied it anew, in remembrance,

mud-lumps I swallowed, in the tower,

language, gloom-lesene,

kumi
ori

DUE SEI WIE DU, IMMER.

Stant up Jherosalem inde
erheyff dich

Auch wer das Band zerschnitt zu dir hin,

inde wirt
erluchtet

knüpfte es neu, in der Gehugnis,

Schlammbrocken schluckt ich, im Turm,

Sprache, Finster-Lisene,

kumi
ori.

(*translated by Brian Lynch and Peter Jankowsky*)

MUSSELSHELL-MIDDEN

This poem abounds with archaeological terms: 'Midden' are heaps of musselshells, remnants of early coastal settlements; stone-clubs (or pebble-clubs) are early tools and weapons of barely worked stone. Together with 'fireflint', 'melting ice', 'dwarf-birch' and 'lemmings' they evoke a barren, tundra-like, post-glacial landscape, in it the beginnings of European civilization. 'Shallow-urn', 'openwork-disc' and 'starfoot-fibula' on the other hand, belong to the much later Bronze Age. Celan seems to see

himself here as the archetypal disturber and outcast for whom the 'All-transforming' —
'Unappeased, unattached, art-less' and 'slowly scraping' is his only companion.

CLOWN-FACED BY NOW
'Haunt-night' is our attempt at finding an English equivalent for the German
'Rauhnacht', the surface meaning of which would be something like 'rough night'; there
is also an association with hoar frost (Rauhreif). The 'Rauhnächte' (originally
'Rauchnächte' — 'smoke nights') are, especially in southern Germany, the Twelve
Nights between the Christian feasts of Christmas and Epiphany, when incense was
burnt in houses and stables, when demons were going around and the dead returned.

BARGE-DRAGGING TIME
'Brought-low' and 'inwarded': the German words 'der Enthöhte' and 'geinnigt' are
taken from the writings of the mystic Meister Eckehart (1260-1328), who taught that
God should be brought down from His height ('enthöht') and taken into Man's
innermost self ('geinnigt'). Celan appears to be using both words in relation to a
particular human being, most likely himself.

'quits' is not the third person singular of the verb 'to quit'; rather it means 'to be
evens, to be quits with somebody'.

YOU BE AS YOU
Celan said that this poem was initiated by his reading of Meister Eckehart's sermon
'Surge illuminare' on Isaiah 60. He quotes in it Meister Eckehart's Middle High
German translation of the beginning of that text. We used the wording in the King
James Bible.

'kumi ori' is again the beginning of Isaiah 60, in the original Hebrew: 'arise,
become light!'

'remembrance': the German word 'Gehugnis' is also taken from Meister Eckehart
where it means 'memory, remembrance, a secret hidden art and knowledge'.

'lesene' is a pilaster strip, an architectural device of vertically structuring large wall
surfaces. It is common in Romanesque church architecture, contemporaneous with Meister
Eckehart.

It should be noted that at the heart of this poem is its bringing together of Jewish
and Christian spirituality, Hebrew, medieval and modern German, and that a
translation here can serve only the purpose of informing a non-German-speaking
readership of its content in general. We have therefore included the original.

Alan Titley

MODERN IRISH PROSE:
A NECESSARY INTRODUCTION
FOR THE UNINITIATED

Much prose suffers from the fact that it is not poetry. That is to say, the ordinary hack prose writer doesn't have the glamour garlanded about him that the poet necessarily claims because he thinks he has access to the mysteries which ordinary discourse can't reach. For all that, modern prose in all languages has been at its best as poetic as most poetry has been prosaic, and writing in Irish is no exception. The poetry which Irish bards of the medieval period produced by virtue of placing a stone upon their bellies and mumbling overnight in a darkened room is no better in style and substance than that which the proseur produces because he has to meet the deadline of an irascible editor, or scribble about the dull quotidian, or tell a story that has been often told before, or satisfy the demands of an educational system that requires that writing be ordinary, yet exciting, yet safe.

This homily is delivered, not so much because the tradition of Irish poetry is so strong that it threatens to overwhelm everything else that has been written, but because, despite the long tradition of Irish prose, equally ancient as that of the versifiers and therefore almost exceptional in Western European literatures, it seems always to be placed secondary to the musers and messers because of their domination of the written word for two hundred years before 1900. It is not, of course, that there is some kind of metaphysical rivalry between prose and poetry since various forms generally come to the fore because of social and political conditions. Poetry flourished in the eighteenth and nineteenth centuries in Irish because it was relatively easy for an impoverished rhymster to rattle off innumerable verses on any subject in field or fair which took his fancy; prose demanded the hard intellectual graft and sufficient leisure which was denied by the political regime. It is for that reason that the twentieth century has been the century of prose in Irish literature; there has been more prose written and read and thought about in this century in Irish than in all the previous centuries put together for all our two thousand years.

The Irish writers who attempted to build anew a modern Irish prose at the close of the last century and at the beginning of this one were not quite starting from the egg; rather they were building from the shattered shell of the seventeenth century and grafting new colours from international species. The great critical debate at the turn of the century was whether Irish prose should be based on the classical standard set down by Seathrún Céitinn at the time of the Counter-Reformation or on the ordinary speech of the people used in their everyday and everynight lives. It was as if English writers wished to model their prose on the unbridled sentences of Thomas Nashe or the heavy iron curtains of John Milton, rather than on the gabble of a Shropshire lad or the cant of a cockney. While this might seem a wondrously strange and weird debate for those who inhabit an unbroken tradition, it is interesting that the Chinese, Greek and Arabic literary scenes suffered a similar wrangle at roughly the same time. As far as my paltry knowledge goes, modernism won the day on every occasion in each of these countries.

It did so in Ireland because writers don't generally give a ship's shine for what the critics say, or alternatively, because they are usually the best critics themselves. It is clear that An tAthair Peadar Ua Laoghaire was not clear what he was about when he embarked on the first Irish novel, *Séadna*, published in book form, after serialization, in 1904. It is equally clear, however, that he satisfied large numbers of Irish readers in producing a novel, that was all things to all people. It is, at the one time, a folk-novel based on an international tale, a study of individual character as in the best nineteenth-century Jamesian plodder, a book for beginners which the sophisticated can appreciate, a medieval allegory of good and evil, a thriller where the suspense is held until the last few pages, a documentary which describes the lives of ordinary people in a rural community, and a postmodernist tale which is self-reflective and self-critical. There is no doubt that it was a theme that suited bang-on the concerns and the limitations of its author; we know that because most of the other attempts at creativity by An tAthair Peadar were successful only as failures, an example of which might be his second novel, *Niamh* (1907), which stretches our credulity a lot more than the eponymous hero was ever stretched. What An tAthair Peadar did succeed in doing was establishing the speech of the ordinary people as the normal standard for everyday prose, and despite dialect bigots' misgivings about his Muskerry muscular diction, the principle was conceded and hankerers after the seventeenth century retired to their studies.

It would be oversimplistic to say that we can divide Irish writers into two camps from the beginning of the century, that is, the traditionalists and the modernists, but it is a pleasantly crude classification that serves some purposes. The traditionalists would argue that the modernists were not being true to the genius of the Irish language and to the facts of Irish-speaking communities, while the modernists would argue that the traditionalists were confusing the nineteenth century and the folksy with life, while not being able to see the semantic wood for the linguistic tree. The truth might be that in any complete language or complete literature you need the lot, and readers of English literature in Ireland will find no difficulty in swallowing the experimentalism of a James Joyce, a Robert MacLiam Wilson or a Sebastian Barry with the same bitter pill as a Brinsley MacNamara, a Frank O'Connor or a John McGahern, who wrote as if the twentieth century never happened. Although there is no inherent virtue in whoring after alien gods or goddesses, Pádraic Ó Conaire proved in his short stories and in his one successful novel, *Deoraíocht* (1910), that much could be learned by applying one's own experience to the technique of a Dostoevsky, a Dickens or a Balzac. Despite his penchant for walking very close to the cliff between horror and melodrama, or for stepping on the very thin ice of depressing realism across the bog of improbable fact, he is still worth reading because we know that somewhere underneath all the schmaltz there is a real writer struggling to emerge, even if he breaks through only in fits and bleeps and glimmers and starts.

The much-reviled-by-revisionists Pádraig Mac Piarais succeeded in implementing a revolution in politics, in education and in literature, which is more than can be said for any of his detractors. While his revolution in politics failed because the guns arrayed against him were too great, and his attempt to change education floundered on the hard-headedness of parents who want their children to be trained in gainful employment as economic timeservers, his influence on literature remained profound because of his sensitivity and courage as a critic. In that, he joins a select band of writers in Ireland whose criticism was always more creative than their imaginative work, and of whom Daniel Corkery and Seán O'Faoláin (as biographer) would be prominent. Pearse had a generosity of soul and a sharpness of critical perception which have set the standard for much that has been written about literature in Irish unto the present day.

One of the main differences between any account of literature in Irish and in English in this century must be the importance accorded to regional and dialectical writing in Irish. Although much writing in English in this century has centred upon coming home through the fields past the lake by lough gorr and twice round the black church neath the green leafy shade in our village of longing amongst women as an only child and mind the dresser, we can readily see that much of its impetus is sentimental where it is not financial. In the case of Irish, it is much more likely to be part of the battle of the dialects, where each region tried to show by literary excellence that its particular forms should be dominant in whatever national standard would eventually emerge.

Although the Munster dialect remained most prestigious for the first quarter century because of the success of An tAthair Peadar Ua Laoghaire's writings and the amazing dictionary of Patrick Dineen, there was a *putsch* by Ulster writers in the twenties and thirties which helped to restore equilibrium and some sense of proportion. Although containing in many ways the most extensive Gaeltacht, Connacht, until the arrival of Máirtín Ó Cadhain as a major writer in the late nineteen forties, remained, like its hurlers and footballers, permanently at the bottom rung of losers and no-hopers, in slumber deep and unknowing. The Ulster revival was spearheaded by Séamus Ó Grianna, who wrote under the pen-name Máire, and his younger brother Seosamh Mac Grianna. One of the great signs of life about these authors is that there is still a lively critical debate about their worth, although this is sometimes influenced by one's proximity or distance to or from Donegal. Critical geographers have noted that their esteem grows in direct proportion to how close the reader is to Rann na Feirste, but they are not likely to be covered with plaudits in the University of West Kerry. For all that, much about Máire is remarkable. He invented a form of the short story that was all his own, and he wrote a series of novels that were invariably interesting until he decided to introduce a plot. His best work is comic masquerading as tragic, and his misfortune was to have wearied the critics and his readers before his best novel, *Bean Ruadh de Dhálach*, was published in the nineteen sixties, long after everyone had given up the ghost and the spirit and the flesh. His autobiographies, *Nuair a Bhí Mé Óg* and *Saol Corrach*, are masterpieces of tenderness and acerbity, and show what he was capable of if he hadn't read Pat McGill or had presumed that Thomas Carlyle was a great writer. His greatest achievement is that he succeeded in producing a substantial body of worthwhile reading material for his own people and for enthusiasts of Ulster Irish from Belfast, occasionally reaching base camp on the mountains of Parnassus but always keeping his end up.

His other achievement was that he added the much-needed ingredient of imagination to that documentary literature which was growing in each Gaeltacht as scholars persuaded small farmers and fisherman that they had something to say. Some did and some didn't. There was, of course, value in documenting the way of life, and more importantly, the language of the Gaeltacht while it remained strong. In this sense, most Gaeltacht autobiographies and old-timers' reminiscences are interesting, although only very few of them should be confused with literature. The most famous of these autobiographies is undoubtedly Tomás Ó

Criomhthain's *An tOileánach* (1929), which was later translated as *The Islandman* and received some international recognition. This form of writing in Irish is almost *sui generis* in so far as it is about so-called ordinary people writing about their so-called ordinary lives, whereas most autobiographies which attain fame are written by the rich or the famous or those who are famous because they are rich. Tomás Ó Criomhthain was no ordinary person, however, but a single-minded literary craftsman who learned to write his language when he was advanced in years and who provided a classic virtually without models. His prose, in the original, is as cold as the water around the Great Blasket, as supple as the seals which he hunted, as clean as the west wind and as tough as the hide of an old cow. He is the most unromantic of writers despite the apparent exotic location and the photography of calendar decorators. He wrote a second classic, *Allagar na hInise*, which is really just a lot of old talk, but which is more poetic in its execution than a shelf-full of old anthologies with greater pretensions.

Seosamh Mac Grianna joined in the cult of autobiographies when he published *Mo Bhealach Féin* (1940) after a few novels and a fine collection of short stories. It is really an imaginative credo and a defiant manifesto against the world, more than any kind of reconstruction of the externals of life, and still remains one of our best statements about the frustrated and misunderstood artist. He was our existentialist before we had heard of the word, our rebel when all the others had gone soft or joined the civil service, our anarchist when others were looking for a code to live by. One always feels when reading him that there was much potential left unfulfilled, much talent that was never quite expressed.

The nineteen twenties and thirties saw the greatest outpouring of prose of all kinds apart from the last few years. Although this outpouring may have been only great in bulk, it was certainly necessary in order to provide reading and working material for the new generation of people either learning or rediscovering the language. The state publishing company, An Gúm, which was founded in the nineteen twenties, provided support for original and for translated books. Many of the world's classics were rendered into Irish and are examples of what good translations should be. Its policy on original novels and short stories was not quite as successful, partly because you cannot order the coming of good authors and partly because writers in Irish suffered the same malaise as their counterparts in English after the foundation of the state. This era of dull and plodding realism seemed to produce the same novels and short stories over and over again under different titles, although a few like Éamonn Mac Giolla Iasachta's *Cúrsaí Thomáis* (1927) or Barra Ó Caochlaigh's *Lucht Ceoil* (1932) can still bear a close reading.

It was not until after the great barbarian war that creative and imaginative prose underwent a transformation. Much was made at the time of Séamas Ó Néill's *Tonn Tuile* (1947), a novel which attempted to depict marital tensions in Dublin during the war. Unfortunately the main character and narrator is — with no hint of irony — such a prig, and the prose is as thin as toilet paper, so that we find it impossible to empathise either with the author's intentions or style. It may have been welcomed more for its apparent modern urban setting than for its literary content in the belief that it heralded a departure from the dominant rural prose tradition up until then. The worst excesses of that tradition were beautifully and hilariously parodied in Myles na gCopaleen's *An Béal Bocht* (1941) some years previously, although the author admitted several times that his novel was written out of a profound respect for *An tOileánach* which it is seemingly sending up.

It was Máirtín Ó Cadhain's magisterial and masterful *Cré na Cille* (1949) which more than anything else broke the back of the realist incubus. If 'the speech of the people' had been the literary catch-cry for so long, Ó Cadhain took it as far as it could possibly go and beyond. For, if we exclude some introductory passages to some of the interludes in which the book is divided, the entire novel is in straight talk. More than that, all the characters are dead and buried in a graveyard in Connemara which means — necessarily — that their movement is restricted and that their development can go only in the direction of decomposition. And in a sense this is ironically apt, since the traditional novel is wonderfully decomposed within a form which is uniquely his own, and traditional society is buried under six feet and tens of thousands of words of bitchiness, and backbiting, and taunts, and sneers, and slagging, and animadversions. If one of the reasons for the cultivation of literature is to glorify language, then *Cré na Cille* does it with power and wonder; it also showed, once again, that the rural novel can be modernist, just as *Tonn Tuile* had shown that the urban novel can be retrogressive. These sociological divisions much loved by those who think that the literature of the dual-carriageway is superior to that of the boreen, or their opposites, who prefer their own real horny bull in a field to artificial insemination in an alley, never had much meaning when it came to the hot stuff of writing. Irish prose had been both rural and urban from the start, and had contained within it the traditional and the experimental. Good writers always understand that it is the critic who sucks his categories for comfort and who keeps putting the psycho back into analysis.

Máirtín Ó Cadhain did for the short story in a series of collections what he had also done for the novel. Although he had published one book of tales before the war, it was a work he was inclined to disown, but he was always proud of the best of his stories in *An Braon Broghach* (1948) and *Cois Caoláire* (1953). These best stories had to do with the toughness of life in his native Cois Fharraige, but they are written without the real sentimentality or the false toughness which marred one of the finest collections of short stories of that time, Liam Ó Flaithearta's *Dúil* (1953). Máirtín Ó Cadhain did not publish another book for seventeen years when *An tSraith ar Lár* (1967), the first of a trilogy of collections of short stories, appeared. This and *An tSraith dhá Tógáil* (1970) contain his finest writing apart from *Cré na Cille*, but they were part of such a good body of writing which appeared in the nineteen sixties that they seemed less remarkable then than they do now.

Any collection of the finest of Irish prose would be overburdened with writing from the nineteen sixties. It was in particular Eoghan Ó Tuairisc, Diarmaid Ó Suilleabháin and Breandán Ó Doibhlin who were innovative and courageous, and in an entirely different way Dónall Mac Amhlaigh and Pádraig Ua Maoileoin who breathed new life into more traditional forms of fiction. It was during this decade that Máire's best novel, the aforementioned *Bean Ruadh de Dhálach* (1966), was published, and even the censors shone on his brother Seosamh's forgotten novel, *An Druma Mór* (1969), which was written in the nineteen thirties but remained in the womb of the Gúm all those years because of political pressure. While it would always be wrong to compare Irish literature with the literatures of the major world languages, there was much written in those years of which anyone could be proud, no matter in what language it was composed.

Irish prose speaks, of course, to our particular condition and situation; if it did not it would be mad. But at its best it reaches out to touch others whose historical life might at least be analogous to ours. It is very likely that we have more in common with Latvian or Serbian or Shona literature, if we were to really know about them, than with the words of the great powers who decide what modernity or sensibility in our time is. There could certainly never be an Irish Kipling, just as surely as there couldn't be an English Séamus Ó Grianna. It shouldn't be any mystery that the concerns of the Irish-speaking community both within and without the traditional Gaeltacht have largely shaped the kind of literature we get; writing in Irish is never just a mirror image of writing in English in Ireland, despite the similarity of landscape and the old familiar faces. Yes, there was much hankering after a simpler rural life and the virtues therein contained in many Irish novels and short stories, but there was also much savage criticism. Yes, there were a lot of political tales of uncomplicated morality, with the goodies and baddies lined up fairly simply on either side, but it is occasionally sensible to be unambivalent about the evil of colonialism. Where writing in Irish seems to differ remarkably from writing in English is that there appear to be a lot less chips on a lot fewer shoulders about the awfulness of Ireland, the oppression of the brutal clergy and the misery of family life. In fact, despite trenchant and critical examination of the past, present and possible future of the country in works as diverse as Brendán Ó Doibhlin's *An Branar gan Cur* (1979), Diarmaid Ó Súilleabháin's *Maeldún* (1972), or Breandán Ó hEithir's *Sionnach ar mo Dhuán* (1988), you get the distinct impression that this is a place where the good life can be lived. Put another way, the anger in Irish fiction is positive rather than defeatist, because if it was defeatist, of course, it wouldn't be written at all at all.

The impression should not be given that Irish prose consists entirely of fiction, whether short or long. Some of the best writing in recent years has been done in literary scholarship. Seán Ó Tuama's criticism of poetry and fiction since the nineteen fifties led the charge to deal with literature as the product of a human mind and human society against the Teutonic tradition of verb-counting and the search for the perfect text which had been dominant in Irish universities since the start of the century. It might not seem so revolutionary now to look upon literature as something that could be enjoyed, but the best of Seán Ó Tuama's essays, collected in *Cúirt, Tuath agus Bruachbhaile* (1990), have a youthfulness and spiritedness and incisiveness about them that comes only from a personal engagement with works of written art. Breandán Ó Doibhlin instituted his own revolution in criticism in Maynooth in the nineteen sixties and his most important essays are brought together in *Aistí Critice agus Cultúir* (1974); Antain Mag Shamhráin's *Litríocht, Léitheoireacht, Critic* (1986) is a prolonged study of the work of the Maynooth critics and a detailed essay on the principles of literary analysis in an Irish context. Gearóid Denvir's *Cadhan Aonair* (1987) is the single most important piece of work on Máirtín Ó Cadhain and is not likely to be surpassed. It is, like the best of this criticism, stylishly written and can be read for its own sake apart from anything it might have to say. Breandán Ó Conaire's *Myles na Gaeilge* (1986) is a model of painstaking and meticulous literary detective work which does for *An Béal Bocht* what teams of biblical scholars have done for the New Testament, lifting up sentences and shaking out their genealogies before us.

This scholarship is evident in many other areas also. There are excellent literary biographies of Seán Ó Ríordáin and of Eoghan Ó Tuairisc by Seán Ó Coileáin and Máirín Nic Eoin respectively. Historical biography has been very well served by Seán Ó Lúing and Leon Ó Broin among others. One of the most important books ever to have been written in Irish, and possibly in

Ireland, must surely be Liam Ó Caithnia's *Scéal na hIomána* (1980) which tells the story of the game of hurling from time immemorial up to the foundation of the GAA. It is much more than this, of course. It is a social history of Ireland which unearths many details of life and puts forward many theories about our past which had never been expressed before. I use this as an example of the kind of important scholarship which has been written in Irish in the last twenty years and which no person who pretends an interest in the general affairs of the country should be ignorant of. Whatever else we say about Irish, it has been and is being used as an instrument of intellectual investigation, debate and exposition with a confidence and facility over a wide range of subjects that it has not had since the seventeenth century.

It is dangerous to write of one's contemporaries because you might meet them around any corner and have forgotten your knife. More novels, however, have been published in the nineteen eighties than in any previous decade and they span the same gamut of types from wild experimentation to boghole traditionalism as they ever did. Séamus Mac Annaidh's *Cuaifeach mo Londubh Buí* (1983) was enjoyed by all who understood literary fun and games with a serious purpose, while Robert Schumann's *Kinderszenen* (1987) played serious games with a definite literary purpose. The short story has been particularly cultivated by Pádraic Breathnach, who has published six collections since the nineteen seventies; while Seán Mac Mathúna's *Ding agus Scéalta Eile* (1982) is likely to become a classic. Even as I write, a massive first collection of about four hundred and fifty pages of stories has been published by a writer we had scarcely heard about until now, Pádraig Ó Cíobháin. This collection, *Le Gealaigh* (1991), could not have been written, one supposes, without the victories won for Irish prose over the last century. In it, realism, fantasy, speculation and wonder in urban, rural and foreign settings are handled with the case and confidence of somebody who knows that what he is doing is worthwhile. As long as Irish prose keeps throwing up surprises like this, it will always be a delight to read.

Brian Friel

FATHERS AND SONS

(An extract from Act 1 of *Fathers and Sons* after the novel by I. Turgenev)

The play opens in May 1859, two years before the serfs were emancipated.

Arkady Kirsanov has graduated from Petersburg University and has just arrived home to spend the summer with his father, Nikolai, and his uncle, Pavel. Arkady has brought with him his revolutionary friend, Yevgeny Bazarov.

Nikolai is a widower, gentle but determined, who manages his small estate enthusiastically but incompetently.

Pavel, his brother, a typical 'Europeanized' Russian of the last century (not unlike Turgenev himself), is a bachelor. Wounded by a love affair in his youth he has retreated from life and lives in correct and austere melancholy in the remote country.

Bazarov is a cool-headed and totally dedicated revolutionary, a textbook Nihilist. Arkady's politics are not as deeply felt but he is dazzled by and in awe of his friend's quiet passion.

NIKOLAI: And how is your father, Yevgeny Vassilyich?

Bazarov looks blankly at him. Pause.

NIKOLAI: Your father — is he well?

BAZAROV: I suppose so. I haven't seen him for three years.

NIKOLAI: He has been away — has he? — travelling?

BAZAROV: Not that I know of.

NIKOLAI: Ah.

BAZAROV: I haven't seen him for three years because I haven't been home since I went to the university.
Silence.

ARKADY: (*Quickly*) Let me tell you about this character. Not only is he the best orator in the university but he is probably the best orator in the whole of Petersburg. He won the gold medal again this year — the third time in succession.

NIKOLAI: Wonderful!

ARKADY: And he is also — (*To Bazarov*) no, don't try to stop me — he is also in my opinion the most brilliant political philosopher the university has ever produced. He is president of the philosophical society and editor of the magazine. It's an astonishing radical publication — the college authorities banned both issues this year! We were brought before the disciplinary council — remember? 'Revolutionaries. Damned revolutionaries!'

NIKOLAI: Oratory is an excellent discipline; excellent. I approve very strongly of — of — of — of oratory.

PAVEL: On what do you . . . orate?

BAZAROV: Politics. Philosophy.

PAVEL: They have something in common, have they?

ARKADY: Come on, Uncle Pavel: you know they have. Politics is philosophy in action.

PAVEL: Really?

ARKADY: Politics is the public practice of philosophy.

PAVEL: Good heavens. (*To Bazarov*) And your philosophy is?

ARKADY: Nihilism.

PAVEL: Sorry?

ARKADY: Nihilism, Uncle Pavel. Bazarov is a Nihilist. So am I.

NIKOLAI: Interesting word that. I imagine it comes from the Latin — nihil — nothing. Does it mean somebody who respects nothing? No, it doesn't.

ARKADY: Someone who looks at everything critically.

PAVEL: If there's a difference.

ARKADY: There's a significant difference, Pavel. Don't be so precious.

PAVEL: Me? — precious? Good Lord.

ARKADY: Nihilism questions all received ideas and principles no matter how venerated those ideas and principles are. The Nihilist makes two assertions: that every belief must be questioned and that the world must be made anew. (*To Bazarov*) That's a fairly accurate summary of our stance, isn't it?

Bazarov shrugs indifferently and spreads his hands.

PAVEL: So you believe only in science?

ARKADY: You're not listening to what we're saying. We don't believe in anything. You can't believe in science any more than you can believe in the weather or farming or swimming.

NIKOLAI: I can tell you farming isn't what it used to be. For decades, probably for centuries, nothing changed. But in the past five years, even in the past three years, the advances I've seen in farming techniques —

ARKADY: I wish you would stop trying to divert me with your juvenile asides, Father.

NIKOLAI: I am sorry.

ARKADY: And I don't want an apology. We are not debating now, you know. This issue is vital to us.

PAVEL: A simple question: if you reject all accepted principles and all accepted precepts, what basis of conduct have you?

ARKADY: I don't understand what the simple question means.

PAVEL: On what basis do you conduct your life?

ARKADY: If something is useful — keep it. If it is not useful — out it goes. And the most useful thing we can do is repudiate, renounce, reject.

PAVEL: Everything?

ARKADY: Everything without use.

PAVEL: All accepted conventions, all art, all science?

ARKADY: What use are they? Out.

PAVEL: Civilization has just been disposed of, Nikolai.

NIKOLAI: But surely, Arkady — if I may be very serious — surely rejection means destruction; and surely we must construct, too?

ARKADY: That isn't our responsibility. Our priority is to make a complete clearance. That's what the present state of the people demands. We must respond to that demand. At this point in our evolution we have no right to indulge in the gratification of our own personal whims.

NIKOLAI: I don't think I had whims in mind, Arkady.

ARKADY: At times it's difficult to know what you have in mind, Father.

PAVEL: Well I'm sure the Russian people will be pleased to know that they are about to be relieved of all those things they foolishly hold so sacred — their traditions, their familial pieties, their sense of faith. Oh yes, that will be welcome news to them. And when do you begin to preach this gospel publicly?

ARKADY: We aren't preachers, are we, Bazarov? We are not going to —

PAVEL: Aren't you preaching now? (*To Nikolai*) This is all nonsense; weary old materialistic nonsense I've heard a hundred times.

ARKADY: All I'm saying is that we believe we have passed beyond the initial stage of social analysis: we know there is starvation and poverty; we know our politicians take bribes; we know the legal system is corrupt. We know all that. And we are tired listening to the 'liberals' and the 'progressives' and the 'reformers' talking endlessly about employment and law reform and the work ethic. And all the time fundamental questions are being —

PAVEL: So you have completed your analysis. You have identified all society's evils —

NIKOLAI: Let him finish, Pavel.

PAVEL: I would prefer Yevgeny Vassilyich would do his own talking. (*To Arkady*) But you intend to do nothing constructive yourselves?

BAZAROV: We intend to do nothing constructive ourselves.

PAVEL: Just abuse people who do.

BAZAROV: Just abuse people who do.

PAVEL: And that's called Nihilism.

BAZAROV: And that's called Nihilism. Is this riveting discussion nearly over?

PAVEL: *Incroyable!* Let me see have I got it right —

NIKOLAI: I'm sure you've got it right, Pavel. Let's leave it for now.

PAVEL: First our saviours will demolish the country and then they will remake the country. But suppose some simple person were to suggest that our saviours were just bletherskites — gold-medal bletherskites?

BAZAROV: My grandfather was a serf, Pavel Petrovich. I believe I have some knowledge of the Russian people.

PAVEL: I'm sure you have a very —

BAZAROV: Indeed I believe I have at least as accurate and as sympathetic an understanding of their needs and of their mute aspirations as those absurd provincial aristocrats who affect English clothes and English customs; who meet a peasant at most once or twice a year; who believe they are civilized just because they speak cliché French; who talk endlessly about Mother Russia but who sit on their backsides and do sweet nothing for the 'bien public' as they call it.

PAVEL: I suspect you're deliberately trying to —

BAZAROV: Words that come so easily to lips like yours — liberalism, progress, principles, civilization — they have no meaning in Russia. They are imported words. Russia doesn't need them. But what Russia does need — and action will provide it, Pavel Petrovich, action, not words — what Russia does need is bread in the mouth. But before you can put bread in the mouth, you have got to plough the land — deep.

NIKOLAI: He's right, you know: ploughing is a very important part of the farming cycle. (*To Arkady*) Sorry. I didn't —

PAVEL: So the two of you are going to reform Russia.

BAZAROV: Remake Russia.

ARKADY: And there are more of us than you'd even begin to suspect.

PAVEL: Good heavens. And this handful of the elite is about to remake our country for us all?

BAZAROV: Yes.

PAVEL: By force?

BAZAROV: (*Shrugs*) If necessary.

ARKADY: All that's needed is a few with dedication. It was a penny candle that burned Moscow down, Uncle Pavel.

NIKOLAI: That's quite true, you know.

PAVEL: For God's sake, Nikolai, you know nothing about it!

NIKOLAI: I beg your pardon, Pavel — it *was* a penny candle burned Moscow down. It's thought to be an old wives' tale but it is based on an historical fact. Father was able to quote chapter and verse on it. (*To Fenichka and Dunyasha, who have entered with a tray and samovar*) Ah! Fenichka! Good! Great! Splendid! And beautifully timed — just when we had all come to a close understanding of one another's position. Have you the sherry? Excellent (*To Dunyasha*) Just leave the tray there. Thank you. Thank you.

Terence Brown

TRANSLATING IRELAND

T ranslation has been a preoccupation of many Irish poets in recent
years. Not only have such poets as Thomas Kinsella, Brendan
Kennelly and Seamus Heaney, in his version of the Sweeney legend,
sought to negotiate the distance between an Irish-language poetic past and the
largely English present, but such writers as Nuala Ní Dhomhnaill, who
composes in Irish, have enjoyed almost an embarrassment of poetic suitors in
poets ready to provide their Irish language poems with English versions.
Indeed the dual language publication is now a commonplace (one thinks of
such recent books as Michael Davitt's *Selected Poems* and Dermot Bolger's
anthology *The Bright Wave/An Tonn Gheal*), causing even a kind of irritation
in those purists who were happier with the state of quarantine in which the
two linguistic traditions existed until very recently in Ireland.

Often enough in the past, translation from the Irish was an act of nationalist
piety, an expression of atavistic need, or even the consequence of a deliberate
programme. One gets no sense of such from the recent work. Rather, the
translations often seem to take for granted that the medium through which
most people in Ireland experience their world and live their lives is English
and that it is wholly appropriate that an Irish poet should write, if he or she
wishes, in that language. The sense of guilt which sometimes dogged English
language poets of an earlier generation no longer seems endemic. What the
fascination for translation from the Irish seems to imply is not a nostalgia for
some truly indigenous expression, nor any revivalist enthusiasm, but a sense
that the complexity of the Irish poet's contemporary experience requires an
interpretative resource which current English language usage somehow fails
fully to supply. It is as if, to adapt the Brian Friel of *Translations*, a linguistic
contour does not as yet match the contour of the fact, and the poet must seek
for alternative linguistic perspectives from which to survey the landscape. Irish
offers one such perspective, an angle that may permit innovatory perception,
radical envisioning. But, as Seamus Heaney has in fact recently testified about
his own fascination with the Sweeney legend, translation from the Irish will
always, as from the indigenous languages of the North American continent,
involve inevitably 'a canonical literature in English [which] creates the acoustic
within which the translation is to be heard'. So such works of translation enter

a world of English language literature. They are not just acts of literary journeywork making available matter which is a closed book to many — they are poems whose English accents have been affected by the work of translation and whose sound effects will imply echoes of other forms of consciousness to those most readily sounded in the poetry of the English-speaking world. So Heaney has written (in *The Poetry Ireland Review*, No. 25) of how when working on the Sweeney text he allowed himself to import 'echoes from the English literary tradition, from the Bible, to perform in metaphor what the text delivered in statement', and how the procedures of Robert Lowell suggested that such a work would bear the pressures of the autobiographical. The exercise accordingly might have resulted in a poem too readily obeying the acoustical laws of an English language echo-chamber. But a protracted work of creative rewriting, Heaney tells us, resulted in the colder, more verbal, music we have in the poem in its published form, as the poet attended 'to the metrical containments and battened-down procedures of the Irish itself'.

Concurrent with this recent reinvigoration of bilingual poetic endeavour has been the related phenomenon of translation of poetry from the European languages. In particular the poetry of Eastern Europe and the Soviet republics has preoccupied many poets. Once again in much of this work one senses a desire to expand the field of contemporary vision and to add to possible ways of conceiving of the present in an English language poetry. For poems from such places come with the imprint of a savage and terrible history on their very structures, bearing the marks of pain in the flesh of their language, courage in the syntactical scruple with which they comport themselves in the face of terror. They afford the Irish poet a way of deepening the local sense of a frighteningly flawed national life while they offer a means of escape from a futility and inanity which must result from the fact that our flawed Irish world only occasionally presses with a defining immediacy on the individual. And as Seamus Heaney again has remarked of these voices from the regions of perma-frost, 'there is something in their situation that makes them attractive to a reader whose formative experience has been largely Irish. There is an unsettled aspect to the different worlds they inhabit, and one of the challenges they face is to survive amphibiously, in the realm of "the times" and the realm of their moral and artistic self-respect.' Such amphibian skills would find plenty to test them in our own 'times' and one discerns in the act of translation from their work a desire to achieve equivalent adroitness and ethical versatility.

Translation as cultural metaphor is therefore a sign of the degree to which in contemporary Ireland inherited definitions of national life, of social origins and expectations, fail to account for much individual and collective experience.

It is a sign also that the language we most usually speak and in which we write, with its history of British (and more recently of US) imperialism has not yet come to seem inevitable, wholly congruent with our world as we know it. So we turn to our Irish past, to Europe, to the poetry of the other, whose accent is that of antiquity or of a savage and complex present, seeking ways to speak of our own less than fully comprehended dilemmas. And in this context it seems markedly significant that in very recent times Irish poetry has embarked on a very curious enterprise indeed, an act of translation more fundamental than anything we have noted hitherto. For in recent poetry it is possible to discern a tendency for poets to write as if Ireland itself had been translated into somewhere else, had begun to participate in the life of the other, the stranger, to write indeed of Ireland as if it were an Eastern European state or a cosmopolitan city of the mind. I am thinking of course most particularly of those poems in Seamus Heaney's *The Haw Lantern* (1987) where the experience of occupation is transmuted into a land of parable in 'The Frontier of Writing' and the history of subjection and uprising is mediated in an allegory of Central European indirection and gravitas in 'From the Canton of Expectation':

> Iron-mouthed loudspeakers shook the air
> yet nobody felt balmed. He had confirmed us.
> When our rebel anthem played the meeting shut
> we turned for home and the usual harassment
> by militiamen on overtime at roadblocks.

Paul Muldoon's poems in *Meeting the British* perform a similar act of transposition of Irish experience to a non-Irish setting, but in this case to the free-wheeling surface world of contemporary *cosmopolis* in which cultural relativism makes its immediate presence felt in designer labels and exotic menu cards. In this volume the shortest way to Tara seems to be by way of New York, where in '7 Middagh Street' Muldoon finds in the mixed tenantry of a famous literary household metaphors of the Irish condition. This poem indeed seems an inevitable consequence of his recurrent preoccupation in his work with an imaginary America as Irish literary tradition and allusion are translated into an urban cosmopolitanism which constantly makes the country seem part of some surreal alternative, composite reality:

> In dreams begin responsibilities;
> it was on account of just such an allegory
> that Lorca

was riddled with bullets
and lay mouth-down
in the fickle shadow of his own blood.

In other poems in the book a sense develops that Ireland is not just somewhere else but everywhere else, its identity so insecure as to be a kind of Swiftian flying island which goes anywhere. In 'The Earthquake' two lovers make love in an earthquake. They could be anywhere but Ireland:

That hacienda's frump
of pampas-grass,

a pair of cryptic
eagles guarding its front door.

So the poem ends 'Ireland has moved; they haven't.'

And in *Going Home to Russia* (1987) Paul Durcan performs an act of quite explicit translation. Ireland is Russia, the Russia of oppression and artistic censorship, an unfree state; Russia is an Ireland of possibility, the place where an Irishman can feel at home:

We Irish had our bellyful of *blat*
And *blarney*, more than our share
Of the *nomenclatura* of Church and Party,
The *nachalstvo* of the legal and medical mafia.

Going down the airbridge, I slow my step,
Savouring the moment of liberation;
As soon as I step aboard the Aeroflot airliner
I will have stepped from godlessness into faith:

. . . .

It is not until I am aboard the carrier
That I realize that I am going home.

But such translations are the stuff of poetic imagining, ways at best of coping with the untranslatable awfulness of our current condition. In translating Ireland, our poets are, it seems to me, in quest of some means to comprehend that condition so that we might be more fully at home in the language of our feelings about this place which is the only home we have.

Hugh Haughton

DENIS DEVLIN AND THE LINES OF COMMUNICATION

Denis Devlin, *Collected Poems*, edited by J. C. C. Mays.
Dublin: Dedalus Press, 1989

Back in 1934, in a now famous essay on 'Recent Irish Poetry', Samuel Beckett hailed Denis Devlin and Brian Coffey as 'without question the most interesting of the youngest generation of Irish poets', and recognized in their work 'the nucleus of a living poetic in Ireland'. Against the 'thermolators' and 'antiquarians', 'delivering with the altitudinous complacency of the Victorian Gael the Ossianic goods', Beckett, showing a touch of modernist complacency himself, aligned himself with those Irish poets who evinced some 'awareness of the new thing that has happened, or the old thing that has happened again, namely the breakdown of the object'. They recognized what for Beckett was the prime artistic fact of the modern situation, the 'rapture of the lines of communication'.

Reviewing Devlin's *Intercessions* in *transition* four years later, Beckett no longer set him up against Irish poetic antiquarianism, but against the English philistinism represented by a reviewer in *The Times Literary Supplement* whom he diagnosed as suffering from a 'morbid dread of sphinxes'. Defining art with memorably rhetorical provocation as 'pure interrogation, rhetorical question less the rhetoric', and faced by the incomprehension of the *TLS* in the face of Devlin's high-tension rhetorical manoeuvring, Beckett asserted that the time was 'not altogether too green for the vile suggestion that art has nothing to do with clarity'.

The sardonic hyperbole of Beckett's essay on Devlin sits easily within the avant-gardiste ethos of the Parisian international magazine *transition*, yet it suggests that Beckett read Devlin's work more as a mirror-image of his own predicament than 'in its own terms'. Ironically, Beckett's move into French after the procrustean comedy of *Murphy* and *Watt* momentously clarified his own language (though not of course his ontology), and enabled him to evade the 'green' issue of writing directly as an Irish writer at all. Since the success of *En attendant Godot*, Samuel Beckett's art of obscurity and lack has not lacked for the light (and night) of commentary, while Denis Devlin's work, despite distinguished and persuasive advocates, has continued to languish in a kind of locally prestigious obscurity. As Dillon Johnson has remarked, 'Denis Devlin is known to be a difficult poet when nothing else is known of him'. Beckett's eloquent advocacy lent prestige to Devlin's case but did little to open up 'the lines of communication'.

Denis Devlin was a fastidious poet who spurned the arts of self-publicity and, after the American success of *Lough Derg and Other Poems*, published in New York in 1946, did not produce another book. Up to the present, his work and reputation have largely survived due to the editorial work and critical advocacy of his friend and poetic comrade in arms, Brian Coffey, whose Dolmen Press edition of the *Collected Poems* in 1964 and of *The Heavenly Foreigner* in 1967 reintroduced Devlin's work into the public domain, adding six substantial new poems or sequences to the canon established by the poet's own two collections, including Devlin's late masterpieces, the strangely earthly and familiar sequence *The Heavenly Foreigner*. Coffey's invaluable editions have long been out of print and *The Poems*, originally printed as a special issue of the *Dublin University Review*, was unavoidably unsatisfactory in many respects, given its double responsibility of republishing the new late poems and reproducing the earlier *oeuvre*. With Devlin's collections published in inverse chronological order, like those in Coffey's own Belacqua Press *Selected Poems* in 1971, and with Devlin's numerous translations largely excluded, it of necessity gave a provisional vision of Devlin's achievement. The situation is now changed. The Dedalus Press's edition of Devlin's *Collected Poems*, edited by J. C. C. Mays, at last makes the bulk of Devlin's formidable work, including many of the translations, properly *available* — though not necessarily *accessible*. Moreover, it carries on its dust-jacket Beckett's early claims for Devlin and, after its title-page, the Parisian master's imprimatur: 'Congratulations on your edition. Amends at last.'

J. C. C. Mays's scrupulously edited collection makes Devlin's idiosyncratic achievement properly visible for the first time. It is constructed around Devlin's two completed books, *Intercessions* and *Lough Derg*, and an uncompleted 'Later Poems', which would have included the bulk of Devlin's projected third book of poems, reproduced here in the form and order in which they were originally published in reviews (almost the reverse order in which they are printed by Coffey). On the principle that 'each volume comprises a statement', the two early books are printed in their entirety, despite the considerable overlap between them. In fact seven poems, including the central 'Est Prodest', 'Bacchanal' and 'Victory of Samothrace', are carried over in revised form from *Intercessions* to *Lough Derg*. Coffey more economically included these as parts of *Lough Derg* only, reducing *Intercessions* to a bare eight poems; the present edition therefore gives a more accurate sense of Devlin's development, while also showing the power of his self-revision — a revision that is less a question of fiddly textual adjustments to punctuation and so on (though it includes these) than of dramatic recontextualization: the early poems read as different kinds of statement in the context of later political poems such as 'Old Jacobin' and 'Pays Conquis'. Between the central three collections, the editor has grouped together all Devlin's previously published but uncollected poems and translations. Brief editorial notes at the back record the publishing and compositional history of all the published poems included here. Devlin's apparently voluminous unpublished and unfinished work has been reserved for a forthcoming complementary collection, to stand in the same relation to this *Collected Poems* as Wallace Stevens's *Opus Posthumous* does to his.

All this means that for the first time we can follow Devlin's progress chronologically while, as far as possible, seeing the individual volumes as he planned them. The editor has included a brief but informative synopsis of Devlin's life as peregrine student and diplomat which will help the reader to construct the tantalizing outlines at least of this intensely unautobiographical poet's biography. More importantly, his lucid, wide-ranging introduction helps us place Devlin's work not only within the historical context of Irish and English writing of the nineteen thirties, but of the development of modern poetry in English. It is a matter of celebration that Devlin should have found in Dr Mays an editor of comparably fastidious catholicity of taste and intellectual authority as himself. The scholarly introduction is really a model of its kind, provoking not only a re-reading of Devlin in the light of the broader history of modern poetry — but a re-reading of that broader history in the light of Devlin's achievement. If Devlin has been seen as a salutary example to other Irish writers of a mobile and international outlook (witness John Montague's tribute to him in his Faber anthology), he is also a puzzling and arresting voice on the international scene. It is to be hoped that this Dedalus Press collection will establish Devlin not only as a poet who has travelled extensively, but as a poet whose poems, too, travel well. Hitherto his work has been dutifully but rather minimally represented in anthologies of Irish poetry; now he can figure in a less marginal role in both the history of Irish poetry in the twentieth century and that of the English-speaking world more generally.

But of course there are still problems, and Devlin needs critics as well as editors. Reading Devlin, you are aware of a sense of anomaly, of strain, of ambition — and of occlusion. Though not knowingly suffering from Beckett's 'morbid dread of sphinxes', I confess to finding Devlin's work dauntingly obscure. Devlin was among the early translators of Eluard and Breton — there is a rather lame translation of Breton's 'Vertebrate Sphinx' with oracularly awful lines like 'A fishhead very very long it is not yet he. The fishhead gives birth to maidens shaking a sieve' — but the obscurity is not, at least after the erratically portentous poems of *Intercessions*, a function of this early interest in surrealism. It has more in common with the riddling sociological scenarios of the early Auden, who is the obvious forerunner of such lines from 'Bacchanal' as 'Forerunners run naked as sharks through water, nose to their prey, have message by heart'. Nevertheless, it is worth remarking that Devlin's revolutionary poem was written in 1933 and predates such large-scale works as 'Out on the lawn I lie in bed' and 'Spain'. In fact the obscurity of Devlin's work has a more astringently intellectual dimension to it than you find in either the Surrealists or Auden, something of the flamboyant opacity you find in Hart Crane or Geoffrey Hill. The first poem in which this is fully developed is the often anthologized but authentically high-flying 'Winged Victory of Samothrace':

Our Lady of Victory!

And your voice, which has the opulent contentment of a June stream,
    babbles
And I feel with relief:
Better in danger with a goddess than float safe like a barge on the sea:
Fingers again at my throat

Baptism by immersion in the numerous sea

With its 'musical hammers' and 'brutal propellers', the goddess to whom this 'intercession' is addressed is not indeed an 'invented lady of stasis', but a modern compound ghost, marked as much by twentieth-century technology as the postures of Catholic devotion and Greek mythology. The poet's voice here is 'numerous' in numerous senses, and this poetic 'baptism' involves poetic as well as other dangers. Devlin's intellectual allegiances commit him to both hieratic ritual gestures, and to vocal and thematic fluidity. This is the source of both his and his readers' problems. 'Better in danger with a goddess than float safe like a barge on the sea' is a good motto but a dangerous one.

The poem reappears with minor revisions in *Lough Derg* a decade later, where it is closely followed by 'Venus of the Salty Shell', a more tonally secure erotic complement, which is dominated not by the cruel brilliance of victory but 'the goddess on the dove-drawn shell / Riding upon the speckled hawthorn waves / Into the rocky waves of the sea-republic'. Though set in the Athenian 'Middle Sea', the effect is of Botticelli's Venus surfing towards the Irish coast, where 'The doves, the hawthorn merge in the wrack and foam'. A poem, written in 1933 to celebrate imminent political transformation, was originally entitled 'News of Revolution', but came to be entitled 'Bacchanal' and it too thrives on classical personification. Likewise, 'Old Jacobin' conjures 'hero-selves . . . summoned from the *Odes*', The Goddess Reason, a new President and Christ. 'The Colours of Love' in turn calls up Venus and her hunting priests to 'explain' his 'heart and the rush of legend on it'. In fact there is *always* 'a rush of legend' in Devlin's political, religious and love poems. Not the legends of the Celtic Revival, but the ceaselessly remodelled classical and Christian imagery of European culture exposed to and exposing the modern world. Goddesses and Republics, Statues and Perturbed Burghers loom large in Devlin's composite Hiberno-Romanesque iconography and it is by such interlacings and cross-references that we begin to make sense of his highly convoluted personal engagement with the public domain, as well as 'the rush of legend' on his heart.

It strikes me that Devlin is a kind of latter-day 'metaphysical' poet, caught between his two possible vocations of priest and diplomat. Part of the strain his poetry contends with is religious, as with his model, Hopkins. Part of it is erotic, as in the pull between the devotional and erotic, Christian and Pagan imagery that runs through it all. Part of it too is the result of the tension between the Ireland he represents and the international scene on which he operates. In adolescence he entered a diocesan seminary, with a view to the priesthood; as an adult he worked as a foreign diplomat of the new national republic; and as a poet Devlin is obsessively interested in the function of 'representing' more than himself. Perhaps the problems of 'representation' he embodies are not 'the rupture of the lines of communication' and 'breakdown of the object' diagnosed by the modernist Beckett, but the burden of representing a people or a congregation in the way that a diplomat or priest has to do. Devlin, as much as Yeats, is centrally preoccupied by the power of symbols and the symbols of power, but, unlike Yeats, he is uninterested in devising a new or reworked symbolic order of his own. His poems investigate a symbolic public domain, which is marked both by Catholic tradition and modern political representation, but marked also by a crisis of credibility, a violent sense of disjunction between the world of political and religious ideals or icons and the credibility of ordinary life. His 'Argument·with Justice', included in both *Intercessions* and *Lough Derg*, dramatizes one pronounced version of the chasm between these realms:

> Virtue all men stand under, what wonder, blinded on thy column
>   transcendental, thou art
> Sterile, since not bedded with man thy secular wooer who could waken
>   thy
> Dreams to bloom; and why blinded?
> Darest not take, not take to thy sight these anarchic, thy
> Realms of thy reign abandoned.

The rhetoric of this intercession creaks with material from abandoned poetic realms, as well as classical and Christian ones, and its strained syntax is a reflex of a tension between ancient and modern, reminiscent of — among others — Hopkins: 'Beautiful named because from time abstract and therefore sacrosanct? Ah, what good!' The poet's idiom is caught between sacrosanct abstraction and contemporary speech. Though it ends with a prayer for Justice to 'come down, though the heavens fall', it is trapped between a transcendental realm (with its marmoreal traditional idiom) and what it calls 'our/temporary measure'. Part of the difficulty of Devlin's poems is their uneasiness with modern speech, his fraught sense of the gap between the magnificent Otherness of transcendence and the inauthenticity of everyday life.

His laboured sonnet about Michelangelo's labours, 'Casa Buonaroti', for example, speaks of the Renaissance artist as struggling 'all life with pigment, rock chisel and sun/To put God in matter, magnify himself' and 'muscle in stone ideas by Time undone'. Where the octet ponders the sculptor's sublime agon with his material, the sestet confronts the spectator's problems of recognition:

> Not devils but the meek minimize the great
> Who bind their eyes as likely as not
> So not is like what they would like it were.
> Samson they enhance us whom our flaws deflate.
> Yet God, from the refuge of his comic thought,
> Moves the momentary tourist with his fear.

Here Devlin's reader has comparable problems in disentangling the abrupt condensations of the syntax and the grammatical ambiguities, especially the notably slippery pronouns. Do 'they' and 'their' refer to the meek or the great? That is to say, do the meek bind the eyes of the great or their own eyes? Pronouns apart, how do we construct the positive sense in the queer grammatical knot of three 'not's? If 'not' is the subject of the final clause, is it an abbreviation for 'nought' or an unidiomatic contraction for 'it is not how they would like it to be'? Then how do we construe the fourth line? As something like 'Samson, those who enhance us are those who deflate our flaws'? Or as 'The great are like Samson, they enhance us who would otherwise be deflated by our flaws'? Or rather as 'They enhance Samson [the Samson in us? or the Samson against us?] when they deflate our flaws'? Do we deflate our flaws by playing them down? Or do our flaws deflate us, when we play them up? The poem ends with the momentary tourist being moved, but even here the pronouns open out mind-boggling ambiguities: does the 'his' in the penultimate line refer to God's or the tourist's or even the artist's 'comic thought'? And does the 'his' at the close refer to the tourist's or God's or Michelangelo's fear? Samson of course was a destroyer of architecture rather than an architect such as Michelangelo, but like him he triumphed over the Philistines. If the reader (momentary or not) is teased out of thought by these vertiginous Empsonian ambiguities and tongue-twisting propositions ('So not is like what they would like it were'), is he or she succumbing to the Philistines who minimize the great, or acting with appropriate awe before the poetic sublime? However we read these hermeneutic puzzles, the poem dramatizes an unresolved strain in Devlin's own work. It is as if the body of spoken idiom were being racked by the artist's relentless pursuit of a poetic equivalent of Michelangelo's sculptural sublime. Reading Devlin, there are times when I have sympathy for the benighted 'momentary tourist' conjured up in the last line.

It was in the poems of *Lough Derg* that Devlin came into his own. This is partly because the best of them admit more of ordinary contemporary idiom, even while insisting on the chasm between the 'prophets' jewelled kingdom' and 'the poor in spirit on their rosary rounds'. Still, compared to Patrick Kavanagh's resiliently vernacular *Lough Derg* of the same year, 1942, Devlin's title-poem is a baroque and esoteric meditation. It takes as its starting-point the Lough Derg pilgrimage described by Catholic writers from Carleton to Heaney, but it is also a dauntingly complex reflection on the history of European religion. It is a baulked devotional poem, an expression of the poet's sense of baffled kinship with the pilgrims, of whom he says: 'All is simple and symbol in their world'. At the same time it serves as a rhetorical gauge of his distance from them and their 'simple' symbols:

With mullioned Europe shattered, this Northwest,
Rude-sainted isle would pray it whole again:
(Peasant Apollo! Troy is worn to rest.)

'Lough Derg' is that comparative rarity in Devlin's work, an acutely and self-consciously Irish poem, which like 'On Mount Muckish' in the same collection makes a place the focus of a poetic pilgrimage into an archaic Irish culture. 'Lough Derg' was written and first published during Devlin's time in the United States, however, and it also aligns itself with poems such as Stevens's 'Sunday Morning' and Lowell's (later) 'The Quaker Graveyard in Nantucket', poems of internal debate about the fate of traditional religion: 'Man his own actor, matrix, mould and casting./Or man, God's image' seeing 'his idol spill'. It has a touch of Lowell's muscular and enigmatic grandeur. 'Glad invalids on penitential feet/Walk the Lord's majesty like their village street' prefigures the wonderfully uncomfortable grandiloquence of such lines as 'The Lord survives the rainbow of his will' from Lowell's 'The Quaker Graveyard in Nantucket'. Since Lowell's poem was published in 1946, four years after Devlin's in Allen Tate's *The Southern Review*, there is no question of the Irish poet's being subjected to the American's influence. It is Devlin who led the way, though no doubt both poets were affected by the formidable shadow of their 'Southern' mentor, Allen Tate. Although the poem travels from ancient Greek culture where 'close priest allegorised the Orphic egg's/brood' through the 'medieval state/Of paschal cathedrals backed on earthy hooves' and on to his own time's 'want of spirit by the market blurbed', its synoptic historical vision closes, not with the scepticism of the Stevens-like 'we pray to ourself', but with a neighbour's pious gesture:

We pray to ourself. The metal moon, unspent
Virgin eternity sleeping in the mind
Excites the form of prayer without content:
Whitethorn lightens, delicate and blind,
The negro mountain, and so, knelt on her sod,
This woman beside me murmuring *My God! My God!*

Devlin's poetry aspires to close the gap between its own intellectual sophistication and such piety, to recover the content as well as form of prayer, and engage with the Platonic Christian icon of the 'unspent/Virgin eternity sleeping in the mind'. Its twists and turns, the hair-raising ambiguities of its syntax and rhetorical insinuations, register the problems of doing so without faking it. They also register the gap between such high style and the speech of his neighbours. To adapt Heaney's words from 'Making Strange', Devlin's work aspires to be 'adept' but not 'dialect'.

Perhaps the price Devlin pays for this is high, but it is one he is prepared to pay. It is in the great poems of his later life that this comes into its clearest focus. In 'Irvine', from *The Heavenly Foreigner*, the poet seems to look back on his early childhood in Scotland, with a rare glimmer of the childhood veneration we find in Heaney and Montague:

Since the time in childhood
When dishes gleamed on the dresser,
And the tall, blue benignant
And black, malignant ghosts
Meant what they said,
Blue for heaven's haven,
Black for the fear of hell

Devlin's poetry is generally less interested in what he calls 'the particles and particulars of nature' than immense and multifaceted forms. Since childhood, he confesses to seeing in such phenomena the 'prolonged sensibility' of a copper-beech and the 'musing spider' of the sea, not nature but 'something else'.

Something there was other
Always at my elbow,
I sang, hunted and hated one;
He sings and hunts and hates me.

It is presumably the otherness of this 'foreign power' which makes Devlin's poetry so heavy with what he calls in 'The Colours of Love' 'absolutist devices'. The price it exacts of him is one he openly acknowledges at the close of 'Irvine':

The world glows with mortal divinity;
The red ash turns grey,
The ash creeps up on the flame
O Heavenly Foreigner! Your price is high.

Not many twentieth-century poets have been so discomfortingly devoted to the absolute or 'the Other' as Denis Devlin appears to be; Rilke's *Duino Elegien*, T. S. Eliot's *Four Quartets*, Claudel's *Odes* come to mind, perhaps even some of the poems in Lowell's *Lord Weary's Castle*. Like them, *The Heavenly Foreigner* asks a high price of its reader, but, like nearly all the later poems of Devlin, it offers real and human rewards, if only in illuminating a poignant and incorrigible need for a foreign heavenliness. Like Hopkins, Péguy, Eliot and Claudel, Devlin is a profoundly Catholic poetic sensibility, and whether in the elusive devotional pilgrimage poems of *The Heavenly Foreigner* or in the great metaphysical love-poem 'The Colours of Love', his writing is the product of a kind of counter-Reformation, even counter-modernist project — an attempt to acknowledge that 'foreigner' beyond 'the breakwater of humanity' or what he calls 'my term, the unavoidable turnstile/In the cathedral porch'. *The Heavenly Foreigner* combines devotional pilgrimage to sacred sites in Europe with a Platonized Romance like the *Vita Nuova* of Dante, and 'The Passion of Christ' is that rarity, a modern meditation on the Passion, written with a strenuously poetic as well as pietist intensity. It is reminiscent of Crashaw or Quevedo as much as the Anglicans Donne and Herbert.

Devlin is comparatively rare among Irish poets in not being overtly vexed about being an Irish poet or about his relation to other Irish poets. The idea that the Irish poet is forced to chose the way of Yeats or the way of Joyce, formulated by Thomas Kinsella and adopted by so many subsequent critics and writers, appears almost irrelevant to Devlin. Even the question of poetic nationality and poetic internationality does not seem to arise. In fact he writes comparatively rarely in direct terms of the nation he represented diplomatically in the USA, the United Kingdom, Turkey and Italy. There are, of course, some exceptions: 'On Mount Muckish' and 'Lough Derg', the 'Dublin' and 'Galway' sections of 'The Heavenly Foreigner', and the late public *tombeau* 'On the Tomb of Michael Collins' which Seamus Deane, who calls Devlin the only Irish poet of his time to attempt 'some reconciliation between poetry and politics', calls (rightly in my opinion) 'a sad failure'. In other poems, such as 'Old Jacobin', Devlin powerfully evokes not only 'the pandemonium of the heroes' of Jacobin France, but, almost between the lines as a structural political innuendo, the figure of de Valera and 'fictions in the misty pubs'. Devlin never turned his back on his country like Beckett, nor set himself up in glamorous or nostalgic exile from it (like Joyce), but his Irish identity is unobtrusively integral to his international world — and *oeuvre*. In 'The Colours of Love' he prays: 'Divinities of my youth/Expound to me my truth/Whether from Judah or Rome/Or my nearer Gaeldom'. His truth was always a question of multiple 'divinities' in opposition or apposition, and all his poems confront drastic polarities and pluralities without being interested in the accommodations of pluralism. Though it makes its way in the world of competing faiths and cultures, it remains squarely rooted in obstinate allegiances established in Ireland, if not in a semi-mythical 'Gaeldom'. Turcoman diplomat he may have been, but he continued to represent Ireland.

Born in Scotland of Irish parents, Denis Devlin spent his first twelve years and the great part of his adult life away from Ireland. He was largely educated in Ireland, first at Belvedere, then in the diocesan seminary at Clonliffe, and finally completing a modern languages degree and an MA at UCD. Thereafter, however, he studied at postgraduate level in Paris and Göttingen and, after a spell lecturing in UCD and as a cadet in the foreign office in Dublin, went on to spend nearly all his life after 1938 in the diplomatic service abroad, dying in 1959 as Irish ambassador to Italy. As a result of this varied service in

Washington, London, Ankara and Rome, Devlin travelled widely and learned a lot about foreignness of many kinds. If he represented Ireland abroad, he also in his work represented abroad to Ireland. Having completed his MA dissertation on Montaigne, he engaged in regular translation from modern French poets into English and even Irish (the Irish translations are included here too). *The Collected Poems* includes the translations of Bréton, Eluard, St Jean Perse, René Char and others which he published in his lifetime, including those into Irish, but with the exception of those of his diplomatic counterpart St Jean Perse and some of the Char (in particular 'Abel', an authentically Devlinesque poem) I do not think he is a very good translator — and indeed his editor intimates a similar judgment. His versions of Valéry's 'Palme', for example, with its bathetic 'Patience, patience be/In the blue vaults of the sky', and Verlaine's 'Parsifal' with its 'Oh, all that children's singing from the Minster' for 'O ces voix d'enfants chantant dans la coupole', remain flat and bathetic, for all their Devlinesque subjects. I suspect this is because Devlin is not interested enough in domiciling the translated poems into plausible idiomatic English — perhaps for the reason that his own poetry too distrusts and even disdains it. His work thrives on a kind of unintegrated 'foreignness'. In fact, abrupt translations between the foreign and familiar are the very stuff of Devlin's poems, as I suggested earlier in considering Devlin's Catholic and Platonic engagement with heavenly abstractions. The translations of St Jean Perse, which Allen Tate praised as some of the 'finest modern translations from the French', are uneven, sometimes bathetic and sometimes idiosyncratically marmoreal, but they suggest a profound intellectual engagement and even an affinity between the two writers. Devlin shares many of Perse's preoccupations, and clearly found an answering chord in his themes of exile and foreignness, his synoptic psalms to the dominion of world religions, as well as in the spell of his long lines and high language. Perse's 'Poem to a Foreign Lady' and 'Exile' lurk behind 'The Heavenly Foreigner'. I am sure Perse helped licence Devlin's later manner, which reads as a dialectical interplay between such high rhetorical openness and aphoristically 'metaphysical' rhyme-scheming. The translations are valuable less for the light they throw on their French sources than for the insight they provide into Devlin's own poetic sources and resources.

The new *Collected Poems* shows just how formidable Devlin's poetic resources were. Whether or not he succeeded in forming 'the nucleus of a living poetic in Ireland' (as Beckett suggested his and Coffey's work should do) is questionable, however, and the difficulties of coming to terms with his work are still formidable. In his introduction, J. C. C. Mays takes a stern line on this:

> The obstacles to understanding poetry of the kind Devlin wrote are
> sometimes held to be references which can be footnoted, which is
> nonsense. Such obstacles are imaginary, and less important than the divide
> which any reader must cross to begin to follow the creation of individual
> poems. How the divide is to be crossed I do not know . . . .

This is no doubt true, but obscure references compound a reader's other
difficulties, and I was grateful for the editor's minimal concessions on this
front, as when he notes of 'Anteroom: Geneva' that 'for what it is worth, DD
frequently accompanied Eamon de Valera to meetings of the League of
Nations in Geneva at the time the poem is dated'. I found it worth a lot. The
same could be said of his remarks on the 'shift from the new Irish Republic to
the French' in one of his finest political poems, 'Old Jacobin'. Mays provides
worthwhile but elliptic information on some particularly obscure performance
such as 'Communication from the Eiffel Tower', as well as on more familiar
major poems like 'Lough Derg' and 'Ankhor Wat' (though I was puzzled as
much as enlightened by his suggestion that 'Ankhor Wat might be thought to
bear more than a passing resemblance to Washington DC'). Nonetheless, most
of the time he prefers to restrict the notes to information about manuscripts,
variants and publishing history, or is content to refer the reader to explanations
in other (often recondite) places. It is good to know that 'The Passion of
Christ' seems to have begun as a series of meditations based on Dürer's *Kleine
Passion* woodcuts, but it would also have been useful to provide readers with a
little information on the pictorial models (if any) of 'The Statue and Perturbed
Burghers', 'Pictures in a Window', 'Venus of the Salty Shell' and, even though it
is relatively familiar, 'Venus of Samothrace'. Again it is helpful to know that the
fascinating late sequence, 'Memoirs of a Turcoman Diplomat' probably began as
a 'series of brief epiphanies', but frustrating to be referred to the editor's
commentary on the poem in a periodical when a little explanatory material in
note-form would go a long way to opening what is a rather hermetic work. In
the same way it is proper for the editor to refer us to Brian Coffey's wonderful
edition of *The Heavenly Foreigner* for an account of its 'personal and literary
background', but galling to be baulked of any signposts towards that background
here. *The Heavenly Foreigner*, like many of Devlin's poems first and last, depends
on a Loyolan 'composition of place', in particular upon the intimate associations
of named places such as 'Mount Muckish' or 'Sirmione'; inexplicably, the editor
footnotes 'Mount Muckish' and 'West Pier' but not 'Irvine' or 'Sirmione',
'Annapolis' or 'Anatolia' which are the titles of other poems in the sequence. In
the introduction he calls 'Est Prodest' (one of Devlin's most elliptic meditations)
'central' and 'paradigmatic', but the notes give nothing away and do not even

explain the Latin title. It seems petty to cavil over such omissions, but the editor is clearly in a position to fill us in on these questions and it is not only the 'gentle skimmer' who might benefit. In the footnote to 'Meditation at Avila', Dr Mays quotes a helpful explanation of the poem that the poet himself gave at a poetry reading in the United States; it suggests that Devlin himself took a less severe attitude on this point than his editor!

Nevertheless, this is a magnificent edition of a magnificent poet. It has been scrupulously edited and proofread (only 'The Passion of Christ' suffers the stigmata of multiple typos) and is handsomely produced by Dedalus. It is a pity, however, that an edition so respectful of Devlin's text should fail to modify page layouts to respect stanza-forms; it repeatedly has a single line or pair of lines stranded on the top or bottom of a page, severed from the paragraph or stanza of which it is part. Given the capital importance of such rhythmic organization to Devlin's high-tension architectural compositions, this is often an additional impediment to clear reading. Though I initially found myself repelled and frustrated by Devlin's warped magniloquence, rereading has increased my respect, and on each reading more poems have opened themselves up, as the exemplary introduction intimates they would. With some exceptions, like 'Victory' and 'Bacchanal', it is not the early poetry praised by Beckett, but the poetry of *Lough Derg* and the astonishing late poems which claim my attention. Devlin's late flowering is as remarkable as that of his English and American near-contemporaries Basil Bunting and George Oppen. There may be comparatively few completely achieved poems in Devlin's *oeuvre*, but there can be few better Irish poems in our century than the best of them; the political allegories, 'Old Jacobin' and 'Pays Conquis', the mythological tableaux 'Venus of the Salty Shell', 'A Dream of Orpheus' and 'Ankhor Wat', the metaphysical and autobiographical sequence 'The Heavenly Foreigner' and the love poems 'Eve in my Legend' and 'The Colours of Love':

At the Bar du Départ drink farewell
And say no word you'll be remembered by;
Nor Prince nor President can ever tell
Where love ends or when it does or why.

Down the boulevard the lights come forth
Like my rainflowers trembling all through Spring,
Blue and yellow in the Celtic North . . .

Ah me! how all that young year I was moving

To take her dissolution to my Breast!

Better no love than love, which, through loving
Leads to no love. The ripples come to rest . . .

I suspect these ripples have not come to rest. Devlin's work is still a *point du départ*. Certainly Irish poetry reads differently when you confront the place of Devlin's achievement within it — which isn't the case with the work of his contemporaries Coffey and MacGreevy, with whom he is usually bracketed. Though Kavanagh's impact on later poetry was undoubtedly greater, it has proved more transitory, I suspect, and the kind of poetry now being written in the island, however little shaped by Devlin's influence, probably has more affinities with his poetry than with the Monaghan man's. Derek Mahon has continued the Irish tradition of French translation associated with Devlin and Beckett, and the modernized metaphysical dimension of Devlin's work, and the international dimension is inescapable in the work of Kinsella, Heaney, Mahon, and Muldoon, as is the kind of intellectual intransigence we find in Devlin. Irish writers, following the line of Heaney's 'Tale of Two Islands' and *Station Island*, may have regularly made their poetic pilgrimages to Lough Derg, but they have become less and less nationalistically insular. Where Devlin's work may prove enclosing, on the other hand, is in its obstinate refusal of the vernacular, the realm of the spoken — where all our important contemporary poets, even the esoteric Kinsella, have staked their claims. Though Devlin's strained linguistic nobility may be an obstacle, the strenuous intellectual mobility of his work is a source of potential inspiration. While robustly confronting the difficulties of the modern, he is capable of writing with something of the rhetorical grandeur of Donne or Lowell, and miraculously without even a hint of Yeats's 'Nobel' touch:

It is with our consent death finds his breath;
Love is death's beauty and annexes him.

Henry Gifford

SEFERIS AND HIS PEOPLE

George Seferis (1900-1971) became the spokesman of his generation in 1935 when he published the verse sequence *Mythistorima* (*Mythic Story*). A mere 150 copies were printed; even his last volume, *Three Secret Poems*, in 1966, had a printing that barely exceeded 2,000. As he noted forty years earlier in his journal, 'Art is for all men, never for the masses.' The politician, he said, addresses the nation ('My fellow countrymen'), the artist simply his individual reader or listener. He had the greatest respect for the popular art of Greece — its ballads in the lively demotic idiom of the villages, or the paintings of the primitive and humble Theophilos, who had once been a door-keeper in Smyrna, the native city of Seferis himself. Such art, he maintained, must be the starting-point for the educated, just as the demotic, for which his father had campaigned, alone made possible the expression of Greek sentiments in a living language. Seferis' whole life was spent in the intellectual pursuit of something he regarded as all-important for himself and the Greeks of his age. He wanted to define and to place beyond the reach of contemporary politicians — about whom as a civil servant he was left with no illusions whatever — the idea of a Hellenic community, not stumbling under the weight of a half-understood heritage, but sure of itself and confident of its own strength in facing a dangerous future.

His generation awakened to the harsh realities of the twentieth century in 1922, the year of the 'Asia Minor disaster'. An ill-conceived military adventure to realize the 'Great Idea' of annexing the western seaboard of Turkey, and so gathering the whole Aegean into a greater Hellas, had ended with a rout even more severe than the Greeks would inflict upon Mussolini in 1941. Smyrna was lost for ever, and a vast multitude of Greeks was uprooted from Ionian shores in the exchange of populations with Turkey. This shock to Seferis and his contemporaries, finding themselves now the citizens of a small state with ruined hopes, was almost paralyzing. They felt, he says, that all spiritual and intellectual foundations 'had been eroded, turned to dust'. This engendered a despair and a disquiet which made Seferis eagerly receptive to the poetry of T. S. Eliot when he discovered it ten years later. But his translation of *The Waste Land*, published the year after *Mythistorima*, found almost no response initially from a reading public whose critical faculties, as he often complained, were very little fostered in the stagnant culture of Greece between the wars. What Seferis missed achingly in his countrymen was openness of mind and breadth of vision. As he wrote in *Mythistorima*:

> Our country is closed in, all mountains
> roofed over by the low sky day and night.
> We have no rivers, no wells and no springs,
> Only a few cisterns and those empty . . .

The spiritual life of Greece in the mid-nineteen thirties is strikingly expressed in a line of verse from the following year:

> A jar that has stayed with a little water
>   beside the ancient columns.

Seferis always saw himself as *thalassinos*, a man of the sea. Smyrna had been one of the busiest Greek ports. When visiting the ruins and choked harbour of Ephesus, he imagined the scene 'in the good years' — with all 'the ships and caravans; a constant coming and going between the sea and the interior; the local people, the resident foreigners, sailors, barbarians, the mingling of interests, religions, races . . .' At the end of the nineteenth century, he supposed, Smyrna and Alexandria had been like that. To Stratis the Seafarer, a persona he had adopted, he attributes the thought: 'In my country every day the room for a man to walk becomes more restricted.' Seferis' cry is constantly for 'spaciousness'. The word he uses, *euruchoria*, goes back to Herodotus, that ever enquiring traveller from Halicarnassus in his own Asia Minor; and Homer, whose birthplace Smyrna claimed to have been, likes to describe the cities he knew as 'spacious'. Seferis felt it was good fortune to have been born 'when Greece had the greatest spaciousness, before the polarization started of the Hellenic populations within the borders of the Greek state'. This 'jostling together' had in his judgment inclined the young — he was writing after World War II — 'sometimes to narrow views'. Hellenism as a living force would be much the poorer without its expression in Asia Minor and in Alexandria — both of them now for ever lost to the new centre. He had begun to 'think seriously', and it was 'a fearfully tormenting thought', that only a new Dispersion 'would allow the Greeks to do anything'. The result of the Asia Minor disaster had been a stifling provincialism.

This contrast dominated his thinking. In August 1950, for instance, he comments in his diary on 'hydrocephalous' Athens, now viewed in the light of Ankara where he was serving as Counsellor of the Embassy. 'A city which has no concern with its hinterland, which is indifferent about its borders, becomes a province . . .' On the next page a fortnight later he contemplates St Sophia in Istamboul — still for Greeks Constantinople, 'the City' above all others which, unlike Smyrna, had not 'lost its shadow'. He finds in the dome 'a spaciousness of lines that breathe'. Alexandria, where he first set foot in 1941 as a refugee from Crete, had impressed him as 'a corner of the great Hellenic world' over which for a thousand years Constantinople had presided even when its territories shrank. The Greek mind, he reflects a few weeks later in 1950, should always be kept 'alive and open'. He returns to this thought when speaking at the University of Salonika in 1964. There he described a visit to the site of Seleucia, once the third city of the ancient world, and 'a great conduit of ideas' between East and West. No traces of it remained by the Tigris, apart from the greenness on the riverbank. Yet 'this *nothing*' gave him, once more, a feeling of spaciousness. Those who complained that Greece was narrow ought, he suggested, to think how restricted were the cities of the modern world.

'We find ourselves', he declared in his Salonika address, 'at a cross–roads: we have never been isolated; we have always stayed open to every influence — East and West; and we have assimilated them wonderfully at those times when we have functioned as a robust organism'. But where was that robustness to be met with, in the confusion, cynicism and self-seeking of Greek life in the desperate years leading up to World War II, and in its aftermath? Yet Seferis' ideal was by no means illusory. In August 1942, visiting the Greek contingent with the British Eighth Army in the Western Desert, he judged the brigadier to be 'a man from the Greece of any epoch. I don't speak,' he explains, 'as a historian: I mean to say e.g. as the olive is the tree of any Greek epoch'. The Cretans who came down from the mountains to resist the German invasion were timeless in this way. (He recalls one veteran 'wrinkled like an olive tree'.) At the back of these comparisons is always the image of General Makriyannis, a peasant hero of the Liberation in the eighteen twenties, whose *Memoirs* in their untutored but sterling eloquence remained perpetually for Seferis an inspiration. 'These unknown men' in the mould of Makriyannis, he contended, 'are the best thing our country possesses'.

Seferis admired in Makriyannis an instinctive Hellenism, true to the moral values that Socrates also held. Ever since the German scholar Fallmerayer challenged the racial identity of modern Greeks with their classical predecessors, the Language Question has formed a major political issue. In his Nobel Oration of 1963, Seferis emphasized that Greece, 'a rocky peninsula in the Mediterranean', had no assets apart from the will of its people to survive, the sea which made them a nation of sailors, and the light of the sun which revealed, as it were a moral landscape, the pledge of a natural justice for humanity. 'Our country is small, but its tradition is prodigious and the thing that distinguishes it is that it has been handed down to us without a break. The Greek language has never ceased to be spoken.' It remained one of the most conservative in the world, 'alive, robust, obdurate and graceful'. This was the continuity that he trusted and loved to trace in all its manifestations. Whenever he came upon a new proof of Hellenic tradition persisting, as in Cyprus, which he visited in the nineteen fifties, he was convinced of his people's capacity to survive. There too his earliest impression had been of a Greece suddenly revealed as 'spacious, wider'. Governed from Athens, Cyprus would most probably have ended up drably provincial. Instead, he delighted in it as being 'Hellenic, without a Greek gendarme or civil servant'. It was a 'change of scene' for the tradition: 'more ancient and more local in speech'.

However, in the twentieth century tradition is everywhere at risk. It can be abused and distorted by the political masters of a country, as was shown by the regime of the Colonels, against which Seferis made a courageous protest in 1969, two years before his death. But there are other, less dramatic but still deeply insidious assaults upon a people's sense of identity and of its place in history.

Seferis' translation of *The Waste Land* was reissued in 1949. The thirteen years since the first edition had brought to Greece and to himself personally manifold suffering. He had watched the ineffectual conduct of the Western democracies in the face of an unchecked Nazi advance; his country had been invaded by the Italian Fascists, and finally crushed by Hitler's intervention; Seferis had accompanied his government first to Crete, then to Egypt, South Africa, and so back to Egypt with a brief interval in Palestine. He had returned to Greece at the end of 1944, where civil war was already simmering. When he wrote a new preface to *The Waste Land*, it was at a time of continuing crisis for his people. 'Greece today', he had noted in April 1945, 'is like a sick man condemned by his doctors, and thrown upon the mercy of God'. He felt 'defiled . . . by the fratricidal slaughter', 'gravely wounded by my country', where under every stone 'you come upon something nasty'. He recorded in 1948 anxiety about the international scene. Seferis was compelled to witness 'the drama of the country and the degradation of people between the Clashing Rocks (Symplegades) of this third world war'. Once to be *heimatlos* had meant to have no nationality; 'today it is the man without a party'.

In the preface he called upon Greek intellectuals to accept that, even in times like the present, there could be no closing of the doors to outside influences. It was easy enough, when viewing the handiwork of Western civilization, to talk about 'the fruits of an extreme decadence'. During the world war Seferis himself had reflected on Europe's spiritual bankruptcy. But they must understand that 'the whole of Greek history had been shaped by journeys, encounters, settlings and dialogues in distant places'. This experience gave 'that unique stamp which we recognize at once and which is called Hellenism'. The poets Solomos and Kalvos, at the beginning of modern Greek literature, had not been 'so scared of the foreigner as to raise walls and to shut him out'.

Fate, he repeats, had placed Greece at a crossroads, now as always; and there could be no shirking the consequences. But here he is forced to admit a fact of ominous import for all nations today. 'The spiritual cultivation of a people, unluckily, is not formed by the poet alone.' Other forces, unstrutinized and with every immunity, are also shaping it. Among them he lists the cinema and radio, 'various cheap foreign or Greek newspapers, drugs and tinned foods, advertisements, propaganda of every sort'. Add to these the political and the military dimensions, and the bringing of news from Shanghai or Teheran to the humblest pensioner tending his garden plot. Events had suddenly made Greece 'one of the epicentres of a world-wide crisis. This has created, between our country and the great powers, contacts so imperative and so penetrating that we shall not be able to suspect their existence for another one or two decades.' The influence of all this goes very deep and is much too rapid. He has to recognize that for most people the media are all sufficient; and thus 'the danger is not small'.

The dilemma Seferis acknowledges to be implacable. On the one hand they could 'confront Western civilization', which is largely their own, confidently taking account of 'its living sources'. This he believes cannot be done without 'drawing strength from our own roots and without systematic hard work upon our own tradition'. Alternatively they might 'turn their backs and ignore' the challenge. That would expose them to being 'outflanked in some way from below' by an influence that would be worse, the product of industrial technology and the market. A weary footnote of 1961 concludes that the outflanking has gone desperately far and without hindrance.

In the former Greek regions of Asia Minor he had found a tradition on the point of expiring. 'The Greek language, churches, houses, inherited gestures. Another two generations and they will all be extinct.' And he records an exchange with a foreigner. Seferis told him: 'I have seen three Christian churches.' The answer came: 'There are many factories here.' 'This was a foreigner,' he comments, 'but what of my dear countrymen?' Nowhere could the debasing effects of Western civilization (he calls it in English the making of 'largely cocacola-ized countries') be more hideously plain than in the Arab lands, which he visited in the early nineteen fifties as ambassador to a group of Middle Eastern states. He spoke scathingly of 'those people who imagine they have attained the height of civilization when they acquire a Cadillac and a gilded chandelier from Central Europe'. The gross material culture which now surrounds us was advancing rapidly in Seferis' later years. He wrote near the end of his life on the interpretation of dreams, and cited one of his own that appeared 'instructive'. At some future time he returned to Athens from a long absence abroad, to unfamiliar houses and unfamiliar people. Before the western façade of the Parthenon he joined an excited throng. Between the columns at a table covered with green baize a bespectacled man was seated; he held an ivory auctioneer's hammer. An American toothpaste company was bidding for the temple. Their victory, he was told, would balance the budget for decades. The jubilant crowd heard the auctioneer announce that the bid had succeeded. Then Seferis found himself the sole spectator as the Parthenon was stripped and its columns replaced by giant replicas of toothpaste tubes.

This grotesque dream has a chilling air of veracity. He felt an increasing gloom in the postwar years, aggravated by concern for the future of Cyprus. That island represented for him a place where the human scale was preserved and where miracles could still happen. Its survival was indeed miraculous, when, as he wrote in *Thrush* (1947)

> the world
> has now become an immense hotel.

Had he revised his preface of 1949 to *The Waste Land*, there is no doubt that Seferis would have added tourism as a major subversive force. There can be no dialogue with the past, he maintained, when you are distracted by tourists from looking at it.

Seferis was sensitive to the landscape of Hellenic settlements — above all in Attica and Smyrna — with a devotional fervour that could sustain him in difficult days. His understanding of history, above all in its modern phase, was tragic, as one would expect from a constant reader of Homer and Aeschylus (and later of Euripides). He had lived to see an immemorial agrarian order, penurious, primitive, often harsh, but still admirable in his eyes, being swept away by the blind onrush of technical change. What he dreaded to lose can be illustrated from a diary note of 1946, on a rare escape from Athens to the island of Poros:

> An astonishing survival: as soon as I find myself in the country, the habits of childhood. The talk of a boatman, the gesture of a fisherman, have an authority for me that I very seldom notice in the company of so many

ministers, for example, or professors or intellectuals. They still belong, even today, to a ceremonious world . . . .

No legislation, no radical reform, can save or bring back this 'ceremonious world'. But Seferis, witness every page he wrote, is a truthful observer, and the most any writer or artist can do is to honour it in his work. Seferis' last will and testament, the *Three Secret Poems* of 1966, fuses his observations of his people's life and his own. One section of the third poem, 'Summer Solstice', celebrates the little garden of the house he had built for his retirement in Athens. The second and concluding paragraph breathes that classic calm and realism which he derived from the Hellenic tradition so many of his best hours had been given to interpreting:

> In the little garden ten paces wide
> you can see the light of the sun
> fall upon two red carnations
> an olive tree and some honeysuckle.
>
> Accept what you are.
>   The poem:
> you must not sink it under deep planetrees
> nourish it with the soil and the rock you have.
> As for the rest —
> dig in the same spot to find it.

The poet must look for his vision in the bare elements of his milieu, and in his own experience, which he comes to understand through mastery of an ancient language, still in touch with the past, and still responsive to his necessity.

Dennis O'Driscoll

AN INTERVIEW WITH MIROSLAV HOLUB

Miroslav Holub was born in Pilsen in September 1923. He lives in Prague, where he has worked as Chief Research Immunologist at the Institute for Clinical and Experimental Medicine.

Your poem 'Homer' does not suggest that you relish the idea of a poet revealing much about his private life.
This was first induced by conditions where you could not tell the whole truth and you would prefer to show your abstention from the text. You are saying as much as you can but a part is missing and you too are missing. You are mimicking the intellectual situation.

Secondly, I don't like it at all — even now. This may be an attitude derived from the scientific habits. When you give a scientific lecture or make a scientific paper, there is no personal background given: no age, no numbers of girlfriends or wives or children. Nothing. So why should it be analysed in poetry?

You can have poetry as just a sort of personal notation, as a personal diary, or as a filibuster against something (usually against the readership or the audience!). But my kind of poetry, if it is poetry at all, is not that personal. It is a communication rather than a confession. It is not a confessional poetry.

So the new circumstances in Czechoslovakia will not prompt you to be more personal in your poetry?
No, not at all. One of the few things which is really good and is derived from scientific life is autocriticism. You even criticize your work in a single scientific paper, in the part which is called the 'discussion'. The scientific habit is simply not to take one's self too seriously and this is, in addition, my personal habit. I am deeply provoked by people — including poets — who take their own personalities very seriously. We should be very serious about poetry. We should be very serious about life, about survival, but not necessarily about ourselves. We are centred on our egos, anyway, instinctively, through biological necessity; but why should there be an intellectual necessity to do so?

What sort of childhood did you have?
I was a single child, a little fat boy who spent half his childhood just trying to get rid of the fat — which I did. Later, I was very active in sports. I have an injury on my left hip-bone from fencing.

What I am defined by personally — here we are dealing with instinctive egocentrism — is that I have never had any diseases. Except as a physician, I was never in hospital, and this is another thing which makes one less self-centred.

What were your wartime experiences like?
I had the good luck that at my high school we had no collaborators among the professors. We had a fantastic textbook which had to be corrected by the German influence. All the names of objectionable scientists, like Darwin, had to be blackened out with heavy lines. We were very well-trained in ideology and anti-ideology and so have been inculcated from an early age in a very sensitive fashion.

We had a weekend house in a mountain resort in Sudetenland and my mother had to flee with a few possessions through tunnels. I was not there at the time but that was the first physical impact. The second physical impact was the bombing. Pilsen is an industrial city, so in critical periods of the war, like '44/45 as the fronts approached, we were once or twice a week in the cellar. I am here only because I was late when I was supposed to be at Pilsen railway station on the paramedic team. The place I was supposed to be was directly hit by a bomb. Nothing was left of the room.

I have actually seen American jets fighting the Germans. I have seen American pilots abducted by Germans in April '45. German peasants in villages near Pilsen used to beat the American pilots to death with sticks. Just because of that, I saw Americans first as suffering individuals. After the war, I became a member of the American Institute and we put up a memorial; but the memorial disappeared immediately after '48. In the textbooks, the schoolkids would be told that Pilsen was liberated by the Russians. In the seventies, when a teacher would again repeat this nonsense, a small kid who wouldn't even remember '68 would say, 'But, Comrade Teacher, I heard it was not Russians, it was Americans!'

I saw people coming from the concentration camps just like cattle in open cars — as I say in the poem 'Sunday' — their dark heads just like cut-out black cardboard. This was terrible. And, of course, I did know some Jewish families who just disappeared somewhere.

You worked on the railways during the war. What did the work consist of?
First of all, I was making piles of wood. Secondly, I was working in the magazines transporting crates from the cars — very, very dirty work. Finally, I was supposed to become a clerk, so I got a telegraph training and was in a little station near Pilsen. In the event of an air-raid, I was assigned to carry the red cap of the station master and the food supply to a shelter underneath the tracks.

It was there I saw the American bombers, the bombs as little shiny bronze things falling down in a beautiful parabola and hitting from all sides the Pilsen prison. I saw the prison building rising in the air and falling apart. It was a beautiful sight, a sunny day . . .

The Third Army came. Nineteen Americans were killed in Pilsen. On May 6th or 7th 1945, caught in crossfire between German snipers and Americans with armoured cars, I looked out of a shelter and saw one American being hit on the foot in front of the theatre. In 1963, I came to Wisconsin and met a guy, a cheese worker. I was introduced as a Czechoslovakian and he said, 'I was in Czechoslovakia. The town was something like Pp, Piz, Pilsen . . . I was wounded in the leg.' I asked him if it was in front of the theatre and he said 'Yes'. Of all Americans, I met the one I had watched being hit by the Germans.

In poetry, we have never lacked themes. If I stopped living right now, there would be enough material. This you can see in any Czech writer, like Hrabal. He enlarges his life experiences by sitting in pubs and listening to people's stories, which I cannot do. I am not gifted to acquire other people's stories and to transform them. But I have enough of my own stories.

Is simplicity something you still aspire to in poetry?
Since 1963, when — having published three books of poetry in almost one year — I discovered I was talking too much, I tried to get rid of myself in a way. I began to look for other styles so as not to repeat myself. I hate to make or bake poems like rolls. All those thirty years, I have been looking for other ways of writing — sometimes more complex, more elaborate, sometimes in an entirely different form such as a little stage act or a short poem.

You were thirty-four when your first collection appeared. This was a relatively late start.
I did begin writing like everybody else. I am a person with well-developed qualities of verbalization; therefore, I speak English, although I have never learned English. I simply find my way through the language. Always, from my childhood, I wanted to be a scientist. My father wanted me to be a physician, which was fortunately compatible. In addition, I discovered in the romantic years (sixteen, seventeen, eighteen) that it would be more interesting for the other sex if I started to write poems.

After the war, I started to write serious poetry — very silly — but conditions educated me a little further from this stage of poetry. It was poetry as a function of words — just a few metaphors, words, subtle feelings and you feel you are doing something extremely educated and intellectual. Then came '48 and, for two or three years, there was virtually no poetry from living people published. My literary tutor told me, 'Look, Miroslav, this is not a time for writing poetry, for being published. This is a detestable time, a detestable regime. We must simply stay silent.' I kept telling him, 'My God, how can I stay silent when I didn't speak? Nobody will figure out I am silent because nobody heard me so far.'

Actually, I started my literary career by just shutting up, so this was the most important period in my literary development and it lasted until 1954. It was a time of total isolation for us. The others were in the Communist Party, shouting in the streets. We felt isolated, alienated from everything and everybody, including ourselves.

I was studying and very diligently editing the scientific magazine *Vesmír*. I actually made my living when I was a medical student, so that my parents didn't have to give me too much money. Then I started to write poetry again, but with new literary friends. I slightly shifted to the poetry which we later called 'the poetry of the little concrete' — no subtle spiritual situations, no dark landscapes but a few clear metaphors aimed on a poetic idea. My very first poem, which was published in '47, was a poem in a newspaper protesting at the expulsion of the Germans from Sudetenland. In '54, when the new voices started to emerge, two of my poems were published by Seifert in his magazine, which I was very proud of. The first poem was undistinguished and introverted. The second poem, 'Sparrows', was rhymed but already in my style. Even speaking about sparrows (and not about nightingales) was a tiny rudimentary protest — the plebeians of the bird kingdom, still here, still singing, staying over the winter, over the harshest times.

Did the idea of a very concrete style occur to you during your years of silence?
It was a counter-style. Basically, it was a style of protest against the official poetry, which was just a poetry for May Day parades or a love poetry by well-known impotent elderly writers.

Had you read poets like Carlos Williams at this point?
Not yet. At this point, we had very few influences because after '48 little could be imported or translated. I had a standing knowledge of French poetry, acquired in the years of freedom ('45-47). I may have known only Jacques Prévert at that time — he was very important. It was later than this that the 'beat' poetry came and the young Polish poets like Herbert and so on.

The discovery of poets like Carlos Williams was a revelation. We thought we were hidden somewhere in a little hole in central Europe under somebody's boot, under the fist of Big Brother. We had to speak with our little voices; and suddenly we discovered the little voices were being used elsewhere. This was telling us that maybe the situation was not so different elsewhere; we were not such a hidden and godforgotten place. The revelation of the San Francisco 'beat' poets and of the Polish poets was a sort of collective discovery. The 'beat' poet who was closest to us was Lawrence Ferlinghetti in his *Coney Island of the Mind* period and in his jazz poetry — visual, concrete, political, fighting poetry.

Did the drugs and madness of the 'beat' poets hold any attraction for you?
In conditions of a more or less sane society, you can afford to be mad as a poet. In conditions of a mad society, you can't afford it because you would be just in the Establishment. You can be absurd in a non-absurd state of affairs. It is of no avail to go for absurdity in an absurd social order.

But surrealism appealed to you, nonetheless.
This was from my French connection — I was reading a lot of French poetry, especially the *poètes maudits*, up to Supervielle. This came from my mother, who was a German and French professor. She loved France and, as a little kid, I was twice in Paris — so it was a kind of dreamland. I don't understand the present-day French poets except some like Guillevic. They are extremely introverted and I can't tell one from the other.

Surrealism was not madness in the essence, only in the vision, resulting from looking at mad things, orders, arrangements, events. So it was a good style, a fitting vision. The inner landscape in certain periods was like a little corner of Picasso's 'Guernica' — those types of disintegration, suffering, shrieks and moans.

What was the effect on your poetry of a classical training?
Czech literary classes were very scholarly: years, titles and so on. But in Greek and Latin, we had to read epics all year — *Iliad* and *Odyssey* and the *Bucolics*. We would learn them by heart, so the heroes like Menelaus or Agamemnon or Achilles became just like our inner property. I was always feeling sorry for Patroclus.

Did your determination to work towards single books, rather than single poems, derive from your study of those classical texts?
No, it's just a reaction against the subjective way of making poetic collections as a sort of physiological function of the lunar cycles of a poet: you simply shed some poems and later you collect them in a bunch and say, 'This was the state of my soul for the last year.' More and more I hate it.

Generally speaking, has poetry played a large part in modern Czechoslovakian life?
From '56 to '68, with the Khrushchev liberalization and so on, the literary life really started. There was a general feeling of progress. In this period, poetry was one of the leading arts. Very much of what happened in lyrical theatre forms, in television and in other literary forms, had a strong poetic basis. After '68, when so many things were dilapidated and banned, I thought it would be interesting to see how the other arts would do without poetry. There were full-grown walls between arts and between persons. In the seventies and eighties, it never attained the status it had in the sixties.

How exactly was the publication of your work regulated in Czechoslovakia?
When I started to publish my books, in 1958, there was almost no restraint on paper. When I started to be published again in 1982, it was a different situation because the printing was extremely expensive and the paper was traditionally in short supply, so the printing would be limited anyway. But, especially between '82 and '86, it was the central intervention which said 'This guy may be published in all possible copies. This poet must have a printing of 10,000.' He would sell about 500. It came to be another kind of absurdity. The publisher would not only have to spend too much paper and too much money on publishing the official poet, but he could make only smaller printings of the others because the official poet's work was blocking the storage spaces, literally. My book couldn't be stored anyway, so they had to make a printing that would just be sold out immediately on the first day.

The poets in short supply would sell out within minutes and the others were never bought — not on grounds of quality or politics but because of the popular obsession with goods in short supply. What was in good supply was traditionally second-class and what was in short supply was interesting.

The real artistic struggle starts now because the dissident literature, the emergent literature, will be published in the first place and I accept this fully. They couldn't appear at all — I appeared since '82 — so why shouldn't I wait? And, besides, I personally know it's very good to be silent for a while. I see no reason, except when I have a very good theme, to write anything more. I am centring more now on the essays — it is entirely my field; there is almost nobody else who could do a literary essay on science.

Some of your scientific prose has been published in English under the title The Dimension of the Present Moment. *Can you tell me something about the prose collected in a further book,* The Jingle Bell Principle?
These have nothing to do with scientific essays; they are in some cases even prose poems. These are productions which I could afford in the non-person

years when I was not obliged to make TV appearances and broad cultural contributions and so on. They are typical products of being a non-person: 'He is a non-person but why don't we print him — without the name.' Just my initials would appear. But, because my style is very typical — in prose I have a more typical style than in poetry (but that doesn't come through in the translation) — immediately all the readers of the magazine would know I am writing.

Is it true that you became a non-person as a result of signing a street petition?
The petition had a good intention which just misfired. There was no sense in having this petition — it made the Russians more angry, owing to a wrong translation. It was a petition to Dubček to push on with the reforms and it aggravated his position. The second thing was my Jan Palach poem. Actually, before August '68, I thought we should all show some restraint. After that, I thought it was better to speak up — and so I commented, making my most detrimental speeches in the Praesidium of the Association of the Czechoslovak Scientific Workers.

You were dropped from the Czechoslovak Academy of Sciences.
I was dropped in '71, having refused to make a statement revoking my political stance. I was lucky enough to work in an institute where we do something directly for the patients. We are producing immunosuppressives and we do clinical diagnosis too. I am free there to do my own things which I love.

My main work comes from the optimistic sixties when I discovered, as part of a collective project, that the lymphocyte is the key cell of the whole immune system, the bearer of the inner wisdom of the body, that it knows about the antigenic properties of the outer world beforehand, that it leads your immune response to all intruders.

What about the Writers' Union and your relationship with that institution?
I was invited back in the latest period. I just asked about the others who were not members and about the other literatures (the samizdat, the exiles and so on). I protested at the police action in January 1989. So there was no other meeting to which they would invite me.

Do you prefer your early work to your late work? Do you share the view that the imagination declines with age?
Definitely you lose with age. You are not getting smarter, but you are getting more experienced. So, while some things are more difficult to do in your mental processes, some things are easier because you know your ways with your mind, your metaphors, your sentences and so on. The only thing for me

is not to get lazy and not to get dependent on anything, on alcohol, on drugs, on superstitions, on false expectations or false consolations — just to do the best one can. I use my free time out of the laboratory only for writing or for sport or for going somewhere with the children. I strictly hate all types of social meetings. When I am meeting socially, it is for professional reasons.

What is the future for the writers who enjoyed great privileges under communism?
My feeling is that we should by no means behave as they did. We shouldn't behave as the Bolsheviks did. The trouble is their careers needed the Party because they have been second-class and have never been educated to go for more. Many of these official writers will never learn to be better, so they will end up by feeling that 'They did to us what we did to them. Much worse, they stopped us for eternity.'

Unfortunately, you can't tell a bad writer that he is a bad writer, even in a creative writing class. But there are a number who may become interesting writers and we should give them every opportunity.

Were you surprised at the suddenness with which communism crumbled in late '89?
The spirit of the sixties was progress. The seventies for everybody brought a hopeless situation. People like Havel just had the guts and the nerve and the audacity and the human quality of self-sacrifice.

In the mid-seventies, when I was a non-person, I was told by the great Czech actor Jan Werich, 'You must write. Intellectuality, irony and satire are what we need for survival. We don't need lyrical, emotional or even political poems; we need something more incisive.' Cracks were visible already since '86 or '87, but that the system was already powder I wouldn't have thought.

How difficult will it be to write in the new Czechoslovakia?
We will now experience the other types of differentiation within society. There will be camps for and against. We will have to take stands. It will not be a unified stance anymore, like all being against the Party bosses. And we have the memories, the dramatic or rich history, which may be used as an attitude or a theme in our writing.

Dalkey, County Dublin
March 1990

Eavan Boland

THE WOMAN POET: HER DILEMMA

I believe that the woman poet today inherits a dilemma. That she does so inevitably, no matter what cause she espouses and whatever ideology she advocates or shuns. That when she sits down to work, when she moves away from her work, when she tries to be what she is struggling to express, at all these moments the dilemma is present, waiting and inescapable.

The dilemma I speak of is inherent in a shadowy but real convergence between new experience and an established aesthetic. What this means in practical terms is that the woman poet today is caught in a field of force. Powerful, persuasive voices are in her ear as she writes. Distorting and simplifying ideas of womanhood and poetry fall as shadows between her and the courage of her own experience. If she listens to these voices, yields to these ideas, her work will be obstructed. If, however, she evades the issue, runs for cover and pretends there is no pressure, then she is likely to lose the resolution she needs to encompass the critical distance between writing poems and being a poet. A distance which for women is fraught in any case — as I hope to show — with psycho-sexual fear and doubt.

Dramatize, dramatize said Henry James. And so I will. Imagine then that a woman is going into the garden. She is youngish; her apron is on and there is flour on her hands. It is early afternoon. She is going there to lift a child for the third time who is about to put laburnum pods into its mouth. This is what she does. But what I have omitted to say in this small sketch is that the woman is a poet. And once she is in the garden, once the child, hot and small and needy is in her arms, once the frills of shadow around the laburnum and the freakish gold light from it are in her eyes, then her poetic sense is awakened. She comes back through the garden door. She cleans her hands, takes off her apron, sets her child down for an afternoon sleep. Then she sits down to work.

Now it begins. The first of these powerful, distracting voices comes to her. For argument's sake, I will call it the Romantic Heresy. It comes to her as a whisper, an insinuation. What she wants to do is to write about the laburnum, the heat of the child, common human love — the mesh of these things. But where — says the voice in her ear — is the interest in all this? How are you going to write a poem out of these plain janes, these snips and threads of an ordinary day? Now — the voice continues — listen to me and I will show you how to make all this poetic. A shade here, a nuance there, a degree of distance, a lilt of complaint and all will be well. The woman hesitates. Suddenly the moment that seemed to her potent, emblematic and true appears commonplace, beyond the pale of art. She is shaken. And there I will leave her, with her doubts and fears, so as to look more closely at what it is that has come between her and the courage of that moment.

The Romantic Heresy, as I have chosen to call it, is not Romanticism proper, although it is related to it. 'Before Wordsworth', wrote Lionel Trilling, 'poetry had a subject. After Wordsworth its prevalent subject was the poet's own subjectivity.' This shift in perception was responsible for much that was fresh and revitalizing in nineteenth-century poetry. But it was also responsible for the declension of poetry into self-consciousness, self-invention.

This type of debased Romanticism is rooted in a powerful, subliminal suggestion that poets are distinctive, not so much because they write poetry but because, in order to do so, they have poetic feelings about poetic experiences. That there is a category of experience and expression which is poetic and all the rest is ordinary and therefore inadmissible. In this way a damaging division is made between the perception of what is poetic on the one hand, and, on the other, what is merely human. Out of this emerges the aesthetic which suggests that, in order to convert the second into the first, you must romanticize it. This idea gradually became an article of faith in nineteenth-century, post-Romantic English poetry. When Matthew Arnold said at Oxford 'the strongest part of our religion is its unconscious poetry', he was blurring a fine line. He was himself one of the initiators of a sequence of propositions by which the poetry of religion became the religion of poetry.

There are obvious pitfalls in all this for any poet. But the dangers for a woman poet in particular must be immediately obvious. Women are a minority within the expressive poetic tradition. Much of their actual experience lacks even the most rudimentary poetic precedent. 'No poet', said Eliot, 'no artist of any kind has his complete meaning alone.' The woman poet is more alone with her meaning than most. To take just one instance, the ordinary routine day that many women live — must live — does not figure largely in poetry. Nor the feelings that go with it. The temptations are considerable therefore for a woman poet to romanticize these routines and these feelings so as to align them with what is considered poetic.

Now let us go back to the woman at her desk. Let us suppose that she has recovered her nerve and her purpose. She remembers what is true: the heat, the fear that her child will eat the pods. She feels again the womanly force of the instant. She puts aside the distortions of Romanticism. She starts to write again and once again she is assailed. But this time by another and equally persuasive idea.

And this is feminist ideology or at least one part of it. In recent years feminism has begun to lay powerful prescriptions on writing by women. The most exacting of these comes from that part of feminist thinking which is separatist. Separatist prescriptions demand that women be true to the historical angers which underwrite the Women's Movement; that they cast aside pre-existing literary traditions; that they evolve not only their own writing, but the criteria by which to judge it. I think I understand some of these prescriptions. I recognize that they stem from the fact that many feminists — and I partly share the view — perceive a great deal in pre-existing literary expression and tradition which is patriarchal. I certainly have no wish to be apologetic about the separatist tendency within poetry because it offends or threatens or bores — and it does all three — the prevailing male literary establishments. That does not concern me for a moment. There is still prejudice — the Irish poetic community is among the most male chauvinist — but as it happens that is not part of this equation.

What does concern me is that the gradual emphasis on the appropriate subject matter and the correct feelings has become as constricting and corrupt within Feminism as within Romanticism. In the grip of Romanticism and its distortions, women can be argued out of the truth of their feelings, can be marginalized, simplified and devalued by what is, after all, a patriarchal tendency. But does the separatist prescription offer more? I have to say — painful as it may be to dissent from one section of a Movement I cherish — that I see no redemption whatsoever in moving from one simplification to the other.

So here again is the woman at her desk. Let us say she is feminist. What is she to make of the separatist suggestion by a poet like Adrienne Rich that 'to be a female human being, trying to fulfil traditional female functions in a traditional way, is in direct conflict with the subversive function of the imagination'. Yet the woman knows that whether or not going into the garden and lifting her child is part of the 'traditional way', it has also been an agent and instrument of subversive poetic perception. What is she to do? Should she contrive an anger, invent a disaffection? How is she to separate one obligation from the other, one truth from the next? And what is she to make of the same writer's statement that 'to the eye of the feminist, the work of Western male poets now writing reveals a deep, fatalistic pessimism as to the possibilities of change . . . and a new tide of phallocentric sadism'. It is no good saying she need not read these remarks. The truth is that Adrienne Rich is a wonderful poet and her essay — 'When we Dead Awaken' — from which these statements are quoted is a seminal piece. It should be read by every poet. So there is no escape. The force and power of the separatist prescription must be confronted.

Separatist ideology is a persuasive and dangerous influence on any woman poet writing today. It tempts her to disregard the whole poetic past as patriarchal betrayal. It pleads with her to discard the complexities of true feeling for the relative simplicity of anger. It promises to ease her technical problems with the solvent of polemic. It whispers to her that to be feminine in poetry is easier, quicker and more eloquent than the infinitely more difficult task of being human. Above all it encourages her to feminize her perceptions rather than humanize her femininity.

But women have a birthright in poetry. I believe — though no separatist poet would agree — that when a woman poet begins to write, she very soon becomes conscious of the silences which have preceded her, which still surround her. These silences will become an indefinable part of her purpose as a poet. Yet, as a working poet, she will also — if she is honest — recognize that these silences have been at least partly redeemed within the past expressions of other poets, most of them male. And these expressions also will become part of her purpose. But for that to happen, she must have the fullest possible dialogue with them. She needs it; she is entitled to it. And in order to have that dialogue, she must have the fullest dialogue also with her own experience, her own present as a poet. I do not believe that separatism allows for this.

Very well. Let us say that, after all this inner turmoil, the woman is still writing. That she has taken her courage in her hands and has resisted the prescriptions both of Romanticism and separatism. Yet for all that, something is still not right. Once again, she hesitates. But why? 'Outwardly', said Virginia Woolf, 'what is simpler than to write books? Outwardly what obstacles are there for a woman rather than for a man? Inwardly I think the case is very different. She still has many ghosts to fight, many prejudices to overcome.' Ghosts and prejudices. Maybe it is time we took a look at these.

II

I am going to move this essay once again away from the exploratory and theoretical into something more practical. Let us say, for argument's sake, that it is a wet, Novemberish day in a country town in Ireland. Now, for the sake of going a bit further, let us say that a workshop or the makings of one has gathered in an upstairs room in a school perhaps, or an Adult Education Centre. The surroundings will be — as they always are on these occasions — just a bit surreal. There will be old metal furniture, solid oak tables, the surprising gleam of a new video in the corner. And finally, let us say that among these women gathered here is a woman called Judith. I will call her that as a nod in the direction of Virginia Woolf's great essay 'A Room of One's

Own'. And when I — for it is I who am leading the workshop — get off the train or out of the car and climb the stairs and enter that room, it is Judith — her poems already in her hand — who catches my eye and holds my attention.

'History', said Butterfield, 'is not the study of origins; rather it is the analysis of all the mediations by which the past has turned into our present.' As I walk into that room, as Judith hands me her poems, our past becomes for a moment a single present. I may know, she may acknowledge, that she will never publish, never evolve. But equally I know we have been in the same place and have inherited the same dilemma.

She will show me her work diffidently. It will lack almost any technical finish — lineation is almost always the chief problem — but that will not concern me in the least. What will concern me, will continue to haunt me, is that she will be saying to me — not verbally, but articulately nonetheless — I write poetry, but I am not a poet. And I will realize, without too much being said, that the distance between writing poetry and being a poet is one that she has found in her life and her time just too difficult, far and dangerous, to travel. I will also feel — whether or not I am being just in the matter — that the distance will have been more impassable for her than for any male poet of her generation. Because it is a preordained distance, composed of what Butterfield might call the unmediated past. On the surface that distance seems to be made up of details — lack of money, lack of like minds and so on. But this is deceptive. In essence, the distance is psycho-sexual, made so by a profound fracture between her sense of the obligations of her womanhood and the shadowy demands of her gift.

In his essay on Juan de Asbaje, Robert Graves sets out to define that fracture: 'Though the burden of poetry', he writes, 'is difficult enough for a man to bear, he can always humble himself before an Incarnate Muse and seek instruction from her. The case of a woman poet is a thousand times worse: since she is herself the Muse, a goddess without an external power to guide or comfort her, and if she strays even a hair's breadth from the path of divine instinct, must take a violent self-vengeance.'

I may think there is a certain melodrama in Graves's commentary. Yet, in a subterranean way, this is exactly what many women fear. That the role of poet added to that of woman may well involve them in unacceptable conflict. The outcome of that fear is constant psycho-sexual pressure. And the result of that pressure is a final reluctance to have the courage of her own experience. All of which adds up to that distance between writing poems and being a poet, a distance which Judith — even as she hands me her work — is telling me she cannot and must not travel.

I will leave that room angered and convinced. Every poet carries within themselves their own silent constituency, made of suffering and failed expression. Judith and the 'compound ghost' that she is — for she is, of course, an amalgam of many women — is mine. It is difficult, if not impossible, to explain to men who are poets — writing as they are with centuries of expression behind them — how emblematic is the unexpressed life of other women to the woman poet, how intimately it is her own. And how, in many ways, that silence is as much part of her tradition as the Troubadours are of theirs. 'You who maintain that some animals sob sorrowfully, that the dead have dreams', wrote Rimbaud, 'try to tell the story of my downfall and my slumber. I no longer know how to speak.'

How to speak. I believe that if a woman poet survives, if she sets out on that distance and arrives at the other end, then she has an obligation to tell as much as she knows of the ghosts within her, for they make up, in essence, her story as well. And that is what I intend to do now.

III

I began writing poetry in the Dublin of the early nineteen sixties. Perhaps 'began' is not the right word. I had been there or thereabouts for years: scribbling poems in boarding school, reading Yeats after lights out, revelling in the poetry on the course.

Then I left school and went to Trinity. Dublin was a coherent space then, a small circumference in which to be and become a poet. A single bus journey took you into College for the day. Twilights over Stephen's Green were breathable and lilac-coloured. Coffee beans turned and gritted off the blades in the windows of Roberts and Bewleys. A single cup of it, moreover, cost ninepence in old money and could be spun out for hours of conversation. The last European city. The last literary smallholding.

Or maybe not. 'Until we can understand the assumptions in which we are drenched,' writes Adrienne Rich, 'we cannot know ourselves.' I entered that city and that climate knowing neither myself nor the assumptions around me. And, into the bargain, I was priggish, callow, enchanted by the powers of the intellect.

If I had been less of any of these things, I might have looked about me more. I might have taken note of my surroundings. If history is, as Napoleon said, the agreed lie, then literary traditions are surely the agreed fiction. Things are put in and left out, are pre-selected and can be manipulated. If I had looked closely, I might have seen some of the omissions. Among other things I might have noticed that there were no women poets, old or young, past or present, in my immediate environment. Sylvia Plath, it is true, detonated in my consciousness, but not until years later. As it was, I accepted what I found almost without question. And soon enough, without realizing it, without enquiring into it, I had inherited more than a set of assumptions. I had inherited a poem.

This poem was a mixture really, a hybrid of the Irish lyric and the British Movement piece. It had identifiable moving parts. It usually rhymed, was almost always stanzaic, had a beginning, middle and end. The relation of music to image, of metaphor to idea, was safe, repetitive and derivative. 'Ladies, I am tame, you may stroke me', said Samuel Johnson to assorted fashionable women. If this poem could have spoken, it might have said something of the sort. I suppose it was no worse, if certainly no better, than the model most young poets have thrust upon them. The American workshop poem at the moment is just as pervasive and probably no more encouraging of scrutiny. Perhaps this was a bit more anodyne: the 'bien-fait' poem as it has since been called; the well-made compromise.

This, then, was the poem I learned to write, laboured to write. I will not say it was a damaging model because it was a patriarchal poem. As it happens it was, but that matters less than that I had derived it from my surroundings, not from my life. It was not my own. That was the main thing. 'Almost any young gentleman with a sweet tooth', wrote Jane Carlyle of Keats's 'Isabella', 'might be expected to write such things.' The comment is apt.

In due course I married, moved out of the city and into the suburbs — I am telescoping several years here — and had a baby daughter. In so doing I had, without realizing it, altered my whole situation.

When a woman writer leaves the centre of a society, becomes wife, mother and housewife, she ceases automatically to be a member of that dominant class to which she belonged when she was visible chiefly as a writer. As a student perhaps, or otherwise as an apprentice. Whatever her writing abilities, henceforth she ceases to be defined by them and becomes defined instead by subsidiary feminine roles. Jean Baker Miller, an American psychoanalyst, has written about the relegation to women of certain attitudes which a society is uneasy with. 'Women', she writes, 'become the carriers for society of certain aspects of the total human experience, those aspects which remain unsolved.' Suddenly, in my early thirties, I found myself a 'carrier' of these unsolved areas of experience. Yet I was still a writer, still a poet. Obviously something had to give.

What gave, of course, was the aesthetic. The poem I had been writing no longer seemed necessary or true. On rainy winter afternoons, with the dusk drawn in, the fire lighted and a child asleep upstairs, I felt assailed and renewed by contradictions. I could have said with Eluard 'there is another world, but it is in this one'. To a degree I felt that; yet I hesitated. 'That story I cannot write,' said Conrad, 'weaves itself into all I see, into all I speak, into all I think.' So it was with me. And yet I remained uncertain of my ground.

On the one hand poetic convention — conventions moreover which I had breathed in as a young poet — whispered to me that the daily things I did, things which seemed to me important and human, were not fit material for poetry. That is, they were not sanctioned by poetic tradition. But, the whisper went on, they could become so. If I wished to integrate these devalued areas into my poetry, I had only to change them slightly. And so on. And in my other ear feminist ideology — to which I have never been immune — argued that the life I lived was a fit subject for anger and the anger itself the proper subject for poetry.

Yet in my mind and in the work I was starting to do, a completely different and opposed conviction was growing: That I stood at the centre of the lyric moment itself, in a mesh of colours, sensualities and emotions that were equidistant from poetic convention and political feeling alike. Technically and aesthetically I became convinced that if I could only detach the lyric mode from traditional Romantic elitism and the new feminist angers, then I would be able at last to express that moment.

The precedents for this were in painting rather than poetry. Poetry offered spiritual consolation but not technical example. In the genre painters of the French eighteenth century — in Jean-Baptiste Chardin in particular — I saw what I was looking for. Chardin's paintings were ordinary in the accepted sense of the word. They were unglamorous, workaday, authentic. Yet in his work these objects were not merely described; they were revealed. The hare in its muslin bag, the crusty loaf, the woman fixed between menial tasks and human dreams — these stood out, a commanding text. And I was drawn to that text. Romanticism in the nineteenth century, it seemed to me, had prescribed that beauty be commended as truth. Chardin had done something different. He had taken truth and revealed its beauty.

From painting I learned something else of infinite value to me. Most young poets have bad working habits. They write their poems in fits and starts, by feast or famine. But painters follow the light. They wait for it and do their work by it. They combine artisan practicality with vision. In a house with small children, with no time to waste, I gradually reformed my working habits. I learned that if I could not write a poem, I could make an image; and if I could not make an image, I could take out a word, savour it and store it.

I have gone into all this because, to a certain extent, the personal witness of a woman poet is still a necessary part of the evolving criteria by which women and their poetry must be evaluated. Nor do I wish to imply that I solved my dilemma. The dilemma persists; the cross-currents continue. What I wished most ardently for myself at a certain stage of my work was that I might find my voice where I had found my vision. I still think that this is what matters most and is threatened most for the woman poet.

I am neither a separatist nor a post-feminist. I believe that the past matters, yet I do not believe we will reach the future without living through the womanly angers which shadow this present. What worries me most is that women poets may lose their touch, may shake off their opportunities because of the pressures and temptations of their present position.

It seems to me, at this particular time, that women have a destiny in the form. Not because they are women; it is not as simple as that. Our suffering, our involvement in the collective silence, does not — and will never — of itself guarantee our achievement as poets. But if we set out in the light of that knowledge and that history, determined to tell the human and poetic truth, and if we avoid simplification and self-deception, then I believe we are better equipped than most to discover the deepest possibilities and subversions within poetry itself. Artistic forms are not static. Nor are they radicalized by aesthetes and intellectuals. They are changed, shifted, detonated into deeper patterns only by the sufferings and self-discoveries of those who use them. By this equation, women should break down barriers in poetry in the same way that poetry will break the silence of women. In the process it is important not to mistake the easy answer for the long haul.

Medbh McGuckian

I THOUGHT IT WAS STILL FEBRUARY

Midway between one house and another,
half of every tree is still brown;
the railings just visible, they don't go the full length,
and one or two raindrops might be added.

My own impossible brand of being
now further away sheds orchids,
picks up unchristened waves and seed-pods of kisses
that breed meaning after they are finished.

You give me your glass to drink out of,
edged with pictures that come up and up
and read like novels (one in red, on love) —
the froth can't manage, blossoms, and breaks.

You have the awkward join to make —
to talk, to unsay, till every other word
is almost one I know,

and the faraway, living smell of the past
that never breaks the silence by a word,
takes the smoky fabric from a different floor,
and turns it into you.

Nuala Ní Dhomhnaill

AUBADE

Is cuma leis an mhaidin cad air a ngealann sí: —
ar na cáganna ag bruíon is ag achrann ins na crainn
dhuilleogacha; ar an mbardal glas ag snámh go tóstalach
i measc na ngiolcach ins na curraithe; ar thóinín bán
an chircín uisce ag gobadh aníos as an bpoll portaigh;
ar roilleoga ag siúl go cúramach ar thránna móra.

Is cuma leis an ghrian cad air a éiríonn sí: —
ar na tithe bríce, ar fhuinneoga de ghloine snoite
is gearrtha i gcearnóga Seoirseacha: ar na saithí beach
ag ullmhú chun creach a dhéanamh ar ghairdíní bruachbhailte;
ar lánúine óga fós ag méanfach i gcoimhthiúin is fonn
a gcúplála ag éirí aníos iontu; ar dhrúcht ag glioscarnach
ina dheora móra ar lilí is ar róiseanna; ar do ghuaille.

Ach ní cuma linn go bhfuil an oíche aréir
thart, is go gcaithfear glacadh le pé rud a sheolfaidh
An lá inniu an tslí; go gcaithfear imeacht is cromadh síos
arís le píosaí beaga brealsúnta ár saoil a dhlúthú
le chéile ar chuma éigin, chun gur féidir
lenár leanaí uisce a ól as babhlaí briste
in ionad as a mbosa, ní cuma linne é.

AUBADE

It's all the same to morning what it dawns on —
On the bickering of jackdaws in leafy trees;
On that dandy from the wetlands, the green mallard's
Stylish glissando among reeds; on the moorhen
Whose white petticoat flickers around the boghole;
On the oystercatcher on tiptoe at low tide.

It's all the same to the sun what it rises on —
On the windows in houses in Georgian squares;
On bees swarming to blitz suburban gardens;
On young couples yawning in unison before
They do it again; on dew like sweat or tears
On lilies and roses; on your bare shoulders.

But it isn't all the same to us that night-time
Runs out; that we must make do with today's
Happenings, and stoop and somehow glue together
The silly little shards of our lives, so that
Our children can drink water from broken bowls,
Not from cupped hands. It isn't the same at all.

(translated by Michael Longley)

Mary O'Donnell

BORDER TOWN

That town seemed comfortless once,
locked in a slither of damp roofs,

wrapped in a winding-sheet of rain,
huckster shops or tattered cabbages,

limp street corners, or
the whine of mechanical saws.

Mothers the shape of soft pillows,
slowly pushed prams, their baskets bulky.

The air was brusque
with the bite of local voices.

Now, when winter scours this plain
like a giant wire brush,

and the wind's a bitch,
untempered by rumpled hills,

when people drawl
in morphine-heavy tones,

I look north
to the half-cross border people,

tongues quick yet awkward,
mood and humour garnered

like nettles beneath the skin.
On a summer market morning

I thought I had ignored, the hills
are goosebumps on nervous terrain,

golden with buttercups,
and the hiccuping streets,

all rise and slump,
are drenched in light.

THE STORYTELLERS

In the storymaker's room,
capital letters, paragraphs,
are embossed with a golden weave
of international intrigue,
blackmail or bribery.
Around the world, every hour,
they recreate thick-thorned forests
of childhood dreams.
In Stockholm and Basel,
Washington or Tunis,
they shuffle papers
when the red light signals 'On',
cast a net of numbing calm
in neutral cadences,
animate the tales of death,
in voices tepid as cooling blood.

Favourite tales consist of warlocks,
witches, pillow-talk betrayals
where the princess tells all,
hints of espionage, astrakhan hats,
plumes of steam at a Siberian railway station,
or the ice-pale eyes of the Romanian
who infiltrates the French Right.

We listen in any language,
sense the passion beyond words,
assimilate nuance
as a voice pauses for a sip of air,
inadvertently hiccups on a word —

pravda, oggi, surtout, Gelegenheit,
addict, salam, —
the tale is never new,
spreads itself anciently
on the shortwave system,
like a wide-cast silver net,
instalments from Grimm or Andersen.

Daily, hourly, we wander
a black forest called Treachery,
lovers in the land of liaison,
our wide robes, tumbling hair,
edged with gold, silver or blood.

Sara Berkeley

BARTOLOMÉ

An old Italian paints small boys
The bloom of their skin is on his breath
No brush smudges it.
His hand dilates the liquid eyes
That never dry, not in the southern glare
Not in the thick nights.

When young, he learned from the rapid palette
Holding it up
Tuning his ear to the colours announcing themselves,
The canvasses taut at the slender tip of the brush.
Youth stole over every painting with its acrid flush.

People came by
And saw for the briefest time
How the brushes hung eagerly above the cloth
But they always waited longer than they ought
And the canvas tightened shut
Taking every stipple closely to itself
In a jealous rush.

Age becomes him
Slipping wrinkled cloth about his limbs
The palette seems much slower
All the tones are kinder now,
his young boys ripple outward from the brush,
He holds the palette still as a vessel full to the brim
And although they have no love for him
In the apricot light
He fathers them.

Julie O'Callaghan

CONTENT AND TASTEFUL

Here I am in my kitchen.
I look content and tasteful.
When my darling grandchildren
visit their grandma, I give them
windmill cookies — the ones with chunks
of nuts that come wrapped
in the orange cellophane package
with scenes of old Holland.
In this oven I cook up a storm.
Ya gotta garnish your recipes.
Cut out pictures from magazines
like *McCall's* or *Family Circle*
and always make your dishes
look like in the photographs.
I keep a few tricks up my sleeve
in these cabinets only I don't tell them
to anybody except my daughter
in Sarasota Florida who's trying
to get to a man's heart
through his stomach.
That's the only exception.
Do you get the aroma of my
Devil's Food cake baking?
Ladies, don't waste your time
with most of these new appliances.
Get your basics, keep 'em clean, buy fresh,
And I guarantee you your mouth
will be watering and your girdle
will be killing you.

Eiléan Ní Chuilleanáin

MEMORIALS

The bus is late getting in to my home town.
I walk up the hill by the barracks, cutting through alleyways
That surprise me, bursting through walls just before I felt them
Getting ready to arch and push. Here is the house.

Nobody who knows me knows where I am now.
I have a pocketful of gravel to wake my aunt sleeping
Behind the third dark window counting left over the bakery.
Here I will not be asked to repeat the story.
Between her and me and the hour of my birth
A broad stony stream is sliding
That changes its course with the floods of every spring.

A NOTE

Here is a note of the time
The nurse went out of the room,
The water was heard flowing.
She has not forgotten the sound.

In the field of four winds
The sand has blown its veil
Across the gouged lettering.
Her dry hands meet and scoop
The grains aside, her breath
Brushes them free: the words,
The glassy silence between them,
Swim up from depths at her call.

She starts again six feet off,
Lays bare the cyphers of the year
The minute the hour.

The sand blows up in plumes
Out of the deeper dints
Hollow like eyes in masks,
The marks the locals name
Where the five fingers sank.

The evening wind has begun
Stroking a long harsh note
On the tall grass in the dunes
As she sets off westward.

Mairead Byrne

AN INTERVIEW WITH ROMULUS AND REMUS

What did you think of the wolves?
Did they excite you?
Make you feel different? More human?
What is it like to be twins?
Did the wolves smell?
Did you find that in any way off-putting?
Did you have trouble expressing affection?
What's wolf's milk like for starters?
What were their names?
Where did they go on their holidays?
Did you find it hard to settle down again in Rome?
We call it Rome now.
I don't mean to cause a fight
but did it ever strike you that *Reme*
might have been an equally good name?
How did you boys get along?
Was it dark out there? And cold?
Are you glad to be home and how
do you get along with women, real women?
I mean, do they compare to the wolves?
Do you think your background will cause problems later in life?
I mean sexually.
Did you ever have it off with a wolf?
You're too young, I guess.
I don't mean to be disrespectful
but, you see, we never heard the full story.
A lot of people wonder about you boys,
being brought up by wolves and all that.
Do you miss them?
Do you know that they're nearly extinct?
Would you let your daughter marry a wolf?
How fast can you run?
Say, what's your favourite food?

Do you eat raw meat and tear it apart with your teeth?
Well, I suppose that was quite common in Rome.
Hey, thanks for your time, boys.
It's been real.
You gotta learn to talk soon, boys.
A lotta people are dying to hear about this.

IN TOWN

No-one I want to avoid.
No-one I want to see.
I have had my great loves.
They have had me.

Maura Dooley

APPLE PIE IN PIZZALAND

We are apologizing to one another
for our shyness. The waitress apologizes
for the lack of sultanas (not like the picture,
she says). I still probe between the slices of
apple as if I expect to find something other than
air. You spin the menu and pleat the paper napkin,
our cutlery scrapes eloquently enough.

On the train here a Canadian told me how
his province holds a lake the size of England.
I imagine you and I and Pizzaland, the green tables,
Doncaster, the fields, motorways, castles and flats,
churches, factories, corner shops, pylons, Hinkley Point,
Land's End and all of us dropped
in that huge lake, *plop.*

Years later new people will stroll on
the banks, remarking how in drought
you might see the top of Centrepoint
and in the strange stillness hear the ghostly
ring and clatter of Pizzaland forks on plates.

Rita Kelly

AR M'ÉIRÍ DOM AR MAIDIN . . .

Caolann an oíche chun na maidine,
sileann an solas, sileachán faoi choim,
diaidh ar ndiaidh trí fhallaing na fuinneoige;
ní féidir é a sheachaint maidin ar bith.
Téann na silíní solais i dtreise
go réidh, go héifeachtúil, gach cúinne, gach log súile,
briseann an lá ar chiumhais coinsiasa.

Doicheall agus déistin fiú
tabhairt faoi in athuair,
sa neamhní neantógach seo
is scriosach gach smaoineamh
agus is seasc gach léargas anama.

Cos thar chos amach,
agus buailim cic i ndraid an lae.

ON RISING IN THE MORNING . . .

The night slithers towards morning,
a furtive light seeps, oozes
slowly through the veiled window:
no morning escapes.
The flow of light grows stronger
gently, powerfully, spearing corners, eye-sockets,
day breaks on the edge of consciousness.

Begrudgingly, nauseously
facing it again,
in this nettly nothingness
all thought is destructive
barren each glimpse of the soul.

Step by step I go out
and kick the snarling day.

(translated by Aodán Mac Póilin)

Paula Meehan

NIGHT WALK

Earth shadows the moon
Leaves just a paring
Of light to get home by.

You follow iced potholes
That gleam in the dark,
Pebbles, perhaps, dropped by a child

When her father and mother
Have left her to find her
Own way out of the forest.

A stream weeps. The lake
Past blackthorn hedges
Is waiting for Finder

To keep her. And you
Still have three miles to go
Three miles to go and

No promise of sleep, but
The long night vigil
And drowning in pools

That go down forever
And there's no way out
And the bottom is never.

Mist grazes a meadow
Spills through a gap
To fresh pasture.

You have to get home.
Someone is waiting.
The table is set.

The kettle near boiling,
The clock ticks louder.
He paces the floor

From chair to window,
Sees nothing outside
But himself looking in.

At the top of the hill
You make out a light
Between pine and willow.

The last mile it measures
Your step on the road,
Human in the darkness.

AUTOBIOGRAPHY

She stalks me through the yellow flags.
If I look over my shoulder I will catch her
Striding proud, her three nipples pointing
From her breast fur, a spear in her hand.
I have such a desperate need of her —
Though her courage springs from innocence
Or ignorance. I could lie with her
In the shade of the poplars, curled
To a foetal dream on her lap, suck
From her milk of fire to enable me fly.
Her face is my own face, unblemished;
Her eyes seapools, reflecting lichens,
Thunderclouds; her pelt is watered silk
And golden; she guides me to healing herbs
At meadow edges. She does not speak
In any tongue I recognize.
She is mother to me, young
Enough to be my daughter.

The other one waits in gloomy hedges.
She pounces at night. She knows I've no choice.

She says 'I am your future.
Look on my neck, like a chicken's
Too old for the pot; my skin moults
In papery flakes. Hear it rustle.
My eyes are the gaping wounds
Of newly opened graves. Don't turn
Your nose up at me, madam, you may have need
Of me yet. I am your ticket underground.'
And yes, I have been suckled at her empty dugs,
Breathed deep of the stench of her self —
The stink of railway station urinals,
Of closing time vomit, of soup lines
And charity shops. She speaks
In a human voice and I understand.
I am mother to her, young
Enough to be her daughter.

I stand in a hayfield — midday, midsummer,
My birthday. From one breast
Flows the Milky Way, the starry path,
A sluggish trickle of pus from the other.
When I fly off I will glance back
Once to see my husk sink into the grasses.
Cranesbill and loosestrife will shed
Seeds over it like a blessing. Soon
The worms will begin to bring it under.

Vona Groarke

FROM A DISUSED HOUSE

If I were being honest, I would have to say
that nothing much has changed.
The rain is through. Nobody comes.
I hardly remember you.

Another day I would say *perhaps you never lived here.*
But the sense of you seeps through the house
in the way (I must say it) of blood.
I don't know. Whatever I say seems wrong.

This place disturbs me. It is not home.
I would describe the room to you
but it is dark. The last bulb blew tonight.
You wouldn't recognize it anyway.

I have boarded the windows up on your side.
Everywhere the stench of mould and shit.
These letters are rotting in my clothes.

I am in the process of not being here.
I don't think I will ever leave.
After Christmas, I will certainly move on.

Someone tried the back door last week.
I thought I recognized the pressure of your hand.

Suzanne Krochalis

TWO GARDENS

Two gardens slip out of memory,
to stand like two troubled guests,
their interesting faces turned
toward us for conversation.

Lush and various, the first was speckled
with a child's trail of stones.
No two shrubs the same, all human
energy churning the soil of home.

The other, an unfinished restoration,
cornering a gazebo
of broken Regency elegance,
scrubbed and ready for gradual repair.

In the first the caretaker bends
over his barrow, no consideration
of the spinning unwinding universe
breaks his resolution.

The second was busy with guests
and the gay host paused over the shoulder
as I played with a baby, his own dead child
nearly breaking the courage of his style.

Ellen Beardsley

HIROSHIMA FAREWELL, 1814

after Rai San'yo

This visit done, all familiar here goes
given up again — our garden gate's click,
the water-wheel's hush; brush of feet
on teak floors polished bright as brass;
farewell teas, this parting glass; song,
our need for song, song's solace.

I'll miss my robes and hats and easy sleep
on silks; that threaded gleam
of our Gingko moonless nights, salient
as father's stern stance or mother's peace.
And I shall miss family's firm embrace
as always, my friends, my place.

Giddy still with departure wine, I slip out
watching familiar islands shanty-shift strange
like this ship's crew. Scared too for all new elsewhere,
I garner last glances of that old Gingko
strung silver on father's hill. It fans farewell
as light slides down this new-moon night.

EHRWALD IN DECEMBER

Stuck here like multi-coloured map pins, we
watch the world grow upwards from our bed. And
what will happen when all that's vertical
finally falls — when Chartres tumbles
to a mere pile of lichen-mottled rock,
or when Seagram's sinks to stamp out
New York's subterranean worm work
or when those twenty-six thousand friction piles
rot under Amsterdam's Central Station —
what of us and what will happen then?

Nothing happens in our rented valley room for now:
the Zugspitze rises outside our window
massive as God; snow dogs and skiers prowl
its iced porches. Our wine's congealed;
our blood's cement. While our knees roll like drumlins
under our duvet, we wait: all that's vertical
elsewhere shudders with cold in its sway.

CHEIRON'S BRIDE

Welcomed warmly and, from the first, embraced
as if one of their own, I now share their fruit
and, clumsy biped, ape their equine strides.

Under dark Magnesia's towering shadows
they have taught me their ways and tastes
and I use my fingers now rarely.

My cup's held like theirs, as if cradled
by hooves. My hands and feet are blackened
and my body swathed in the chestnut hide

left by dead Nessus. His tail, now mine
blows flaxen behind me as I pretend
to gallop fast and free, out of danger and fun.

My own flaxen hair, like a mane, grows daily.
'Please never cut it again', begs Cheiron.
His gentleness, no guise of some buried demon,

alarms and I resist his embrace. I still remain
content, but wary, and only slowly warm
as my heavy shroud of sadness sheds

to show the spring coat of a promising centaur.
Should he, my last immortal man, ever die
all will, again, fall to dark furore.

Julia Carlson

PERFECTION IS TERRIBLE

Linda W. Wagner-Martin, *Sylvia Plath*. London: Chatto and Windus, 1988
Anne Stevenson, *Bitter Fame: A Life of Sylvia Plath*. London: Viking 1989

When will the mythmaking that surrounds Sylvia Plath come to an end? Dutiful daughter, feminist, sacrificial victim, she is now the victimizer.

There is no shortage of material on Plath. From childhood, she kept copious journals. After she left home for Smith College, she became a compulsive correspondent. Memoirs of her abound, and three more (by Richard Murphy, Dido Merwin, and Lucas Myers) are included in Anne Stevenson's new biography. At this point, no biography of Plath can be definitive, however. Much material still remains unavailable, some of it in sealed library collections. Important documents will never be recovered, including Plath's last journals, one of which her husband, Ted Hughes, lost and another of which he destroyed after her death. And it is well-known that Hughes refuses to discuss their life together.

By his very aloofness Hughes has contributed in no small way to the mythology which surrounds Plath. His sister, Olwyn Hughes, who acts as literary agent for the Plath estate, is now entering the mythology herself as a kind of fairytale guardian, protecting Plath against the eulogy of 'feminists' and setting the record straight by ensuring that the 'negative' side of Plath's character gets its fair share of attention. In her capacity as literary agent, Olwyn Hughes shaped Wagner-Martin's version of Plath's life by insisting that large sections of the manuscript be omitted from the final, published version. Now she has given substantial shape to Stevenson's biography, so much so that Stevenson refers to it as 'almost a work of dual authorship'.

No one claims Sylvia Plath was an easy person to like. In their memoirs former friends and lovers recall having been dazzled or bewildered by her, hurt or infuriated. No one seems to recall enjoying her company. Her relationships with people were dominated by the fact that she remained an annoyance, a challenge, or an enigma, even to those who were closest to her. Certainly, she attracts mythmaking for this reason; however, she attracts it even more because she spent her short lifetime repeatedly creating her own myth of herself — as All-American girl, as brilliant student, as perfect wife and mother, and, finally, as martyr.

Plath grew up in suburban America during the nineteen forties and fifties. Her father, Otto Plath, whom she idolized as a child and raged at in 'Daddy', was authoritarian and kept a cool distance from his children; a scientist by profession, he once ate a cooked rat in front of a group of students in order to demonstrate that all responses are 'conditioned'. Her mother, Aurelia, was self-sacrificing and transferred her dedication from her husband to her children after his death. Immediately after Otto Plath's death, Aurelia signed a document written by the eight-year-old Sylvia which stated, 'I Promise Never to Marry Again'. Several years later Sylvia successfully blocked her mother from taking the position of Dean of Women at Northeastern University in Boston by accusing her of betrayal — 'For your self-aggrandizement you would make us complete orphans.' Throughout her life Plath was to remain deeply dependent on and resentful of her mother, writing her adoring letters at the same time that she was lashing out at her in *The Bell Jar*.

The insecurity and anger Plath suffered after her father's death were at the centre of her emotional life, but she tried desperately to conceal them both from herself and from others by looking for perfection and control in every aspect of her life — domestic, emotional, intellectual and artistic. Writing in her journal as a teenager, she described herself as 'the girl who wanted to be God'. The mythology she subscribed to was often that of American post-war femininity and domesticity, her ideals those she had learned from her self-sacrificing mother and women's magazines of the period. However sympathetic one feels towards Plath, it can be difficult to reconcile the burning intensity of her work with the banality of many of her ideals.

At high school in the Boston suburb of Wellesley and later at Smith College, which she attended on a scholarship, Plath cultivated the image of an All-American girl. She developed a 'popularity strategy' in high school; at Smith, she put herself under intense pressure to embody what she called 'a Smith girl', achieving good grades, dating Ivy League men on weekends, and creating a general sense of well-adjusted, cashmere-sweater normality which she could ill afford. She represented herself as enthusiastic; her smile won over one English professor, who saw it as 'not the ambitious, ingratiating falsely open smile of someone eager to please and be accepted', but 'a radiant smile . . . of happiness at what was being offered, being shared.' The smile, as forced as it was desperate, appears in most of her published photographs from this period and is plastered across Doris Day-like pictures of her modelling ballgowns and bathing suits in the Cambridge *Varsity*, for which she wrote on fashion when she was a Fulbright Scholar at Cambridge.

The skill with which Plath played the role of All-American girl was rewarded when she became a guest editor at *Mademoiselle* magazine in the summer after her junior year at Smith. It would be difficult to overestimate the significance of this appointment. For conventional American young women, *Mademoiselle* was an arbiter of taste, and every summer the twenty women who were selected from across the county to occupy these posts became properly regarded as the most talented young women in America. Although Plath had already published in the magazine, it was only when her editorship was announced that Smith professors feted her at private dinners.

What had seemed to epitomize Plath's dream disturbed her deeply. She was overworked at *Mademoiselle*, overwhelmed by the city of New York, and insecure outside the structured world of academe. On her last night in New York, she became so depressed that she threw most of her clothes, many of which she had splurged on for the purpose of wearing in New York, out of her hotel window and had to borrow clothes in order to go home. Several weeks later she was found in a coma after having taken an overdose of sleeping pills. Pathetically, one of her first remarks when she woke up in the hospital was, 'I so wanted to be a Smith woman!'

The energy Plath put into being an all-round achiever was matched by the energy she put into a search for a husband. For her, there was no question of choosing between marriage and a career. She could not imagine her life without the structure of a home and husband and longed for a 'blazing love that I can live with . . . to cook and make a house, and surge force into a man's dreams, and write, if he could talk and walk and work and passionately want to do his career.'

She drove many men away with her overeagerness. Peter Davison, who remembered being fascinated and baffled by her, also felt that she slipped into his bed somewhat too easily and was 'too exigent'. Other men, such as her Wellesley next-door neighbour, Dick Norton, whom she caricatured as Buddy Willard in *The Bell Jar*, became victims of her savage accusations of betrayal. During her senior year at Smith she strung along two entirely different men — handsome, well-meaning Gordon Lameyer, an Amherst graduate who had gone into the Navy, and Richard Sassoon, a Yale student with a Continental flair and a taste for the sadistic. She spent considerable energy corresponding with them both, making her letters literary and provocative and assuring each that he was her 'major man'. Lameyer, who was in love with and hoped to marry her, later wrote a memoir, 'Who Was Sylvia?', where he revealed how confused he had been by her. Sassoon, with whom Plath was in love, deserved her accusations of betrayal: many of his love letters were actually assignments for creative writing classes, and he tried to slip carefully out of her life by forbidding her to communicate with him — a command she refused to obey.

Plath was still reeling from Sassoon's rejection when she met Ted Hughes. She idolized him from the start, describing him first in 'Pursuit' as 'the black marauder', whom she predicted would be the death of her, and then as 'the strongest man in the world . . . brilliant poet whose work I loved before I met him, a large, hulking, healthy Adam . . . with a voice like the thunder of God — a singer, storyteller, lion, and world-wanderer, a vagabond who will never stop.' They had a whirlwind romance straight out of her dreams, marrying on Bloomsday after knowing each other for only five months. To her they were soulmates and he her 'male counterpart'. She identified with him as an artist and believed he would free her as a writer. It was a dangerous identification and one which inevitably led to accusations of betrayal.

For the first two years Plath did find a degree of freedom in the security of marriage. Their relationship gave her the energy and the confidence to write more openly. Hughes directed her reading and gave her the courage to abandon plans for an academic career. Living with him in Boston, going to weekly sessions with the psychiatrist who helped her through her first breakdown, and attending Robert Lowell's writing seminar at Boston University, she found for the first time courage to struggle to find her own voice as a poet and to incorporate into her work 'real things', 'real emotions', 'real situations, behind which the great gods play the drama of blood, lust and death.'

When she and Hughes returned to England, it became clear that the breakthrough she was making in her writing was not one that she was able to effect in her personal life. She became jealous and possessive, obsessed with the idea that Hughes would abandon her for another woman. Her reprisals for imagined affairs could be violent, and he once came home late from a meeting to discover that she had destroyed all his work in progress, various notebooks, and his favourite edition of Shakespeare.

As a writer, Plath always showed extraordinary ambition and wrote as much for public approval as for personal release. At Smith, and later at Cambridge, she submitted nearly everything she wrote for publication. She jealously watched the success of other writers whom she regarded as competition, especially 'this damn adrienne cecile rich, only two years older than I, who is a yale younger poet and regularly in all the top mags.' After she and Hughes had children, Plath insisted that he and she divide up days, one writing in the morning and one in the afternoon. Given her strong sense of identity as a poet, it was a dangerous sign that many people she met knew her as a wife and mother first and as a poet second. After having spent an evening with her and Hughes at their flat, Al Alvarez, who had already published her poems in *The Observer*, was stunned to discover he had just had dinner with Sylvia *Plath*.

As this episode suggests, Hughes's career eclipsed Plath's when they returned to England. To fill in the gap, she put herself under enormous pressure to become the perfect wife and mother. She became obsessive in her domestic role, cleaning and furnishing each apartment or house they moved into and straining finances by purchasing new furniture, appliances and American-style gadgets. Additionally, she took on the role of secretary for herself and Hughes, typing their work and correspondence and ensuring they each had manuscripts under submission. English friends marvelled at her energy, but it concealed desperation in the face of her rapidly disintegrating marriage. If she was possessive of Hughes, she soon felt stifled by him and came to believe that, instead of giving freedom, their marriage was like a death. In 'The Rabbit Catcher', written only a few months before their separation, she wrote: 'And we, too, had a relationship — / Tight wires between us, / Pegs too deep to uproot, and a mind like a ring / Sliding shut on some quick thing, / The constriction killing me also.'

It wasn't until her separation from Hughes that Plath found real freedom as a poet, 'producing stuff I had locked in me for years.' She was ecstatic but terrified at the prospect of living as a professional writer. In her personal life she ricocheted between the extremes of total efficiency and total collapse, suffering serious bouts of flu and pouring out her tale of Hughes's rejection to anyone who would listen. As this tale grew, it became one of martyrdom, and she began to see Hughes as the latest in a long line of men who had betrayed her. She vented her rage at him in poems such as 'Fever 103', 'Ariel', 'Lady Lazarus', and 'Purdah' where she wrote of a betrayed woman who survives to mete out vengeance.

Plath finished her final two poems, 'Balloons' and 'Edge', only days before she committed suicide. The contrast between them offers a frightening index to the mood swings she was going through. A warm, tender celebration of life, 'Balloons' describes balloons flying around in her flat and being played with by her children. 'Edge' is chilling, a celebration of death as perfection: 'The woman is perfected./ Her dead/ Body wears the smile of accomplishment.' Suicide had been a subject of many of Plath's final poems, but the image of rebirth had been equally powerful. In her final poem, however, she suggests that she no longer saw martyrdom in relation to Hughes, but in relation to herself. She is both creator and destroyer — the God she longed to be as a child.

Linda W. Wagner-Martin and Anne Stevenson have written two strikingly different biographies of Plath. Wagner-Martin's solid account is well-disposed towards Plath and strongest when she treats of Plath's life before her marriage. Wagner-Martin views Plath as a product of the American fifties, who was politically committed and 'a feminist, in a broad sense of the term: she never undervalued herself or her work.' Stevenson's biography complements Wagner-Martin's by focusing almost entirely on Plath's life after her marriage. Stevenson writes from the premise that Plath's real character, in particular the destructiveness which manifested itself in her marriage, has been concealed by feminist mythology. As a psychological study, *Bitter Fame* is the more complex of the two biographies and offers greater insight into Plath's relationships with people and her mental illness; however, it is always clear that one of the principal unacknowledged aims of *Bitter Fame* is to vindicate Ted Hughes.

Here are several examples of how the biographies differ in their treatment of major and minor events in Plath's life. Describing responses of people to Plath at Cambridge, Wagner-Martin is respectful; her Plath 'impressed fellow students as being . . . older . . . worldly and highly competitive.' Stevenson's Plath was a comic figure, unaware that she 'stood out oddly' and that Hughes's friends 'looked on in perplexity' when it became clear he was falling in love with her. In 1960, shortly after her daughter's birth, Plath went with a friend to a Ban-the-Bomb rally in Trafalgar Square. Wagner-Martin sees this as evidence of the political Plath exhausting herself by trying 'to do everything she ordinarily would' after the birth of her child. Stevenson uses the episode to reveal that Plath went principally because she knew Hughes would be there with Dido Merwin, of whom she was jealous. Discussing Plath's suicide, Wagner-Martin identifies Plath as having just 'come into her own as a woman' and suggests that she committed suicide because of 'changes in her personal life'. There is little reference to family problems in Stevenson's account; she reproduces a doctor's verdict which suggests that Plath's mood swings were caused by a chemical imbalance.

Although Wagner-Martin often strains material for the sake of her thesis, her optimism never equals the negativism which characterizes Stevenson's biography. It is most pronounced in the three memoirs — by Lucas Myers, an American poet who knew Hughes and Plath at Cambridge, Dido Merwin, the former wife of W. S. Merwin, and Richard Murphy — which are reprinted as appendices. In each Plath emerges as rapacious — as 'trying to swallow Hughes whole' in Myers's memoir, as embarrassing Richard Murphy by making a pass at him and offering to rent his house with him in it. In Dido Merwin's particularly vindictive memoir, Plath is 'a natural-born appropriator', while Hughes is tolerant and protective of her, 'if anything, too nice'. There can be little doubt that each of these writers felt a need to speak in defence of the silent Hughes, but thanks to them and to the interpretation which Stevenson imposes upon many events in Plath's life, there is now a new mythology in place with Plath as the victimizer and Hughes as the victim — strong, long-suffering, good. And straight out of *Jane Eyre*.

Mary Benson

A TRIP TO DUBLIN

In Pretoria he was known as Mr Benson of the Hospital and when we bought anything — shoes or a book or material for frocks that Ma would make up — we simply said, 'Put it down to Mr Benson of the Hospital's account.'

When he died I was furious at an obituary in the *Pretoria News* which told of how he gave sweets to strangers. I think they even made that the headline. I wonder now, was I furious because it belittled him by taking a triviality out of context while not giving him credit for all the valuable things he did, or was I furious *because* of his habit of offering sweets, like the time when I pushed him in a wheelchair through London airport on our way to Dublin, and he insisted on stopping to give toffees to two American infants, all curls and bows.

What made it worse on that occasion was that I'd had to argue to get him into the wheelchair at all. 'Can't be seen in that thing!' he'd protested. Even in his eighties he was vain. 'Get in!' Then, after I'd shoved the unaccountably recalcitrant wheelchair from one end of the terminal to the other, I found I'd left the brake on. No wonder my arthritic wrists ached. And the trip to Dublin was meant to be my treat for him. I had set out that morning with such good grace, intending it as compensation for not being exactly welcoming when he'd turned up from South Africa, hoping to settle with me in London.

Not that he would for a moment have admitted that I could be in any way unkind to him. He adored and forgave, or seemed not even to notice, my faults. And I had adored him when I was a child. Those early years in Pretoria were full of fun and sunshine. Each morning we woke to a clear blue sky; our beds on the stoep looked out on jacarandas, their mauve radiance fixed in memory, although they blossomed only briefly in October. And while I bathed, he stood at the basin, shaving, and sang:

She told me her age was five-and-twenty,
Cash in the bank she said she'd plenty,
I like a fool believed it all,
'Cos I was an M U G.
At Trinity Church I met my doom,
Now I live in the top back room . . .

Smiling into the mirror as he made pink tracks through the white foam each side of his Roman nose, telling about Ireland: 'We are descended from one of the Kings, yes, we were the O'Banaghans of Castle Banaghan in County Sligo. More than one of them was hanged.' It was years before I heard the joke about every Irishman being descended from a king. But I believed, for hadn't he been a frequenter of the Viceroy's receptions at the 'Cassle' as he pronounced it, in Phoenix Park. 'With the Cavalry in full dress — Lancers, Hussars, Dragoons — their spurs jingling. And "Flora-dora" at the Gaiety!' Then, with a flourish of hand and voice, 'Once upon a time when I was a boy at my father's school, I fell from the topmost branch of the old elm tree and broke my arm!'

'Broke your arm!'

'That was before I Knew the Truth.'

The Truth. Perhaps only an Irishman could at the same time be an ardent Christian Scientist *and* Secretary of a hospital and fail to see the humour in it. He'd even converted the matron of the hospital.

Before breakfast he sat with his Bible and *Science and Health with Key to the Scriptures* and while he did the Lesson or breathed prayers to Father-Mother-God I crouched at his feet. Mrs Mary Baker Eddy, could she be married to God? Motes of dust danced in the sunlight that flooded through the window of his study. 'Thy kingdom *is* come. Thou are ever-present,' he declared confidently. The hooter sounding from the railway yards across Potgieter Street told it was breakfast-time. He bent his close-cropped handsome head for a final communing with God, then rose refreshed, tall and smiling. Soon he would choose a rosebud for his buttonhole as he strode through the garden to his office in the hospital.

Children long for parents to be more than they are, or ever could be. We cannot imagine and allow for the fact that they, like ourselves, are products of a time and place and family. And out of their love for us they want, above all, our 'happiness' — but on their terms. 'I do want you to be happy,' he'd say as he gave me chocolate bars when what I wanted was his genuine attention.

But as we set off for Dublin, it was I wanting to make him happy, on my terms. In the plane I asked, 'Aren't you excited at the thought of seeing your brothers after all these years?' 'They'll be so old,' he said glumly. But perked up to flirt with the air hostess, who wrapped him in a blanket and brought snacks.

In Dublin, Pa, the renegade, prepared to encounter the upholders of the faith he had long ago abandoned. Keep off religion, we agreed on our way to Uncle Ambrose, who lived in a boarding house for clergy widowers.

Ambrose was a small, thinner, younger version of himself, apple-cheeked above the confines of his dog-collar, and with a more pronounced Irish accent. The walls of his big dark room were covered with framed photographs of choirboys, going back twenty, thirty years; entire choirs as well as individual choristers, there they were, artless and scrubbed in white surplices, forever boyish. His passion was innocent, he saw nothing peculiar in it: as he'd once told me, his father liked three 'B's — boys, boats and birds — while he himself liked two 'B's — boys and birds. He awarded a silver cup to an annual singing competition for boy soloists and was to die a year later when attending the event — surely a blissful way to go.

Among the photographs were religious paintings. 'Of course,' said Ambrose, observing our attention gripped by a particularly lurid scene of Jesus radiating light, 'I don't know about art, but . . .' I hastily changed the subject, remarking on a nice photo of Aunt Rosamund, short grey hair, wide mouth smiling. Rosamund, transplanted from England by marriage to Ambrose, had encountered leprechauns at the bottom of the vicarage garden and in old age emerged with touching brightness from shock treatment in a mental hospital. The last time I had seen her we'd met for tea in their favourite restaurant before going to the pictures. 'There's just one thing,' Ambrose confided while she was in the Ladies, 'she likes to talk to commissionaires.'

Outside in the street stood a commissionaire. Rosamund made a beeline. Ambrose hurried me on. We were an odd procession, he narrow-shouldered in dark suit with black clerical hat, impatiently leading the way; I tall and thin, arthritic feet in yachting shoes padding after him, and Aunt Rosamund in little black-buttoned boots trotting to catch up, eyes sparkling as, ahead of us, outside the cinema appeared another commissionaire.

What did she say to them? Was there a marvellous secret in her past? Had she perhaps loved a military man?

Now Pa, the subject of religion safely skirted, was reminding Ambrose of some youthful prank. 'What about you, Cyrie,' Ambrose responded, 'to be sure you were the naughty one, you climbed the forbidden tree and broke your leg!' 'My arm!' Pa corrected him. Two old men each in his mind's eye seeing the other in Eton jacket and high white collar. While from the wall their revered, long-deceased father watched, a bearded patriarch, Doctor of Divinity. 'A great schoolmaster,' the plaque in St Patrick's Cathedral called him, and when I'd read a biography of George Tyrrell, who had been one of his pupils, Tyrrell's praise for the grandfather I had never known excited me: 'Dearest and best of men, a ready wit, bubbling over with interest.' I wondered if Ambrose had read the biography? 'What, Tyrrell the Jesuit!' But clearly he'd been impressed all the same. In dreams Tyrrell had returned to the school, to the headmaster reaching out enthusiastically from the pulpit as he regularly exclaimed, 'Really boys, I do think that *without exception* this is the most remarkable text in the whole Bible!' Or, on a cold dark night, tearing along with a boy on each arm as he led a class to the cricket field to show them Jupiter's moons through the telescope he'd just bought.

He'd treated all the boys as if they were his sons. What could this have been like for Pa, among the youngest in a family of twelve? Of the twelve only four married, and of their six children one died young and one, myself, remained unmarried and childless. Anglo-Irish decadence?

Ambrose had strayed onto politics. 'Of course, I wouldn't dream of reading the Irish press,' he declared and, with a glance at the Union Jack displayed on the mantelpiece, added, 'I get the *Daily Express*.' Glimpsing my hastily suppressed grin, and blind to inconsistency, he sternly reproved, 'It's all wrong, you know, your going against your government.' 'I always say,' said Pa, intent on peacemaking — besides he was proud of my opposition to the Afrikaner Nationalists — 'that I left Ireland for South Africa to avoid a bunch of rebels. At least here they have a sense of humour.'

A whole teatime avoiding the tricky subject, but Pa could no longer resist it. 'You know, Ambrose, since I discovered Science,' he bragged, 'there's been never a day's seediness.'

The outrageous claim jerked me into accusation. 'What about your hernia!' I hissed, looking back in pain and anger on all those times in childhood when, at tennis, one moment he was cackling gleefully as his sliced shots confounded his scurrying opponents and the next he was bent double, face contorted in agony, hand masking eyes as he Knew the Truth. Was it a heart attack? In Science you must not 'Name'. Might he die? The family waited in dread. Eventually a 'Demonstration' was made and he would give a 'Testimony', expressing gratitude to 'our beloved leader, Mary Baker Eddy'. Long afterwards he explained it was a ruptured hernia. 'Is that all?' By then I had broken away. 'Then why not have an operation, it's quite simple?' 'No. It's a good thing really, keeps me up to scratch.'

Did I want him to be truthful because I loved him or did I want to punish him? That night I lay awake, wondering. Old and forlorn he looked when we said goodnight. He'd confessed that the prospect of meeting Uncle Willie filled him with alarm. 'But why, Uncle Willie is a dear?' 'He's my big brother' was Pa's explanation and, surly with shyness, throughout the visit next day he remained a new boy in the presence of a prefect.

Willie, aged ninety, and living in a nursing home for elderly clergy, seemed not to notice. 'You should've seen your father at eighteen,' he said with a chuckle. 'Just before he left us and set off for the Cape Colony. Ach, a grand young fellow he was, a smart dresser. He was a clerk at Amiens Street Station, d'you know, but he disliked work in an office. He used to stroll up and down the platform smoking a cigarette as if he owned the entire railway!'

Willie, a Canon and Chancellor of the Church of Ireland, had been a terrific preacher, like his father almost tumbling from the pulpit in an exuberance of faith which compensated for the smallness of the congregation. His organ and piano playing were just as passionate. Now here he was with a tendency to fall over. 'Feeble, you see, in arms and legs, but I *can* dress myself and I thank God, yes I do often, for sparing me so long to repent of my sins.' He was writing an epic poem. 'How's Ambrose?' he wanted to know, though he saw him every week. 'We always argue, he and I. He has very definite opinions.'

As we came away Pa announced, 'I've done my duty. I have seen them both and there's nothing more to say.'

'Listen,' I was merciless, 'I've paid £100. You've got two weeks to go yet.'

'Dublin was so different in the old days.'

Pa's Dublin. We went in search of it in a hired car. The day was fine as we drove across the wind-rippled Liffey. I was less sure of the atmosphere inside the car. I had grown sensitive about our Anglo-Irishness, had laughed out loud when, browsing through a book of Irish history, I'd come across Engels on the Anglo-Irish: tall and handsome with Roman noses, their pleasures and their debts, regarding themselves as aristocrats. It seemed to me the driver had summed us up in a flash.

A huge advertisement captured Pa's attention. 'All the poor people paying their pennies for their stout,' said he, the teetotaller. 'Maybe it makes them happy,' said I tartly.

A Catholic church lay ahead. Passersby were crossing themselves. 'Place is full of XYZs,' said Pa and looked puzzled at my sharp nudge. 'Ah, Phoenix Park! It was here the regiments paraded in full dress — so colourful. We'll never see the like again! There, there's the Castle!' He was transported: 'I was just fourteen, at one of the Viceroy's receptions the English officers served us tea. I do believe Lord Roberts served me. Could that be so, could he have been only a colonel in 1894? Of course, in the old days, the whole of society was Protestant, we never met XYZs socially.'

Surely the driver's neck had flushed redder? 'We'll soon be in Kingstown,' said Pa. 'Dun Laoghaire,' said I.

A Martello tower offered an escape — although Pa was not the intellectual I had come to require, I liked to think of him and Joyce as contemporaries; they had left Dublin at much the same time, Joyce for his art, Pa for an outdoor sporting life — 'Joyce's tower, where he stayed with Gogarty!' I pointed out.

'Sandycove,' said Pa, 'where I fell out of the boat and nearly drowned. The sea was so rough most of the crew were seasick. But not I!'

Pa and his memories — long-dormant images and sounds and smells permeating each moment. I heard his utterances but went on superimposing fragments of literature over his reality, picturing Stephen Dedalus gazing from the parapet at the sea, Buck Mulligan called it snot-green.

Now the sea was blue-grey and smooth and as we turned to drive inland a mist was rising over emerald hills. We passed large estates with great old trees beyond splendidly constructed grey stone walls. 'High walls everywhere,' for some reason Pa minded. 'The walls,' and he leaned forward to address the driver, 'why don't they rather have fences? You can't see the gardens with those high walls.'

'They were built,' said the driver loudly as if he had been awaiting he opportunity, 'in the Famine. When the people were starving. Terrible times. No jobs. And the English put them to building walls.'

Again I lay awake, hearing the day's discordant voices, feeling the vibrations. The night was a time for remorse, and for clarity. With a curious physical sensation as of a slanting towards sense I saw I had always been an extension of Pa's ego, to be shown off, whether to visiting Christian Science lectures — 'Recite something from Mrs Eddy's works!' — or to the musical comedy actresses he brought home to tea and I, the only too eager accomplice: prattling to the one, 'Ancient and Modern Necromancy, Alias Mesmerism and Hypnotism, Denounced!'; turning cartwheels for the others. 'We're such pals,' he liked to say and I, for most of my life, had been a loving daughter. Why couldn't I accept him now with generosity, was it sheer terror of losing my independence? The waste of lying awake, assessing my failures and his. Rather try more kindness by day. Tomorrow I would take him on a pilgrimage to Stokers' house.

The Stokers for as long as I could remember had recurred in his personal mythology. His Aunt Susie, blue-eyed Dublin beauty of nineteen, had married Dick Stoker, a doctor in the Indian Army who swept her off to Tibet, then pioneering British Columbia's wilderness. Their framed pictures looked down from our walls in Pretoria. Dick's brother, Bram, red-headed eccentric, had written *Dracula* and had been Henry Irving's manager. But most important was Sir Thornley Stoker, distinguished surgeon, consultant to the Viceroy — it was he who had taken Pa to those receptions at the Castle — clearly he'd been very fond and proud of his young protégé who had served in the Boer War and then, at the age of twenty-three, been put in charge of Pretoria's hospital and poor relief.

From St Stephen's Green we walked toward Ely Place. 'Sir Thornley was renowned as a connoisseur,' Pa explained. 'He collected Chippendale and the chandeliers were magnificent.' I had read Gogarty's description of the surgeon's habit of buying a museum piece after each big operation. George Moore, observing a new chair, had teased, 'A cancer, Sir Thornley, or a gallstone?'

Pa stopped abruptly. 'There, that's the house!' He stood and stared. The once imposing Georgian house with its once elegant front door was propped up by wooden girders as after a bombing. A bedraggled white cat rubbed against the railings which once Moore had provokingly rattled with his malacca cane. We peered through a grimy window. 'You should have seen the chandeliers,' said Pa.

We hurried off. Eventually he spoke: 'How strange the long twilight is, not like at home.' Home. Yes, the sudden plunge into darkness, the explosion of stars so brilliant you felt you could reach up and touch them. But here we were, far away, in the old world, together. 'Do you remember how you used to show me Orion?' I asked.

We took a bus through streets bustling with people leaving their offices. 'See that hotel, beside the railway bridge?' Pa's face was radiant. A small, shabby hotel, I couldn't make out the name. 'That's where the barmaid worked! I used to take her out. When I was back on leave. In 1906.' The memory overwhelmed him and for once I was attentive to his inner world. 'She took me to church with her.' He chuckled. 'The only time I ever set foot in a Catholic church.'

Sound of hooves and carriage wheels, cries of cockles 'n mussels, a barrel organ playing — was that the background to their whispers and laughter and sighs? Lamps dimmed by fog drifting in from the sea.

The bus drove us on and away. I shared in his silence.

'She must be in her eighties now,' he said suddenly. 'Or dead.'

John Banville

COOLGRANGE

An extract from a novel in progress

It was early afternoon when I reached Coolgrange. I got down at the cross and watched the bus lumber away, its fat back-end looking somehow derisive. The noise of the engine faded, and the throbbing silence of summer settled again on the fields. The sky was still overcast, but the sun was asserting itself somewhere, and the light that had been dull and flat was now a tender, pearl-grey glow. I stood and looked about me. What a surprise the familiar always is. It was all there, the broken gate, the drive, the long meadow, the oak wood — home! — all perfectly in place, waiting for me, a little smaller than I remembered, like a scale-model of itself. I laughed, it was not really a laugh, more an exclamation of startlement and recognition. Before such scenes as this — trees, the shimmering fields, that mild soft light — I always feel like a traveller on the point of departure. Even arriving I seemed to be turning away, with a lingering glance at the lost land. I set off up the drive, a walking cliché, with my raincoat over my shoulder and my battered bag in my hand, though it's true I was a bit long in the tooth, and a bit on the beefy side, for the part of the prodigal son. A dog slid out of the hedge at me with a guttural snarl, teeth bared to the gums. I halted. I do not like dogs. This was a black and white thing with shifty eyes, it moved back and forth in a half circle in front of me, still growling, keeping its belly close to the ground. I held the suitcase against my knees for a shield, and spoke sharply, as to an unruly child, but my voice came out a broken falsetto, and for a moment there was a sense of general merriment, as if there were faces hidden among the leaves, laughing. Then a whistle sounded, and the brute whined and turned guiltily toward the house. My mother was standing on the front steps. She laughed. Suddenly the sun came out, with a kind of soundless report. Good God, she said, it is you, I thought I was seeing things.

I hesitate. It is not that I am lost for words, but the opposite. There is so much to be said I do not know where to begin. I feel myself staggering backwards slowly, clutching in my outstretched arms a huge, unwieldy and yet weightless burden. She is so much, and, at the same time, nothing. I must go carefully, this is perilous ground. Of course, I know that whatever I say will be smirked at knowingly by the amateur psychologists packing the court. When it comes to the subject of mothers, innocence is not permitted. All the same, I shall strive to be simple. Her name is Dorothy, though everyone has always called her Dolly, I do not know why, for there is nothing doll-like about her. She is a large, vigorous woman with the broad face and heavy hair of a tinker's wife. I do not mean to be disrespectful. She is impressive, in her way, at once majestic and slovenly. I remember her from my childhood as a constant but remote presence, like a marble figure at the far side of a lawn, statuesque, abstracted, impossibly handsome. Later on, though, she grew to be top-heavy, with a big backside and slim legs, a contrast which, when I was an adolescent and morbidly interested in such things, led me to speculate on the complicated architecture that must be necessary to bridge the gap under her skirt between those shapely knees and that thick waist. Hello, mother, I said, and looked away from her, casting about me crossly for something neutral on which to concentrate. I was annoyed already. She has that effect on me, I have only to stand before her and instantly the irritation and resentment begin to seethe in my breast. I was surprised, I had thought that after ten years there would be at least a moment of grace between our meeting and the first attack of filial heartburn, but not a bit of it, here I was, jaw clenched, glaring lugubriously at a tuft of weed sprouting from a crack in the stone steps where she stood. She was not much changed. Her bosom, which cries out to be called ample, had descended to just above her midriff. Also she had grown a little moustache. She wore baggy corduroy trousers and a cardigan with sagging pockets. She came down the steps to me and laughed again. You have put on weight, Freddie, she said, you've got fat. Then she reached out and — this is true, I swear it — and took hold of a piece of my stomach and rolled it playfully between a finger and thumb. This woman, this woman — what can I say? I was thirty-eight, a man of parts, with two degrees, and a doctorate in science, a wife and a son and an impressive Mediterranean tan, I carried myself with gravitas and a certain faint air of menace, and she, what did she do, she pinched my belly and laughed her phlegmy laugh. Is it any wonder I have ended up in jail? Is it? The dog, seeing that I was to be accepted, sidled up to me and tried to lick my hand, which gave me an opportunity to deliver it a good hard kick in the ribs. That made me feel better, but not much, and not for long.

Is there anything as powerfully, as piercingly evocative, as the smell of the house in which one's childhood was spent? I try to avoid generalizations, as no doubt the court has noticed, but surely this is a universal, this involuntary spasm of recognition which comes with the first whiff of that humble, drab, brownish smell, which is hardly a smell at all, more an emanation, a sort of sigh exhaled by the thousands of known but unacknowledged tiny things that collectively constitute what is called home. I stepped into the hall and for an instant it was as if I had stepped soundlessly through the membrane of time itself. I faltered, tottering inwardly. Hatstand with broken umbrella. That floor tile, still loose. Get out, Patch, damn you! my mother said behind me. The taste of apples unaccountably flooded my mouth. I felt vaguely that something momentous had happened, that in the blink of an eye everything around me had been whipped away and replaced instantly with an exact replica, perfect in every detail, down to the last dust-mote. I walked on, into this substitute world, tactfully keeping a blank expression, and seemed to hear a held breath being let go in relief that the difficult trick had worked yet again.

We went into the kitchen. It looked like the lair of some large, scavenging creature. Lord, mother, I said, are you living in here? Items of clothing, and old woman's nameless rags, were stuffed between the dishes on the dresser. The toes of three of four pairs of shoes peeped out from under a cupboard, an unnerving sight, as if the wearers might be huddled together in there, stubby arms clasped around each other's hunched shoulders, listening. Pieces of furniture had migrated here from all over the house, the narrow little bureau from my father's study, the walnut cocktail cabinet from the drawing room, the velvet-covered recliner with balding arm-rests in which my Great-Aunt Alice, a tiny, terrible woman, had died without a murmur one Sunday afternoon in summer. The huge old wireless that used to lord it over the lounge stood now at a drunken tilt on the draining-board, crooning softly to itself, its single green eye pulsing. The place was far from clean. A ledger was open on the table, and bills and things were strewn amid the smeared plates and the unwashed teacups. She had been doing the accounts. She glanced from me to the papers and back again with amusement. I turned away from her, to the window. Out on the lawn a large girl in jodhpurs was leading a string of Connemara ponies in a circle. I recalled dimly my mother telling me, in one of her infrequent and barely literate letters, about some hare-brained venture involving these animals. She came and stood beside me. We watched in silence the ponies plodding round and round. Ugly brutes, aren't they, she said. The simmering annoyance I had felt since arriving was added to now by a sense of general futility. I have always been prone to accidie. It is a state, or I might even say, a force, the significance of which in human affairs historians and such like seem not to appreciate. I think I would do anything to avoid it. Anything. My mother was telling me about her customers, mostly Japs and Germans, it seemed, they were taking over the country. They bought the ponies as pets for their spoilt offspring, at what she cheerfully admitted were outrageous prices. Cracked, the lot of them, she said. We laughed, and then fell vacantly silent again. The sun was on the lawn, and a vast white cloud was slowly unfurling above the sweltering beeches. I was thinking how strange it was to stand here glooming out at the day like this, bored and irritable, my hands in my pockets, while all the time, deep inside me somewhere, hardly acknowledged, grief dripped and dripped, a kind of silvery ichor, pure and strangely precious. Home, yes, home is always a surprise.

She insisted that I come and look the place over, as she put it. After all, my boy, she said, some day all this will be yours. And she did her throaty cackle. I did not remember her being so easily amused in the past. There was something almost unruly in her laughter, a sort of abandon. I was a little put out by it, I thought it was not seemly. She lit up a cigarette and set off around the house, with the cigarette box and matches clutched in her left hand, and me trailing grimly in her smoking wake. The place was rotting. So bad was it that here and there even she was startled. She talked and talked. I nodded dully, gazing at damp walls and sagging floors and mouldering window-frames. In my old room the bed was broken, and there was something growing in the middle of the mattress. The view from the window — trees, a bit of sloping field, the red roof of a barn — was exact and familiar as an hallucination. Here was the cupboard I had built, and at once I had a vision of myself, a small boy with a fierce frown, blunt saw in hand, hacking at a sheet of plywood, and my grieving heart wobbled, as if it were not myself I was remembering, but something like a son, dear and vulnerable, lost to me forever in the depths of my own past. When I turned, my mother was not there. I found her on the stairs, looking a little odd around the eyes. She set off again. I must see the grounds, the stables, the oak wood. She was determined I would see everything, everything.

Stephen Matterson

THE MURMUROUS BLOOD
OF ANTHONY HECHT

In his third book, *Millions of Strange Shadows* (1977), Anthony Hecht included the poem 'The Ghost in the Martini'. It is a fascinating poem, typical of many in Hecht's lucid narrative-lyric style. A renowned middle-aged poet at a reception is being lionized by an attractive young woman. Asked what he was like at twenty, the poet takes the opportunity to talk flirtingly about a callow introvert whom the young woman would not have liked. Just then the reproachful ghost of the younger poet starts to speak from the twist in the martini, angrily condemning the willed forgetfulness of the older man, who can so readily make light of the heavy costs involved in the poetry. The ghost speaks with lachrymose, bombastic exaggeration of the hardships he has suffered, but, even so, the middle-aged poet has no adequate answer to the ghost's accusation:

> You only got where you are
> By standing upon my ectoplasmic shoulders,
> And wherever that is may not be so high or far
> In the eyes of some beholders.
>
> Take, for example, me.
> I have sat alone in the dark, accomplishing little,
> And worth no more to myself, in pride and fee,
> Than a cup of luke-warm spittle.

Hecht does allow a happy ending of sorts, as the middle-aged poet takes advantage of the ghost's momentary silence to escape with the woman:

> Better get out of here;
> If he opens his trap again it could get much worse.
> I touch her elbow, and, leaning toward her ear,
> Tell her to find her purse.

'The Ghost in the Martini' has a lightness of touch that is one of Hecht's finest characteristics as a poet, and it also displays his frequently deceptive casualness

— few other poets could have punned on 'trap' with such aplomb. In this poem, as in others, he nimbly walks a line between dark horror and light comedy with, here at least, a lucky conclusion. The ending, though, is also a knowingly temporary evasion of horrors, and it demands recognition of the cost which that evasion exacts.

For all its nearly skirted potential terrors, the haunting in this poem belongs among the more benign manifestations of Hecht's ghosts. During World War II Hecht served in the US military, as a German-speaking counter-intelligence officer. In this way he was involved in the liberation of Europe and the opening up of the Nazi death camps. Although his poetry makes few direct references to his experiences of this time, it is frequently informed by a sense of aftermath, and of carefully subdued emotion. Trauma is obliquely rendered; like the ghost in the martini, it is only rarely confronted fully. Like Nick Adams in Hemingway's post World War I stories, Hecht's protagonists cannot evade the self-consciousness of their very survival, even though this cannot be confronted nakedly. They find no special virtue in having endured, having come to know survival's accidental, arbitrary nature:

> Merely to have survived is not an index of excellence,
> Nor, given the way things go,
> Even of low cunning.
> Yet I have seen the wicked in great power,
> And spreading himself like a green bay tree.
> And the good as if they had never been;
> Their voices are blown away on the winter wind.
> And again we wander the wilderness
> For our transgressions
> Which are confessed in the daily papers.

In this poem, 'Rites and Ceremonies', Hecht untypically faces his own ghosts fairly directly. He comes to terms with them through a generally modernist and specifically Eliotean strategy of constructing a form of ceremony, personal but echoing those traditional forms, such as the Requiem — or the rite of exorcism — by which death and evil have been ritualized and controlled.

The poem is uncharacteristic, though, both in its direct confrontation with a past, and in the self-consciousness attending the confrontation. More typically, Hecht's protagonists are consciously wounded by the past, knowingly diminished as humans by the horrors of the twentieth century, and are unable either to evade or confront this knowledge. The inability to do either ensures that they are haunted, and that there are moments when their hard-won composure is disturbed. Both 'A Hill' and '"It Out-Herods Herod. Pray You Avoid It"', respectively the first and last poems from *The Hard Hours* (1968), are concerned with the instability of identity when confronted by the ghost. In 'A Hill', the narrator suddenly has a vision of a hill replacing the elegant Italian city in which he walks:

> And then, when it happened, the noises suddenly stopped,
> And it got darker; pushcarts and people dissolved
> And even the great Farnese Palace itself
> Was gone, for all its marble; in its place
> Was a hill, mole-coloured and bare. It was very cold,
> Close to freezing, with a promise of snow.

At first this seems to be a vision of nihilism, of seeing the pretensions of the civilized suddenly stripped away to reveal bareness. But the vision is brought up to date, in a revelation which is at once more personal and more disturbing:

> I was scared by the plain bitterness of what I had seen.
> All this happened about ten years ago,
> And it hasn't troubled me since, but at last, today,
> I remembered that hill; it lies just to the left
> Of the road north of Poughkeepsie; and as a boy
> I stood before it for hours in wintertime.

Various elements unite to give the poem its unforgettable qualities of lucidity and terror; the fact that the experience (if any) associated with the hill remains undefined; the inability to forget, to close off unpleasant or traumatic experiences from one's past and consider them completed; the inability to evade the experience in both time and place. But above all the poem terrifies with the sense of being haunted by something too disturbing to name, yet too jarring to allow a life to focus properly. If it could be named, the suggestion is, then it could be conquered. There is also the intensity of loneliness, carried forward in time to an existential moment of despair.

The enigmatic, troubling experience of 'A Hill' is nowhere repeated exactly in Hecht's work, but the horror takes on more tangible forms in other poems. Often at a moment of joy or pleasure, the protagonist will be haunted, reminded of an unsettled life. This is the case in '"It Out-Herods Herod. Pray You Avoid It"'. The father with his children at Christmas time watches the old morality plays updated and screened on television. However, he knows that the phrase to 'out-Herod Herod' means not just, as in Polonius's terms, to overact, but it also grimly indicates a slaughter of innocents more vicious than

Herod's. Instead of celebrating Christmas, the troubled father finds in it now the chilling realization that he would have proved an inadequate protector for his children:

> And that their sleep be sound
> I say this childermas
> Who could not, at one time,
> Have saved them from the gas.

The occasions of involuntarily remembering pain and sorrow recur frequently in Hecht; they are the 'hard hours'. But, as a counterbalance, Hecht often emphasizes the virtue of forgetfulness, the clarity which can come when the past is forgotten, or is distant enough to be recalled without the distortions of pain. In his most recent book, *The Transparent Man* (1990), the long poem 'See Naples and Die' begins with a narrator expressing gratitude for this achieved lucidity:

> I can at last consider those events
> Almost without emotion, a circumstance
> That for many years I'd scarcely have believed.
> We forget much, of course, and, along with facts,
> Our strong emotions, of pleasure and of pain,
> Fade into stark insensibility.
> For which, perhaps, it need be said, thank God.

To this narrator, Mnemosyne can be a nuisance; Lethe a blessing. 'See Naples and Die' is told by a man who feels the need to be insulated from pain, from suffering, who becomes 'too numb' to know the pain of remembered happiness. While in Naples, early in their marriage, the man and his wife, Martha, accidentally witness a procession of deformed patients from the local hospital for the handicapped. Martha is emotionally overcome by the encounter, and runs back to the hotel. The narrator later tries to console her, talking of the need to be shielded from the world's suffering. He tells her

> That life required us to steel ourselves
> To the all-too-sad calamities of others,
> The brute, inexplicable inequities,
> To form for ourselves a carapace of sorts,
> A self-preservative petrific toughness.

This statement of belief appeared also in 'The Venetian Vespers' from the book with that title published in 1979. There, the unnamed narrator tells us:

The mind
Can scarcely cope with the world's sufferings,
Must blinker itself to much or else go mad.

Martha refuses to accept this; she 'said *No* several times, not as a statement,/ But rather as a groan.'

After their marriage has ended, the husband sees himself and Martha as too sensitive to the pain of others, too aware of misery to find happiness. His hard-won clarity is a movement forward for Hecht, since earlier his characters tended to harden themselves against the world, forcing themselves to endure through a willed insensitivity towards it. 'The heart turns to a stone, but it endures', he writes in 'Clair de Lune'. More specifically, 'See Naples and Die' represents a development away from the earlier long masterpiece, 'The Venetian Vespers'. The poem's unnamed narrator is on the verge of sanity, longing for the stability of a heaven that he characterizes as 'arrested movement', an escape from the turbulent demands of the world and his family history. As he reconstructs his past for us, we are given to guess at an almost Jacobean family drama of defeated father and usurping uncle.

The narrator's fear of madness, of despair, is very real, and to counter it he longs for coolness and civilized balance. He can encounter the family ghosts only when he has withdrawn from life, and he is aware of the costs he has paid for his personal peace. He sees life 'as a spectator sport' and appreciates his own celibacy:

Viscid, contaminate, dynastic wastes
Flood through the dark canals, the underpasses,
Ducts and arterial sluices of my body

. . . . .
At least I pass them on to nobody,
Not having married, or authored any children,
Leading a monkish life of modest means.

In Hecht's work, the refusal to acknowledge the blood's demands is the price paid for tranquillity, as in 'A Letter', a poem of sustained composure, ending with the lines:

But I would have you know that all is not well
        With a man dead set to ignore
The endless repetitions of his own murmurous blood.

The cost is not ignored, or lightly borne. But it is nevertheless real. 'The Venetian Vespers' also includes Hecht's most desperate example of a man determined to cling to a minimal, if arbitrary, order system constructed against despair. The narrator recalls a rootless fellow soldier who carries with him an Emily Post book of etiquette. The book is a reassuring 'fiction of kindliness', a fiction of ordered manners in atrocious conditions. In spite of the book's consolation of organized life, the soldier is killed in an attack, and his memory is another ghost the narrator must encounter:

> And there he crouched, huddled over his weapon,
> His brains wet in the chalice of his skull.

'The Venetian Vespers' has a range of reference and subject, a subtly engaging development of character, and a compelling narrative, which combine to make it one of this century's finest poems. But it is a poem of withdrawal from life and its demands. The narrator is becoming a hollow man, close to misanthropy, emptied of memory, and willing oblivion and death. He has a dark counterpart in another poem from *The Venetian Vespers*, Shirley in 'The Short End'. Alcoholic and self-enclosed, Shirley is nevertheless haunted by a terrifying memory of human isolation. Out driving one day, she and her husband encounter a thirty-eight-day live entombment of one George Rose. The paralysing vision of human isolation becomes her reality, in spite of her attempts to avoid what she obsessively views as her fate. Like the narrator of 'The Venetian Vespers', though in her own way, she has withdrawn from life; her last appalling vision is of George Rose lewdly dancing before her.

'The heart turns to a stone, but it endures.' In 'The Venetian Vespers', misanthropy is the self-defensive reaction to an otherwise self-destructive sympathy for others. The hardened heart will endure, because it is hardened, though its very hardness is the price paid for the survival. Those lines from 'Clair de Lune' echo Othello's cry; 'My heart is turned to stone; I strike it, and it hurts my hand'. The Venetian background of *Othello* makes the play pertinent to 'The Venetian Vespers' (Hecht quotes from it in one of the poem's epigraphs), but it is more broadly relevant to an understanding of Hecht. It is worth noting that Hecht frequently cites Shakespeare in his work. Shakespearean quotations recur in the titles of poems: Hecht's 1986 collection of essays, *Obbligati*, includes articles on *The Merchant of Venice* and *Othello*, and in *The Transparent Man* there is the elegant 'A Love for Four Voices', based upon *A Midsummer-Night's Dream* in the way that Auden's *The Sea and the Mirror* was a 'commentary' on *The Tempest*.

Hecht's essay on *Othello* is of special interest. He examines T. S. Eliot's well-known judgment that in his final speech Othello is 'cheering himself up'.

Hecht worries at this statement until he can make his own rationale of it. In a proleptically modern way, Othello is reconstructing his identity after a crisis which makes him lose his humanity and his sense of an ordered world ('And when I love thee not,/Chaos is come again'). The task of Hecht's characters is a similar rebuilding of the self, a restoration in which their humanity will not be compromised. Most do not manage it; instead, finding a shield from the world or retreating into misanthropy. One might long to be free of ghosts and terrors, but to be successfully free is also to be hollow. To imagine oneself free is a form of self-delusion. Hecht's characters face the challenge of being able to recall and acknowledge horrors without being overwhelmed by them. Similarly, they must not become humanly impoverished by denying pain and suffering altogether. The balance is difficult to achieve, and gaining it incurs many costs. It is in the earned ability to confront ghosts, Hecht indicates, that we live at our most fully human.

This sense of humanity is perhaps the most accessible and obvious of all Hecht's virtues as a poet. He has insisted on the values of human sharing, generosity and acceptance in the face of appalling horror and cruelty. His is not a poetry with an agenda, a programmed way of looking at history and the world — he can be a delightful and a profound occasional poet, a lucid writer of light verse, and a writer who achieves the twin aims of parody as a tribute and a correction. His parodies of Matthew Arnold ('The Dover Bitch') and Wallace Stevens ('Le Masseur de Ma Soeur') are deservedly famous. Both, though, are very much part of Hecht's other work, in their insistence on the responsibility of art to be true to its human subject rather than sacrificing that subject to an ideal. As in the later work of Auden (incidentally defended by Hecht in *Obbligati*), the reader senses an intelligence which flexibly and piercingly assesses the world, rather than one which seeks to impose an order on it. That Anthony Hecht is one of the finest living poets ought to go without saying. That he has something important to say to us needs to be emphasized again and again.

Tom MacIntyre

THE WORD FOR YES

I was spending a little time in hospital. Not unexpectedly, he arrived. There's something of the born visitor to him.

Lip hanging like a side of bacon, he chose a cool distance. I thought it useful to fire first.

— You're pure nineteenth-century melodrama.

He offered a distempered grin, spoke in his ambiguous bear's paw of a voice.

— Baa-baa, black sheep, have you any wool?

I rose like barm.

— Yes, Sir, yes, Sir, *three* bags full. *One* for The Master, *one* for The Dame, and *one* for The Little Boy who lives down the lane.

He left. I lay back, jubilant. This once, at any rate, I'd gone through him for a short cut.

We didn't meet for a long time. Who was avoiding whom? No idea. Take that back. We were avoiding each other. Qualify that. I was avoiding him, can't speak for the related proposition.

Why avoiding him? For the same reason that you, friend, on sound general principles avoid certain pushy specimens among your intimates.

We met again in Leningrad — made sense to me. On Feb. 14th — that too made sense. Associations? St Valentine's Day massacre, Al Capone, wasn't it? Plus a much deeper association touching a woman who eluded me. Of which more later. Maybe.

(She was a high-flier, that much I'll vouchsafe. And she had company up there, the entire Fleet Air-Arm, if truth be told.)

Anyway. Leningrad. Valentine's Day. Early hours of Valentine's Day. Often called the *small* hours, a misnomer, surely. Aren't they, as a rule, spacey, sprawling, leached of the finite?

We're in a large ballroom, the pair of us. We have it to ourselves, own it. The floor is marble, lozenged black-and-white. That design belatedly intrigues me — but let it pass.

We're waltzing, to no music but our own, as the poets say. Waltzing, however, on the horizontal. Sliding, better perhaps. Sliding/whizzing about the highly polished marble floor in a close horizontal embrace.

Like two perilously sober drunks.

The embrace is sufficiently close, controlled, to prevent me ever seeing his face. That's an urge, by the way. Not a necessity. I can smell who it is.

We spin about the floor. He — I concede now, conceded then — is the one in charge.

We could be there yet but, no doubt, he had other things to be doing. The whirl came to a stop, my head in close proximity to his loins. And I'm looking at his bared privates, scrotum tight, cock erect.

Some weeks later we met in Moscow. Arbat Street. No, I'm making that up. Wish it had been — Arbat so textured — but no. Some street or other, centre of the city, dusk.

The circumstances were, as often (it will be apparent) in our meetings, *louche*.

Dusk, as I say. Heavy traffic. And I'm strolling along naked. The evening is unseasonably mild. I don't say that in self-justification but it was. Nobody in the least bothered (*pro tem*) by my naked state. Except me. I admit to unease. Edginess.

So what was the rationale? There was none. All I can say — I'm being quite open — is that I so behave at irregular intervals. Undress. Go for a walk. A run.

Arbat Street then — or whatever street it was. I'm becoming antsy about my exposed pelt. This fret has congealed to a burden when a passing motorist, male, nondescript — your average guy trying to turn a rouble, *à la mode* among the Muscovites — pulls over, waves me in.

I get into the back. No words exchanged — there is the language problem. I find a pullover on the seat, and make free to requisition it. Solace of the gansy. In far foreign fields.

The car proceeds.

While you'd wink, checkpoint up ahead. At speed, it's our turn. I glimpse the face of the one — *the* one of the pair — manning the barrier. Oh, yes. The driver lets down the window.

A head-and-shoulders fills it. And a coiled arm. There's no hesitation, plainly I'm expected. The coiled arm uncoils, extends itself with supple authority. The hand collects mine, pulls it forward, crisply checks it against the driver's.

He's not slow, say that for him.

I found myself liking him more. Warming, cagily, to his sense of humour. Incipient, at least. But meanwhile we remained strangers. And at odds.

The question, as always, who'd now make the move?

Recently I was compelled to change house. I found an apartment overlooking a park. I'd scarcely moved in when, glancing out the window one evening, I see him directly opposite, among the trees, looking right up at me, my abode.

The alacrity shocked me.

The audacity.

And brought us, once more, that little bit closer. His demeanour among the trees? Watchful, yes. But what else? Bit lost. Standing there under the trees.

More precisely, I had the sense he was showing me his face. Offering it, could be.

It will be evident we're moving towards a rendezvous.

Sabbath rendezvous, I've felt for some days. Something to do with Sunday quiet. Something to do with us, the pair of us. Merely a hunch.

But on Sundays expect to find in me a special state of waiting.

I amble to the window to check the park. Sunlit. Deserted. Too early in the day for much activity. Nip in the air.

I focus on a particular tree, tall healthy fir. And, as if in abeyance for my eye, action.

Among the topmost branches, a horse and rider appear. Next, horse and rider float fluidly down through the branches — causing hardly a stir, land below, and set off across the park in a confident canter. And quickly out of my vision.

Held by the window, I'm aware there's someone beside me. Second spectator. I know it's he.

I turn to him. His drawn eyes. Still on the park.

— Who was that? I ask.

— The bridegroom.

— And the bride?

He doesn't reply.

— I want to know you.

— I know.

He looks directly at me.

Your breath is stained, I think. Mine too.

— All right?

— Right.

We strip for the encounter.

No handshake.

It begins.

Gerald Dawe

AN INTERVIEW WITH THOMAS KILROY

Playwright and novelist, Thomas Kilroy was born in Callan, County Kilkenny in 1934. He lives in County Mayo.

You've written that you were 'born with a Protestant mind in a Catholic body' and were 'soon secularized'. What did you mean?
It's a matter of taste as much as any specific reference to religion. I'm using the terms Catholic and Protestant to make a distinction of taste which inevitably comes out of the whole religious/historical currency attached to those two terms. So that when I say I admire the intellectual and moral passion of the Anglo-Irish writers, I'm talking about the kind of moral qualities which are both moral and aesthetic. I was also talking autobiographically in that I do feel that one of the problems I had as a youngster growing up was that, although I didn't know it, I was in some profound way alienated from my own culture. In fact I think I was traumatized as a child by the culture I was in. It was almost a case of being born in the wrong place. That something within my own nature resisted and rebelled in a very natural way against the shaping forces of that culture which were predominantly Catholic.

We are talking about where now, Kilkenny?
We're talking about County Kilkenny and the whole schooling system, and, as it were, the tribal teaching. And we're talking about a period of the late nineteen thirties, forties, into the early fifties. A period when the hold of a very rigid puritanical Catholicism on Irish culture was present. I didn't realize it at the time but my instinctive nature was drawn towards a kind of privacy, a sense of personal judgment and a heavy reliance on rationalism.

Where would this have come from? Your reading?
No, I think you're born with these kinds of qualities. I'm talking about a natural predisposition.

And was it reinforced by the family?
The family was deeply Catholic and the family was loving, but it wouldn't have in fact protected me from the kind of things I'm talking about.

Kilkenny was the family home going back generations?
No, no. The background there was west of Ireland. My father and mother were both transplanted westerners living in County Kilkenny and to that extent they were and always remained somewhat outsiders in the community. Policeman's family.

Without stretching it too far, I'm curious about what you say regarding the Church because you have only to listen to every news-bulletin, headline, and there is reference to authority of one kind or another in Ireland at the moment. Who is the vindicating authority, who makes the judgments we live by? Is it the State or is it the Church? So much of your own work is really engaged with sorting that out, with issues of authority. Is that a fair summary?
Well it is because I very rapidly came to espouse the individual conscience as the central pivot and it came to mean a great deal to me. And the point you've just made, why isn't the question being asked about the individual conscience, and it isn't. It's not being raised at any level in this current debate [about Abortion]. When in fact it is the individual conscience that the individual woman is left with in the loneliness of the trip to England. I think a strong Protestant consciousness in Ireland would have helped in this debate on social morality. I'd go so far as to say that the decimation of the Protestant community in the south of Ireland is one of the two great tragedies in the history of the modern Irish State. The other is partition. But when I grew up, the whole sense of Protestantism was something very alien and the Protestant communities in that part of the world, very beautifully written about by Hubert Butler, would have been in terms of class quite completely removed from the world that I moved in. So I am talking about something which is, I think, instinctive, rather than learned. It became reinforced . . .

It's not the wee boy looking over the manse wall at the apple and pleasure-garden?
Oh no, not at all! In fact I had no fascination with the Protestant world as a child; none whatsoever. But there was something within me which was deeply troubled by the condition I was in and it was for that reason a very unhappy childhood.

Do you think that that unhappiness, or the awkward sense you had of your place in the immediate society, created a rift which your imagination was drawn to probe and examine when you became an adult and a writer?
Well I do. I subscribe to the notion that fiction of any kind is autobiography with the facts changed and that somewhere, like a palimpsest, way back in the background, is the shadow of the person and no matter how *non-*

autobiographical a work may appear to be, it's infused with autobiography to the extent that the *mind* of the work is entirely autobiographical.

But you could never interpret a Kilroy play as being autobiographical? There's an important distinction between the autobiographical thrust of a play or the autobiographical oxygen out of which a play comes and the kind of confessionalism that we are in now, where really the more of yourself that gets on the stage or into the poem, the more valuable the work is as 'expression'. Your plays and your fiction indeed are not about self-expression of any kind.
No they're not in that sense.

So what is the relationship between these two things — between the sense of autobiography in your writing and how it ends up? What's the linkage between the two?
I think all writing, to some degree or another, is drawn from the shaped autobiography of the writer and this is very often mental, emotional, quite unrepresented by the factuality of the life but represented by the impulse and thrust of that individual mind.

It's not possible, really, and it's an illusion, for writers to think they are engineers who are moving around bits and pieces of furniture on a stage, or images in a poem, when really there's a very powerful link between who they are and what they write: not a correspondence but a confluence.
Yes, I think the more vital the work, the more infused it is with personality and this is what interests me in writing. I'm as much interested in that personality of the mind as I am about any subject-matter, what Henry James once called 'the quality of mind of the producer'.

Well, if you think about it from Mr Roche to Talbot to Bracken and Joyce, to Angela, all your plays and the prose so far, if you think of them like a wheel, the hub is always the psychology of an individual. How does that tally with the other element I think is most powerful in your work — the dealing with ideas, rather than psychological studies?
The way I'd like to see it is that, while it may in fact be concentrated upon an individual state, psychological state, what is important about that state is that it is a *moral* one and for me, at any rate, the impulse that draws me to a particular character is the moral see-saw on which the character is placed and this is what I'm trying to dramatize — how this moral see-saw tips.

So we are back to this notion of palimpsest and duality. That there's a double quality to language and the individual moral state which is actually suffused with political significance. You can't have it split down the middle or separate. In the same way that the work cannot be considered objectively separate from the writer, in the same way, the individual characters (and you are drawn to these 'historical' figures) that they embody, or radiate, have a sense of moral or political significance.

That's right and I think this goes back to the Anglo-Irish mind in a way. I don't think you can make any distinction, or that you should make any distinction, between passion, feeling, the moral sensibility, and the ideas which flow from that. They are all part of one. It's *that* network which I inhabit.

What I'm trying to move us along to is that, as a writer, critic and for some time a teacher, you've been involved with American writing and that from an early stage in your writing you moved to America for some further kind of distance (or just because you liked being there) and also the fact that you've been drawn so much to Chekhov, and that you have written with a certain degree of trouble about some of the excesses in Irish writing which have caricatured it, outside Ireland — so what does this creative and critical 'impatience' amount to? Is there a literature that you admire?

I think in many ways the kind of things that stimulate you as a writer very often do not correspond to the particular journey you are trying to make yourself. I don't think influence works in that kind of way, necessarily. My involvement with American literature is almost promiscuous. In that I would read with great enthusiasm and excitement a whole range of work which would represent many different styles and interests in the American imagination. It's difficult to pin it down to any kind of boxes. The one thing I would say is that there is a kind of writing which repels me and that is the writing of easy sentiment or easy feeling; writing as a form of exhibitionism and sensational display.

Are we talking about people like O'Casey, for instance?

I think we are talking of a lot of O'Casey where there is great natural skill and reflection on the life that he lived and knew but there's also a very easy access to feeling in the work which actually becomes sentimental.

Without pushing you into a box, would you see yourself as a writer trying to cut away that sentimentality, easy access, or do you just go ahead and do your own thing without being conscious of resisting that allurement which is there in Irish writing?

I don't think it's a programme. All I'm simply saying is the kind of thing I recoil from and which I think my own work does not represent. I think I might also be saying something about the difficulty that I might experience in having my own work received.

Your most recent play, The Madame MacAdam Travelling Theatre, *received some severe criticism. Are you thinking about that?*

Yes, well, the Field Day production of this play was uneven, sometimes a bad show and on some nights a very bad show, indeed. It was a strange combination of negative circumstances, in the text, in the production, which I would never want to repeat. The whole tone of this play depends upon the fact that everything on the stage has to be highly theatricalized and this never quite happened the way I wanted it to. That kind of artifice, too, bothers some people because they are so heavily fed upon realistic images, on television and on stage. I also think the play may have been a victim of the contraction of taste in the Irish theatre. There's this hunger everywhere for simple black and white judgments. This is good, that is bad. It's the authoritarianism of a world where the old forms of authority have become obsolete.

Could that be that we are also back to Kilkenny — in the sense that we are back to a sense of dislocation, or what you felt ill at ease with, your resistance to the tribal, familial community world, deeply suffused with Catholic teaching, morality and aspiration, and its sense of itself — that there is a fissure running through from the young Kilroy of nine, ten, eleven, or when you became conscious of this divide, right to the Kilroy of the present; where this other Ireland which we are hearing so much about at this time is separated morally, emotionally, intellectually; an actual gap that you are conscious of? Is that true?
Maybe that's true. We should remember, though, that a great deal of Irish life is simply hilarious. Even its serious problems have a habit of turning into farce. Besides, confrontation creates its own energy in the writer.

What is it the writer is confronting in the first place? What is it about the 'community-world' which troubles you? Is it the easy double-standards?
I would put it this way. The general shape of life as it is lived on this island is something that I find a lot of difficulty in sharing in. I live apart from it a good deal of the time. I mean it fascinates me.

As a writer?
Yes, complete fascination, but I feel constantly on the periphery of it in terms of my own life.

Now you don't mean that you made a decision to feel this way; this is something you were propelled into feeling?
Cut-offness, or whatever? No, it wasn't anything like a personal decision. No. It has caused problems in what I've been trying to write and how I've been trying to write because, for instance, the mode of writing I employ a great deal of the time is irony and one of the problems with irony is that it relies upon a kind of complicity with your audience or with your reader. And if that

complicity is not there, there's a strong sense of the writer being superior to the material and I think that that has happened to me in *Madame MacAdam* . . . sometimes the failure is inefficiencies of the writing but it can also be because the code is not shared.

Yet, isn't this strange? Your version of Ghosts *was a very potent siren-call about shared codes.* Madam MacAdam *is a play available to any intelligent attender of theatre, yet you did experience difficulties with that play. Is there prejudice with the shared code as it stands? An expectation that a play must be a certain kind of thing, commodity?*
I think it comes down to the fact that the values in writing can be identical to the values in a culture, in which case you get a writing which is, at the worst, populist, consolatory, but at its best, celebratory. When they diverge you get an antagonism, competitiveness even. This is true of much Irish writing this century. But there is a great loss when one is not an intrinsic part of one's culture. I've certainly felt that loss and I think some of my writing comes out of that loss. But loss is there to be filled, fracture is there to be healed. And that, finally, is what I try to do in my plays by going beyond the local.

Glenrevagh, County Galway
1992

Fred Johnston

INDIAN SUMMER

We sat on frail tubular chairs in a gravel garden behind the little pub. The sun gleamed on everything. It was unusually warm. His muscles vibrated and shone like disturbed oil. We talked about people we knew and old places. The children, fresh returned from Athens, exploded among the thorny bushes in shattering laughs; they had swallowed the Greek sun whole. My thin arms looked fishy white. He trained, kept himself in trim. He carried no extra weight. Under a chair, a child's toy Luger pistol. I once met a girl who was the grand-daughter of a German general, he says. The children, cantering like miniature ponies in the sloping grass towards the blue bay, have never known violence of any kind. A picket fence surrounds the gravel garden. If this weather lasts . . . . Through the dark cool pub and into the street, which is also a slope towards the white spraying fountain and the angled green public square, the gentle snickering of a radio. The sun lubricates everything, sets dead machines running again. All summer we have waited in the rain, under skies the colour of corpses. The uncanny sunshine has set us free, and we talk of trips abroad into unknowns, as we did when we were teenagers. It is difficult to be downhearted; the sun has brought with it our lost innocence. We fear nothing. As we pass back into the pub, I look down and see how the sunshine glints and hums along the black barrel of the Luger.

On a vague black night, alive with stars and distant storms, strolling along towards Salthill, a restaurant where friends gather like moths, and the arcades blazing with disappointments. Taxis hustle past like ghosts. Tonight Marcel, trying to be friendly and finding himself seated alone when the music was over, told me he had heard me on his radio in Brittany. You had left, peddling home on a bicycle with red wheel-rims and frame, making it clear you travelled alone. Conversations started up like flares and died again. A good tiredness fell upon us when the playing was over. You rushed away, looking around as if you had lost direction, needed reassurances. Then you left with waves, and I joked with you: take me with you. I'll sit up on the cross-bar. Silly. Marcel watches all. Pour jouer la musique traditionelle Irlandaise; why else do any of us come here? Listen: when you leaned over to speak to me, when you laughed and I laughed together like timed chiming clocks, the spontaneity was enough to make me drunk. Now the lines of demarcation are drawn . . . . Too many mysteries for me, or so I tell myself. You make everything so perfectly respectably clear. Then you smile. And what is more, your friend nicknamed Bebe wants to take me dancing some night. She has no illusions. She is very different from you. She runs after me in the street. Armfuls of smiles and grins. Pure Alsace. I knew her kind in Algeria; pure extract of peach, distilled sunlight, wave upon wave of devil-may-care. But I don't wish to go anywhere with Bebe really. She is what I'd call a nice girl. Bebe is the other side of you, the side that smiles and fools me. Through her, I can just about glimpse the France in you which laughs and plays street-games; later, it is music. Bebe Ah! Here the greatest difference lies — is at home anywhere. You are most at home in a cocoon of silence. Broken only now and then by music and dispensed smiles. We have been making jokes of a murmuring kind about a certain musician. We have been unkind, most united in our unkindness. We have the capacity for great cruelty. Your eyes, green as oceans, strip me right down to this cruelty. We all played well tonight; the fiddles, the pipes, the guitar, the goatskin bodhrans, the mandolin, all combined to send up a well-tempered skirl of reels and jigs. and I sang. Having momentarily forgotten that I have a smattering of your language, you did not bother to lower your voice when, turning to Marcel as I broke into the tune 'The Blarney Pilgrim', you told him laughing that it was probably the only tune I knew how to play all the way through. This is not cruelty, merely naivety, and I am surprised that a woman of your shyness and intelligence . . . . Never mind. Bebe comes in, full of grins, like a great chattering animated puppet. I am quite fond of her exuberance. She calls me Darling, in a mocking sort of way. Bebe occupies so much of your time that I grow jealous. Marcel is looking for a flat, a room, anything. He doesn't mind paying. I think he has taken upon himself, quite unconsciously, the role of your guardian. In any case you went home alone and I ran for a bus to the restaurant in Salthill. The night had excited me. It was hot, promising rain. Not since Chernobyl have the strollers on the promenade been conscious of the rain. I remember, in the restaurant, how people avoided downpours they might otherwise have walked through. A friend of mine, pregnant, terrified, smoking nervously in this same restaurant. For myself I don't give a damn. For the baby, it's a different matter. She was very angry. Slugging freezing orangeade, I resolve once again to tell you, despite any consequences, how pretty you are. It will most likely occur during our tuning-up before an evening of music commences. It must be said safely, with all due diplomacy. When we played together last, dear heart, we were not yet informed by the media of a nuclear accident aboard a Soviet submarine off Bermuda. If we, God forbid, were ever to kiss, what natural or man-made catastrophes might we anticipate? Bebe — another night on the promenade, wanting to discuss Bergman. I had no interest. I insisted on walking her home. Nothing more, needless to add. She says I remind her of her brother. Dear heart.

Peter Hollywood

LEAD CITY

'Those are not monsters out there; they are not beasts, packs of wild dogs on the prowl, wolves. No. Nor are they demons or vampires, ghosts or ghouls. They are men.

Take no solace from this.

I must go into their lead city.'

She waited impatiently for him to read the letter. Farrell was aware of her trembling as she sat across from him, watching him. Eventually, she could no longer hold herself in check; she judged that he had had enough time to take in the message and said:

— What can it mean?

Farrell looked up at the pale woman and was at a loss. He was about to say something when she again spoke.

— You were the only person I could think of that might know about these things.

— Things?

She nodded her head and lowered her voice, although they were alone in Farrell's house.

— Guns and things, she confided.

Farrell rose sharply from his seat.

— Jesus Christ, Mrs Price. What the hell do you mean by that? Christ, he fumed. Is that what you people are saying? Do you want to get me shot or something?

He saw the woman wring her hands and tears begin down her face. He stood still a moment and took a deep breath. Then he walked past the woman and went out into the kitchen. The fluorescent light threw his reflection up onto the window and he gazed at it briefly as he filled the kettle from the tap. He poured a glass of brandy and returned with it to Mrs Price.

There was a polite party underway just down the avenue from them. Strains of music came through to them, backed up softly by laughter and voices. It had been at a similar party, to which he had been unexpectedly invited, that he had made the acquaintance of the Prices.

— I didn't mean anything by that, she said. He liked the new steadiness in her voice. It's just what with having read your book and all, you seem to know things. My husband admired your book immensely; sure you know he did. I even think he's a little envious of it.

— I don't think this is anything to worry about, Farrell broke in. It's obviously something he's working on.

She shook her head.

— He only uses that paper for letters. It's so expensive. No, it's definitely a message, she assured him.

— And you haven't seen him or heard from him since yesterday?

Wearily she went back over the details with which she had arrived laden to his door: her husband's recent moodiness, culminating in her own discovery of two bullets in the desk drawer in his study.

— No gun? Farrell repeated the question he had put earlier.

— Just these. She reached for her bag and drew out the two bullets.

Farrell went slightly pale. Then he was more amused than alarmed. This was a respectable neighbourhood; there were never any dawn raids or house searches. Another time, another place, he might have worried. Having the bullets there, however, rolling them in his left hand, brought home to him the extent of the woman's concern.

— I take it he's never had a gun? he asked.

— My husband writes poetry, she stated.

Farrell didn't see that not possessing a gun necessarily followed from this, but he let it go.

— I'm afraid, she said. He's been under a lot of stress recently. From his publisher. I just don't know what to think.

Martin Price drank. That he was on a bender now was Farrell's opinion as he drove down into the city. He had walked Mrs Price back the short distance to her house, assuring her that all that was needed was a quick search of the bars her husband frequented. Farrell had gone along on a few drunken circuits with Price and some of Price's publishing friends. Price, he felt sure, was a creature of habit.

As he drove along, Farrell caught glimpses of solitary fireworks bursting pallidly apart above the city's glare. There were stars in the October sky also but these too were faint. The traffic mostly comprised taxis, ferrying passengers to a variety of night-spots, but the circulation was halted at regular intervals by police checkpoints. A security ring of steel encircled the commercial centre of the city. Farrell managed to get parked quite close to the centre.

Going in and out of bars, in only two was he aware of some of the clientele noting his brief passage with suspicion; on the whole, people let him glide through their smoky presence unnoticed. The bars by this time were loud and crowded and, in his sobriety, Farrell felt himself tense, the odd man out. Finally, in The Crown Bar, his progress was checked. He was pressing past a group of people when one of them recognized him.

— Well, my God. The person spoke aloud for the benefit of his company. If it's not Ernest Hemingway.

Farrell turned and vaguely recognized the man as someone he had met in Price's company. Farrell himself would have admitted a bigger debt to Leonard Gardner with regards to the book he had written, though he was sure there was some Hemingway in it as well. In any case, he disregarded the gibe and asked after Price.

— Don't tell me he's your new literary mentor, the man persisted.

Farrell sighed.

— Something like that, he said. You haven't seen him then?

The man was not listening. He was paying attention to something one of his number was saying to him. When he looked at Farrell he was sizing him up. Farrell arrested the man's punch in mid-air. The man's eyes bulged as his fist remained seized in Farrell's grip. With his right hand, Farrell considered knocking the man down but in the end he released the man, who backed off from him. One of the onlookers approached Farrell.

— Price was drinking in McGuiness's earlier on this evening, she told him. He was pretty much out of it though.

McGuiness's bar was popular in the early evening, an after-work venue. By the time Farrell walked in, the clientele had thinned out. Price was sat by himself at a table, a stale, half-drained pint of stout in front of him. He didn't notice as Farrell got himself a pint and moved over to join him. Farrell ran his eye over the other's bulk but was unable to gauge whether or not Price was carrying a gun.

— Your wife's worried sick about you, Farrell said as he pulled out a seat and sat down opposite Price.

Price focused on Farrell's face and was roused from his stupor.

— Well speak of the devil, Price said. I was just talking to somebody about you earlier on; some old boy, said he'd seen you fight.

— Your wife says you've been missing since yesterday.

— I think he was just trying to get a drink out of me, though. Price looked up at Farrell. I've been working, he said. Doing some research.

Price heaved himself up from his slumped position and, leaning forward, beckoned Farrell to draw closer.

— I've been wondering what it must be like to be a gunman; what it must be like to be walking about amongst all these ordinary people deciding maybe to shoot one of them.

— You'd need a gun to do that, Farrell suggested.

— Got one, my boy. Got one. See; I've got contacts too.

He was briefly boastful; then he shot a glance behind him in case he had been overheard.

— Where is this gun? Farrell got Price turned facing him again.

Price brought his hand suddenly up from under the table.

— Here, he said. Bang. His finger was pointing at Farrell's chest in a child's imitation of a gun.

Farrell hardly moved, but the blood drained momentarily from his face.

— My God, Price exclaimed. I actually got to you there. I was beginning to think that nothing frightened you, Farrell, but I actually made you jump, didn't I?

— There's nothing very funny about guns, not even pretend ones.

— Oh I've got a real one too. Again Price looked over his shoulder. Only it's in the car.

Price was drunk; but he had been drinking, Farrell calculated, at such a pace that a dull sobriety had begun to creep back in at the edges of his senses. He was therefore prepared to press him further.

— Why do you want a gun?

— I'm not like you, Farrell. In all the while I've known you you've never seemed afraid. This city never seems to get to you; but it gets to me, it frightens me.

— So you think a gun's going to protect you, keep you safe? Farrell asked.

— No, that's not it. I just thought maybe the gun would help me . . . . Price searched for the right words. Fit in, he said finally.

Farrell shook his head to indicate that he didn't quite follow.

— You see, if you're one of the guilty ones you've no great reason to be afraid. That's probably why you're never too much bothered by anything. Let's face it, you're no fucking innocent.

Even drunk, Price stopped to gauge the effect of this on Farrell; Farrell simply looked at him.

— Go on, he said.

— You know what my biggest fear is? It's walking down the street, minding my own business and being shot purely at random, or maybe getting blown up because I'm in the wrong place at the wrong time. Being an innocent bystander. What a fucking stupid way to die. Price was speaking almost in a whisper now.

— An illegal gun, even using it, won't make dying like that any less stupid. You want to feel guilty: minding your own business like you said a minute ago is as good a way as any.

— You know all the fucking answers, don't you? Price snapped, trying to struggle to his feet. You're part of it all, he said.

Farrell's hand came down on Price's arm so that he couldn't move away from him, so that Farrell could be sure he was paying strict attention.

— Listen. I've had it with the way you people think of me. Christ. Even your wife earlier on this evening. I have a prison record for something I did when I was too young to have known any better. I wasn't even inside for any length of time. But it gives you people a bit of a thrill doesn't it? Either that, or it gets you all hot and bothered. In the end we all have to serve, my friend. Even you.

Price sat immobile, staring into Farrell's face.

— Now, where did you park your car? Farrell was calm once more.

Outside, a few fireworks exploded confusedly over on the edges of the city. Price didn't appear to notice. Some late-night revellers staggered past them wearing ghoulish Halloween masks; one of them, in a Frankenstein mask, stumbled against Price and Price let out a yell of fright. There were howls of laughter.

By the time they reached Farrell's car, the crisp night air had done for Price, and Farrell had to slump him like a dead man across the back seat. Farrell was tempted to take Price straight home, but he thought of the gun and frisked him for his car-keys.

Price's car sat in the middle of the deserted car-park. The cinema-goers had long since gone, as had the opera-lovers and the pub-quizzers and the eaters in the various restaurants. The coast was for the moment clear. Farrell opened the car and went straight for the glove compartment, where he found the gun. He took a scarf from the passenger seat and wrapped the gun in it.

Given the possibility of checkpoints, Farrell knew he was taking a risk, but he felt momentarily responsible for the deep sleeper in the back of his car.

Getting into his car, he wedged the gun against the driver's door. That way, if he saw a checkpoint in the distance, he only had to open the door slightly for the gun and scarf to tumble out into the night. He didn't like the idea of the gun lying around for some fool or, worse, a child to come across it; but it was the only plan he could come up with.

In the event, the only stop he made was of his own accord. Leaning over the railings by the river, he pitched the gun into the water to settle into the silt and mud beneath the surface.

The following day, Price's wife answered the phone and told him Price was still recovering in bed. The next day, he was still too unwell to come to the phone.

— As long as he's on the mend, Farrell said.

— Yes, Mrs Price quickly replied. Yes of course.

On the third day, the person who answered the phone hung up the receiver on hearing Farrell's voice.

When the letter arrived, a week later, Farrell recognized the expensive paper. In it Price said he could remember very little of what had passed between them, but he thanked Farrell for his expert help. He went on to indicate that he would appreciate it if Farrell would stop trying to contact either himself or his wife.

Farrell put the letter down while he went to get himself a beer from the fridge. That the past these people dreamed up for him was not his real past didn't seem to matter to them. But it mattered to him. Being some invented, fictional figure bothered him more than being suddenly cast aside by them; though even that didn't fully explain what really made him angry. He picked up the letter again.

'Perhaps for a while there I was using you; you seemed dangerous to me and I think I was fascinated. But then I got in over my head. My dabbling nearly got me into a great deal of trouble. I was lucky to get out in one piece. The truth of the matter is there's a lot of evil out there and I don't want to have anything to do with it.'

Price was expecting stuff back from his publisher. When the padded envelope arrived in the midst of a pile of Christmas cards, he therefore had no reason to be suspicious of it. He slit open the envelope and tilted it up to empty out its contents. He was stunned when two silver-plated bullets rolled out onto his desk-top.

He could hardly move as he stared in horror at the objects. Then in a sudden frenzy he ripped and tore the envelope apart, but there was nothing besides the bullets. He felt suddenly sick as he thought of how people were dying almost daily in the city. Then, just as panic was about to take him over, he thought of Farrell.

Of course, he thought. Farrell would know what to do.

John Dunne

PURTOCK

Extract from a novel

Everything I am or ever was, all I have pilfered from this begrudging world, my whole life, my fame and what you call my downfall, has come from one thing only. Love. I owe everything to love. Not the sweat between man and woman; not the helpless dependence that parents and their children confuse with love; not the passion for country or idea that men will kill and die for. I am talking of that sensation rushing through your blood; seething in the marrow of your bones; seeping like light from your fingertips; that *bewitchment*, the one and only love, that makes you want to touch your fellow creatures and, through the simple alchemy of hands, give healing to their lives.

The finest house, flashiest car, biggest bank account, most beautiful ageing wife in this mean provincial town, do not belong to the banker, doctor, big farmer, solicitor or businessman.

Because of love, they belong to me. To me, Michael Joseph Purtock, humble offspring of the eternal midland bogs.

To me, whose ancestors toiled with flatcher, fork and slane; with barrow, slipe and donkey-cart; who suffered centuries of crooked spines, palms crisscrossed with threads of pain. Season after season, they wrested sods of turf from the squelching earth: stacked and dried them under endless sunblazed skies. Generations of poor simple countrymen, intimate with the ways of skygoat and curlew, the shriek of the otter, the fox's bark at twilight. Modest, faceless people who worked the spongy earth and felt they were in touch with the lurching of the planet.

I can see the eyebrows raised in doubt. The house, car, money, wife. How could he achieve all this? This peasant. This yokel, this *bogman*. You won't have long to wait. I will tell my story to all you strangers, foreigners even, with your cameras, microphones, lights. To you, my unbeloved townsmen, who once stood outside my door in thunderstorm and heatwave; who now, with tales of Miracle Mickey and The Mad Maneen, sell what you swear is my past for pints of slopping porter, fists of ten-pound notes.

I inherited no money, house nor land; went to no university; committed no flamboyant crime, grew fat on no rich business deals. You can believe the lies, the rumours flying like turf mould in the wind. You can believe what you like, but listen to me now, and I swear on my mother's grave that every word's the truth.

Some of you will sneer at the very mention of my beloved bogs. But do you know that in a certain European language the word 'bog' is synonymous with 'god'? There, what do you say to that!

Words. You will learn of my attachment to those sacred scraps of sound you spit at me today. I have always venerated words: their sound, their meaning, their happy or disastrous effects.

I play with words, savour them, marvel at the complexity of their making. Think of *tomb*, for instance. Feel how the tongue glances off the palate, skims the inside of your teeth; how the lips construct that black hole so appropriate to the meaning.

I cry when I remember certain words. I cry for Mary Margaret. Poor never-forgotten Mary Margaret; the tang of creosote on your lips.

All this talk of love and words, I hear you say. Go on then, throw away these words, crumple them in your disbelieving fist, burn them in disgust. But someone will read what I have to say. Someone who, once, was handed to me from his mother's trembling arms, a brittle smile trying hard to mask the pleading in her eyes. I will tell my story to you, or to anyone who listens. To you now, into whose hands these pages filled with truth have somehow found their way.

Picture this:

The screams have all subsided, the helpless cries are vanished into air. The frightened midland night settles down again.

Dogs locked in outhouses, roped to farmyard trees, leave one ear open and dream of fleshy bones.

Around the cottage, elder trees stand erect again, their branches darker etchings on the blackness of the sky.

Inside, kneeling against the bed, a man has collapsed into sleep. He has scrubbed his hands but blood still darkens underneath the nails. Around the room, buckets of water go slowly cold. A liverish blob still bubbles on the hearth.

Inches from the man's head, a woman also sleeps, her face streaked with matted hair and sweat. But look! She is lifting a pale arm and, never once opening her eyes, she moves a palm across her voided belly. Her sleeping hand creeps along the bedclothes and — look! look! — it has found me: Michael Joseph Purtock; only minutes old, my blue lips puckered round the fullness of her breast.

Think long on this, for this is how it all began. Fill your eyes with the pathetic scene before you; your nostrils with the stench of burning afterbirth. See how the moon hangs astounded in the window!

This is the genesis of Michael Joseph Purtock: clodhopper, rustic, *bogman*. Renowned Abecedarian, Miracle Mickey, Mad Maneen. Alchemist of Love. Inventor of the Rule of Love. Mortal victim of this accursed town.

It is the day before Easter and I am thirteen hours old. A neighbour woman has been to see my mother and left a bottle of holy water propped against the pillow.

My father takes three sips, blesses himself, and offers the bottle to my mother. Raising herself on one elbow, she drinks and traces a vague cross on her forehead.

Now he fills a spoon and solemnly approaches me. I can imagine this precisely. As the cold edge touches my lips, I start to cry and the water dribbles down my chin. He looks at my mother but her eyes have closed again. He fills the spoon a second time but it's no use; my face is blue with screaming. My mother turns away and, while he tries to get the water back into the bottle, hides me in her arms.

All that afternoon, while the village preens itself to welcome back the risen Christ, my parents lie beside me. Whenever my screams subside, my father aims his told-you-so smile at my mother's sunken eyes: when I start again, he storms into the kitchen and attacks the flagstones with a broom. Twice, someone knocks the door, then taps the window-pane. Each time, they are driven away by my father's growl:

'The babby's alright. It's just a bit of wind!'

All that night, while eggs are boiled in washing blue; while children dream of who will eat the most, my mouth is a crimson well of noise.

It is morning now. My mother slides away from me and her hand becomes a fist pounding on the pillow. My father fidgets with his belt. Suddenly he rubs his eyes, opens his mouth, but turns without speaking to the Jesus his grandfather carved from a sod of turf. He whispers something and scurries from the room.

I lacerate his prayers as he pulls the donkey from the stable. Any other year at this time, my parents would be returning from the vigil on Easter Hill, their voices filled with wonder at the dancing of the sun. But look at my father now: one minute beseeching Jesus to stop my screams; the next, swearing at the donkey to stand while he fills the cart with straw.

Look how he plunges through the doorway and emerges with wads of clothes; goes inside again and, this time, appears with my mother shrieking in his arms. Soothing her frantic hands, he wraps the clothes around her and, for an instant, it seems that she and I are vying to bawl the loudest.

My father is gone a third time, but, look, here he comes striding through the yard with me, in swaddling clothes, clamped against his chest. I melt into my mother's arms as he returns to lock the door. He shouts at the donkey and my mother — poor Madonna of the bogs — starts to howl again.

It is fifteen miles to town and, all along the road, stragglers from The Hill cross themselves as we gallop past their eyes. Women roar at children who drop their coloured eggs; curtains part; birds scatter; dogs chase the wheels as my father lashes the donkey with a stick. I am squealing like a *banbh* in the straw . . .

By the time we reach the first houses, the donkey's back is bleeding. When it slows into a ragged trot, my father throws away the stick and falls onto the seat, his face nodding in his hands.

A gang of children follows us into The Square. Past the blinded windows of the lawyer, around the statue of the Virgin and the courthouse; past the cinema where no desperate heroine would ever screech like my mother and I that Easter morning.

My father has never been to a doctor in his life. At the church railing he asks someone for directions and a young girl comes forward to peer into the cart.

Can you see the picture? A little girl in her Easter bonnet; a cartful of noise with its cortege of giddy urchins. A town given something to laugh about for years; the first sign that The Mad Maneen has come to brighten up their lives. And how they relished my arrival and locked it in their memory. Look, today, how my screams are sold to foreigners.

The girl halts at a Georgian door and stands gaping as my father scatters the children with imaginary stones. He pats my mother's hair, climbs the steps to bang the knocker, then leans on the handrail like someone going to vomit. The girl points to something in the window and he hammers the door again.

A woman's head appears and stammers that 'himself's gone out for his dinner'. As my father jabs the air, the window slams, and the children shout the name of some hotel.

The donkey's head is jerked around and my mother's arm dangles like a famine victim's from the cart.

As we pass the churchyard a second time, she has fallen silent, but I'm still bawling loud enough to frighten every corpse.

My father kisses her hand, tucks it beneath the clothes, then leads us up the avenue and through a maze of cars.

He pulls me from my mother's grasp and strides towards the lobby.

Within minutes he is out again, his anger flying like daggers at the youth gawking from the doorway. My mother suddenly hauls herself up, clutches at her nightdress, and shrieks 'Where are you taking my baby?' He pushes her back on the straw, drops me on her chest, and tries to drag the donkey through the flowerbeds. It just nibbles at the perfect lawn. Dancing with rage, he tugs the animal's ears and batters the diamond on his forehead.

Cursing every doctor in the country, he scatters clumps of snowdrops with his boot, then attacks the exhausted animal, first with handfuls of clay, then a young tree. Again and again he lashes it across the eyes until it stumbles backwards through the flowers. Back and forth we plough, until someone shouts from the doorway, and my father pulls us towards the road again.

Now he is pounding on the presbytery door.

When the housekeeper appears, he roars that his son is going to die, and storms past her into the hall. A door opens and the parish priest looks from the woman to the madman with the baby in his arms.

Who knows how that cleric was persuaded — how many masses, First Fridays, loads of turf? — but before my mother knows I'm gone, I'm back in her arms again, a strong and perfect Christian with my grandfather's name.

As the donkey shambles off, my father keeps muttering that the child will be alright, the man above will save him.

Is it any wonder I became The Alchemist of Love? Born on Good Friday, baptized on Easter Sunday?

At twelve months, not only did I know my own age, but I could sit for hours, calmly producing page after page of immaculate cephalopods — a feat which, in any culture you care to name, would elicit gasps of admiration for the most precocious two-year-old. Imagine, I could've been an artist too!

In the English language there are seventeen vowels and twenty-seven consonants. By the age of two, I had them all. Every single one. I could impress you with my knowledge of close, plosive, fricative and flapped, but all you need to understand is I was no tongue-tied Philip Pirrip. Observe me as I waddle through the yard, squawking like some exotic bird,

MICHAELJOSEPHPURTOCK! MICHAELJOSEPHPURTOCK!

But I am no braggart. James V was king of Scotland before he reached his second year. Grimaldi, king of clowns, was performing at the same age. So, I ask you, what's a prodigy? Someone who's different from the rest. That's all.

Leonardo claimed that every man at three years old is half his eventual height. He may have known how to paint on walls, capture enigmatic smiles, but when it came to paediatrics he should have shut his mouth. It's your average two-year-old who's reached the halfway stage.

What am I trying to prove? Nothing. Nothing at all, but, on the morning of my second birthday, my mother took a tape from her sewing box, stood me against the kitchen wall, and, to her horror, found all her prayers unanswered.

A what? Don't ever use that word again! What do you think I am? Something in a circus? Some sort of freak tumbling after Snow White? Listen. At the age when parents drool over every squeak their little darlings make, I could recite the entire vocabulary of the bogs.

You asked about my parents.

My mother was a deeply religious woman immersed in superstition. In her prayers, Jesus, Mary, and The Child of Prague jostled with the *púca*, *dullahán*, and May Day hare. Like all our neighbours, she never went to mass, yet ran to kiss the biretta when the priest appeared from town.

I inherited her eyes, perfect skin (I didn't need to shave till I was twenty), her modesty and infinite patience. But I drew the line at seventh sons, falling pictures, robins in the kitchen.

I loved my mother for her hands (can you hear my father's laughter as she washes them in the dew?). I loved her for the untimely whiteness of her hair, for the way she never stopped telling me how much she loved me.

My father. Peasant and avatar of the bogs. I loved him for his hands, for the strength of his slane, for his helpless tears whenever I hurt him. I loved him for his hatred of the town, for his cap that never hid the port wine stain, for the donkey's hoof, the thread of blood on his cheek. I loved him for his face when Nan-the-Habit laid him out.

Why do people hate the bogs? Why will they scrimp and save to visit windy sea-side towns; cities smothered in filth; mountains transformed by visions into money-traps for the curious, the lonely and the dying?

But how many will 'broaden their minds' by entering the watery kingdom of the boglands? If it wasn't for me, do you think there'd be a sinner here today? Michael Joseph Purtock, tourist attraction, economic saviour of the Midlands.

You think I'm arrogant? Should I lie down and whinge because of what they're doing to me? I was born to laugh at hurricanes!

Why do people travel? I'll tell you why. It makes them feel important. The more they see, the more their dominance is confirmed. 'Look at us, we bested mountains and rivers, tamed the sun, shaped the air to accommodate our dreams!' And every work of art becomes a mere reminder of their power. This picture, book, symphony, cathedral . . . 'One of ours did that!' And you accuse me of arrogance.

But their vanity is threatened by the bog, intimidated by its apathetic vastness. Hearts beat faster, a shiver crawls along the spine, and something keeps telling them how helplessly alone, how utterly insignificant they are in this *terra incognita* of endless air and water.

Did you know the bog is 95% water? Less solid matter than milk.

And how do they disguise their fear? They call it boredom. 'But it's so featureless. How could anyone exist here?' I'll tell you about existence. The quaking ground, the invisible gurgling of streams, the smallest sprig of heather, the most transparent insect, have all been here for millennia without you, and will continue for ages more to come. And what have you? Seventy? Eighty? Ninety? A hundred at the outside. Mayflies. Poor deluded mayflies the lot of you.

Tell me this. After love, what's the second most important thing in life? Sex? Health? Power? Money? Happiness? Death? None of these. It's sleep. Sleep that knits up the ravelled sleave of care. I've hardly slept a wink in ages. How can I, with their lights poking my eyes every few minutes? I am living an insomniac's nightmare. Like Macbeth, they have murdered sleep. Why? Because they fear my dreams, that's why. Because they know I dream the truth.

And the questions they keep asking. 'Did you love your mother?' 'Did you love your father?' 'Why were you an only child?' 'Did anything ever happen in your childhood?' Jesus, do they not know who they're talking to? I am Michael Joseph Purtock, Dreamer of Truth, the one and only Alchemist of Love.

While they were still fingering dirty pictures, I had studied books they've only heard about. *The Interpretation of Dreams*, *Psychopathia Sexualis*, *Claustrophobia in the Midlands*: I've read them all. Read them all and laughed.

When my mother started whitewashing the kitchen, I knew for certain my father was going to die.

Picture this:

It is the fifteenth of July, a blazing cloudless day. We are lying on our backs, wondering how such heat could last for forty days. Now and then, I lean towards Mary Margaret and lick beads of sweat from her forehead. Now and then, she opens her eyes and does the same to me.

Can children be in love? What is love? All I know is my happiness depended totally on hers. Have you a better definition?

I ease away from her and scan the air for butterflies. I know she is pretending not to notice. That's love too. I want to trap one in my hand and kneel before her. I want to press her hands on mine, let her feel the beating of my heart.

A Common Blue hovers above a tussock, but before I can react, it has ebbed into the sky.

I turn around and she is smiling, her face paler than the Large White we followed through her father's garden. I am going to tell her how I wish she was my sister when the noise makes us jump.

The Zulu Galvin is attacking the donkey with a sprong. With every stab, it twists and turns between the shafts; skeleton's teeth chomping the air; a beard of froth erupting in drops of silver rain.

When the cart takes off across the bog, The Zulu curses every donkey in the village and fires the sprong like a javelin towards the sun.

The men are huddled in a circle, and through a gap in their legs I recognize the brown boots, the navy laces he laughed at when I brought them from The Widow Tynan's. He is lying on his back, a crimson thread trickling from his ear. Uncle Joe presses a rag to the far side of his head, but I just stand there, embarrassed that my father has wet himself in front of Mary Margaret.

I don't know how we got him home but I remember waiting for the doctor.

My mother's brush slaps the kitchen wall and I picture specks of whitewash in her hair. Every few minutes, footsteps cross the yard and she roars at them to go away.

He is lying perfectly still, his startled eyes fixed on the ceiling. How can anyone stare so long without blinking? Why is there so little blood? Does Mary Margaret know he wet himself?

The door bursts open and my mother rummages in a drawer. Clothes I've only seen in magazines fly around the room, and when I go to snatch a nylon from my father's face, she snarls and holds a mirror to his mouth.

'What's keeping him?' she snarls again, and before I realize she means the doctor, she is gone.

I stand beside the bed and clench my fists until they hurt, certain that my pain will summon up the alchemy of love. The Rule of Love believeth all things; hopeth all things; endureth all things. The Rule of Love never faileth.

I touch the stubble on his chin and remember how he used to nuzzle me in bed. Tears force my eyes open. His are still the same. Fixed to something wondrous on the ceiling. Eleven years of love are pouring from my fingertips but my father never even blinks.

In the kitchen, my mother sits with the brush poised before her like a mirror. She mumbles something I can't hear, then springs forward and tears my father's otterskin from the wall. Rocking back and forth, she is suddenly the oldest woman in the village, crooning to that piece of skin, fondling it like a cat sleeping in her lap.

I run into her arms, and when I think she's going to kiss me, she just whispers 'you shouldn't leave your daddy'.

She follows me inside, telling me over and over 'your daddy's going to be alright'.

His lips move and I believe her. His perfect words fill the room and I believe her.

'The fox is a quare sly baste.'

A grin seeps across his face and he starts to bray. My father starts to bray. A black hysteria of noise throbbing with the memory of blood that Easter morning:

'They wouldn't cure him, Mary. The bastards wouldn't cure the poor maneen!'

My mother covers her ears, but still it comes, shrieking through the history of The Mad Maneen, shrieking through the immanence of hands, the seven years I lay in this very bed, shrieking until she dances up and down, tearing her hair.

And then it starts to die away, shrink back inside the cavern of his mouth and, as we creep towards the bed, a single tear gathers in his eye. I have never heard such love as in the final words that dribbled from my father's mouth.

'I'm sorry, Neddy, I didn't mean it. Show me your poor eyes.'

He tries to lean forward but there's a sound like water going down a sink and he collapses on the pillow. My mother flings herself across the bed, one minute stroking his face, the next pounding on his chest, and when I try to intervene, she hisses at me to go out and stop the clock.

I stand for ages on my father's chair, breathing in the smell of whitewash. I don't know what to do. To this day I still don't. How do you stop a clock?

Gerald Dawe

AN INTERVIEW WITH LES MURRAY

Poet and editor Les Murray was born in 1938. He lives in Bunyah, New South Wales, Australia.

A lot of your work concerns itself with the past and your family and your experience of living in Australia, coming from a certain kind of background. Can you fill us in on that background?

My mother's people were coal-miners, engineers, and all that. Grandfather on that side I never met. He died rather young as a result, I guess, of dust on the lungs. His ancestry was Cornish and English. So I was more conscious of my father's world, a Scottish world, with a bit of Irish in it. My father's mother's people were Paynes from Wexford, but the Murrays, from Roxburghshire in Scotland, had gone to Australia in the late eighteen forties and settled on the Manning River and kind of stayed put. Stayed Scottish in fact for a long time. In fact, even up to Grandfather's time they'd sometimes break into Scottish accents. Quite isolated, and very strict Free Presbyterians, do you know? Quite out of the mainstream altogether. It was a fascinating, a so enclosed and yet spacious world in the hills there — dairy-farming and cattle-raising and so on.

Tell me, do you feel that you've moved away from that through writing, or is your work an imaginative exploration of that world?

The latter I would say. I've moved away from it only far enough to see it more clearly. But I still value it and I still continually go back to it. It's a kind of lode-star in the centre. And I've gone back to it again. I've gone physically back to it. We moved back from the city finally this year [1986] to the district I came from. To the next door farm, in fact.

There are poems, particularly in the earlier work, which are specifically related to your experiences as a young boy growing up in a specific world. Do you feel your writing has to go back to touch that to be real? You use the word 'lode-star'. Do you feel that the imagination needs to be rooted in that way?

I do. I wouldn't say that as a prescription for everyone. But I've always felt that if I lost contact with that, somehow I'd be deeply lost. And that I'd be what the Aboriginals call a man without dreaming. Spinning. The kind of vertigo that I would fear.

You live now, full-time, as a poet?
Yeah, yeah, partly because I'm a subsidized industry. We have a rather decent set of fellowships in Australia. They're not continuous; you can't live from year to year on them but you can get enough of them to string together in a sort of way. Also my wife's earnings as a teacher have been the real backbone of our family economy. But yeah, it's funny. I think your career in writing often describes a spiral-course: you go back on an old subject-matter and look at it again from another level of development and then you go away from it for a while. And I've done that a few times.

Do you feel, though, that there is a claim upon you in Australia as 'being a poet'?
Ay, yeah. I come from a class of people in Australia — we pretend Australia's classless, but in fact it has a class system that is all the more pernicious in some ways for being subtle . . . and denied. I come from the rural poor. Not a very large class in Australia and at all stages of history deeply despised; and I tend to hope to be a credit to them and I naturally draw upon those loyalties.

You could say that your poetry is an articulation or a voice for that experience of growing up from a group of people who are in a sense 'despised' or treated with contempt by the received.
Yeah, that's true. I wouldn't make too much of it. You know, I don't go in for heavy resentment, but I do know the asperities of that situation which is, I suppose, all the more perplexing for being denied. You see my timing was off. I came to the city at just about the same time as the critics — you see we do tend to have a critic-led literature, if not a demographically led literature — I think the ultimate determinants of Australian literature are demographic critics; ah, the word was out that we were now to be urbanized and sophisticated. That kind of writing was now in demand and I had the opposite background.

So you immediately clashed with received opinion?
Ah, yes. And I've been in that kind of clash ever since. And occasionally it gets gross, but more of the time it's subtle, but I do tend to be read by those people, and a good many others.

As a poet do you feel that you have to move outside Australia or are you quite content being where you are?
Pretty content being where I am. I like going for trips occasionally abroad. I did have to go at one time on a sort of Grand Tour. That was my real university, after I finished the literal university. I went working for a few years and then I went to my real university which was a trip to Europe. About Europe I wrote very little indeed. I've hardly written about it, but it was a

wonderful vantage from which to look back upon my real subject-matter.

But through your wife you do seem to have entered into a wider kind of 'European' experience?
Through my wife, and through reading and meeting other people, yeah. My wife comes from Budapest, although her mother's Swiss; her family's terribly complicated. Their name's Italian, their ultimate Swiss-Italian ancestors served Napoleon and happened to end up in Hungary by accident. And there's still a family of Morellis in Budapest. There's only about one left now. Yeah, I got a kind of pipeline into a central European world there.

And of course Australia itself is full of different waves of migration?
Yeah, a third of people in Australia would have been either born overseas or born to parents born overseas. This has probably always been true; it's just that the spectrum of places that they come from has been getting wider all the time. At one time it would have been heavily English, Irish and Scots, with light garnishings of other peoples. But now it's every nationality and human group you've ever heard of.

You have a poem 'Jozsef'.
That's my wicked grandfather-in-law: a fascinating old boy. Old Jozsef, he loved that poem. It had to be translated to him to a degree. His English wasn't quite up to it, but Valerie translated it for him. It was all the old scandalous stories that he told about himself. He once attempted suicide. He was a pistol-champion, you see; he'd won many duels and stuff but he missed his own heart! He thought it was further over to the left (as many people do) than it was. The pistol-bullet went in and hit a rib at the back and skated right around and came out the front and landed in an old Dunhill cigarette lighter which we still possess.

Those kinds of human details: your poetry is full of them.
Yeah, they're a sort of nougat compressed out of stories, you know.

To what extent do you feel that, without being too self-conscious about it, a poet's first real commitment, after his feeling for language, is to that kind of sympathy for (dare we use the old word) 'ordinary' people — people's own experience?
I tend to lean that way. I wouldn't be prescriptive about it but I do tend to lean that way myself. And I find in the unceasing fascination with what we call in Australia 'yarning'. My poems are, as you say, often made out of yarns.

Does this mean that you view with a critical eye what you call in one of your essays 'the opposition between our derivative high culture and a more distinctive vernacular culture'?

Yeah, what we've said is probably the root of that bother I have. I do feel most of all the agenda of received subjects and attitudes which you can tick off. You know that I tend to be in opposition to that. Because *any* agenda, any world-view, will exclude a tremendous amount in order to exist. And I'm interested in the excluded.

And it makes it all the more difficult to keep an eye on things when there is a received literary sensibility which seems to be dragging you in one direction.
Yes, it's a powerful tidal force. You've got to fight it all the time. It tries to simplify the world in order not to have the fatigue of sympathy and of thought. It's like Utopia, you know: 'Please for God's sake bring time to a stop because it's too complicated'.

Yes, that's right.
I don't think the world is too complicated. I can actually handle it, even with time running.

Exactly. You have a marvellous feeling for the diversity of things. There's one poem, in the beginning of Selected Poems, *'Driving Through Sawmill Towns'.*
That's the little remote country places that I come from. That's forestry country; it's very near us. It's anywhere in the Dividing Range, I suppose. The Dividing Range is actually a large but not very much noticed feature of the Australian landscape. It's about four thousand miles long, right from Northern Queensland down to Tasmania, a great bow-like arc of mountains, but none of them very high. It's a slightly larger Appalachians, and very much the same phenomena occur and the same sort of people occur.

Yes, reading those earlier poems I was reminded in some way of William Faulkner territory.
Yes, yes, and James Dickey. He's a poet I have a lot of sympathy for.

And those last lines of yours: 'Men sit after tea/by the stove while their wives talk, rolling a dead match/between their fingers/thinking of the future'. What does the future hold?
Just write more poems. I won't cover it all you know. I'll go round and round a good many times yet, just enjoying it and finding out more of what it means. The next book (*The Daylight Moon*) tends to go back into that country stuff . . . coincident with my moving there. The last part of the book gets all bushy again.

And tell me, you're also involved, outside of writing poems, with editing.
Yeah. Used to edit a magazine called *Poetry Australia* and then, lately, I was asked to do *The Oxford Book of Australian Poetry*. They wanted a scholarly book which was good for the educational market and they didn't get one. They got an altogether strange and scruffy book which allowed no more than three

poems to anyone. I didn't want any of that obsessive ranking and grading nonsense. You know — 'If so-and-so has nine poems, then so-and-so must have seven' — all that anxious sort of —

Proxy egotism?
Yeah, yeah. Proxy egotism is right. Yeah: I also didn't want lots of biographical and critical prose interposing themselves everywhere as if poetry was some kind of exotic indulgence which had to be propped up with lots of prose. I wanted to throw people in at the deep end and make them read poetry, so I wrote the briefest possible introduction and gave no more biographical information than dates of birth and death, if people had taken things that far. And people didn't necessarily all get three poems. Some of them got one or two. And even that wasn't hierarchical because sometimes they got one poem because it was a long one! Other times they got only one poem because it was the only good poem I could find!

And you've also written The Australian Year?
That was a book about the Australian seasons. It's an interesting subject. That was not my idea to write it; it was the idea of a lady who has now become the publisher of our oldest literary press, I guess, Angus & Robertson. She said we'd never had a book about the Australian seasons and I said this is true and she said 'And you're the one to write it' and I said 'This is probably true' and then I wondered how the hell am I going to get out of this. She wouldn't let me out of it. So it came out and it's not a bad book I think. You see the Australian seasons is a very complicated subject. We imported four seasons from the Northern world for which we have English names. They *sort of* fit. The further south in Australia, as the south gets cooler, the better the fit is. In Northern Australia they mean nothing because the seasons there are the wet and the dry. The monsoon wet and the droughty dry. In lots of Australia they scarcely mean much when the seasons are really summer and non-summer, you know bloody hot and hot . . . But there's also an old Aboriginal way of seeing things. Aborigines don't think in terms of seasons; they think in terms of times. A time when a particular species of food or animal is in abundance, which will be correlated with something else. I'll give you an example. When the red hop bushes flower in the forest near where I come from, that's the time to eat oysters, on the sea coast. All these things are intricately interconnected with the Aboriginal mythology which is very geographical. Every story has a place; it all happened in particular places. And Australia is a great network of songs about these stories. The only Aboriginal season is, in a way, the return of water. The great Australian contrast is between dryness and the return of

water. Most, or all, native plants and animals are keyed to the return of water and reproduce when the rain comes or even the water comes. Perhaps the rain was hundreds of miles away but the water's come down the river and at that point, in a very precise way, the different species will start reproducing . . . a certain species will suddenly turn on and start laying eggs. It's very exact.

So, in a way, you're really going deeper into another layer of The People?
The Aborigines are the primal imagination of Australia. They have been here a very very long time and have worked things in *their* way. You see not being farmers,. never never being growers of things, they never invented a system of seasons the way we did, most of Australia was never cold enough for the seasonal contrast to be hard enough. The Northern thing is burgeoning, harvesting, and then the cold death of winter . . .

What you're really saying is that the English words for seasons are out of place here?
They have a place, but they don't fit exactly. They make a better fit the further south you go; they make a fair fit but not a completely accurate one.

Could you use that then as a metaphor for the language?
Yeah, you could. English makes a fair fit in Australia but there's a lot more you need besides English. In a funny way, every word in Australia, every English word used in Australia means something slightly else in Australia than it does elsewhere. That would be true of the West Indies, or Africa or America too.

So you are conscious when you write that you are using a language which is nominally English but it is Australian?
Yeah, I am writing over a wonderfully high mountain of possible misunder-standings! A lot of commonplace things that are here are just not known in Europe, and words take on different meanings. Like in America, the word 'creek' took on a meaning of 'stream'. It did here too. They tried out 'rivulet' and 'brook' and stuff, but somehow they wouldn't fit. Creek would.

You find that a creative possibility though?
Sure. There's lots of things in Australia which don't have English names at all. Species of fish and birds, and plants, that have no common English name, or perhaps twenty.

So we can move from seasons into language. What about politics?
Yeah, I'd say it's all subtly weird and different. In politics in Australia it tends to be deeply derivative. You're buying political concepts from abroad and not

cutting them to fit but just laying them down and sort of forcing the local facts to fit those. I mean terms like 'Left' and 'Right' and 'Conservative' and so on. One of the notorious cases would be 'Liberal' which doesn't mean the same thing here at all as it means in, say, America.

Do you feel, for instance, that the Australians are looking over their shoulder?
All the time. Politics is probably one of the most derivative things in our culture. It wasn't always. We had a period in the eighteen seventies, eighties and nineties — up to the First World War, when a lot of distinctive things happened in Australia. There was the invention of the Secret Ballot and of Child Endowment Payments and a whole load of pioneering social legislation that went on. That was the most creative period in Australian politics. Probably the *only* creative period. It's *totally* derivative nowadays. And it can be fairly nasty in fact. Since the nineteen sixties there's been this new atmosphere of The Agenda and of people policing each other and that kind of atmosphere of indulged resentment.

Do you find that culturally Australia is becoming 'transparent'? That it is becoming overly concerned with its own identity?
Yeah, sure. It happens in cycles too. The last time it happened would have been around Federation, late eighteen eighties, to the early years of this century. The same time as these quite enlightened, interesting, distinctive political developments were happening. There was a lot of self-conscious nationalism. You can always tell; when people start growing native plants in the garden, it's a great sign! There's always a quotient of bullshit in every good thing. It just so happens that there's been a particularly high quotient of bullshit since the nineteen sixties in Australia.

And has that damaged writers, do you think, here?
A lot, yeah. Working not from their own vision of the world but from some vision that they felt obliged to follow —

That which can be Australian, or can be American or English —
Yeah, yeah.

Rather than the centre coming from within themselves?
That's right. Yeah. That's the great weakness. And that's what I call 'colonial' and I get disliked for calling it that.

Thanks.

Quenbeyan, Australian Capital Territory
1988

Les Murray

ASPECTS OF LANGUAGE AND WAR ON THE GLOUCESTER ROAD

I travel a road cut through time
by bare feet and boots without socks,
by eight-year-old men droving cattle,
by wheels parallel as printed rhyme
over rhythms of hill shale and tussocks.
    In the hardest real trouble of my life
    I called this Gloucester road to mind,
    which cuttings were bare gravel, which rife
    with grass, which ones rainforest-vined.
The road starts at Coolongolook
which means roughly Leftward Inland
from *gulunggal*, the left hand,
runs west between Holdens' and James'
where new people have to paint names
on their mailboxes, and where stumps have board-slots
from when great trees were jibbed like yachts
and felled above their hollow tones.
The road comes on through Sawyers Creek
where the high whaleback ridge becomes a peak
and where my father, aged nine years,
faced down the Bashing Teacher, a Squeers
who cut six-foot canes in the scrub
and chewing his tongue in a subjective ecstasy, lashed back-arching children.
Mind your mhisness! — *Time someone chipped you!* —
Short blazed at tall — and the knobbed cane withdrew.
My father was cheered shoulder-high in the playground then
and the bunched rods vanished. But previously slack
parents loomed, shouting. And after them, the sack.
    Here too a farmer heard *Give up*
    cigarettes or your life! He coughed a sup
    of Flanders gas, cried *Jesus Christ and that,*

Doctor, I'll give up my life! And what
was burning inside him smouldered on
for decades, disclosed only once
in '39, teaching dodges to his sons.
(1939, an aunt smiles, *the year
when no woman had to stay a spinster.*)
The road runs through Bunyah, meaning bark
for shelters, or firelighters' candlebark
to blow on in a *gugri* house, a word
for fire hut that is still heard
though few farms still use a googery.
Few? None now. I was gone a generation.
Even parrot-eating's stopped: *The buggers,
they'd been eating that wild-tobacco berry:
imagine a soup of boiled cigars!* —
    I'm driving to Gloucester station
    to collect my urban eldest from the train,
    and there are the concrete tips
    of bridge piles, set like a tank trap
    up a farm entryway. The huge rap
    of a piledriver shivered few chips
    off the bedrock when they were banged stubbornly
    by an engineer who would not be told
    Black rock at eight feet'll stop you cold!
    What did locals know, lacking a degree?
    I loved the old bridge, its handrails,
    ballast logs and deck, an inland ship.
    Kids watched how floods' pewter rip
    wracked limbs over it. Floods were our folktales.
    Now we drive above missed schooldays, high
    on the Shire's concrete second try.
There at the hall, drums and accordeons
still pump, and well-lit dancers glide.
In the dark outside move, single and duo,
the angrily shy and the bawdy ones:
blood and babies from the dancing outside.
    We held Free Church services too, though,
    in that hall. For months I'd cry aloud
    at the rise in the east of any cloud

no bigger than a man's hand.
A cloud by day led me out of Babyland
about when Hiroshima had three years to go.
The Free Church, knuckle-white on its ridge,
now looks north at the Lavinia Murray Bridge,
at my great-grandmother's Chinese elm tree
and the Dutchman tractoring peaceably.
That faint scar across the creek is butts
of a range for aligned wartime rifle shots.

    What fearsome breach of military law
    sent you, Lieutenant Squance, to command
    that platoon of worried men-on-the-land
    the Bunyah Volunteer Defence Corps
    in those collapsing months after Singapore,
    brassbuttoned fathers, deadly afraid
    for life and family? Your British parade
    manner gave them some diversion:
    milky boots, casual mutiny, aspersion,
    your corporal raving death-threats in your face
    for calling his clean rifle a disgrace,
    brownpaper sandwiches sent to you with tea
    after parade one Saturday —
    I think, though, you'd have stayed and defended
    us, and died as our world ended,
    Mr Squance. Belated thanks are extended.
There's a house where I had hospitality
without fuss for years when I needed it.
Now it's dying, of sun-bleach, of shadowed
scarlet lichen, of the poisons of abandonment.
I'm thinking, over the next rises,
of children who did not have their lives,
who died young, and how one realizes
only at home that, unknown to younger wives,
faces lie in wait in finger-felted albums'
gapless groupings of family. The sums
of those short lifetimes add to one's own age,
to its weight, having no light yarns to lift them.
Peace or war, all die for our freedom.
The innocent, the guilty, the beasts, all die for our freedom.

I was taught the irreparable knowledge
by a baby of thirty next door in his wheelchair
who'd thrash and grimace with happiness when I went there.
I see the road, and many roads before,
through a fawn snap of him as a solemn little boy
before meningitis. And it is first for him
that I insist on a state where lives resume.

    The squatter style grinds eastward here, or 'down'
    (both *ba:rung* in the old language) and spreads out from town.
    One property here was Something Downs for a bit:
    over there through the hills I can glimpse part of it
    just short of the pines round my one-teacher school
    with its zigzag air raid trench and morning flagpole;
    from there I remember birthdays, and how to shin
    fast over fence rails: *You're last! — I'll be first in Heaven!*
    I pass by Lavinia's gate,
    the first woman Shire President in the State
    and not dowager at eighty, but reigning, in her fox fur,
    descending on Parliament, ascending with the cropduster
    whose rent for an airfield was shopping flights to Gloucester.
A flagman stops me with a circled word.
I halt beside him, wait till he can be heard
over a big steel roller's matt declensions
as it tightens gravel down into two dimensions.
He points at a possum curled like an ampersand
around a high dead branch, spending the day
miserably where its light caught her away
from her cache of darkness. *There's her baby's hand*
out of her pouch. — She's dreaming. — Wonder if we
are in her dream? — Wonder if she's ever seen a hill? —
What lights would we have, on what cars, if we were nocturnal?
Look lower, native bees. Round a knothole spout
a thought-balloon of grist breathes in and out.
Look, one on your arm. — Their mixture must need salt.
Hell will have icecream before this road gets asphalt.

    I drive off, on what sounds like a shore.
    In Upper Bunyah there are more
    settlers without nicknames, or
    none they know. The widower on that hill

used to have one (and he was the raving corporal).
He once had some evangelists staying
in his house, demonstratively praying,
so one day his two dozen cats annoyed him
and he took the small rifle and destroyed them,
shot them off rafters, sniped eyes under his bed —
cups exploded in the kitchen as poor Tibby fled —
the men of prayer too ran headlong from his charity.
Sweet, for one, are the uses of barbarity.
His later wife had a chequebook and painted in France.
Why does so much of our culture work through yarns
equivalent to the national talent for cartoons?
It is an old war brought from Europe
by those who also brought poverty and landscape.
They had scores to settle, even with themselves. Tradition
is also repeating oneself, expecting inattention,
singing dumb, expecting scorn. Or sly mispronunciation
out of loyalty to the dead: *You boiling them bikinis*
for that Vichy sauce? We were the wrong people risen
— forerunners in that of nearly everyone —
but we rose early, on small farms, and were family.
A hard yarn twangs the tension
and fires its broad arrow out of a grim space
of Old Australian smells: toejam, tomato sauce,
semen and dead singlets the solitary have called peace
but which is really an unsurrendered trench. Really prison.
It is a reminder all stories are of war.
Peace, and the proof of peace, is the verandah
absent from some of the newer houses here.
It is also a slight distance — as indeed
grows between me and the farm of my cousin
who recently was sold treated seed grain
in mistake for cattle-feed grain:
it killed cows, but he dared not complain
or sue the feed merchant, for fear
he'd be barred as a milk supplier
to the Milk Board, and ruined, and in consequence
see his house become somebody's rural residence.
Such things can make a farmer look down, at his land
between his boots, and dignity shrink in his hand.

Now the road enters the gesture of the hills
where they express geologic weather
and contend with the landscape, in spills
of triangular forest down fence lines
and horse-and-scoop dams like filled mines.
What else to say of peace? It is a presence
with the feeling of home, and timeless in any tense.
    I am driving *waga*, up and west.
    Parting cattle, I climb over the crest
    out of Bunyah, and skirt Bucca Wauka,
    A Man Sitting Up With Knees Against His Chest:
    baga waga, knees up, the burial-shape of a warrior.
Eagles flying below me, I will ascend Wallanbah,
that whipcrack country of white cedar
and ruined tennis courts, and speed up on the tar.
In sight of the high ranges I'll pass the turnoff to Bundook,
Hindi for musket — which it also took
to add to the daylight species here, in the primal 1830s of our numbered Dreamtime
    and under the purple coast of the Mograni
    and its trachyte west wall scaling in the sky
    I will swoop to the valley and Gloucester Rail
    where boys hand-shunted trains to load their cattle
    and walk on the platform, glancing west at that country
    of running creeks, the stormcloud-coloured Barrington,
    the land, in lost Gaelic and Kattangal, of Barandan.

Terence Brown

POETRY AND PARTITION: A PERSONAL VIEW

A curious partitionism has been affecting literary life in Ireland in recent times. Difficult to pin down but oddly pervasive nevertheless, a kind of poetic triumphalism in particular about the Northern poetic flowering (the term renaissance has to be avoided unless it can be defined at length). No single voice can be identified as prosecuting the cause of literary partition, but as a general critical tone, a note of local pride that can verge on self-congratulation, one senses a Northern condescension towards the South and towards Dublin in particular in a lot of what one reads and hears these days. And the South is trying to set the record straight about itself, thereby accepting the terms which Northern self-assurance has laid down. We have had Seán Dunne's *Poets of Munster*, as if to answer Ormsby's excellent and scrupulously adroit collection *Poets from the North of Ireland* (its title stylishly weaving its way through the Irish question) and to assert a Southern resurgence, and now along comes Sebastian Barry's *The Inherited Boundaries: Younger Poets of the Republic of Ireland* (solving the Irish Question by ignoring it?). And a young poet, Seán Lysaght, has recently published an article in *Poetry Ireland Review* (17) which employs the term, which one hears used in quite a lot of conversations these days, 'Southern poetry'.

The anthology wars haven't helped. Paul Muldoon's *The Faber Book of Contemporary Irish Poetry* was a decidedly Northern flourish, deftly, even cheekily, managed (seven poets from the North to three from the rest of the country) which excludes most notably Richard Murphy and Austin Clarke (though John Hewitt has also to abide Muldoon's question), while Thomas Kinsella's *The New Oxford Book of Irish Verse* can find space for Padraic Colum's piece of Irish Georgian bric à brac, 'The Old Woman of the Roads' (now there's a poem for the feminists to get after), but no place for W. R. Rodgers (whose erotic religious lyrics 'The Net' and 'Lent' would have complemented the Christian verse of the anthology's earlier pages) nor for John Hewitt (whose poem 'On the Difficulties of Translation' would have complicated in an important way the theme of translation and scholarship which runs through the book). Indeed Thomas Kinsella in the introduction to his collection delivers himself of the kind of dogmatic *obiter dicta* which must raise Northern hackles and induce angry counter-attacks, thereby intensifying the sense of division. He writes:

. . . it is clear already, with the most insistent of these, that it is in the context of a dual responsibility, toward the medium and toward the past, that Seamus Heaney's and Derek Mahon's poetry registers so firmly, rather than in any 'Northern Ireland Renaissance'.

The idea of such a renaissance has been urged for some time (with the search for special antecedents usually settling on Louis MacNeice) and this idea by now has acquired an aspect of official acceptance and support. But it is largely a journalistic entity.

What is wrong with this, it seems to me, apart from the slightly aggressive vagueness of its certitudes ('clear already', 'urged for some time', 'aspect of official acceptance and support', 'largely a journalistic entity') is that it seems to imply that poetry, to be significant, must register in the context of a responsibility assumed, compact of the medium and the past, whatever that might mean when you try to tease it out. Are such as Michael Longley and Paul Muldoon excluded and Seamus Deane, for example, included on the basis of such criteria? What does 'the past' mean in such a formulation? Why should any poet be required to concern himself with anything anyway, never mind assume responsibilities? And is it the Northern poet alone who has to be judged by this demanding if vague standard, for earlier Kinsella has granted that 'for the modern Irish writer' the tradition which has been retrieved and which provides 'a link with the significant past' can be ignored: 'this is merely an opportunity, and not a requirement'? So Valentin Iremonger can be represented by such a slight poem as his 'The Toy Horse' with its Audenesque manner and its Blakean moral, but Derek Mahon's 'Derry Morning' and his 'The Woods' are valued because 'the past is significantly present'. What price his 'An Image from Beckett' or 'Going Home', tantalizingly poised as they are in an imagined future?

It was not surprising of course that the Northern writers and their critics should have relished their successes of recent years. There was a long tradition of literary and cultural condescension about the North in the South of Ireland. Belfast (that city which Tom Paulin once declared 'holy ground') was customarily referred to in tones somewhere between a sneer and a guffaw. It induced even in the normally suave humanist Seán O'Faoláin a sense of horror when in his *An Irish Journey* he reported:*

One felt that nothing could, indeed, have possibly come of that nineteenth century Sunday sleep, and the red factories and the grey buildings, and the ruthlessness with which the whole general rash of this stinking city was

---

* To be fair to O'Faoláin, one must remember that he could be even-handedly offensive. Dublin also felt the lash of his tongue.

permitted to spread along the waters of the Lough but the bark of rifles and the hurtle of paving stones and the screams of opposing hates . . . All the hates that blot the name of Ulster are germinated here. And what else could be germinated here but the revenges of the heart against its own brutalization . . . There is no aristocracy — no culture — no grace — no leisure worthy of the name. It all boils down to mixed grills, double whiskies, dividends, movies and these strolling, homeless, hate driven poor.

That the North and Belfast might generate a poetic renaissance was in the early sixties when I first came to Dublin to university scarcely to be credited. Most of the lecturers in English at Trinity College exuded an air of Anglo-Irish self-satisfaction, giving one to know that a proper relief at having escaped barbarism for civilization was the only acceptable attitude to provincial origins. A Northern poet was somebody like Louis MacNeice, or W. R. Rodgers, who had had the good sense to get out. And as the Northern crisis rumbled into life, I remember the irritation which *The Irish Times* provoked in me by its patrician, patronizing tones as leader article and letter to the editor alike pontificated on all things Northern in the stereotypical terms for which the sobriquet 'Black North' is the easiest piece of shorthand. I often felt seriously alienated (preferring indeed the atavistic republicanism of *The Irish Press* to the more genteel and denigratory forms of Southern nationalism). I felt the South was impossibly petit-bourgeois, affecting the manners of a suave bourgeoisie without the performance and totally lacking in any appreciation of working-class reality (which for me meant Belfast). The *Dublin Magazine* was almost the only literary periodical on the scene and it exuded an air of the precious literary coterie. In the daily papers and in such intellectual organs as existed there was almost no interest expressed whatsoever in the scientific, technological and urban matters that were the daily concerns of many of my contemporaries who had read science at Queen's University in Belfast. The South seemed to be living on its cultural fat. In the bookshops there was plenty of English and American poetry but not much of the home-grown variety. And the only critical text on Irish literature by an Irish author that was easily available was Daniel Corkery's *Synge and Anglo-Irish Literature*, written over thirty years earlier.

Things were stirring however. By the late sixties the Dolmen Press was fully into its stride and I remember the excitement of reading Kinsella's *Nightwalker and Other Poems* (1968) which took the modern world for granted in its uncompromising way, putting paid to a lingering Celtic Twilight. In 1964 Kavanagh's *Collected Poems* had been published, with a second printing in 1968, making 'The Great Hunger' widely available for the first time. *Hibernia* was flexing its literary muscles in ways that were to make its review section the most exciting, opinionated and vital of anything going in the nineteen seventies. Flann O'Brien's *At Swim-Two-Birds* came back into print in paperback. MacNeice's *Collected Poems* came out in 1966. Beckett and Joyce were easily available from Calder, Faber and Penguin. Francis Stuart came home. So did Tony Cronin. There was new Irish writing every weekend in *The Irish Press*.

While all this was happening, the Northern poets were making their way. The London publishers, particularly Faber — whose Charles Monteith had a local interest in the province, began to take notice. Heaney's *Death of a Naturalist* (1966) led the way, appearing to the enormous critical acclaim which shed light on his fellow Northerners whose work was to appear, also in London, in fairly short order, Longley, Mahon, Simmons. The rest is, as they say, history.

It seems indisputable to me that these poets and their successors would not have received the attention they did had Northern Ireland remained at peace. In the context of a tragic two decades, their work has received much extra-literary attention (of which the recent *Newsweek* extravaganza was only the most vulgar example) and no one would grudge them that, were there not the risk that the cultural condition of contemporary Ireland as a whole might be seriously misrepresented and adversely affected. What I mean is this. The oft-canvassed view that the best Irish poetry at the moment is Northern ignores the fact that the North as a clearly defined cultural entity does not exist. Heaney has in fact written more of his poetry in Wicklow and Dublin than in the North and it shows in his preoccupations and development. Nevertheless, the assumption that the North has some kind of proprietary claim on him accounts for Sebastian Barry's recent disavowal of Heaney's influence on poetry from the Republic of Ireland (as if Heaney's *Station Island* was not itself in some senses poetry from that Republic). Montague is from the North, but is *The Dead Kingdom* a Southern or a Northern book? The question seems unanswerable to me; perhaps it cannot even be convincingly posed.

But the assumption that, as Sebastian Barry has it, 'Paul Muldoon, Tom Paulin, Gerald Dawe, Medbh McGuckian, and their confrères and consœurs, do not share a sensibility with these . . . poets of the South' leads to the following muddled claim:

> This is a poetical condition, not a political one, but in the politics of poetry it has had a bad effect: the work of the younger Northern poets has received a (due) prominence, partly because of its excellence, partly because of the Troubles, and partly because of Faber and Faber; and they have come to seem, in England and probably elsewhere, the full story, or most of it. They are a fine part of the story of an island, but they are no part of the story of the Republic.

In writing such a passage Barry is in fact indicating how much a part of the Republic's story the Northern thing has been. It has induced respect blended with a slightly envious sense of being overlooked', a determination to make that neglect good and a factitious, reactive, and not very convincing, partitionism. For of course Barry wants the story of the whole island fully recognized, the South's role in that poetic saga afforded its true place. For he would not be responding in this muddled, understandable, way if the poetic pace in the last decade had been set, say, by some odd chance in the Isle of Man, or indeed in Wales.

I don't believe myself that the island story in the last two decades is in fact so very complex, though within the broad outlines of the plot, complexities abound. I believe with Derek Mahon that what gave the Northern flowering its peculiar force and significance (alongside the extra-literary matter of the political crisis) was that 'it hadn't happened before' (*Poetry Ireland Review*, 14). This gave to many of those involved a sense of personal and collective significance and a group solidarity impossible, perhaps indeed undesirable, in a more richly composed cultural environment. In the south of Ireland, in Dublin in particular, the early and middle sixties represented something of a trough in the social and cultural life of a nation. The Revival and the immediate reaction to its imaginative hegemony had given way to the period of the literary diaspora (Beckett in Paris, almost unknown except as the author of *Waiting for Godot* until his Nobel Prize of 1969, MacNeice dead in England in 1963, John Montague and Francis Stuart also abroad). The sense of cultural decay that I remember of the mid-sixties in Dublin was only a change of gear as Ireland adopted to a social renewal that by the end of the decade was to have a generation of Irish young people in secondary school for the first time, their eyes firmly set on higher education. And the kind of social revolution, so frequently adduced as an agent in cultural and poetic change in the North (that famous Education Act of 1947) was set on foot. I believe we are beginning to see the effects of that at the moment as the children of the late sixties get into their adult stride. But for such as these, the Peter Sirrs, the Aidan Carl Mathews, the Matthew Sweeneys, the Sara Berkeleys, there is none of the attention that met a group of young poets in the Northern nineteen sixties who could be greeted as a nest of singing birds all the rarer for the notorious desolation of their habitat. Nor can there easily be that sustaining solidarity that engaging in something for the first time provides in an environment of assumed hostility. Rather the young poet, in Dublin say, must reckon with a city where books have always mattered, where the park statues challenge and rebuke, where the texts studied on a university course create a territory of the imagination compact of Swift's Liberties, Joyce's Nighttown and Beckett's Foxrock. He/she must cope with a literary capital oddly disabled by the commercial dominance of London (it is of course absurd that we seem still to expect Oxford or Faber to put an imprimatur on what we ought to be able to publish ourselves with equivalent authority), yet still a capital, that draws the ambitious, the talented and the charlatan alike, a city of legends and loveliness, of seedy provincial pretentiousness and of dedicated, often isolated, individual excellence. A city where at least three major writers now live and work and where literary politics are assumed to be as perplexing and destructive as any other form.

So in the end what I'm saying is that there is one literary Ireland, the partitionism of current debates and of the anthologies merely a stage in the cultural life of the island. As the Northern revival comes to be more taken for granted (and the sense deepens that such a thing cannot happen twice) its achievements will be set in a wider context of the literary history of the whole island. Then it will, I believe, come to be seen as a less isolated phenomenon (even as it will, I believe, come to be appreciated more fully by all) with its links to and analogies with literary activity in the rest of the country and with effects on that and affected by it. In time, the current forms of aggressive defensiveness will diminish in a country more composedly ready to welcome good writing from all its provinces. And by then there will be new tensions.

Gerald Dawe

THE BRIGHT HOUR

1. *Genesis*

The baize tablecloth is velvety with age
and the tassels torn. You lie on the sofa
watching Tottenham Hotspur walk all over Sheffield Wednesday.

Whitewash on the backyard peels in scales
and the slack weeps in its makeshift shed.
The rain drip-drops down gutters and drains.

Let there be another Ice Age, a God to speak with Moses,
the skies open up and rivers part —
this is where a young man finds himself,

at half-time making tea by the sink,
below glass-panelled presses that give back a look
of the great-grandfather on his mother's side.

2. *V-Day*

There you are, the one in the Military Band
seated on an X. A tram's welded to the spot
between air-raid shelter and that roman clock.

Behind, the City Hall is like a mausoleum
protected by Queen Victoria, soldiers of another war,
and the unperturbed masters always at the ready.

I wonder what you're playing and how many of those
who stand idly at the railings see what is coming —
after the Victory Parade and new estates go up,

after the children, when the doubts came,
shuttering through venetian blinds for the first time
one Saturday morning early.

The day steely blue, along Royal Avenue your woman is walking.
Photographers stand among the crowd like spies
prying on the future; but who cares, the music is beguiling.

3. *Men*

In the cabbage patch at the end of the garden
he drags stalks out and shakes them free of earth.
Shirts steep in a basin and everywhere

the light takes over from his silence —
the huge lough, hills on the far side brilliant,
and the houses, way above and down below us,

like tiers of an ancient settlement.
Across the way the woman's head is like a rag doll's,
her man's blootered and between the cupped hands she rolls,

window wide open, the cries operatic, his face bloody:
and wouldn't thank you, I hear them saying,
for interfering either.

4. *Pilgrim's Progress*

As for William Bailey Chartres,
sports editor with the *Ireland Saturday Night*,
we never met. I can only go by the pictures —

his dapper suit, the carnation and cane,
that inquisitive moustache.
Little man walking the town,

known by everyone and by none,
would we ever have got on, with your imperial wishes
and three-times-of-a-Sunday church?

5. *Mission Hall Under Demolition*

Not a sound from the place but pews
and a little air in shafts of light.
Who stood up there and what did he say,

the Bible held like a ledger?
His distracted flock are far from him
this bright hour, the houses behind

a ghostly site of wall-less rooms
and fireplaces that hang like cages.

6. *Happy Families*

They used to say, 'Don't sing before breakfast
or you'll cry before tea' —
great aunts at mockcrab sandwiches and medium-dry sherry.

In the front room their wisdom astounds me,
recitations and broken marriages,
'Uncle' Oswald vamps on the piano, like a seal

his bald head turns to face them all,
and bright Ethel, lovely Ethel,
smiles like an actress on *me*.

7. *Days-Off*

Sometimes I can see those roads
and inside the graven houses —
it's Sunday, a man appears and disappears

in the tree-light, the long walls curve
along sequestered avenues to our house
where Granny snoozes in her favourite chair

to 'Sing Something Simple' and out on the lough
a ship reverses engines and is silent:
'I'll tell you this and no more, something's going to give'.

8. *Fosterage*

From the mantelpiece Nell Gwynne touts
oranges and apples to an empty room.
You are in the front clipping a hedge back.

The woman next door sips her Austrian coffee
and hears The War all over again,
dressed like a man to avoid The Russians.

Two down Mrs MacAuley hosts some more kids,
the crucifix on her mottled chest
is a blade of silver caught in the sun.

9. *Loyal Sons*

                    i

We loll about the grass most afternoons.
Then one evening going home
Trevor asked for a light and the man

in the bus queue was you,
obliging, tired after a day's work,
and that was it —

an inconspicuous summer night,
our heads in the clouds.

                    ii

Lord, I am far gone.
The castle at Carrick dissolved into thin air.

Who's stepping ashore this time —
King Billy's horse munching hay
or a load of guns off some cranky trawler?

There's us, anyway, full as kites,
pissing up against the restored battlements.

Conor Kelly

LAMENT OF AN AGEING ROCK STAR

after Sir Thomas Wyatt

They flee from me, those big-boobed, tight-assed chicks
Who screamed and spat with lust each time I played
My punk-infested, self-taught guitar tricks,
Then threw their sodden underwear on stage.
All I ever wanted was to get laid.
And I did. In God knows how many rooms,
I sent my seed spitting towards countless wombs.

Once, on a world-wide tour, I played Bangkok.
After the show I prowled the backstreet dives
Seeking the ultimate sexual shock;
A naked whore smoked fags between her thighs,
Then pulled out razor blades from her insides,
A bloodless birth. As I crept to the door
A withered crone muttered, 'See more. You see more?'

I've seen all that I ever dreamt I would.
But everything has changed. Now no one buys
My records, no one knows my face and should
A chick from the old days undo my flies
And lead me towards her sweat-stained paradise,
I'd lie there afterwards and think, 'Aw, shit!
Is this what it all comes to? Is that it?'

Michael Foley

INSOMNIA IN THE AFTERNOON

1.
It's fragments of ancient Westerns I have shored against my ruin.
(Like nuke city mutants weird things haunt the derelict brain.)

Glenn Ford to Van Heflin, Glenn riding a train to captivity too
But relaxed, philosophical, stylish: *I bust outa Yuma before*.

2.
And still the fanatically grinning blind harmonica man
Plays with unflagging gusto on the Underground steps.
Blows into it, more like, his dance more a lurch.

Cheery childish sign: EX-SERVICE   WOUNDED IN ACTION   GOD BLESS

3.
Dark name-plates discreetly glow.
Sheets gently stir on the bulletin board.

Subdued controlled hum — like on board a great ship.
Superb craft and trained crew — going somewhere.

4.
It's the time of the project the marketing mix
(Knock on doors tout your wares laugh a lot kiss ass).

Morning. High on an inner wall
The sun placing calm parallelograms of gold . . .

5.
Mike you're OK. Make jokes and they'll
Beat your door down. Go back, friends.

It is easy to seem interesting
— But valuable secrets are scarce.

6.
It's a spell makes me seem a prince.
Break it and send me home
Cold silent ugly ecstatic alone.

Plop! A frog in dark pond slime: *profound resonance.*

7.
Instead the voices clear and strong
Resources Committee agreeing it has to get its skates on.

Firece and implacable opposition to the hegemony of essence!

Somewhere a broken king jerks off alone.

8.
It's a desert so arid they have to rein in.
'What could live here?' Burt questions, aghast.

Lee Marvin ponders, then gravely replies:
'Scorpions . . . *and men tempered like steel.*'

9.
Neither radical compassion nor sublime contempt.
Deserted the crag and unburdened the cross.

Kings, generals, presidents, film stars and whores.
We are all workers now, we all 'get on with the job'.

10.
But my briefcase of folders and memos
Has a book of poems, a novel and a high-fibre lunch.

Echo on, siren roar of the subsidized canteen!
I like to take my secret nourishment alone.

11.
In 'the enforced essential privacy of late individualism'
i.e. hunched, with hunted eyes, tensed for a knock.

Every now and then I make it all the way back home.
Welcome to Serenity   Population: One

12.
Where you can gaze past the kettle and the single chipped mug
To view of a great river basin
— A main drainpipe with tributaries on a wall of old stains.

But above that again the roofs. *Look up!*

13.
Functional and drab at ground level old buildings blossom on top
Into cupolas, minarets, ramparts, turrets, towers
Fantasies of belief and defiance surviving corrosive dirt.

Everywhere there are symbols of faith for the faltering heart.

14.
Though it's not vibrant colour or strong line
Draws the eye back to ordinary clouds.
They rage sometimes . . . mostly they drift.

I'm stupider — but I feel more.

15.
By the path of least resistance
To the garden of remembrance . . .

Decaff and a muesli bar. Darkening sky.

Someone else can arm-wrestle the taciturn gods.

16.
Old pros learn to lie on the ropes
Taking shots on the arms.

But with no hope of victory why go on?
Brain damage, happily, spares us such thoughts.

17.
O frictionless world of perfect spheres!
The iron laws of mathematics once ravished my soul.

Pewter light. Going home time soon.
How would it be to be smart again?

18.
To dispute with the masters on how to live
— Crag or Cross, Nietzsche or Christ?

On the long weary silent way home a sign:
Tudor Way leading to Cedar Grove Gleneagles Harmony Heights.

19.
Insubstantial vague light unsurprised unappalled
We blow back and forth through the shit storm of the world

Only settling at evening bizarre double life
Event-driven by day, couch potatoes at night.

20.
A large one — to put fire in the lukewarm innards
And tears in the dried-up eyes.

Drink and be dull again beyond confusion.
We're meant to get thick as we age.

21.
But the lady news readers are strong
Calm at the hour of desolation, spared our bodily decay.

I would like to serve one of them humbly
Hand-washing her pants with fanatical care.

22.
Again silence. Gold ingots pass the back window
Last train to the north.

Double glazing around us
Our bone china trembling is all we can hear.

23.
Sweet Christ, it is time! Return
And show us how to live in our world.

You get tired of disgust and fastidiousness
But it is hard for the infirm to affirm.

24.
Christ will never return. Only I know how truly he suffered
How truly he lived the grim fate of a man

Taking even male-pattern alopecia on himself
(*But the hairs of your head are all numbered* — Matthew 10:30).

25.
Send me a flawed human Muse marked by life.
I will kneel down and kiss her stretch marks

My eyes closed not in distaste but worship
The living braille traced out by rapt trembling hands.

26.
Sweet Muse, give me my great work
Love in the Polluted City

(Later to be a hit musical
Kiss Me Where it Smells).

Gerard Fanning

IS THIS A SAFE PLACE, OR WHAT?

Even the greatness of Beechey's journeys
Dims illegibly by the light in this cabin.
In the drowsy odour of kerosene
Fuse elements expose,
And in the dewy interludes
Where we built our seamless lives,
Tears dissolve the day.
As the boat slaps on its beaded moorings,
Cars thread the inlet slips
And two by two, frail magenta lights
Echo music down the bones of old darkness,
Setting off minute timbre bells,
That let us doze in the slippage of dreams.

We are shelved in the lea of the lough's great loves,
Tied to the wooden levee —
And the hurricane lamp sauntering on the imaginary bank
Could be Wolfe or Beechey
Pencilling the boils on Adelaide Rock.
But is this a safe place, or what?
Do our grieving mistresses still entreat *The Times*,
Pretending one more lost soul
Is important in their lives?
Or are we always monitored somewhere,
A blip failing to return from the lakes
For the start of another week?

Martin Mooney

THE LOST APPRENTICE

He arrived late and was turned away from the shift.
Blue light seethed on the road outside the factory,
there was no bus, and the streets were unfamiliar
with their skin-coloured shops and pavements sprouting grass.
He probed his grievance (was it his fault that today
was already this hot, or that he'd missed his lift?)
and followed the trail of a slow green backwater
towards distant traffic snoring on the overpass . . .
He idly cursed his siphoned luck, and was last seen
under the high bricks of a derelict warehouse,
asking directions perhaps . . . When we found his gear
his new tools had rusted; but the bubble of air
in his spirit level was where it should have been;
his milked and sugared tea was warm in its thermos.

John Montague

UP SO DOUN

I open underwater eyes
and the great lost world
of the primordial swims before me
a living thicket of coral
a darting swarm of fish

(or the moon with an apron
of iceblue tinted cloud,
rust bright Mars or Saturn's
silvery series of spheres)

how quiet it is down here
where wandering minnows explore
the twin doors of my eyelids
lip silently against my mouth

(how still it is up here
where I dance quietly to myself,
stilt across a plain, hardly
disturbing the dust on the moon's shelf)

I had forgotten that we live between
gasps of, glimpses of, miracle;
once sailed through the air like birds,
walked in the waters like fish.

PACIFIC LEGEND

In their houses beneath the sea
the salmon glide, in human form.

They assume their redgold skin
to mount the swollen stream,

Wild in the spawning season;
a shining sacrifice for men.

So throw back these bones again:
they will flex alive, grow flesh

When the ruddy salmon will return
a lord to his underwater kingdom.

Frank Ormsby

A NORTHERN SPRING

CLEO, OKLAHOMA (1948)

'I knew he'd be a big shot'. My mother's words,
in the third person, as though I'd already gone.
She stepped back through shadows, relinquished me
to sun and bunting, a street of cheers and smiles
from there to the depot. The Mayor struck a pose
for a possible statue,

but the bandsmen stayed in tune until I waved
from the steps of the Greyhound. Already I belonged
to somewhere else, or nowhere, or the next
photograph. The Mayor spread his arms
and had trouble with History.

There was dust everywhere. It was too late to cry
or too early. I heard the Mayor say:
'We've had History before now, folks, in this town.
There'll be more History soon.'

DAYTON, OHIO

I watch for them in the mornings. If they are free
they slip from the rhododendrons. George takes the reins,
Chuck rolls cheroots and hunkers on the boards
among my father's milk-cans.
The cart squeals on. They read to me as we go —
letters from home, the girls of Dayton, Ohio.

In the light evenings, when we kneel to pray,
my mother watches me. Her face is sad.
She hears, through murmured sleepy litanies,
names from a scuffed atlas drum in my head:
Gdansk, Archangel and lately, like a slow
train in a distant tunnel, Dayton, Ohio.

A CROSS ON A WHITE CIRCLE

A cross on a white circle marked a church
and a cross on a black circle a calvary.
Reading the map too hastily we advanced
to the wrong village and so had gone too far
and were strafed by our own fighters.
In the time it takes to tell Bretteville sur Laize
from Bretteville le Rabet, twelve of us died.

MAIMED CIVILIANS, ISIGNY

We did not see the wreckage or hear the cries.
The train had stopped smoking around its dead
somewhere back in the tunnel, the planes had gone
when we got to the tunnel entrance and found them there,
civilian casualties from the core of disaster.
We thought of ourselves, and chose to think of them
as grounds for optimism —
the men would master crutches, the bandaged girls
marry in wheelchairs.

First words, first rites, the work of consolation,
Calvados and chocolate on their scorching tongues.

FROM THE GERMAN

When I delivered the grenade cleanly through the slit
of the gun emplacement,
I buried my face in seaweed and covered my ears.

Today, forty years after, I hear it explode
in a wheelchair-veteran's book of reminiscences
'translated from the German',
and know for the first time what ended there:
Walter's dyspepsia, Heinrich's insufferable snores,
big Hofmann's correspondence course in Engineering.

And tonight, oddly alive to me as they never were,
though forty years dead, elusively they rise
to baffle grief with an inviolable presence,
some treacherous gift of innocence restored
I cannot believe in and would not refuse.

AT THE JAFFÉ MEMORIAL FOUNTAIN,
BOTANIC GARDENS

1
Lipman and Cohen, butchers, Hercules Lane,
Manuel Lightfoot, Smithfield, 'taylor and Jew'.
Names in the old leases, gone to ground
since the year the first sailing-ships from Europe
breezed up the lough.

Wolff, Jaffé, Weinberg, purposeful merchant Jews
of Hamburg and Jessnitz. Later the refugees
on sleepless treks from places where they had grown
and spoke the language,
who improvised a style of making do
from trunks and travelling bags and the will to prosper.

2
What might they leave their children,
the dead Jews of Lübeck, Lublin,
packed in Antrim clay?
Faith and unhappy memories?
The desert flower that blooms after loss,
its red heart colouring obstinately against the urge,
insistent, inward, of the petals' bordering dark:
griefs not to be assuaged, the carrier blood's
murmur of vengeance?

3
A wind off the Lagan strays across open ground
at the Jaffé Memorial Fountain.
Half summerhouse, half temple, a room without walls,
its tenants river-smells, in-transit birds,
the dung-and-sawdust ghost of the Circus Hofmann
on a European Tour,

it stands for the ones who earned their monuments,
the ones whose lives were quiet streams hidden
for centuries in the foundations.
I think of dispersals, settlings, the random inheritors
of dispossession who kept an image of home;
of Solly Lipsitz walking his labrador
in the streets of South Belfast,
Chaim Herzog's birthplace on the Cliftonville Road.

Harry Clifton

THE WALLED TOWN

If I lived where there were still wolves
Or the myth of wolves, my town would have walls,
My neighbours, instructing themselves
On fresco cycles, like televised government,
Would never read or write at all,

Too lazy for politics, just as we are today
When a Nordic motorcyclist, the first one for ages,
Fills the square with his terrible horsepower
And seems, by his very attitude, to enquire
'Did Frederick Barbarossa come this way?
And how could his army, collective as fate,
Pass through so tiny a gate?'

He looks and he listens. Dirty linen, and catcalls.
A pretty divorcee in a miniskirt
Who deals in antiques, and raises a child on her own.
And footballs, the thud of footballs
On the inside walls of limit, of the known . . .

What does he see in us? Something innate
Like his own lost childhood? Could he live among us
Praying to a cardiac muscle on a plate,
Our sanctified relic? Or is it our view of the plain
He wants to commandeer, for his next campaign?
Could he satisfy, if he took our women as wives,
His hunger for integral life?

Michael Coady

REVOLUTIONS

In nineteen twenty
his father
toted a gun
and a dream

which he took on the run
through ditches and barns
before he went
into wallpaper.

The son in his turn
took over the wallpaper
keeping the shop
as he found it

and doing three rounds
of the town park
every night
whatever the weather.

You could set
your watch
to his nightly
revolutions.

Frank McGuinness

LULLABY

for Christopher Morash

The man in the moon
Looked into your eyes

Sleep sleep sleep child

The birds of the air
Came from Paradise

Sleep sleep sleep child

The man in the moon
Looks into your eyes

Sleep sleep sleep child

PRISONER OF WAR

I must kiss the silver enemy.

I remember home, wife, child — family.

I remember room, bed, hand — come to me.

I will kiss the silver enemy.

SISTER ANNE BRESLIN

These days I move between sleep and dream.
Dreaming is easier on the bones.
I swim through my sleep to a strange rock.
The rock's in the ocean, the ocean's in my bones.

I am turning into wind, into pink water.
Wind and water took a vow of silence.
I rock in the bed between sleep and dream,
Trying to remember when there was silence.

Noise is a word away from nuisance.
I am a nuisance but I once was water.
I wore down my fingers to the touch of stone
And built my house from the self-same rock.
Fingers to stone, noise to nuisance —
Dreaming is easier on the bones.

John Hughes

NAGASAKI

I arrive in the city
to sell the skull
of Saint Thomas Aquinas
to a retired policeman.

A passer-by tells me to panic.

I prise open the nearest door,
climb to the third floor,
and walk in on a geisha
listening to herself on the radio
describe how she navigated by the stars
out of her dead mother's womb.

She asks why she sweats blood
when I touch her where I shouldn't

I wake up clinging onto
the second horseman of the Apocalypse
in his disguise as the tail-fin
of a high-altitude American bomber.

THE ROYAL ASYLUM

The wind blows a newspaper into the gardens
at the rear of the Royal Asylum's A-wing.
The Empress Dowager picks it up
and reads that her son has declared war
on a country she has never heard of —
there is a huge photograph of him
sitting in the shade of an oddly familiar tree.

She buries the paper in the compost heap
and turns her attention back
to the felling of the oak
five successive emperors hanged themselves from.
Her son is perched high in that tree,
waiting for it to give him the order
to surrender unconditionally.

JEREMIAD

In such troubled times as these
small wonder there is a crow perched on her forehead,
and that her mother and five brothers
put her death down to the fact
she always dressed in black.

I begin my investigation into her murder
by erecting a gallows
for a heretical hare and a blasphemous stoat,
and reprieving them when I remember
I am in a cell for the insane

The next thing I am shooting piebald horses
in Santa Rosa, New Mexico,
on the eighteenth of March 1917.
I am called Roland Barthes
and I am about to step on a scorpion of the same name.

Robert Johnstone

THE BOOK OF INVASIONS

There ought to be compensations,
If silence and darkness are death,
if rock allows no translation

between us and all the bright earth,
if God is this burden of stone,
hungry as sponge for a sense of worth,

leaky and fissured as limestone,
if our language can only show,
in daylight, when we're not alone,

chronicles of quarrels, yet we know
to expect the unexpected:
a lamp is lit, a page glows,

in the attic inside my head
you are writing out the names of orchids.

Brendan Kennelly

THERE CAME A PLEASANT RAIN

It was one of those conversations
You can only have when walking
So that afterwards you think
It almost didn't happen.
A man with bleeding knuckles
Staggered up to us and said, 'The bastards
Done me out o' fifteen quid
An' beat me up! Why don't ye hit me too!'
We didn't and walked on
Past drab houses like thinkers
Thinning in the sun.
There came a pleasant rain.
Andy went on about death
And I almost understood.
His eyes drank in the living.
'I might live in London, Paris,
But the house in Strand Road
Keeps me shackled here.
I'm a knapsack man at heart.'
Past the railings where the girl
From the country was blown up
By a twilight bomb,
Past the Lincoln and Kennedy's
To the threshold of Psychology.
'It's towards the building of a faith.
I believe in the struggle to believe.'
The green door opens like a book.
He goes laughing up the steps.
'Send me that oul' poem. Good luck.'

Peter Fallon

IF LUCK WERE CORN

They have found a baby in a lake
not far from here. Slowly the pieces fit.

Her parents slept in the next room
and a girl gave birth. Nine months
their daughter grew and carried
on her own. They didn't know.
They were in the dark.

What happened her
was always meant to happen
to another, somewhere else,
reported in small type,
whispered for a while.

If luck were corn
you'd thresh hers with a whip.
The baby died.

She thought she'd hide the swaddling clothes
in Hanlon's idle byre, the body in the lough,
and carry on. Who'd know?
There wouldn't be a word about it.
No one would be a bit the wiser.

Flesh of her flesh, bone of her bone —
her brother found the body.
Fishing. He didn't know. He told the guards.
The rest you know yourselves. The rest
was in the papers. An inquest. Enquiries.
The question of charges.

That was one week's talk
on Herbstreet's step,

the usual sympathy:
And she only a child herself,
and wasn't that a cross to bear;
and the common savagery:
Boys will be boys . . . and girls will be mothers,
she has cried the laugh she had last year.

Till Jimmy stopped their say.
He said, You're great, just great.
You'd walk the length of Sheelin,
you'd carry water in a riddle,
but if you drained the ponds
in your back yards
you'd find more than you bargained for.
You'd not let on,
but the like of that's gone on to yours
since the year of one.

Andrew Elliott

RODIN'S HEADACHE

*But there was one muse/mistress above all others, Camille Claudel . . . Unlike the rest
she was herself a gifted sculptor and she had a mind and desires of her own. Rodin met her
in 1883 when she was twenty and a student. The relationship lasted fifteen years; her face
and form appear repeatedly in the works of those years — including the nude studies at the
top of* The Gates of Hell.

Edwin Mullins

Holding his head in her hands like a phrenologist
She is feeling through that meagre cap of hair
For all the little bumps of his genius — the skull
Beneath the skin, the softness of his temples,
The little things he never notices or bothers with —
Until now, with a flick of his wrist, he waves her off

Without thinking; back into the middle of their studio
With its marmoreal walls and its windows rattling
Under the enormity of a tumultuous Paris sky
In which the clouds are split in only one place
By a sleeve of gold and from out of which
Like the benevolent right arm of God

Showing off the work of his child to another God
A single shaft of light shines in upon the statues
Of *Balzac* or *The Thinker*, gilding them like saints,
But in doing so leaves her among the shadows and draughts
Her mind is weaving into a shawl that she drapes
Around her shoulders, and clutches at her throat

For the cold comfort it can give her as she squats
In the dawn of a new century of Art, her fingertips
And toes and the tingling tightness of each nipple
Ossifying under his eyes as they probe her
To the core, before he picks up his tools
And goes on chiselling into marble.

PEEPSHOW

In resurrection they neither marry,
nor are they given in marriage, but
are like the angels of God in Heaven.

                              Mark 12:25

Lying there with you Hannah under the antique quilt
We'd bought ourselves for a special Christmas treat
And as my mind dissolved into *le petit mort* —
Bits drifting off like islands through the cosmos
That was pitch-dark and tingling with starlight —
I found myself suddenly to be standing with my hands
Cupped to the window of a nineteenth-century cottage
In what — for some reason or another — I knew
To be a colony of The Shakers; the air and the sky
So stiff with light that I had difficulty at first
Seeing in through the small square panes
Encrusted with salt off an ocean, a glitter of crystals
That dissolved with my breath until I could see in
To where there were women at work —
Some old, some young, some in between —
Everything motionless but for the spritely flickering
Of needles through the scraps of common cloth,
All so dead and creepy Hannah it jumped my mind awake!

And yet, when I'd recovered, gone out to the loo
And come back in relaxed and drained,
I couldn't help but wonder if any of those women
Really had in the end ever made it to the life beyond —
As all of them must most certainly have expected to.
In fact Hannah I wondered if they had been watching us
Just then, imagining them all perhaps grown young again
And crowded like the milkmaids in *Tess*
To a tear in the threadbare clouds of Heaven,
Each jostling with her elbows, their wings in the way,

As under lamplight and a hundred years on
We cavorted over their labour of love;
Two bedroom gymnasts with our heads full
Of *The Joy of Sex* and with no thoughts at all
For God or Piety . . . two playmates
Whose only interest — unashamedly — was in the spilling
Of our juices so wantonly that that patchworked square
Of fading work we'd inherited from an age
More straight-laced than our own would be stained
By us for all times with little Maps of Ireland.

Tom MacIntyre

69

my anus juices
like the grape,
tongue and teeth
I tell flavours,
the room smells
of the forest floor.

'There was a book
owned a tall book-case
of my childhood —
Girl of the Limberlost.'

She inclines
a verdant eye.
'Never read it,
no one read it'.
Good steady pace
a red thread
travels the wall
above the mantelpiece.

'*Girl of the Limberlost.*
Cover could've been
ash-blue or dove-grey
or, could be, maroon.'

The book drifts
from shelf to shelf.
'How you doin'?'

Her belly smiles.
The book-case gleams.

We lie there
deep in clover.

Matthew Sweeney

DIVERS AT THE LAURENTIC

The divers have left the Laurentic
to the crabs and flatfish.
Already they're past Malin Head.

And now they'll veer South,
along the East coast, or West,
until Ireland disappears.

For three weeks their dredger
sat in our bay, while they
felt around in the wreck

that settled there in 1917,
courtesy of a German mine
or a snorkelling U-boat.

They know they're not original.
They have predecessors
who, forty years before,

broached the Laurentic's cargo
of gold bars
to the tune of five million.

They know a sixth remained
and it's now on the move
under their unknown flag

while at a wake, on land,
men spend the night
talking about sunken gold.

Conor O'Callaghan

THE HISTORY OF RAIN

These are the fields where rain has marched
from time to time. This is the year that
is measured in consistent downpours, until it spills
on the foreground of a basin covered, the tone of dull enamel.

In the half rush to shelter these unripe blackberries
and woodbine drifts at the level crossing distract a generation
that knows the probability of sitting through August, the blight

of reticence raising a month past an average fall.
Or that later sees the lost patch momentarily bleached
as if by an hour of recorded sun and the history of light.

In the photo of nineteen forty is my granduncle with his uncle.
Late that tall summer they fold their sleeves and step
into the front yard to watch a swarm of veined clouds pass.

It is as if the full world could still end here,
away from the horizon of more populated storms.

Forgetting that soon they will run back to the house
and the wireless babbling, and listen to the gentle clapping
on slate and galvanised roofs where the sky begins,
suddenly uncertain at the border of an even longer decade.

THE DREAM OF GERONTIUS

There is a story about Edward Elgar,
the composer. How for weeks
in the middle of a harsh winter
he found insomnia, silence and sickness
the only prayers he could hear.
And the evening he returned to work

until *The Dream of Gerontius* was complete.
Having heard voices outside,
and, in falling sleet,
helped a neighbour bind
a blizzard of sheep
away from darkness and the road.

In a letter to a friend
some years later, he seemed
moved by the ease of it all,
by the passing sounds and the ease
with which each note fell,
almost taken to be real.

He said he thought the simple
movement was the same
as that from night-blindness to understanding shapes.
As each time, finished in the drawing room,
he would blow against a lamp
and find himself uncertain in a pallid gloom.

Until the last shapes of his age
separated, and night snowed
against the mirror, the cream drapes,
the notepaper, the piano,
the lampshade,
the mantelpiece, the bay window.

Michael Gorman

SHE ELOPES WITH MARC CHAGALL

Across fields of rotting cabbages
That nobody wanted to buy
The girl I loved went flying
To the other end of the sky.

Up she flew
Over the enormous satchels
Of the homebound primary scholars;
Over the disused dancehalls
And empty factories;
Over the wandering dogs
In the tinker encampments;
Over the five upturned wheelbarrows
Outside Grogan's Hardware Store
On Main Street, Swords;
Over the fleet of Escort vans
Selling fruit, fuel and vegetables
On the Dublin–Belfast road.

When I went to the doctor, he said
'In a week or two, it'll be Easter,
The sun will shine after tea,
You'll be yourself again,
Sure of who you are,
Clear as a bell,
With all the time in the world
To find someone else.
In the meantime,
Should that scalding sensation
In the pit of your stomach persist,
Try writing some verse.'

Tra-la-la, la-la,
When it's springtime in Ireland,
The fog comes in from the sea,
The birds revive in the mornings,
The earth smells sweet under me.

At night the Rockabill foghorn
Summons her back from the dead,
I remember her cheeks in blossom,
The way that she turned her head.

Easter came and went.
Despite the quack's advice,
I'm no better now
Than when I began.
I torment myself
By chanting their names:
Maggie, Maggie,
Marc Chagall.

GOING THE DISTANCE

Memory is the only thing we get from existence.
Delmore Schwartz

He was not content to see light moving
Or to follow the pattern of birds in flight,
No, it had to be, 'Who am I tracking the light?',
'What's up with the birds?'

A shrink might put it down to pleasing mother —
Entering his school expenses in a ledger
Waiting to reclaim her share,
Insisting that he study in the kitchen
To save electricity.

Or to wifey number one, Gertrude Buckmann,
Parading neglect,
Writing Miserare Me on hospital windows.

Or to the general company he kept.

Happy Delmore is meeting John Berryman
In the Metropolitan Museum of Art.
He has just been invited to tea
By Mr W. H. Auden.
When jealous Henry hears the news,
He faints right there and then
In the corner, under Picasso's blues.

The others, Randall Jarrell, Roethke, Cal,
Were hardly what you'd call a bag of fun.
But Delmore had the dirt on everyone.

Young Princess Elizabeth visited Japan
To receive instruction in fellatio.
Eliot was compromised into marriage.
Punting at Oxford, he halted, by a quiet spot
Near Cherwell. When Vivienne implored
him to 'Put the pole in, Tom',
Thomas misunderstood, half-heartedly complied
And, later, felt obliged.

Sure that wifey number two
Was having an affair
With, who else, Nelson Rockefeller,
Delmore entertained a young woman.
Christmas, she brought a tinsel tree.
Thinking it wired for explosives,
He doused it in the bath.

In this photograph of him
Sitting on a park bench,
He looked utterly mad.
Eyes of unfocused pain,
That kind of fear
Which comes from nowhere
And shreds the heart.
A tabloid at his feet,
The tale of some forgotten heiress.
I see on today's paper

An Australian, aged 41,
Has been found dead
In a field near Castleblaney.
His body was covered in an old rug
And some plastic caping.
An open suitcase of personal belongings
Lay beside him in the field.
For the past three years
He lived rough, slept upright
In a shoe-shaped box-car
built, to specification, by a local firm,
Fastened to a pillar at The Old Louth Hospital
Across from Dundalk Garda Station.

Maybe, Delmore, after all,
there is no blame,
Not even America.
Out of what Cal called
'The chicken-hearted shadows of the world',
Exotic failure creeps as frequently
As does, the bitch, success.

Go on, say it, start again.
'What, in your opinion, constitutes success?'
'And what is failure? . . .'
'What, precisely, did the suitcase contain?'

BELHAVEL LAKE (1896): THE OLD STORY

That Sunday,
Father brought me down
To the Montgomery place
Near Belhavel Lake,
When they were all away.
It was full of furniture, inside,
With pictures on the walls.

You might have heard tell
Of the Belhavel Trio,
The famous Leddy Brothers.
They played all over.
London, Boston, New York.

As he lifted me up,
The sun was shining.
I'd never seen pictures before.

The place was knocked, soon after.
Men came from the North
And carted the stones away.

'Footballer down,' she shouts
At the playpen, 'Footballer down.'

But the young went away.
The Rifles and Roper,
Wild Wisdom, Mick Greaney,
What chance had they?

Ah, you're a rogue
And I'm another.
You'll hang by the rope
And I'll hang by the rubber.
Weren't that crowd badly
Carting the stones away?

The rubber'll break
And I'll be saved
But you'll be hanged forever.

Boys, Oh Boys, Oh Boys.

Michael O'Loughlin

SNAPSHOTS FROM JEWISH AMSTERDAM

1. *The Wibautstraat*

It's years since this city froze.
The water is soft and stinking,
the tourists' boats circle aimlessly.

In the evenings I emerge
from the city's watery maze
like a weevil from a cheese

to stand here near your monument:
a four-lane highway
out to the suburbs

where I too could have been born
in the resurrected '50s
to hopeful parents

in public parks
holding us up like offerings
to shiny new Kodaks

and in the evenings,
kicked a ball with Johann Cruyff
down endless concrete summers.

Now I loiter and listen
for the whirr of angels' wings
the screech of diamond on diamond.

Nightly, grey water sluices
through my veins while I wait
for the first brittle grin of ice.

2.   *The Poetry and Pathos of Social Democratic Architecture*

The trick is to make red brick
perform like natural stone, to build
the diamond city that lives in the blood,
that wants to crystallize
in words and acts
but so often settles back
smouldering, like lumps
of half-burnt coal on the landscape.
Fuck Hegel. This is different.
This is the diamond we are born with
or better, the diamond we are
no matter how softly accoutred
the head gnawing itself
in hunger, like a hard flame.

3.   *The Diamond Workers*

An obvious one. Saved,
like the best wine, only till last

they did what they had always done
until, on the day of the last razzia,

they stood with their arms in the air
and let the diamonds trickle down

to form a pool of salted light
in which they stood, stranded.

Later, a soldier gathered them up
with a sweeping brush.

4.   *Max Beckmann in Amsterdam, Winter 1944/1945*

The road from one day to the next
crosses a narrow bridge
across the Amstel river,

takes him through the emptying streets
rehearsing the operas
of the future.

The winter is hungry for men
its swollen sky
and gluttonous light.

Like ambulant masscards,
the people he passes are ringed
with icy black auras.

At the zoo,
the hippo floats
in the foul water

like the world's sum total
of intransitive verbs.
His mind full of hippo,

Beckmann feasts his brush
on Quappis' thighs, and waits
for the squadrons of platitudes
to arrive at the City Gates.

5.   *Near the Portuguese Synagogue, Winter 1990/1991*

Hell has frozen over
and the children skate upon it,
their steel carves the ice
into a jewel of perfect absence.
So let the diamond fall from your hand,
leave it uncut,
a raw fragment of stone in the heart:
let the business-like dusk reveal
a box of left-behind light.

Seán Dunne

A SHRINE FOR LAFCADIO HEARN, 1850-1904

Like Hokusai painting on rice-grains,
He tried to trap Japan in a story:
His one good eye so close to the page
He might have been a jeweller with a gem.

So much to tell: kimonos and cranes,
Cemeteries to stalk at evening, slow
Shoals of candles like souls
Along rivers beneath a massive moon.

Even the sound of sandals on a bridge
Stayed in the mind for an evening,
Matching the shadow of fishermen
On still waters: a painted print.

Or a face smiling to hide its grief,
The touch of passing sleeves part
Of a plan that maps the future,
A heron seeking the heights on a wall.

Every act with its own ancestry.
He saw the singular made special:
A solitary spray in a vase
Far from childhood's opulent wreaths.

Loneliness ended in Matsue: that raw
Pain no longer gnawing like the Creole
Songs on a sidewalk in New Orleans.
Instead he heard a flute's clear note.

He was a lantern drifting from the shore,
Dissolving like the tone of a struck bell.
Sipping green tea in Tokyo, he heard
Ghost stories from an impossible past

And died past fifty from his Western heart.
Afterwards, he was a story still told, set
Firmly as rocks in a Zen garden.
Incense burns near cake at his shrine.

In the sound of sandals on a bridge
I hear him sometimes, or catch him
In the swift calligraphy of a scroll,
Smooth curve of a lacquered bowl.

A breeze through a bamboo-grove,
His memory passes for an instant.
Snow falls on his grave and on plum-blossom.
He is fading like a fisherman in mist.

John Goodby

THE BLACK SWAN

I

The only sound, Gavita, is interminable strumming
rain at this hacked green circumference. It falls leadenly,

sheer until the hour before sunset. Then a drenched soloist
in the *macas*, some inconsolable insect's *veh, veh, veh,*

is the unscratchable itch of the world. One still, small voice
slowly fires up a million. I listen. I eat more rum.

Rain-forests are bad Gothic revival; ebony, palm,
balsa, star-apple, plantain, clerestories tackled

with lianas, bristling and vinous. Lordly *madrinos*
soar above the darkness, canopied in a last bloodied light

(as light dies, so spittoon-augurs arrive bearing beef tea,
swabs, indignities, float me free of this hammock. As if

I might live they bundle me indoors before dewfall, before
the moon-shadow of the jaguar wavers across the stream).

In the twilight factory, moth-thickened and camphorous,
my half-corona draws to a coal through its blood-filter

wheezing stickily; *veludosas vozes, vozes
velados*, velar and labiodental fricatives

bittersweet on the teasing, peeled tongue. They unglue
my lips to kiss the rain-glazed, vegetable heart of death.

The veranda roof drips its aftermath of black consonants.

II

What is 'white', anyway, but vowelled apologias? Fatuous,
operative howlings at a tubercular moon?

Why should these hands — made to harvest stars — spider among
files, railway timetables, the bad debts of humanity?

Slave prodigies are groomed by their fathers' owners to trace
the retreat of black-letter armies across the drifted page

of Europe; discern soon enough in their spittle-and-cuff-
burnished mirrors the heritage of the orang utan,

the animalistic and rapacious leer of the ape.
I echoed the mocking papal laughter of Hackel, embraced

the creative mindlessness of the egg. I would hate white,
the elementary magnolia, Darwin's first flower,

the drained lips editing my speech. That gossiped 'his affairs
with white women should have made a man of his colour proud'.

We would breed a race of *black übermenschen to avenge*
the 'Goat' and 'Monkey' of their Panassian barber-sharps.

But I am Lucifer, the Trismegistus. I eclipse
the senile boredom of their heaven as clotted flies fume

and rumour around Alexandria's torched libraries,
swarm from Babel and Babylon and Carthage sown with salt,

Lord of the Flies. For my soul is badly bent to Africa.

THE SHINING PATH

If shit was gold, the poor would
be born without arseholes.
Peruvian Proverb

When Abismael dropped the Old Testament s
he became a Horseman of the Apocalypse
claiming descent from Inca Tupac Amaru III
with dislikes that spared only Albanian olive oil
and Chinese cashews. A Mormon in a lace cravat,
he scorned Che Guevara as a 'chorus girl' —

'We will transform the dialectic of Peru.
Perez — I use his mother's name because Perez
has a mother's mind — doesn't know he's in a war.
A monkey who dresses in silk remains a monkey.
We opened with Washington Irving on Mohammed
and will close with the first two acts of *Macbeth*.

Remember: Ayacucho translates as *Corner*
of the Dead. Once within the Indian Stain
you will be cursed as a *pistaco*, milk-drinking
wielder of a white knife under that Burberry,
trimmer of Indian torsos to melt down and grease
the wheels of your European industries.

Beware of an exploding child, dog, duck, donkey.
If you hear sounds like popping maize behind prison
walls, just whistle 'Pepito de mi corazón'
and walk on. If you are caught, my name is Shampoo.
I wash brains. They will sever your head and feet
and sew them back on backwards to prevent pursuit.'

IN THE TROPICAL HOUSE

Butterflies seemed to hatch behind ears,
from hair — the Constable, Paris Peacock,
the Lacewing — as we strayed under dripping glass,
you perhaps seeking a White Tree Nymph,
me in attendance on a Bamboo Page.

They might have conjured any possibility
Magellan's Birdwing, Dark-veined Tiger,
Common Mormon, the Postman and Mocker
Swallowtail as they lazily settled on leaves
or opened their books of hours in the shade

although the feather-pronged moths would never feed
in the adult stage. Despite their eye-spots
and snake-headed wings, the Giant Atlas,
the Monarch and the Indian Moon Moth
could look to no future except love and famine.

Was the Owl Butterfly a butterfly at all?
You might have been that Painted Jezebel on the bridge
above the toy waterfall. I consider it, still
alighting from or on those harder names;
Red Pierrot, Sulphur Emigrant, the Great Duffer.

Thomas Kinsella

TWO FRAGMENTS

Dura Mater

I
A potato smell came out from the kitchen door,
and a saucepan smell, with a piece of meat boiling.

She came along the passage in her slippers
with a fuzz of navy hair, and her long nails
held out wet out of the washing water.

Come here to me. Come here to me, my own son.

Stiff necked, she put up her pursed mouth
at her grown young — whatever idea she had of it
in the half-laugh and the bad temper in her eyes.

Will you look at him. How do you stick him at all.

And offered, and withdrew, a Cupid's Bow puckered,
closed lids, a cheek of withered silk,
the little smell of her hairline powdered over.

II
The withheld kiss returned
onto her stone forehead. Dura Mater.

To take it, a seal on her stone will,
in under the screwed lid.

III
He came out, stooping forward
with hands held down before him
still joined in the gesture of prayer,
his feet heavy but employed with care.

The sides of hair receding around his scalp
were moistened and dyed dark,
the face downcast,
the eyes soft but emphatic.

The air was filled with music.

*

He stepped into the funeral coach outside,
with quick irritated hand gestures
repeated without meaning,
a motiveless urging in the uplifted, inviting voice.

IV
I entered the lobby at the hour appointed,
a crowded place, low-ceilinged and obscure.
I found the place to wait, beside a great
illuminated plant in a stone pot.

Sudden and silent, he was there beside me.

I have come to speak with him, after so long,
because I have a question. But first to our places.
The instruments to hand on either side,
seated opposed, we settled down and ate.

I put the question. Certainly. Of course.
I am sorry you had to ask. There should be something
next week in the post, or the week after.
I'll see to that. And we must keep in touch.

Iain Crichton Smith

IN THE AUTUMN

The music of poetry is the music of life.
'I do not know what I am doing here,'
she says. 'Clean glasses surround me.
The children have gone to school and I am alone.
My husband is out at work and I am alone.
What shall I do with myself in this autumn,'
she says, looking out at the trees whose leaves are yellow.
'The glasses stand up clear but I do not feel clear.
My head has a fog in it and a frost also.
If I were like the trees I would not feel this
useless ache which surrounds me and distorts me.
The music of poetry is the music of life.
This autumn has the pang of departing wings.'

FANTASIES

She stares at the tree,
mindlessly.
'My husband locked me in the byre.
I shall run away to the town
where I shall buy a new ring.
And I shall have my hair done,
though I have no money.'
This is all fantasy
on a clear day
among the rich swish of leaves
above her ruined head.
The tree is stationary
under the blue sky
though the leaves are like coppery rings.

Her husband says,
'She always wishes to run away
and as for our pension
she spends it on trash and wine.'
Ah, her head shakes like leaves
but the tree, fixed in fact,
endures beyond fantasies.
Her husband she stood
in the shelter of once,
before these images
sang in her head,
and before the byre
was a prison of wood,
and before the cattle died,
unmilked, unfed.

THE CRY

All night I thought I heard
a terrible crying
till the cockerel stood up in his spurs
as ordered by the sun.

My bed was warm
but it shook with that crying
that crossed the acres of dew.

The train is setting off
to the bare country
where the chimneys are thickening
with the smoke of bones.

The cries were those of cattle
weeping among the wood,
knowing that the rays of the sun
would be blood-stained axes.

Michael Longley

PERDIX

after Ovid

In the wings of that story about the failure of wings
— Broken wings, wings melting, feathers on water, Icarus —
The garrulous partridge crows happily from a sheugh
And claps its wings, a hitherto unheard-of species,
The latest creation, a grim reminder to Daedalus
— Inventor, failure's father — of his apprentice, a boy
Who had as a twelve year old the mental capacity
To look at the backbone of a fish and invent the saw
By cutting teeth in a metal blade; to draw conclusions
And a circle with the first compass, two iron limbs,
Arms, legs tied together, geometry's elbow or knee —
Which proved his downfall, for Daedalus grew so jealous
He pushed the prodigy headlong off the Acropolis
And then lied about him slipping; but Pallas Athene,
Who supports the ingenious, intercepted his fall,
Dressed him in feathers in mid-air and made him a bird,
Intelligence flashing to wing-tip and claw, his name
Passing on to the bird (it is *perdix* in the Greek) —
The partridge that avoids getting airborne and nesting
In tree-tops or on dizzy ledges; that flapping along
At ground level, laying its eggs under hedges, has lost,
Thanks to the memory of that tumble, its head for heights.

AN AMISH RUG

As if a one-room schoolhouse were all we knew
And our clothes were black, our underclothes black,
Marriage a horse and buggy going to church
And the children silhouettes in a snowy field,

I bring you this patchwork like a smallholding
Where I served as the hired boy behind the harrow,
Its threads the colour of cantaloupe and cherry
Securing hay bales, corn cobs, tobacco leaves.

You may hang it on the wall, a cathedral window,
Or lay it out on the floor beside our bed
So that whenever we undress for sleep or love
We shall step over it as over a flowerbed.

Augustus Young

TOUCH OF EVIL

Hats off to Orson Welles (1915-1985)

What is the difference between evil and corruption?
Evil does not seek material gain (and usually gets it).
The corrupt get caught.

Someone is going to hit me from behind.
I may be blinkered but I am not blind.
In the movie car-chase the streets unwind

like bandages in a miracle cure.
The actors act themselves, the pay being poor
(immunity from screen death is secure).

What does it matter what you say about
people? Every action is dubbed in doubt.
And with words you act your fantasies out.

So Captain Quinlan in cross border wars
shudders to conclusions about the Stars
(Dietrich and Heston live on candy bars).

He knows the truth's a killer and bad news:
this bad good cop long shadowed by past booze
is heat incarnate, makes the room-fans fuse.

(Alias Orson in this Mexican
B-movie set, the budget overran,
deadlines to be met. He carries the can.)

A great coat in the tropics keeps him warm
on the trail that will kill him once it's dawn.
(Outside the studio is a snow storm.

This is not in the film, only the still.)
A chac mool of a man in for the kill:
if cancer does not get him corrupt officials will.

The film beneath so slight a thought is spit.
His poncho is a gaucho shroud, and fit
only to cloak a double tequila hit.

He wears death on his sleeve, and vultures flock
to feed from his flabby hand, and die of shock.
Cheap hotel rooms wait for the final knock.

'Some sort of a man.' Marlene's ad lib knells
a roll of credits, and what private hells
open for the real death of Orson Welles.

THE END's a blank screen or a wall of death.
(Double you is for Welles, Orson ill-met
by midday moonlight in a movie set.)

From nineteen fifty-eight to eighty-five,
he played Harry Lime as God in disguise,
and Falstaff as Poor Devil, come alive

born in the slobbery swamp of Captain
Quinlan's character (not Citizen Kane):
this one-armed Ahab, legless Tamburlaine.

Ps AND QUEUES

The art of waiting in a queue
is finding something else to do
like watching other folk in line
doing their nut, and feeling fine
thinking of Mozart and Malthus,
and higher things that are no use
to man or beast. You wait your turn
like Joan of Arc, and slowly burn.

THE CORK JAZZ FESTIVAL 1991

for Imelda Marcos and Fats Waller

The terror of new shoes
strikes the tender, flowering
the feet into blisters.

The first are changed almost
as often as nappies
so not to rot the toes.

Still as our growing slows
the ordeal's less frequent.
They stand the pace of life.

Shoes are changed for formal
occasions such as Fun
Runs and first marriages,

And how they squeak and pinch —
for skin's thin, arches fall,
and leather's grip is cruel.

The wardrobe fills with them.
And carelessly footwear warps
like unused tennis rackets.

Why don't we throw them out?
Oh! shoesies represent
acceptance that life's pain.

The last pair are chosen
for appearance sake, when lying
in state in the coffin:

No concern for comfort:
In death's eternal fit
nothing can hurt the feet.

J . C . C . M a y s

BRIAN COFFEY'S
WORK IN PROGRESS

In the minds of most people who have heard of him in Ireland, Brian Coffey's reputation is linked with that of Denis Devlin and Samuel Beckett. All three left Ireland during the nineteen thirties and all three attempted to write in ways outside and counter to the realist tradition which was dominant. This is a useful point of departure, but an equally useful comparison might be with Basil Bunting in England or with George Oppen in America. They too published in the nineteen thirties and returned to poetry in the late nineteen fifties after an extended period of silence and exile. In the case of Bunting and Oppen, too, the later work is what their reputation will rest upon, and the peculiarly extended period of its gestation gives in its special quality. *Briggflatts* and *On Being Numerous* and *Primitive*, on the one hand, and Coffey's *Advent* and *Death of Hektor*, on the other, are authoritative in their different ways because they are testamentary.

Bunting, Oppen and Coffey have all been deeply critical of present-day society, yet have cast their criticism in the form of love poems. There are parallels to be drawn between Oppen's reaction to Marxism and Coffey's to Irish nationalism, and Bunting's sense of humour and Coffey's version of the same. There are obvious differences, such as derive from Oppen's Jewishness and Bunting's special interest in musical form. One difference to be celebrated is that Brian Coffey is happily still very much alive, and at the age of eighty-two has several important projects in hand. It seems to me in the spirit of his work not to look back but forward, to anticipate his next two publications, and to offer some comments on what they promise.

The first we might expect is a translation of *Les Chimères* by Gérard de Nerval. A version of 'El Desdichado' was published in *Irish University Review* (Spring 1975) and the complete set of poems is due to be published in Fred Beake's magazine, *The Poet's Voice*, later this year [1987]. Coffey's 1975 version, interlineated with the French original, reads as follows:

> I am the tenebrous one, widowed, disconsolate,
> Je suis le Ténebreux — le Veuf, — l'Inconsolé,

Prince of Aquitania at the torn-down tower.
Le Prince d'Aquitaine à la Tour abolie:

My sole star is dead and my lute constellate
Ma seule *étoile* est morte, — et mon luth constellé

bears the black sun of melancholia.
Porte le Soleil noir de la *Mélancolie.*

In the night of the tomb, thou who didst comfort me,
Dans la nuit du Tombeau, Toi qui m'as consolé,

give me back Posillipo and the Italian sea,
Rends-moi le Pausilippe et la mer d'Italie,

the flower which so won my heart desolated
La fleur qui plaisait tant à mon coeur désolé,

and vine-arbour where vine-shoot with rose allies.
Et la treille où le Pampre à la Rose s'allie.

Am I Eros or Phoebus? . . . Lusignon or Biron?
Suis-je Amour ou Phébus? . . . Lusignan ou Biron?

My brow is red yet from the kiss of the queen.
Mon front est rouge encor du baiser de la Reine;

I have dreamed in grotto where siren swims . . .
J'ai rêve dans la Grotte où nage la Sirène . . .

And twice a conqueror have crossed Acheron
Et j'ai deux fois vainquer traversé l'Achéron:

inflecting turn about on Orpheus' lyre
Modulant tour à tour sur la lyre d'Orphée

the sigh of the saint and the cry of the fay.
Les soupirs de la Sainte et les cris de la Fée.

Coffey's version, it seems to me, is not of interest in its own right — at least, in the customary way. Some lines barely make sense (8, 13), others are hardly English (11). There are poeticisms (4) and awkward inversions (3, 6). What is obscure in the original is no less obscure here, and for a version which aims at independent status and a kind of comfortable coherence one would be better advised to turn to Derek Mahon's *The Chimeras* (Gallery Press, 1982). Mahon delivers a poem which is an elegant and clever answer to the technical and interpretative questions posed by the original. At the same time, Coffey's version is not entirely reliable as a crib. Though it follows the original closely in the main, the last line appears like a perverse departure. It would have made no difference to the metre to have made 'sigh' and 'cry' plural, so why did Coffey not do so? Again, after the first quatrain, he progressively abandons Nerval's rhyme-scheme — a feature Mahon exercises considerable skill in matching.

The point is, Coffey's version does not aim to be a substitute. Nor does it attempt an exact equivalence. His literal mistranslation in the last line must be intended as a provocative reminder of this fact. Someone who went to school in France and later spent several years working at a doctoral thesis for the Sorbonne, as well as many years since at translation, is not ignorant of what he is attempting to do. Coffey's version courts a degree of strangeness, making English read as if it had been originally written in French, and is tinged with nineteenth-century mannerisms, in a deliberately calculated way. His version of 'El Desdichado' is a translation in the sense described by Walter Benjamin as transparent: 'it does not cover the original, does not block its light, but allows the pure language, as though reinforced by its own medium, to shine upon the original all the more fully.' The effect resembles, in a single text, that gained by the simultaneous reading of French and English versions by Jean Douve and his translator, Michael Edwards, at the Second Cambridge Poetry Festival in 1977 (at which Coffey also read).

Coffey's aim differs from that of translators such as Mahon, therefore, who seek to replace originals by equivalent independent poems. It more closely resembles that of Celia and Louis Zukofsky in their translation of Catullus. The closeness with which the sound of the translation matches the original is at the expense of normal English. The original is contained in the sound of the translation, so that its shadowy presence combines with the words we read. Coffey's revisions for the version to be published by Mammon Press move further in that direction: 'console me' in 5, 'flower which so pleased my heart' in 7, 'sighing' in 14. Again, however, there is a distinction to be made because Coffey's version is not offered as an end in itself. There is no suggestion of *tour de force*, no suggestion of expertise exercising itself for display, as in the Zukofsky translation.

One may well ask why bother? What is the point of a translation which, with apparent perversity, eschews exactness? Which does not attempt to stand as an independent poem in the language in which it appears? Which by itself is sometimes ungainly, sometimes odd, not always comprehensible? The answer is that Coffey's version is a reading and is deliberately not a crib or another, derived poem. His version rides the contours of the original and enacts a process in which rhythm and syntax are more important than rhyme and current usage. It is entirely subservient, though in the sense that a bareback-rider is subservient to his mount. The aim of the exercise is not to subjugate or assimilate, nor to thrill the spectators. It is to communicate the spirit of the untamed mount, not to temper its spirit, nor to compromise the audience in an experience of pseudo-mastery.

Coffey's version is justified by the idea of *poiein* in the Thomistic sense, that is, making as opposed to doing. The translator works to place his reader inside the original, differently, in a different language. The transposition does no more than make the qualities of the original more evident, even its obscurities, and to that extent such qualities are put to the test. Translation is part of making in that it makes objective, gives facticity: the new world or language into which the original is thrown establishes a context for evaluating Nerval's values. At the same time, the evaluation gains its authority by non-evaluative means.

What I am saying cannot be proved by quoting individual lines, or by comparing individual phrases in English and French. It is a matter of taking the version as a whole, following the way it moves alongside the original (rather than its sound, in the narrow sense), seeing it as a calculated displacement and seeing what this implies. The subject remains the same, the nexus of poet and lover, but the rendering involves estrangement and judgment. The French is not turned into English, quite, and that is the point. The English is partly French. The achievement of such a version lies in the insight it offers into the original, rather than in its attempt to be a self-sufficient or even modest rival, yet this is offered from an entirely independent position.

I labour this point because the single discussion of Coffey's translations I have heard failed to understand it. Professor Felix Leakey gave a lecture some years ago at University College Dublin, in which he compared versions of 'Le Bateau Ivre', among them Beckett's and Coffey's. It would be foolish to claim that either translation is superior to the other, because they proceed by different principles. While Beckett also attempts to work from the life contained in Apollinaire's lines, in his more assertive method results in a more independent poem of his own. He creates an original, derived from another poem, whereas Coffey's version is obviously dependent. The distinction between the two translations is that Beckett's derivative kind is free-standing, but stands on ground prepared by somebody else. Coffey's dependent kind always leans against or 'hangs from' its original, but the ground it stands upon is its own.

The way in which Coffey's version of a Nerval sonnet involves a reader in its justification is typical, and leads to the other forthcoming piece I want to discuss. This is *The Prayers*, an extract from which was published in *Chanterelles: Short Poems, 1971-1983* (The Melmoth Press, 1985). The extract fills some six pages at the end of the book, and I have no idea how it might fit into a larger scheme. Nor do I know how far the project has advanced beyond these six pages, nor of plans for the publication of the whole. It nonetheless promises to be a work of major stature, on a level with *Advent* and *Death of Hektor*.

The extract is too long to quote in full, but it opens:

Where it goes on   Here not anywhere

when not anywhen   Here   Now

For why go probe whose heart

The lines that follow describe a spiritual state which has been penetrated with subjectivity, 'Now here an inside find' 'Inside become without', and the method mimics this. Its content is — as in the case of the sonnet — defined by what the content does. Thus the movement is eddying, immersive, 'no escape from lump once begun'. The rhythms enact a process whereby they come together and petrify, even as the lines move forward to 'self-abyss and null'.

The opening shows what to me is the central, essential Coffey. The first two lines establish a beginning in the here and now, dependent on distinctions which are folded over one another with evident care. Simultaneously, by echoing the opening sentences of Beckett's *The Unnamable*, the distinctions are made to participate in a debate about value. The method of the entire extract is contained in the two lines, and the third line stands apart from and outside the predicament they describe, looking forward to the question with which the extract closes:

What hand   what care saves here

The pacing of the argument is not as simple as dialectal progression, not a straightforward oscillation between balanced opposites, just as the opposition contained in the opening lines is enfolded asymmetrically. The opposition is restated as between inside and outside, twice-over in increasingly emphatic ways in the paragraphs which follow, until a point is reached when the reader is tagged, slotted 'into frame'. The situation is thereafter clarified, retraversed, advanced from and summed up in a variety of contrasting verse forms and moods. And the last third of the extract develops further the encircled entrapment of:

> Escape no-when no-where
> They keep one live theirs

The paragraph and groups of paragraphs are therefore in a live relation, registering the fluctuations of a lyric voice in such a way that we almost immediately internalize it. The poetry becomes, in Keats's words, a 'voyage of conception'. This is perhaps the justification of the title of the poem, which is less about spiritual struggle than the enactment of a state of rapt listening. Something similar has been said about the poetry of Laura Riding by Paul Auster, who quotes Malebranche to the effect that attention is the natural prayer of the soul. Prayer in this sense is the method, not the content. The content is the wreck of innocent, romantic impulse; solipsistic nausea; spreading fear; failure of nerve.

Internal correspondences between the parts are the most important form of allusion, but the kind of allusion contained in the opening lines of *The Unnamable* works on the same principle of analogy. Operating in this way, there are allusions to John 19.23 ('seamless garment'), Homer ('forfeit Ithaca remote'), Blake's 'mundane shell', Keats' *Lamia* 45-65 ('As if in what dusty brake bright cirque-couchant'), Beckett's *Ping* and *Lessness*:

> As if the facile blue and silver shell
> of dreaming day away did harden
> to ceiling jet walls black grey floor
> as if spacy air did shape to cubes

The point is, such allusions interact with their source-texts in the same way that Coffey's version does with Nerval. They interact in ways which create meaning and are not just ancillary to it. They feed on the other texts as the poem feeds on itself, and are particularly important as a means of establishing value. Thus, the allusions to Beckett create a bridge with modern cultural traditions and thereby create a context for Coffey's counterstatement. The allusions to Blake and Keats work differently in that they are corroborative: they show the applicability of quite different analyses to the present instance. Together, in various ways, the allusions enlarge the scope of the implicative method. They prevent oppositions such as are contained in the opening lines from becoming engrossed in a web of analogy.

The movement of the extract has something in common with the movement of Coffey's previous long poems, but it is worked through here in yet another way. The opening statement is reminiscent of *Advent* and *Hektor*, and so is the way themes emerge from their opposites, and the way the whole ends on a suspended note, which supplies a finale but does not complete the process it describes. The difference arises from the largely negative direction in which the present extract moves. The satire is not social or political, like *Leo* or *The Big Laugh*. There is no spluttering anger, though there is numbing pain:

> wear away wear away
> lump make limp make lump

The satire in this instance has been introjected, and the lines communicate failure, horror, bleakness. There is no upbeat and no sign of hope; no woman, no piety and no place for sentiment. The sound established by different kinds of analogy is both continuous with and distinct from Coffey's previous poems. It is more various, tending less to settle down into settled rhythms — whether in the upward-turning direction of *Advent* as a whole or the clanging protest of *Hektor*. The three- and four-stress lines, with expandings, are magnetized by a vortex of futility from which escape is impossible and simultaneously necessary. As I said, I do not know how the extract fits into a larger scheme, but it promises to be something different from what we have had before.

These comments on Coffey's work in progress will perhaps make clear why he commands such respect, even if not among a large number of readers. His kind of poetry 'pries to the interior' and makes a distinctive music. Perhaps this music has something to do with the method of analogy which, in several extensions, is so central to his way of making. One remembers a voice which, when one looks for a quotation to pin it down, is always in part elsewhere, contained in some kind of echo. The voice is a quality of mind in the way it moves: one is really remembering qualities like intelligence, tact and bravery. At the same time, they are not qualities which take one far in this world, and when they are appreciated, it is usually in the train of qualities which are more obvious.

I may have given the impression of poetry so immersive that the outer world disappears, as it tends to do in the poetry of John Ashbery. This is not the case: the outer world enters the extract from *The Prayers* to create moments of stunning poignancy. The following paragraphs set inside against outside, inner freedom against the constraints which compel escape, in a way which is as visually precise as it is charitable. The degree of unreality is carefully measured in the first paragraph, and one might set the rising emotion contained in the pauses of the second line against what differently comes across in the leaden pauses of the ninth:

> Free all free that cool that mild
> lake swan grass isle tree
> so different from outside here
> at hand constant foe
>
> The bonds live sharp black
> fringe false reaches exhaust one slay
> Miles beyond swamps drab summer moss
> later winter leagues in driving sleet
> berries none nuts none verdure none but blighted

The same images are completed several pages further on: 'summer moss' is overtaken by an extended image of 'ivy carpet' creeping on 'graveyard floor', 'dry-rot', 'cold dark like within a stone'. And at this point the poetry begins to enter the inner ear.

Given the restricted awareness of Coffey's work, it is difficult to estimate its final worth. Not that wide acceptance seems to matter to him, and he has probably been better off without it. I suspect that the association of his name with those of Beckett and Devlin, in Ireland, has not done him much good. The way in which Beckett has written about his own private concerns has proved to be attractive to many more readers and large audiences, even though in the process his superstar status has obscured what he is writing about. Devlin's name crops up in Irish literary history and anthologies more often than Coffey's, and I suspect the reason is, being dead, he can be more readily assimilated to a paradigm of the thirties' writer in exile. Coffey, following last, is a name to be mentioned as it is passed over — the more quickly because he is the more resistant to romantic misprision. The effect has been to leave him free both to follow a single vision undistracted and to develop it in multifarious forms.

My choice of a translation alongside an extract from a long poem was motivated by more than the wish to discuss work in progress. There is evidence, following the republication of *Advent* and *Hektor* by Menard Press, that the readership for Coffey's work is enlarging; but it would be a pity if he was thought to be a writer of long poems only, and, if he is, then those long poems will be misunderstood. Consider again the implications of his method of translation. Whereas Derek Mahon's version of Nerval delivers an elegant derivative, Coffey's version most obviously declines to do the normal thing and goes for something more ambitious: it takes the reader into the making of the original. It is only when one understands what such a method of translation shares with the long poems — and how it is implicated with their values — that one sees fully what they are about.

The translation refuses to deliver a centred lyric presence. It aims at an existence between texts, which depends on both and yet is neither. The allusions in *The Prayers* from one point of view look not properly assimilated, but, from another, prompt a reader to range beyond the pathos of lyric statement to larger questions of value. Both pieces of writing are postmodern in an individual yet recognizable way. The moment of epiphany on the first page of *The Prayers* is recognized as a temptation as well as a comfort, wonderful yet past. The text evolves like a spoken monologue, yet it is not spoken by an individual. There is no locus for meaning, only movement, dynamics, relationship. Derrida's view of meaning as *différance*, the infinite play of differing and deferring, is particularly helpful in understanding the peculiar sound made by Coffey's poems.

In historical terms, and Coffey is alert to the numbing analogies between post-revolutionary Ireland and Russia, he might be described as a Celtic Mayakovsky, a Neo-Thomist Futurist. The forces with which he engages are political and moral, even when his writing appears to be literary and experimental. It presents a challenge to orthodox nationalism, by suggesting an overlap between Proletkult and the Celtic Revival and by developing an alternative model. It is more engaged than Beckett's response to the same literary-political-social dilemma; and if it is less funny, it is less despairing; if it is less spectacularly desperate, it has a life beyond the page. Beckett's excruciating brilliance leaves many readers marvelling, with the result that he writes himself off. Brian Coffey's fewer readers are in less danger of losing themselves in literature. Also, if the meanings in his writing inhere in play, in relationships such as Derrida celebrates, the way they connect with the world of value makes them responsible in a fundamentally different way.

Coffey is original in the best sense, that is, aware of predecessors all the way back to Aristotle, and constantly surprising as he has moved into the future. He has created what amounts to a large, varied body of work — all of it of interest and a considerable proportion of it of a kind which sets his achievement alongside that of Bunting and Oppen, as I said. This is not a rhetorical flourish. A collection which included *Third Person, Missouri Sequence, Dice Thrown Never Will Annul Chance* (a version of Mallarmé) and perhaps some other translations, *Leo* or *The Big Laugh*, then *Advent* and *Death of Hektor* would comprise an astonishing body of writing by any standards. Bunting and Oppen, much as they are to be admired, would not seem the more impressive:

just different. Beckett, read alongside Coffey, in an Irish context, appears less a solo performer. And then again, as I said, Coffey has not stopped writing. We can look forward to the full version of Nerval and to *The Prayers* and, God willing, to yet still more.

John Jordan

CHAPTER AND VERSE

Tom Paulin (ed.) *The Faber Book of Political Verse*
London: Faber and Faber, 1986

Mr Paulin, who is thirty-eight this year and lectures in English at the University of Nottingham, became known in the Republic of Ireland not as the accomplished if deceptively prosaic poet that he is, but as the author of the first Field Day pamphlet, *A New Look at the Language Question*, in which he adroitly registers his distaste for the prose of the late F. S. L. Lyons, Owen Dudley Edwards, Benedict Kiely and Frank Delaney, the last-named accused of having infected 'southern Irish writers' with his 'saccharine gabbiness'. The pamphlet, published in 1983, revealed Paulin (he will not object, I believe, to being surnamed) as erudite, most serious-minded, and puritanically conscientious. I found myself reacting in a parochial Catholic way that shocked me. My first, exploratory, reading of the Introduction to Paulin's anthology of political verse also made me feel alien, unIrish, uneducated; I will try to compress my reactions to my first reading of the Introduction with my more measured reactions to it in re-reading.

Paulin initially makes a trenchant attack upon the 'close reading' of poetry. He describes as 'Manicheans' those who 'dismiss as mere politics' everything outside the 'garden of pure perfect forms' which is Art. He makes a devastating but unconvincing attack on the 'close readers': 'The practitioner of close reading agrees with Henry Ford that history is bunk and enforces that belief with a series of fallacies . . . these supposedly fallacious ways of reading literature are designed to hinder the reader who believes that there is often a relationship between art and politics, rather than a clear-cut opposition between formal garden and contingent scrapheap.' The first poet mentioned by Paulin in his discourse on poets who write about 'political reality' is Burns, described as 'a radical republican', who nonetheless 'could combine a dedicated egalitarianism with a pride in the House of Stuart that was both personal and national'. Burns is singled out as 'one of the most notable victims of the aristocratic, hierarchical, conservative tradition which Arnold and T. S. Eliot have floated as the major cultural hegemony in these islands'. While granting that Eliot offered 'a strategic defence of Burns's verse', Paulin denounces as 'a major act of cultural desecration' Eliot's 'subversion of Milton's reputation'. Eliot, abetted by F. R. Leavis and the *Scrutiny* critics, the New Critics and 'that reactionary theologian, C. S. Lewis' (Lewis wrote about theological matters, but never, so far as I know, claimed the status of theologian), 'was able to rewrite English literary history and almost obliterate the Protestant prophetic tradition'. Paulin, quite trenchantly, indicates in that last sentence his primary literary loyalty (I do not know if it is also the basis of whatever religious belief he may hold). Immediately after he counts himself among 'those of us who still revere Milton as the greatest English poet and the most dedicated servant of English liberty'. The first of these judgments, while questionable (even when we take it for granted he is excluding the dramatic verse of Shakespeare), is permissible, the second is unquestionably dubious. Paulin appears to be taking it for granted that the Church of Rome and the Church of England are not to be considered worthy of 'English liberty'. Paulin's antagonism to the Church of England (and the Church of Rome by extension) boils over when he writes, 'Together, Arnold and Eliot ensured that the magic of monarchy and superstition permeated English literary criticism and education like a syrupy drug'. That phrase 'the magic of monarchy and superstition', if 'papacy' were substituted for 'monarchy', would not sound strange from the mouth of Rev. Dr Ian Paisley. And Paulin is surely flogging a dead horse when he writes that 'in time it may be generally acknowledged that Milton is no more a non-political writer than Joyce was — or Dante, or Virgil'. That is a smart but shallow sentence. The 'politics' of Joyce were of a kind and quality utterly different from those of either Dante or Virgil. Nor do I credit that anyone today even remotely acquainted with Milton's work would maintain that it is 'non-political'.

On the third page of his Introduction, Paulin becomes decidedly more convincing. He hails *Paradise Lost* and Dryden's *Absalom and Achitophel* as 'the two greatest political poems in English' and 'works of the committed imagination'. Milton, 'the most dedicated servant of English liberty' was also 'a republican, a regicide, the official propagandist of the English parliament', while Dryden became 'a monarchist and a Tory after the Restoration'. Paulin does not mention that Dryden became a Roman Catholic and remained one after the ascent to the throne in 1688 of William of Orange. He says of Milton and Dryden: 'their political beliefs are fundamental to their poems and our reading is enriched by a knowledge of those beliefs and an understanding of the social experience which helped to form them. (I say 'helped' because in the end we accede to a political position by an act of faith — Milton's essential faith was love of liberty, Dryden's love of order).' From Milton and Dryden, he makes a brilliant leap to the dilemmas of poets of the last sixty years in Eastern Europe. 'In the Western democracies it is still possible for many readers . . . to share the view . . . that poets are gifted with an ability to hold themselves above history . . . However, in some societies — particularly totalitarian ones — history is a more or less inescapable condition.' He instances Zbigniew Herbert (b. 1924: five poems translated from the Polish). Tadenz Rózewicz (b. 1921: two from the Polish) and Miroslav Holub (b. 1923, one from the Polish) as exemplars of 'ironic gravity and absence of hope'. He goes on to consider the different fates of two Russian coevals, Mandelstam (1891-1938: four translations) and Pasternak (1890-1960: Robert Lowell's masterly translation of 'Hamlet in Russia, A Soliloquy'); Mandelstam died in the Gulag, Pasternak survived the Stalinist purges but contrived to leave a body of cryptically plaintive but seemingly resigned verse. Pasternak's case brings him to an important point in his definition of what are for him political poems. They do not 'necessarily make an ideological statement. They can instead embody a general historical awareness — an observation of the rain — rather than offering a specific attitude to state affairs.' Paulin returns from the contemporary Russians to Dryden whose *Absalom and Achitophel* he describes as being, politically, 'a brilliant dirty trick, an inspired piece of black propaganda', but, aesthetically, 'a great masterpiece'. Paulin takes it for granted that the Whig leader was quite justified in opposing the accession of James Stuart, Duke of York, who happened to be a Catholic. Somewhat abruptly, Paulin leaps forward again: some instances of Yeats's political stratagems are given. The couplet 'And did that play of mine send out/Certain men the English shot?' from 'The Man and the Echo' in *Last Poems* (1936-1939), Paulin takes as a confession of 'the poet's impurity, his responsibility for political violence.' The poem 'Easter 1916', dated 25 September 1916, was privately printed in 1917 for some of Yeats's friends. It was not published commercially until 1921 in the volume *Michael Robartes and the Dancer*. Conor Cruise O'Brien, in his by no means fulsome essay 'Passion and Cunning: Politics of Yeats' (in A. Norman Jeffares and K.G.W. Cross (eds), *In Excited Reverie*, 1965) has one magnanimous statement to make: 'By the time when "Easter 1916" and "The Rose Tree" were published, in the autumn of 1920, the pot had boiled over. The Black and Tan terror was now at its height throughout Ireland. To publish these poems in this context was a political act, and a bold one: probably the boldest of Yeats's career.'

But Paulin is not prepared to accept the boldness of Yeats's act. He even suggests that the Labour-orientated *New Statesman* was the *safest* outlet for 'Easter 1916', since the magazine was engaged in a campaign against the British government's campaign of 'official terrorism': 'A statement which might have isolated and exposed Yeats in the autumn of 1916 now helped to consolidate links between British socialists and Irish nationalists.' If so, the links were frail and short-lived. Paulin castigates Yeats's 'self-confessed circus-act which appears to have fooled many spectators into believing the poet was somehow above the vulgarities of politics.' And he 'would guess that Samuel Beckett had the great ringmaster in mind when he created Pozzo in *Waiting for Godot*'. Paulin, clearly, has little more affection for Yeats than he has for Eliot, although he includes eight poems, as against an extract from Eliot's 'Little Gidding' (Section III). Ezra Pound, the friend of Yeats and Eliot, and quite definitely a luminous poet despite his crack-brained Fascism, has not even a reference in Paulin's anthology.

Paulin with what never appears to be ostentatious erudition, sketches the seven traditions he adjudges to have contributed to the history of political verse in English. Thus one wonders why the publishers did not demur when the editor included translations from Irish ('Fear Dorcha Ó Mealláin' translated by Thomas Kinsella and Egan O'Rahilly — why the anglicization of the second Gaelic poet's name? — translated by Eavan Boland and by Frank O'Connor); Italian (Dante's portrait of Ugolino in the *Inferno*, translated by Seamus Heaney); German (Goethe and Heine, translated by Paulin; Brecht, translated by an unknown; Enzenberger, b. 1929, translated by Michael Hamburger); Polish (I have referred to these translations above); Russian (apart from those already mentioned, two women poets, Tsvetayeva and Anna Akhmatova, and the suicide Mayakovsky, all translated by Paulin); Spanish (Neruda, translation of the Chilean master by the American poet Robert Bly); French (André Chénier, translated by Paulin and Rimbaud translated by the late Robert Lowell).

The seven traditions receive tell-tale spatial treatment. The 'Popular' gets less than three pages; the 'Monarchist' less than five; the 'Puritan-Republican' twelve; the 'Irish' a little more than three; the 'Scottish' three; the 'American' a little more than three; the 'Anti-Political' two pages. About 'The Popular Tradition' Paulin has some surprising comments. 'It shapes itself in anonymous ballads, popular songs, broadsheets, nursery rhymes like "Gunpowder Plot Day"' and — this I find engaging — 'its visceral energies can be felt in both Kipling and Yeats'. How visceral? 'This rich proletarian tradition looks to the prelapsarian Adam and Eve as ideal images of a just society . . .' In the sixteen forties, the Leveller John Lilburne, the ascribed author of *Vox Plebis*, wrote, 'For as God created every man free in Adam: so by nature are all alike freemen born.' Paulin traces the 'image of free Adam', with a side-kick at Episcopalians

— why not Roman Catholics? — who regard such an image 'pejoratively', through Milton and Marvell to Arthur Hugh Clough (1819-61). Paulin very justly hails 'The Fallen Elm', 'a bitter and tender elegy' by John Clare (1793-1864) 'which seems to rise up from a vast, anonymous historical experience'. Paulin links Clare's elegy with the activities of an organization few Irishmen will have heard of, the United English, who like the United Irishmen looked to French Republican aid 'to free this Contray'. The oath of the United English has been recorded in the spelling of an Irish accent. Paulin unexpectedly introduces Browning's 'The Lost Leader', in which the 'lithe dactylic rhythms are shared by many Irish rebel songs'. The Lost Leader, of course, was William Wordsworth, who accepted the laureateship in April 1843. The speaker of the poem sees the acceptance as a betrayal of the working-classes. Paulin might have made the point that the first line 'Just for a handful of silver he left us' links Wordsworth with Judas and those he 'left' with the disciples of Christ.

After Browning, Paulin finds that 'the popular verse' tradition in political poetry weakened, until now the tradition is best represented by 'pop' poet John Cooper Clarke (b. 1948) and the younger West Indian (Paulin or his researchers fail to say from which island) Linton Kwesi Johnson (b. 1952). At the end of 'The Popular Tradition' Paulin is severe about Ted Hughes (who compiled a magnificent if methodically eccentric anthology, *The Rattle Bag*, with Seamus Heaney, Paulin's fellow Field Day director). He writes, 'The student of Ted Hughes's poetry will notice that it draws strongly on a popular vernacular, but his recent acceptance of the laureateship suggests that he has been co-opted by the rival monarchist tradition.' Goodness gracious me. Paulin stops short of accusing Hughes of leaving 'us' for a handful of silver. In 'The Monarchist Tradition' Paulin hails Spenser as 'a Protestant prophet' and alleges that his 'mystic patriotism, belief in social hierarchy and reverence for institutions "sprung out from English race", which characterize monarchism' (and which also characterize *The Faerie Queene*) are not his true colouring. In looking forward to the 'new Hierusalem' and identifying the English as God's 'chosen people', he is anticipating the 'radical Protestant beliefs' held later by Milton. Paulin reminds us that Milton believed 'our sage and serious poet Spenser' to have been fully committed to the puritan cause. It is many years since I heard the UCD specialist in Langland, the late Father T. P. Dunning, describe (off the platform) Spenser as 'a cur'. I confess to having been shocked, but Paulin's brief account of Spenser might lead many to think of him as an Elizabethan time-server.

Paulin cites Shakespeare's 'conservative pessimism' as belonging to 'the opposing tradition' of Spenser and Milton which we must, I suppose, call 'liberal optimism'. Paulin allows for Shakespeare's 'populist anger' in Sonnet 66, 'Tired with all these, for restful death I cry', and includes it alongside two excerpts from *Coriolanus*, which Eliot described as Shakespeare's 'most assured artistic success', but which Paulin describes as anti-populist. Given Paulin's by now entrenched commitments to revolutionary Puritanism, the fact also that he admits it 'would require a large and separate anthology to give a comprehensive account of Shakespeare's political vision', I cannot see why Paulin included any Shakespeare at all. And his description of him as 'a conservative pessimist' *pur et simple* suggests that Paulin is baiting the naive and the gullible among his readers.

Characteristically, Paulin then attempts to establish Gerard Manley Hopkins in the Monarchist Tradition. Certainly, Hopkins was loyal to Victoria as a British citizen, loyal to the Church as a member of the Society of Jesus, but I cannot grasp Paulin's contention that Hopkins saw 'the working class as occupying a fixed position in the divine social design – it is a lowly member of the body politic and leads a bestial, mindless existence, careless of the "lacklevel" or inegalitarian nature of society.' Without mentioning the fact, he returns to another convert to the Roman Church, Dryden, since *Absalom and Achitophel*, like 'Tom's Garland' of Hopkins, answers Milton's 'radical vision, his belief in the free individual conscience'. Paulin's recurring vindications of Milton as the apostle of 'the free individual conscience' suggest that 'conscience' has no function in the intellectual and spiritual lives of those born into hierarchical Churches, whether they stay in them or not. This is a form of bigotry no more or less distasteful than Christian presumption of evil in genuine agnostics or atheists. Paulin is on more solid ground when he detects the 'paternalist strain within English conservatism' which informs Ben Jonson's "To Penshurst", hostile to, among other things, 'mercantile capitalism and recent money'. Paulin finds 'this anarchistic disdain for the cash-nexus' in the opening section of Tennyson's *Maud* and 'it is an influential strand in Yeats's social thought'. Given Paulin's declared preferences, he has a remarkably cogent passage linking Yeats with the Elizabethan-Jacobean Ben Jonson and the early and late Augustans, Dryden and Pope: like them, Yeats 'has a horror of the destruction of culture by the rough beasts of egalitarianism'. We have met the phrase 'conservative pessimist' in connection with Shakespeare. It is used again in connection with the translator of Ecclesiastes in the King James Bible, and, surprisingly, in connection with Eliot's 'Little Gidding', it is used not disdainfully. In that poem 'he imagines a cultural consensus where the English people are at last united "in the strife which divided them". Charles I

— the beaten, broken "king at nightfall" — combines in Eliot's historical memory with "one who died blind and quiet" and that unnamed figure is the poet whose reputation Eliot did so much to maim. The regicide Milton is here allowed a ghostly presence in the canon as the ancient wounds are healed by Eliot's sacramental vision.' Paulin admires the poignancy of Eliot's 'salving lines' and, whatever our political stance, 'it is impossible not to admire his achievement in writing this type of religious and patriotic verse'. But Eliot is still in the corner. Admiration for 'Little Gidding' 'ought not to make us collude with Eliot's displacement of the major tradition of English political verse and we must be alert to the Burkean or High Anglican conspiracy which has so distorted literary history'.

In 'The Puritan-Republican Tradition' Paulin repairs the mischief he attributes to the influence of Eliot, and he does so brilliantly and with missionary ardour. He admires the puritan imagination which reads the Bible 'in a directly personal manner' so that Psalm 114 in the Authorized Version 'is a song of freedom that exults in the litheness of a released vernacular'. For Milton, Stuart absolutism, which Jonson helped to beautify, was 'a sojourn in Egypt where a "people of strange language" oppressed God's chosen people, the English'. We are asked to consider that Milton is echoing St John in his sonnet defending his treatises on divorce. Like Cromwell, he believed in 'the free way', not 'the formal'. He is therefore opposed to 'a classic hierarchy'. Yeats in his senate speech on divorce invoked the rights of Irish Protestants 'won by the labours of Milton and other great men'. Paulin allies Shaw with Yeats in this 'resolute Anglo-Irish tradition' and might mislead those who are not Irish, and of course Irish Catholics, into believing that the Church of Ireland looks benevolently on divorce. I wish also that Paulin had given chapter for his contention that this 'resolute Anglo-Irish tradition ... paradoxically finds its most complete aesthetic summation in Joyce's superbly "catholic" imagination'. What Paulin has to say about Milton's world-view is intensely interesting. Since he regards *Paradise Lost* as 'the greatest poem in the English language', that is not surprising. What puzzles a non-Protestant like myself is his contention that 'Theology and politics fuse completely in the Protestant imagination, and it is essential that we read Milton in that knowledge, hard as Protestant hermeneutics are to convey in an England which appears to have forgotten its remarkable history.' Reading Paulin on Milton, one almost forgets the existence of Luther, Calvin, Zwingli, of all the great 'protesters' against Rome. England itself is impugned for its slackness in adherence to Miltonism. Paulin glosses the Archangel Michael's speeches in Book XII with quotations from the Second Epistle of St Peter and Revelations. Protestant frustration is attested by the closing passages of *Samson Agonistes* and the conclusion of Yeats's 'In Memory of Eva Gore-Booth and Con Markievicz'. Clearly, Paulin is Milton's Evangelist. Paulin's reverence for Milton indeed creates the illusion of him being the essential Protestant, a dangerous ploy when we remember his attachment to Cromwell, whose campaigns in Ireland may not have been quite as atrocious as they were recounted when I went to school, but whose name is still anathema to those who have heard of it (fewer these days I suspect).

It is a relief to turn from Paulin on Milton to Paulin on Andrew Marvell, whom he makes sound much more interesting. He is especially good on 'Upon Appleton House' which, in its fantasy, is anti-Roman Catholic, rather than actively propagandist for the Milton-Cromwell Second Reformation. Paulin also gives us Marvell's 'The Mower against Gardens', which might have been written by a monarchist cavalier. Marvell's 'An Horation Ode upon Cromwell's Return from Ireland', while it certainly offers a heroic image of Cromwell, offers an almost saintly image of Charles I awaiting the axe on the 'tragic scaffold'. Paulin passes over the 'Ode' and so does not have to explain away Marvell's calm and poignant lines about Charles which picture his exit from mortality as almost saintly:

> *He* nothing common did or mean
> Upon that memorable scene:
>   But with his keener eye
>   The axe's edge did try:
> Nor called the gods with vulgar spite
> To vindicate his helpless right,
>   But bowed his comely head,
>   Down, as upon a bed.

Paulin manages to include Gray's 'Elegy' in 'The Puritan-Republican Tradition' because of its 'compassion for the rural poor'. Such a placing strikes me as eccentric: Paulin *likes* the 'Elegy'; therefore it must be assimilated to the tradition with which he has most sympathy. Blake's 'entire canon', with 'its firm biblical foundations and Miltonic vision', is 'a member of the popular tradition'. We have now come to the point where it appears that for Paulin, 'the popular tradition', and 'the Puritan-Republican tradition', if not synonymous, tend to dovetail. Although Paulin has hailed Browning's indictment of Wordsworth as 'The Lost Leader', he quotes copiously from the second version of *The Prelude* (1850). (There is also one extract from the original version of 1805.) Paulin's strict joy is occasionally relaxed by the inclusion of an unexpected extract, such as the noble invocation of the 'Genius of Burke'. However, referring to the sonnet 'Great men have been among us', Paulin finds that Wordsworth 'presents himself sternly in the line of succession' to those 'who called Milton friend'. From Wordsworth, Paulin passes to Clough, 'a shamefully neglected poet who was closely interested in British, Irish, European and American politics'. Clough was in his early thirties when radically committed in 1848, 'that year of revolutions', and 1849. Brief discussion of Clough affords Paulin another opportunity to douse Arnold, Clough's friend. Although Clough 'later became an embittered reactionary', Paulin, with commendable honesty, says that 'It is an ambition of this anthology to redeem Clough from the neglect which his work has suffered', but also 'to suggest his links with Auden in a tradition of upper middle-class radicalism and sympathy with "the old democratic fervour".' Paulin is warm about the earlier Auden, although there is a pejorative note when he describes that poet as crossing over to 'the monarchist or Anglo-Catholic tradition' and makes the sweeping, almost damning, statement that 'The puritan-republican tradition ends in England with the early Auden, though some critics would claim that its inheritor is Tony Harrison'. (Harrison, b. 1937, is represented by 'On Not Being Milton'). 'A tragic impoverishment' is how Paulin describes the 'diminution of this tradition'. One is mildly surprised when he appends, 'so too is the attenuation of the rival monarchist tradition'. After lack-lustre references to Philip Larkin (1922-85) and Geoffrey Hill (b. 1932), represented as *laudatores temporis acti*, he concludes 'Sadly, it would seem that political verse is virtually a lost art in England now'. Clearly he is grieved that the 'conservative literary puritan' Donald Davie (b. 1922) joined the Church of England and supported 'the reactionary Anglicanism' of a periodical, *Poetry Nation Review*, I have not seen.

When Paulin comes to 'The Irish Tradition' he is entertaining but eccentric. Aogán Ó Rathaille is described not only as 'an adherent of the Jacobite order' but 'an exponent of a distinctive type of Irish snobbery which we can variously detect in Wilde, Synge and Yeats', Paulin's use of 'snobbery' is self-defeating, since it exposes him himself to the charge of 'snobbery', a proletarian disdain for those poets who have indicated attachment to the medieval order. However, both 'The Irish Jacobite and the Irish rebel traditions of political verse are opposed by a populist Orange tradition which believes in hierarchy and deference — a deference to the new Williamite order which can be combined with hostility to England.' He cites lines from the anonymous (and admirable) ballad 'The Orange Lily' to illustrate 'that aggressive feeling of cultural inferiority which still afflicts the loyalist imagination'. In Yeats, Paulin finds that his 'magisterial aristocratic style' in his later verse 'delights in certain intent cadences drawn from the ballad traditions of both protestant and catholic culture'. Paulin finds a formal echo of Yeats's 'The Fisherman' in Seamus Heaney's 'Casualty' from *Field Work* (1976) and also a spiritual repossession of Yeats's concern in 'The Fisherman' to find an audience of 'my own race'. Paulin is especially warm about Heaney, born in the year of Yeats's death, 1939. He has written the most succinct summation of Heaney's unique position among Ulster Catholic poets: 'his warmly inclusive vision has always rejected those nets of class, religion and ethnicity which Stephen Dedalus describes in *A Portrait of the Artist* . . . we must also recognize the manner in which Heaney's work rises out of the post-partition Ulster Catholic community, out of a rural society which has always felt itself trapped within the modern concrete of the State of Northern Ireland.' The last sentence in this context is important and poignant, scarcely to be grasped by professed admirers of Heaney in the Republic who read him as an up-to-date traditional nationalist: 'To oppose the historic legitimacy of that state [Northern Ireland] and at the same time refuse the simplicities of traditional nationalism is to initiate certain imaginative positives and offer a gracious and level trust.' Paulin treats Paul Muldoon (b. 1951) almost as cordially as Heaney. He posits a Northern vision 'which lies beyond a self-regarding, emotional Irish nationalism and an equally self-regarding British complacency, and in their very different manners both Heaney and Muldoon give that possibility a strict and definite shape.' He concludes with a trenchant statement that must have irked many good souls: 'Only nationalists, whether British or Irish, claim monopoly of "truth".'

In 'The Scottish Tradition' Paulin maintains again that, fundamentally, Burns was not a Jacobite, despite the evidence of 'Charlie, He's My Darling', and counters that evidence with Burns's 'The Tree of Liberty', in which the French Revolution is hailed as the exemplar for a similar upheaval in Britain. Paulin very sensibly recognizes in Hugh MacDiarmid (1892-1978) the apparent paradox of Marxist internationalism and commitment to MacDiarmid's Scottish nationalism. He sees MacDiarmid's 'In Memoriam James Joyce' as a brilliant indictment of 'that strain of Anglican whimsy and antiquarian eccentricity in English culture' and he hails 'his parody of Arnoldian judgment'. And he praises also MacDiarmid's indictment of 'that tedious moralism which is such a dominant force in English literary criticism and which is so careless of formal beauty'. Paulin seems unaware that his own critical standards are not devoid of 'moralism', admittedly of a lively kind. He finds in Douglas Dunn (b. 1942), as in MacDiarmid, 'a rigorously Calvinist tendency ... which expresses itself in his angry, disciplined attack on Sir Walter Scott for turning "our country round upon its name/And time" (from 'Green Breeks'). To my mind, Dunn's poem is not absolutely anti-Scott, for it ends with the presumption of magnanimity in the not altogether *kitsch* and 'mendacious' poet-novelist: 'Be not amused, Scott. Go and give him thanks/He let you patronize his "lower ranks"/Go, talk to him, and tell him who you are/Face to face, at last, Scott; and kiss his scar.' Astonishingly, the proposed encounter in eternity between Scott and 'Green Breeks' reminds me of Eliot's juxtaposition of Charles I and Milton 'folded in a single party' in 'Little Gidding'.

Paulin disposes, surprisingly, of 'The American Tradition' in political verse in about three-and-a-half pages. It strikes me that he has in this case restricted his range of choice by narrowing his definition of 'political'. He does not, incidentally, include anything by Philip Freneau, whom he describes as 'the first American political poet', but tells us that his 'George the Third's Soliloquy' is echoed in 'George III', a luminous and ironic poem by Robert Lowell (1917-77) which sees the shade of George in a modern clown of 'tragic buffoonery', Richard Nixon.

Paulin hails Whitman's free verse 'for its Jeffersonian, populist confidence in republican democracy.' 'One's-Self I Sing' Paulin describes as speaking 'for the pleasure-loving side of the puritan imagination'; this statement requires considerable glossing for readers who have not been taught that 'the puritan imagination' is 'pleasure-loving'. Paulin's inclusion of Robert Frost's 'Mending Wall' is a little puzzling; but it is a political poem in the sense that the neighbour conducts his life on the basis of proverbial sayings like 'Good fences make good neighbours'. More space is given to Robinson Jeffers (who made an inexplicable appearance in John Montague's *The Faber Book of Irish Verse*, 1974) whose 'spartan conservatism' is, not surprisingly, admired by a poet and critic who believes Milton to be the greatest English poet in the classic canon, although he would flinch at the adjective 'conservative' applied to Milton. However, perhaps Jeffers's kind of conservatism is not orthodox; in 'Shine, Republic' he writes, 'The love of freedom/has been the quality of Western man'. Later he writes, 'For the Greeks the love of beauty, for Rome of ruling; for the/present age the passionate love of discovery/But in one noble passion we are one; and Washington, Luther/Tacitus, Aeschylus, one kind of man'. The spartan element emerges when Jeffers addresses America: 'You were not born/to prosperity, you were born to love freedom.' Jeffers 'is a critical analyst of American freedom'. With unexpected enthusiasm Paulin salutes the American 'Jane Austen incognito' Elizabeth Bishop (1911-79), who obliquely criticizes Jeffers's analysis in her account of Trollope's visit to Washington during the Civil War. The descendant of New York State Tories, Elizabeth Bishop is 'silently amused at the vulgarities of democracy and offended by the thuggish, gimcrack recency of the country's neoclassical capital.' Like her friend Robert Lowell, Bishop is 'a social critic who believes in original sin, not primal innocence.' But both Lowell and Bishop give way to the Blues singers — 'they are the most authentic American political poets and their work challenges the more comfortable written tradition'.

Paulin's conclusion to his Introduction is, in a sense, a self-challenge. Poems which adopt anti-political attitudes are essentially conservative, it may be argued, but 'such an absolutist reading usually wrongs the sacral moments of being which this type of poetry can offer'. Paulin reckons that Derek Mahon's 'A Disused Shed in Co. Wexford' has 'sacral moments of being', as does Marvell's verse and Southey's 'The Battle of Blenheim', which is both 'an anti-war ballad' and a 'humanist vision of historical suffering'. Such poems spring from a 'condition of supremely unillusioned quietism.' Beckett's characters and many Russian and East European poets occupy 'that bare drained landscape'. These Eastern European poets are not, finally, 'anti-political': 'In confronting a sealed, utterly fixed reality the East European imagination designs a form of anti-poetry or survivor's art. It proffers a basic ration of the Word, like a piece of bread and chocolate in wartime.'

I have put down my objections to Paulin's anthology and to certain of his statements in the Introduction. But although I cannot fathom his presentation of Milton as a puritan liberal humanist and his acceptance of him as a celebrator of regicide, nor his reluctant admiration of Eliot, nor indeed his quasi fascist omission of the supposed fascist Ezra Pound (who certainly paid for his 'war-crimes'), I must record my perhaps perverse pleasure in Paulin's combination of scholarship, wilfulness, unabashed prejudice, and admirably toned prose. For the record, his most admirable critiques are of Marvell and Elizabeth Bishop. And Paulin's own three volumes of verse should be read in the chiaroscuro of his Introduction.

W. J. McCormack

HOLY SINNER

Seamus Heaney, *The Government of the Tongue. The 1986 T. S. Eliot Memorial Lectures and Other Critical Writings*. London: Faber and Faber, 1988

Asked to contribute to a collection of writings for presentation to Nelson Mandela in the year of his seventieth birthday, Seamus Heaney immediately offered a poem called 'New Worlds', adding the comment that it was one of his 'eastern European poems'. The reaction and the comment do not now seem uncharacteristic of the man, though ten years ago the conjunction of Poldsmoor Prison with Russia or Poland might have raised an eyebrow among the Ancient Hibernians. Heaney's second volume of essays admits into its title a political term unthinkable back in the days of dying naturalists and doors into the dark. These details signal changes in the poet's attitude to the much discussed 'unhealthy intersection' of literature and politics, changes which he himself characterized as a new wish 'to write a bare wire' rather than the 'Keatsian woolly line'.

In addition to the obligatory tribute to the bard of Inniskeen, and a splendid essay on Sylvia Plath, the collection includes pieces on Chekhov, on Miroslav Holub, Osip and Nadezhda Mandelstam. Nervousness haunts the fussy title of the opening essay — 'The Interesting Case of Nero, Chekhov's cognac and a Knocker' — a title which rivals a Cruise O'Brien newspaper column in its plethora of dropped names. One feels, and not comfortably, the occasionalness of some of the pieces, their emergence in one or other of those great literary occasions where Biffo the Bear Meets Miss Piggy. Yet as the intent of the essay is to justify a dedication to poetry amid bomb explosions and military intimidation, this nervousness should not be taken lightly.

Nevertheless, a collection of essays, notably concerned with the relationship between poetry and violent politics, surely lacks something if it lacks something on Yeats. And do the terms of the Eliot Memorial Lectures preclude one from discussing Great Tom's unpleasant attitude towards the Jews, an attitude slyly if silently perpetuated after the War when, in introducing a Faber and Faber book on Poland between 1939 and 1945, Eliot found it unnecessary even to advert to Auschwitz or Treblinka? Such omissions oblige the inclusions to look to their laurels. Another essay — 'The Impact of

Translation' — takes off from a consideration of Czeslaw Milosz, and the omission of individual names from this title disguises the relatively narrow range of material under scrutiny. But the evidence is abundant that Heaney reads Mandelstam and Milosz not so much in search of answers to Irish issues as in search of new ways to pose a question in which the inherited Ireland of the early poems no longer has a place. What kind of vacuum might this be?

'The Impact of Translation' should be read in conjunction with the review (also published here) of Thomas Kinsella and Seán Ó Tuama's *An Duanaire 1600-1900: Poems of the Dispossessed*, but by now the paralleling of 'foreign' and 'Irish' material will have become so schematic as to eliminate any such neat categories. What is striking about 'The Impact of Translation' is that it pays no attention to the impact of translation in Ireland where, within the last ten years, poetry originating in French, German, Spanish (the Iberian and South American varieties), Russian, Hungarian, Italian, Swedish, modern Greek, Romanian, and doubtless other languages too, has been written in considerable quantity and with an appreciable concern for quality also. The omission is self-denying, for Heaney participated in a unique collective act of translation (together with Michael Longley, Paul Muldoon, Ted Hughes and others) when he worked with the Romanian-born Joanna Russell-Gebbet on versions of poems by Marin Sorescu.

The poet, living in a society of recurring if isolated acts of violence and knowing the historical momentum by which these acts are moved and even motivated, does not wholly surprise us if he turns to other cultures where violence, terror and oppression have persisted. If such conditions have pertained where great poetry has yet been written, then the place cannot fail to interest the Irish poet, however distant the place may actually be. But the converse of Heaney's silence on the impact of translation in Ireland is that his Slavic interests are oddly persistent *and* gappy. He is primarily concerned with writers from Eastern Europe who live in the West (Brodsky and Milosz) and to a lesser extent with writers (Holub and Herbert) who have travelled in the West and are somehow protected at home by their reputation abroad. Sorescu, whom alone among those names Heaney has 'translated', is a wholly anomalous case, essentially a poet with a comic, even absurdist, vision of reality; opportunities to read him either as a truth-teller in some admirable political sense or as a persecuted lyricist are rare indeed. Moreover, Romania is a brutal despotism, hostile to Soviet socialism and explicitly racialist in its persecution of its (mainly Hungarian and German) minorities. To be sure, this preponderance of untypical cases is balanced by Heaney's interest in the extreme, fully terminal case of Osip Mandelstam, who was killed in one of

Stalin's camps. Yet the slenderness of his list is damaging to any case for analogical interpretation: why is there little allusion to Boris Pasternak, who survived Stalin, or to the victims and survivors of Nazism? The Romanian-born Paul Celan exemplifies both victim and survivor.

The general cultural framework in which Heaney's Slavic interests are maintained might be best described in the following sentence: 'A grant-aided pluralism of fashions and schools, a highly amplified language of praise which becomes the language of promotion and marketing — all this which produces from among the most gifted a procession of ironists and dandies and reflexive talents, produces also a subliminal awareness of the alternative conditions and an anxious over-the-shoulder glance towards them'. The sentence might be read as a description of Faber and Faber *in flagrante delicto*, of *The Sunday Times* combining investigative journalism in Crossmaglen with colour-supplement ads for the Folio Society's *War and Peace*, of — finally — the American circuit of university-based poets endlessly meeting each other in conference and (sometimes) in congress. The sentence, in other words, might be read as deeply hostile to the intellectual environment in which Seamus Heaney works. But the crucial point is that the sentence is his own; coming from 'The Impact of Translation', it is not utterly distinct from the self-accusation so thoroughly worked for in 'Station Island'.

Examining the sentence more closely, I do not think that 'alternative conditions' properly accounts for the relation between East and West as locations for the poet. But in other regards, the sentence catches at the global level the brutal inanity of the British press on death in Carrickmore. There is not, I think, a poet (or novelist, or playwright etc.) for whom the conditions are available as — even coerced — *alternatives*. Heaney cannot simply become Herbert, any more than Brodsky, being expelled from the Soviet Union, ceases to be Russian. Moreover, while Brodsky was in penal confinement in the Soviet Union, his impact in Ireland — through western translation of course — was arguably greater than in the years since his naturalization in America and the commencement of his regular visits to Dublin. In poetry, 'conditions' can hardly be classified in any neat way, and certainly not in some binary system deriving from wholly non-literary 'alternatives'. Regarded instead as other or different conditions, they gradually appear to be less uniform, less susceptible to generalization. And the risk Heaney takes in fixing on Milosz or Holub is that the individual writer becomes the basis for a generalization. Talk of 'difference', of course, may only encourage the endless interplay of signifiers to resume its dance of death from Oxford to Texas, like some cartoon version of the final days in Bergman's *The Seventh Seal*.

More convincingly, Thomas Mann lours austerely across the shockingly fragmented literature of modern Europe. I have written elsewhere of the disaster for contemporary Irish culture that 'Protestant Ireland' should have failed to produce a similar critical intelligence. Now the other side of that imposed coinage — the sectarian — Heaney's inherited history reveals a similarly damaging lack of comprehensive self-scrutiny. There is much evidence of his feeling guilty — 'Station Island' is constructed round the paradox, the scandal indeed, of a figure hearing 'confessions', though it is he (the central voice) who is most culpable in this company of intimate ghosts. Yet the larger, and unspoken, inheritance of nationalism remains dangerously unaware of the very immediate impingement of its options (in 1916, in 1939, in 1969–72) on Europe. The notion of 'alternative conditions' derives blatantly from post-war political categories, without consideration of the origins of these categories. The result is that his essays, as he acknowledges here and there, spring from a mid-Atlantic view of things. England is now adequately represented by the strikingly provincial Larkin, whom Heaney admires in an unconvincing essay. Of Ireland, we read little except of Kavanagh and the difficulty of the poet in a time of social upheaval. If Kinsella's work as translator is approved, Kinsella's own far more exploratory poetry awaits judgment. All this makes Heaney uncomfortable; but until nation, place, and myth are reconsidered at least as thoroughly as Larkin is, the critic remains a victim of an inarticulated history.

After the renowned *Doctor Faustus*, Thomas Mann wrote a lesser-known novel, called in English *The Holy Sinners*. It is the telling (by an Irish monk as narrator) of successive acts of incest in a family which ultimately provides the saintly Pope Gregorius. We may read Mann's novel as an allegory of writing itself in an age of comprehensive guilt, an allegory in search of a new category — of innocent guilt perhaps. Through this, the artist might negotiate with the obliterated victims, whom he cannot show he has not betrayed. And, with even a lesser surety, he might begin the more demanding negotiation with victors; without the possibility of such ironic election, he wins only a dichotomous assurance of difference from these, and only through death. Seamus Heaney's 'Slavic interest' may be interpreted as comparable to the Irish traces in this novel. They acknowledge and recognize a way not available, a way somehow emblematic of a qualitative integrity no longer to be relied upon here 'in the West'. That Heaney does not focus on Paul Celan or on any other absolute victim of political totalitarianism indicates his recognition that Ulster should not be confused with eastern Europe in the degree of its violent history. Pomeroy is not Pomerania, even on a bad day in County Tyrone.

W. B. Yeats advised that one should not attribute too much reality to

World War I; and Irish critics, ever obedient and tardy in equal proportions, have taken his advice in relation to the Second. There is one Irish novel of the late nineteen thirties which provides a remarkable opportunity to draw Heaney towards consideration of that marginalized Irish literature (Elizabeth Bowen, Samuel Beckett, Francis Stuart) which is deeply anticipatory or responsive to the War. Flann O'Brien's *At Swim-Two-Birds* was published in 1939, and crucial to its elaborately planned formal derangement is the recurring voice of Sweeney, the deranged maledicent bird/man who has been cursed by his victim, a Christian saint. Pastiche medievalism here takes on the comic tonalities of alienation, and O'Brien is closer to Beckett than to Mann in this and other regards. The original Sweeney had been cursed to live in trees, and his reincorporation into the Christian community — a fine, hard, ironic rewriting of the incarnation — proceeded with exquisite slowness, matched by precipitate flights and alarms. O'Brien's Sweeney is a phoenix burnt in the modernist inferno of his fictional satire. The title poem of Heaney's 'Sweeney Redivivus' now explores the comfortable agony of accommodation and success:

> And there I was, incredible to myself,
> among people far too eager to believe me
> and my story, even if it happened to be true.

Even when these present essays are individually excellent, as in the discussion of Sylvia Plath, one shivers in the draught of a gaping vacuum, the neglect of a theme which Plath herself did not avoid. Heaney's family inheritance lacks the full, dreadful, melodramatic character of Plath's, of course. Yet Irish militant nationalism has a more recent history that the cultic, and analogies for the poet's dilemma in relation to it do not begin *ex nihilo* in 1945.

Edna Longley

MISPLACED FIGURES OF A PARTIAL MAP

Peter Fallon and Derek Mahon (eds), *The Penguin Book of Contemporary Irish Poetry*. London: Penguin Books, 1990

Critical discussion of Irish anthologies usually stops at 'Who's in, who's out?' Personalities take precedence over the wider politics of canon-making, and both take precedence over the question of good poems. Indeed, judging by their introduction, little sense of aesthetic mission gripped the Penguin editors themselves: 'This book tries to suggest the map of achievement and variety by Irish poets in the last thirty or forty years.' The muddy prose betrays unclear purposes, apart from that of exporting the product to Britain ('The Irish publishing industry is now a busy and extensive one'). Another oddly worded sentence tells the punters where Ireland is: 'Increasingly the give-and-take between Irish and American poetry is felt, sharing as it does a comparable relationship with the English language, and determined as their countries are by *transatlantic neighbourhood*' (my italics). Should we trust these map-makers, I wonder?

Fallon's and Mahon's belief that Ireland is situated somewhere near Long Island derives from continuing uncertainty about the *loci* of our poetic traditions since Independence/Partition. In the nineteen twenties and thirties desire for a de-Yeatsization of Irish poetry, and for literary decolonization, often led to unsuccessful Modernist experiments on American or continental lines. Good poems by Beckett, Clarke and Kavanagh surmount the formal confusions of that era. And MacNeice, testing Yeats and Eliot against one another, achieved new syntheses. Yet some confusion lingers on in the work of the two poets conventionally supposed to have inaugurated a new dawn — Thomas Kinsella and John Montague. The *Penguin Book* brings no fresh air to the uncritical piety which has, perhaps, helped to arrest these poets' development.

The anthology begins with 'A Lady of Quality', cloned from the well-set stanza of Auden's 'Summer Night 1933'. But when Kinsella gave up a jelly-mould notion of stanzaic form, his content wobbled, as in 'The Route of the Táin':

For a heartbeat, in alien certainty,
we exchanged looks. We should have known it, by now:

the process, the whole tedious
enabling ritual! Flux brought to fullness
— saturated — the clouding over — dissatisfaction
spreading slowly like an ache: something
reduced shivering suddenly into meaning
along new boundaries
                    — through a forest,
by a salt-dark shore,
by a standing stone on a dark plain . . .

Surely this is bad, inflated writing? Kinsella builds a shaky bridge to the
metaphysical, by suspending adjectives and nouns between abstract and concrete
('A faint savage sharpness'), and by applying a thin metaphorical veneer ('grey
waters crawled with light'). Also, to repeat a word, like 'dark' in the passage
above, should be a significant punctuation, an event. Kinsella gives us repetitions
without resonance. 'We ourselves, irritated . . . Scattering in irritation'; 'The
main branch sharpens away gloomily . . . along this gloomy pass'.

John Montague's poems generally have stiffer backbones, more precise
phrasing, better-specified pain. But his patterning sometimes obscures an impasse
between the rhythmic impulsions of Yeats or Auden, and the unemphatic
syllabics of his American models. Low-pressure syntax, which favours partial
constructions, fully realizes itself only in 'All Legendary Obstacles', where
motion and emotion fuse:

All legendary obstacles lay between
Us, the long imaginary plain,
The monstrous ruck of mountains
And, swinging across the night,
Flooding the Sacramento, San Joaquin,
The hissing drift of winter rain.

Here the big adjectives and the place-names count for their full value.
Elsewhere, as in the sad but verbally predictable poems about his mother, you
never quite feel that Montague has risked being surprised by form, language, or
himself. Perhaps Kinsella — as some critics argue — does take risks. But if he
jumps into psychic deep-ends, he lands in formal shallows. Hence the echoes of
Eliot's and Hughes' free verse. His two most interesting poems here, 'Hen
Women' and 'Ancestor', personify the 'dark', and thereby attain richer thematic
and rhythmic presence. But the introduction's reverence for an 'iconic' and
'exemplary' (that overused and dubious adjective) figure seems misplaced.

Later in the anthology one finds more satisfactory examples of freedom in form and form in freedom. There are the transcendental closures of Seamus Heaney's sonnets in 'Clearances'; or, alternatively, the poignant gaps at the end of Paul Muldoon's 'The Wishbone':

> Yet we agree, my father and myself,
> that here is more than enough
> for two; a frozen chicken,
> spuds, sprouts, *Paxo* sage and onion
>
>   *
>
> The wishbone like a rowelled spur
> on the fibula of Sir — or Sir —.

Or contrast the play between stress and cadence in Heaney's brief quatrains:

> Some day I will go to Aarhus
> To see his peat-brown head,
> The mild pods of his eye-lids,
> His pointed skin cap.

(noting the role of 'd', 'p' and 'l' sounds) with Ciaran Carson's elongated haiku-lines:

> I snuffed out the candle between finger and thumb. Was it the left hand
> Hacked off at the wrist and thrown to the shores of Ulster? Did Ulster
> Exist? Or the Right Hand of God, saying *Stop* to this and *No* to that?
> My thumb is the hammer of a gun. The thumb goes up. The thumb goes
>   down.

Both poets exploit the force of monosyllables in quite different ways.

MacNeice once reminded writers of free verse that the English iambic line had not been the *same* line over the centuries. Similarly with sonnets, quatrains and other stanzas. Perhaps all poetry belongs somewhere on a spectrum which runs between 'sentence-sounds' (to quote Frost) and 'shape and music (to quote Heaney). It's a long way from Carson's action-packed syntax to the centripetal poise of Derek Mahon's stanzas (though I find the Cork garage a poor relation to the Wexford shed). Carson's extraordinary poems test a crucial frontier, as do Muldoon's mutating sonnets. It's interesting to compare the sonnet-stanza of the latter's 'Gathering Mushrooms' with the ten-liner of Mahon's 'A Disused Shed' and to ask *why* two of the best poems 'about the

Troubles' involve mushrooms.

Although hardly up-to-date, the selection from Paul Durcan indicates that his formal procedures are tighter than one might think: two cryptic couplets; the ballads 'The Kilfenora Teaboy' and 'Backside to the Wind'; the tender sonnet 'She Mends an Ancient Wireless'; the sustained lilt of 'Birth of a Coachman'. And, even at his loosest, Durcan's intonations are unmistakable. There should have been more of his satirical tones — only 'Irish Hierarchy Bans Colour Photography' and 'The Divorce Referendum, Ireland, 1986'. I notice that the Republic's body politic gets off more lightly than the North's: why, in the bowels of Christ, nothing from *Cromwell*?

Equally unmistakable are Medbh McGuckian and Michael Hartnett. McGuckian's style, fluid as Virginia Woolf's, indeed seems 'As meaningless and full of meaning/As the homeless flow of life/From room to homesick room' ('On Ballycastle Beach'). Her poems, for me more radically subversive than Eavan Boland's, make some of the male structures in the anthology look obsolete, like the fiction of Woolf's Edwardian antagonists. I still find 'The Flitting' one of McGuckian's richest dislocations of how man, woman, domesticity, art have traditionally related:

> Her narrative secretes its own values, as mine might
> If I painted the half of me that welcomes death
> In a faggoted dress, in a peacock chair . . .

Hartnett, apart from the self-indulgent 'The Retreat of Ita Cagney', produces some extraordinary music:

> The ashleaves froze without an ashleaf sound.

and

> A wounded otter
> on a bare rock
> a bolt in her side,
> stroking her whiskers
> stroking her webbed feet.

Tom MacIntyre's (too few) translations from the Irish have a related quality. I am not competent to judge the poems in Irish, though Nuala Ní Dhomhnaill's breadth may be proved by how, in translation, she 'becomes her admirers'.

But too many poems in this anthology are devoid of recognizable signature or distinctive form. The first-line test is a good one: has the poet seized an irresistible momentum from the flux of experience and language, or is he merely looking out the window, telling you it's a nice day, and casting round for a subject? I fear so, in the following cases: 'My window shook all night in Camden Town', 'Tonight in the cold I know most of the living are waiting' (Anthony Cronin); 'Bright burnished day, they are laying fresh roof down', 'In the cold dome of the college observatory' (Eamonn Grennan); 'In the air-conditioned drone/Of a room' (Harry Clifton). Surely an anthology should be full of nuggets, not this watery stuff. 'Why can't he make a *poem* of it?' as Larkin enquired. Some contributors confuse poetry with autobiography (not noticing how the father in Muldoon or Heaney is symbolic, archetypal, fictional); some (Grennan, Fallon) with detailed meditations on their environment; some — this being Ireland — with explicit bulletins on the state of the nation. I suspect that Mahon's influence has cut down on the latter. But Irish critics who attack the English 'domestic' poem might remember that there's more than one way of trivializing the impulse.

As for the younger set: Thomas McCarthy, Michael O'Loughlin and Peter Sirr introduce new shapes and shades. Sometimes McCarthy overextends a poem he should cut more boldly. But the sestet of 'The Phenomenology of Stones' and the last stanza of 'The Wisdom of AE' are astonishing:

> And his deepest vision was that feminine thought,
> the lack of a killing view. His thoughts altered
> the deepest enmities. Like a woman who gathers
> her husband's arrogance into a basket of love,
> he took our wars into the palm of his thought
> and stroked the poisons from where we had fought.

Michael O'Loughlin has a cool, graceful, economical line, and does know where to begin and end:

> I move around the city, denounced
> To the secret police of popular songs.
> A name flares in the darkness.
> Moon-sister, twin.
> Who are you? I don't know.
> My mouth tastes of splintered bone.
> I thought I'd left this place a long time ago.
>
> ('Posthumous')

Peter Sirr may be a little too aware of 'writing', of the post-modernist and semiotic odds: 'a shaded nipple just visible/under the woolly *O* of Holland';

'observing how/The troublesome genitive falls into disuse/In an afterglow of language'. Yet Sirr works at language with an ambition that pays off in 'Understanding Canada':

> Tonight
> he is understanding Canada
> curled up under the standard lamp
> with his thoughtful look, eyeing me
> like a Whiteoak dreaming of Jalna . . .

True ambition has become rarer since the Irish publishing-industry became as 'busy and extensive' as the British. Marginalization of Irish/ Catholic/ Protestant/ Women/ Northern/ Southern poets often at least made them try harder . . .

Rather than aesthetics, the Penguin introduction gives us the politics of publishing and of South-North literary rivalry. Its preliminary reading of 'traditions' defers to, but defers MacNeice ('associated with the English tradition . . . His ironic inflections are audible in the early work of [X, Y and Z]'). Whereas: 'More than MacNeice, more than Yeats, Kavanagh may be seen as the true origin of much Irish poetry today.' We then proceed to Liam Miller and the 'centrality' of Kinsella. (What about the centrality of Faber, OUP, Secker, Bloodaxe?) Having so easily broken the connection with England, the editors move on to declare their idealistic 'polemical purpose', *viz* 'to correct imbalances created over the years by editors, publishers and critics [who can they mean?], and to dispel the illusion that Irish poetry has been written exclusively by persons of Northern provenance, whether they live in Belfast, Dublin, Dingle or Berkeley, California'. Temper, temper. They even endorse Kinsella's notorious claim that 'the Northern phenomenon' remains 'largely a journalistic entity' (another peculiar phrase from the maestro). Immersed as they are in literary politics, Fallon and Mahon have forgotten the larger politics within which writers of Republican outlook strive to deny all Northern difference. I submit that the anthology's very text demonstrates how the cultural, formal, and socio-linguistic dynamics of the 'Northern' poems differ from the other material. This is a circumstance which should give rise to interested analysis, rather than to self-betraying cultural defence. In the meantime, perhaps some Northern poets would do well to maintain their dual presence — with its shifting contextual significance — in this anthology and *The Penguin Book of Contemporary British Poetry*.

Before he read the *Penguin Book*, an anxious personage from Southern literary circles asked me if it was 'sane' (presumably as compared with the insanities of Muldoon and Kinsella). By this I think he meant: 'Has a fair muster of the standing army been paraded; is the poetic universe the right way up again, with Dublin calling the shots according to its 'central' right; has 'Irish poetry' once more become a single tradition with a 'true origin'? I have my own arguments with Muldoon's *Faber Book of Contemporary Irish Poetry*. But its sins of omission may be preferable to including a dozen poets who, by my reckoning, do not deserve their place in 'the *Penguin*'. However, at least, there now exists a plurality of anthologies, engaged in a quarrel with one another. I hope that readers will approach that quarrel in aesthetic terms, and not fall back on old complacencies which Fallon and Mahon seem unhealthily eager to resume.

Jerzy Jarniewicz

THE CASUALTIES OF HISTORY
Two essays: 'Extract from work in progress'

Recent events in Eastern Europe have overthrown governments and numerous well-established institutions, destroyed political careers and launched new political careers, redrawn maps and withdrawn foreign troops, repainted urban landscapes and reshaped human expectations. One way of looking at these galloping events is to see what has happened to *words*. As a writer, and not a professional politician, I find it most fascinating and revealing to concentrate on the changes in the usage and the meaning of words that occurred in the turbulent years of Polish history.

When over forty years ago, as a result of an election fraud, the communist party took over the political power in Poland, one of the first things the regime did was to change names of several institutions associated with the old, overthrown system. Underlying this decision was clearly a shamanistic belief that by changing the name you change the institution itself. That is what happened with the POLICE, which was hastily rechristened as MILITIA. The official propaganda presented the newly formed (newly named?) militia as an organization which had no resemblance to and no continuity with the old mechanisms of repression active in the pre-war, semi-authoritarian state. Needless to say, the militia very quickly started to play the role of a new means of repression, becoming a highly centralized institution at the disposal of the Party, designed to suppress any manifestation of dissent and to control all possible spheres of social life. It was not a surprise then that during street demonstrations against the martial law, crowds attacked by The People's Militia shouted back at them: Gestapo! — thus proving the inefficiency of the magical powers of the communist lexicographers. In 1989, when communism was overthrown, the word 'police' returned triumphantly: all police cars had to be repainted. Words, just like individuals, monuments and institutions, can become victims of history.

For forty years of practically one-party rule in Poland, the word 'party' has meant the Communist Party (although Polish Communists always avoided using the word 'communism', preferring to call their organization less riskily The Workers Party). 'Are you a party member?' was the question which meant nothing more than 'Are you a communist?' The effect of this illegitimate identification is that today newly formed political parties do not use this word in their names: they are called unions, alliances, congresses, federations. These political groups, steering away from the dangerous word 'party', launch individual politicians rather than produce consistent political programmes. In popular opinion, it is the individual who is known and respected, and not the party he or she belongs to. Party politics is always suspicious and brings to mind practices of the former years. In the long run it may prove to be a serious shortcoming of the Polish political scene.

Among the words most affected by historical changes in Eastern Europe one should first of all mention: socialism, left, communism. When in 1980 Solidarity was born as a mass movement (10 million members!) of workers and intellectuals (or rather the intelligentsia), its slogan was 'Socialism — yes, distortions of socialism — no!' At that time hardly any leader of the democratic opposition would voice doubts about the need for a socialist system: the movement of 1980 was to improve the system from within, not to destroy it. Words like 'free-market' or 'unemployment' did not appear in the pronouncements of the opposition leaders. Martial law, introduced one and a half years later, was a clear indication that the 'owners' of the Polish People's Republic (as the communists were called then) had no intention to reform, to negotiate, to reach a consensus, to share their power with anyone. It was then that many dissidents realized that the system cannot be reformed. Any minute change means its end. Milosz wrote that, with the introduction of martial law, hope was murdered. Now it was either/or. The divisions were clearer than ever. History demonstrated that, by introducing martial law, the communists started an inevitable, suicidal process of the destruction of their system.

Nine years later, in 1989, Polish opposition leaders sat at the round table talks and discussed possibilities of a peaceful departure from what they called then the 'Stalinist model'. For some time hardly anybody would use other words to describe the system they were fighting against. At that stage only such a formula was acceptable to the Polish communists and it harmonized well with the changes in the Soviet Union. Thirty-five years after Stalin's death, thirty years after Khrushchev's secret report denouncing Stalinism, leaders of the Polish opposition defined their political goal as the elimination of Stalinist elements! That clearly was a case of what I would call 'tactical semantics' . . . Yet this was a very brief period: after the overwhelming victory in the elections of 1989 (99 per cent of senators were Solidarity candidates), nobody felt the need to pretend that the real objective was the destruction of communism and not only of its Stalinist version.

But once the process started, it could not be stopped. The communists in their propaganda have very skilfully and successfully appropriated the notion of socialism — to the point of making socialism and communism indistinguishable terms to a common citizen. Unashamedly, communist organizations called themselves 'socialist'. At the same time, obsequious historians were busy rewriting history in order to eradicate all other forms of socialism: all those who cherished different views on what socialism means were either declared renegades and sentenced to non-being, or presented in such a way that concealed all crucial differences and problematic issues — after which modifications, these unorthodox socialists could be put in the line of the only true history of socialism running from Marx through Lenin to Brezhnev. In communist Poland, where everyone had to study the history of the working-class movements, just a few realized that there were essential differences between, for example, Rosa Luxembourg and Lenin. That the word 'socialism' has become that vulnerable was also due to the vagueness of its meaning. Is socialism an economic dogma that does not allow for the private ownership of the means of production? Or does it concern only the distribution of goods and accepts state interventionism in this field? Or does it simply mean that the state should provide social security with free health service, free education, labour legislation? If socialism as an economic theory has failed, does it mean that its other forms are equally abortive? However harmful it may be to the state of Polish political thought, it was not unexpected that when communism collapsed, socialism also fell victim of the dissatisfied, disillusioned and angry people. The odium attached to the word 'socialism' gave birth to (a) almost unanimous acceptance of the idea of free market, (b) popular distrust of any political movement that associates itself with socialist tradition. Except for one insignificant group, there is no party of the Polish left that would call itself socialist. The only palatable term akin to socialism is social-democracy, and this too has been made suspicious since the former communists during just one night underwent mystical transfiguration and called their new party Polish Social Democracy. This miraculous process of change did not take place at Mount Tabor, but in the Warsaw Palace of Culture, named after Stalin and known to be the most shocking example of the socialist taste in architecture: marbles, spires, chandeliers, colonnades, dozens of figures of idealized, muscular, healthy, optimistic workers — larger than life. The change of the Party's name was yet another instance of the perversities of political semantics: only a few years earlier, the list of words that functioned in the communists' lexicon as words of abuse included: anarcho-syndicalist, revisionist, reformist, Trotskyist, and social democrat. These were very dangerous words, used to attack and denounce the political opponents of communism.

On the other hand, the unreserved support for the idea of free-market made it the most popular word now in the Polish political dictionary, used as lavishly as the word 'socialism' was formerly used — by politicians of various, mutually incongruous political orientation. 'Free-market' is a shibboleth, a word understood differently by different people, but that is not important: what matters is that today it legitimizes one's political career. It is interesting that in this turbulent political situation nearly every concept is questioned, even 'democracy' — one of the leading politicians has recently called to abandon the dogmas of democracy, believing that it is not possible to get rid of the totalitarian system by means of pure democratic changes, the situation demands authoritarian, decisive leadership which will be able to create conditions for later development of the truly democratic system. But even though democracy is questioned, the concept of 'free-market' shares with the Pope the dogma of infallibility.

The spectacular collapse of communism did not only mortally infect the word 'socialism', but also affected the more general term 'the Left'. It is a significant fact that many Polish politicians who were apprenticed in the opposition and whose background and political views are clearly leftist, take pains to avoid the use of the word 'Left'. The division between Left and Right is now widely considered anachronistic and inadequate. An *émigré* Polish philosopher, Leszek Kolakowski, claims that the division lost its meaning after the outbreak of World War I, when the Leftist belief in internationalism proved only a wishful thinking as national interests won over the class issue. The words 'Left' and 'Right', says Kolakowski, have lost their sense. It is possible now to imagine the following conversation: A. 'So you say you're a Leftist, but this means you support Stalin, Pol Pot and Ceauşescu. And Hoxha's regime in Albania.' B. 'Oh no. I support Mitterrand, not Stalin. But you are right-wing. Does it mean you give support to Pinochet, to the apartheid in South Africa, to the anti-semitic groups in Poland?' A. 'Certainly not. I do not support Pinochet, but John Major.' Instead of using these ambiguous and misleading labels, Kolakowski suggests speaking of open and closed mentality. The former would be the one that adheres to the ideas of tolerance, social equality, rational discussion. The latter is characterized by tribal, chauvinistic and xenophobic thinking.

Unfortunately it has to be made clear that years spent in opposition to the totalitarian regime do not necessarily guarantee the open mentality. It is a romantic myth to believe in the redeeming powers of participating in a just struggle. Fighting with evident injustice, as was the case in Poland, does not always make one more tolerant, understanding and open-minded. Struggling against the common enemy is an abnormal situation which develops its own logic — and often it has to be a simplified logic, the main assumption of which is that the world has a manichean character and is divided into black and white, good and evil. Following that logic, one takes for granted that 'the enemy of our enemy is our friend' to the conclusion that Polish trade unions used to treat Margaret Thatcher and Ronald Reagan as cult figures. Following that logic, one is inclined to believe that 'if you are not with us, you are against us' with the consequence that a few public figures who kept apart from political discussions of the last decade were ostracized by public opinion. Following that logic, one tended to make political views the main criterion in assessing people, without any real regard for their competence, intelligence, skill, or artistic talents.

Living in a totalitarian state was like living in a permanent state of emergency, where many values and norms have been suspended. It could not be a favourable milieu for developing the open mentality. The present-day political scene in Poland is in many ways an aftermath of that state of emergency. The chaos generated by communism and introduced to the world of words and ideas, the real casualties of history, will still haunt not only my part of Europe.

THE WANING OF UTOPIAS

'Heard melodies are sweet, but those unheard are sweeter', writes John Keats in his 'Ode on a Grecian Urn'. Confined in the world of space, time and matter, subjected to the irreversible processes of change and decay, unheard melodies of perfect harmony lose much of their potential beauty. Reality tends to dissatisfy by brutally dragging down our most cherished ideals to the horizontal world of earthly dimensions. An open spectrum of unlimited possibilities, including everything that might be — from potency to act. There can be no symmetry between what is and what might be; the latter always possesses the unique and enviable privilege of taking no account of flesh, blood, sweat and tears; the privilege of ignoring the prosaic and unexciting domain of yards, pounds, and minutes.

Dissatisfaction with the factual world goes hand in hand with the dream of an ideal and perfect reality. This dream may become a model for the rearrangement of the dissatisfying world, turning into utopias visions of perfect communities living in harmony, free from anxiety, unhappiness, poverty, hunger, frustration, inflation and other possible dangers. In the hands of fervent revolutionaries, utopias work as practical guidebooks: instructions of how to mould the world into a shape resembling the inspired vision.

Dissatisfaction with the actual world may be directed towards the past or to the future. It often happens that people idealize certain periods from history, real or mythological, and perceive them as Arcadias: lands of innocence that remind us so often of our own childhood when everything was simple and unproblematic. The world used to be better; present ailments may be cured by a return to the ways things were. It is an idealized past: our memory tends to select the most beautiful aspects, shifting into the dark hole of forgetfulness everything that could introduce discord. This is nostalgia.

But there are others who, dissatisfied with present reality, project their visions into the future and see them as realizable potentials, guide-posts even on the road of their missionary activity. This is utopia.

Utopia is totalizing: it is the product of one's inner belief that everybody should live in happiness. It disregards those who would dream of a different kind of a happy life, those who understand the meaning of this very vague word in a different way. Utopia is blind to the fact that human beings often behave in an irrational way and often are ready to resign from happiness in order to affirm their individual sovereignty. Programmed, declared happiness may be oppressive; curtailing one's freedom. In Aldous Huxley's novel *Brave New World*, one of the chief characters, John, rejects the comfortable, affluent life and retreats to a desert where he wilfully exposes himself to suffering and pain. This may seem the most unreasonable act to perform in the light of what we usually understand by the word 'happiness'. However, what is most important to John is the need to exercise his free will, his freedom, without which human beings cease to be human. And this freedom includes the freedom to be unhappy.

Utopia is reductive; by defining the 'happiness', it perverts a meaning which is in fact open and undefinable. In the same way, trying to define a 'human being' usually enslaves man in a dead formula, excluding simultaneously all those who do not conform to the definition — they are non-humans, who may be variously called madmen, perverts, dissidents, *üntermenschen*, Blacks or Jews; in any case, there is no place for them in the well-programmed machinery of the utopian community. There is no room for them among humankind fixed in a clear-cut formula. If happiness is reduced to purely social, political, or economical terms, then all the anxiety that stems from biological limitations of a human being, or from the existential context, is declared to be mystified, immature consciousness — and to be ignored, neglected and ridiculed.

Utopia is dogmatic; the elementary dogma is that man is essentially good. What makes people behave in an evil way are social conditions which can be altered. If social injustice, social inequality, poverty, hunger, unemployment, exploitation are removed, people will be kind to each other; aggressive and destructive acts will be unheard of, altruism will flourish. This belief in the essential goodness of mankind has been responsible for a long-lasting blackmail. For years we have been told by the most powerful utopian thinkers of this century that the concept of the evil nature of man has been always used by authoritarian, repressive institutions — the Church, the Family, the State, to legitimize their power and privileges. Whoever spoke of the evil nature of mankind was accused of taking part in a conspiracy with the forces of repression, a conspiracy aimed at keeping people in ignorance and subjugation.

Today we can observe the spectacular dilapidation of the castles of utopian thinking. Two great great totalitarian monstrosities, Nazism and Stalinism, have taught people to be suspicious about any system which tries to define the value of an individual by the degree of his or her participation in a bigger organism — state, nation, class. Together with the unmasking of the true face of states that try to control all aspects of human life, there has come the distrust of any theory that ventures to encompass everything by generating reductive definitions and systematic explanations. Poetry of today, responding to this historical experience, looks at the world through a microscope rather than a telescope: it scans everyday trivia, the low and the insignificant, the ephemeral and the intimate. Leaves of grass, wet pebbles, wooden knockers, black spiders, old shoes, and hot pavements inhabit much of modern verse. This narrowing of perspective to a small area protects us against totalitarian aspirations, and serves as guarantee of the authenticity of experience, free from mystification and any manipulative intentions.

This turning away from the all-embracing systems is also a manifestation of distrust towards any thinking that reduces the variousness of the world, including the human world, to one aspect only, be it economics, biology, or some other abstract concept. Poets are now drunk with 'the things being various', sceptical of any organizing, autocratic schemes and imposed structures.

Yet possibly the greatest discovery of recent times is the recognition of human limitations, a long-forgotten truth and a turning away from the idea of perfection. Eastern European philosophers, such as Leszek Kolakowski, once a Marxist, speak most sincerely about the crucial significance of the concept of evil to our civilization. Man is not God, and never will be. This truth, however cruel it may sound, is a safeguard against the temptations of the Promethean pride, arrogance and aspirations which — as recent history demonstrated —

often turn against mankind itself. The real lesson that recent history has taught us is to doubt, to accept that human limitations cannot be eradicated and to learn how to live with them. To act as gods and attempt to build Eden here on earth proved to be the most serious danger mankind has ever faced. On their way to the ideal world of Utopia, people forgot that in order to pass the gates of Heaven one has to die. There is no other way to the heavenly bliss than by death. In the meantime, those who would rather live, listen to the nightingale who sits in the dark tree in the corner of the garden and sings for a few minutes, and then is gone, frightened by the creeping cat who has just woken up from a short slumber.

Seán Dunne

POETRY AND POLITICS:
NATION V. REGION
IN NORTHERN IRELAND

Frank Ormsby, *A Northern Spring*, London: Secker & Warburg; Loughcrew, Co. Meath: Gallery Books, 1986

Frank Ormsby (ed.), *Northern Windows: An Anthology of Ulster Autobiography*, Belfast: Blackstaff Press, 1987

Frank Ormsby, *A Store of Candles*, Loughcrew, Co. Meath: Gallery Press, 1986

A curious partitionism, writes Terence Brown in *Krino* No. 2, has been affecting literary life in Ireland in recent times.

Such partitionism affects more than literature and there is no reason why literature should not be affected by it. The nature of partition (what a fusty, de Valera-ish word it seems now) is inevitably reflected in many of the activities which take place in the divided area. This can be as true of literature as of politics or economics.

It has also played its part in the schism of literary emphasis between North and South. Literature has been one of the most obviously successful aspects of life in Northern Ireland over the past two decades, even if much of it was written by Northern Irish writers living in the South or in England. It has been sucked into the political situation even if it does not deal with it, its very obliqueness or concern with non-partisan ordinariness sometimes interpreted as ivory-tower aloofness or smug indifference.

And there has been a concomitant tendency among some critics to regard poetry from the South as relevant only if it can somehow be linked to the national question, to our politics and our questions of identity. The poetry of privacy is seen as irrelevance. Even a poetry as achieved, say, as Richard Murphy's is seldom mentioned in the pages of *The Crane Bag* or *The Irish Review* because it does not fit the agenda as set by such publications. It becomes absent from the indices, a marginal achievement seldom mentioned in dispatches.

The historical and political links between Northern Ireland and Britain have affected poetry as much as politics. Most of the Northern poets publish with British houses: Ormsby's two books of poems under review are among a growing number coming out in London and Dublin simultaneously, though one of them — *A Store of Candles* — appeared originally in 1977 from Oxford University Press. 'Cold Comfort Fermanagh' Andrew Waterman called it then, which was half-true, but too smart-aleck to be more than that.

Most poets in the South have taken their books (especially their first books) to presses established in Dublin, like Gallery and Raven Arts, themselves part of a continuing process set in motion decades ago by Liam Miller's Dolmen Press,

Inevitably, with the extraordinary amount of attention focused on writers from the North, at the same time as the Troubles have continued like a slow bleeding, one wonders if, in the absence of the Troubles, such attention would have been focused with the same intensity.

This is not to crudely imply that writers, to quote Edna Longley's rebuttal of a similar statement by Thomas Kinsella, have 'set up a civil war as a publicity gimmick'. It is quite simply a fact, to which the British government or the international press have not been blind, that a profusion of cultural talent has arisen against a background of political tragedy and inadequacy. Inevitably, the success or failure of the writers, or simply their existence, receives added attention as the province is placed under the media microscope.

Only a fool would deny that some wonderful writing has come out of it all, or say that it is all only a Troubles offshoot. There are those in the South, however, who feel that the nature of the emphasis has created an imbalance in attention. Two anthologies in the past two years — my own *Poets of Munster* and Sebastian Barry's *Inherited Boundaries* — have asserted that there is more to the story of recent poetry in Ireland than a clutch of fine writers from Ulster.

Some of the problems arise because the North is at once a province and a separate country, with a different allegiance for most of those who live there, and with a specific set of problems and backgrounds engendered by the nature and problems of the Northern state. As a result, the ethos and problems of writers living there can be as remote from a writer living, say, in Cork as the problems which face writers in the Lebanon, to which country the North, with its intractable, convoluted problems, bears some resemblance.

Allegiance to a different country, or as in the case of some Catholic writers, the decision to reject such an allegiance, or to agonize over their role in its acceptance or rejection, is not quite the same thing as regionalism, an idea which preoccupies Frank Ormsby both in his own poems and in the kind of books he edits.

His anthology *Poets from the North of Ireland* remains an important book eight years after it first appeared. Curiously, I can recall no one stating at the time of its publication that it was enforcing a literary partitionism. In his introduction, Ormsby does not assert that writing from the North is in any way *sui generis*, and his North, both in his anthology of poems and his anthology of prose, includes Donegal and Monaghan, though oddly the prose anthology includes Patrick Kavanagh, while the poetry anthology does not.

One of the writers whose work is represented in *Poets from the North of Ireland* is George Buchanan, from whose autobiography, *Green Seacoast*, an excerpt is included in *Northern Windows*. Buchanan used a statement of Karl Heim's as the epigraph to his book and that same statement serves as epigraph to Ormsby's new anthology:

The past is not disposed of, as we might have expected; it is, in a very special way, still there and still alive. It has entered into the Now; so that it never becomes old, however thickly the grass grows over it.

Northern Windows, far more than *Poets from the North of Ireland*, illustrates the truth of Heim's statement. It is in their memories of childhood that these writers most illustrate the kind of world in which they lived, for the incidents of childhood become paradigms of one's time and place.

Heim's insistence that the past is not disposed of is illustrated by the opening sentence in the first excerpt of the book. It is from the *Autobiography* of William Carleton: 'It is unnecessary to say that for some years after the Rebellion of '98 a bitter political resentment subsisted between Protestants and Catholics.' For some years indeed, and to anyone reading that now, the past seems less another country than a province of the present moment.

Besides the quotation from Heim, there is another important passage in *Green Seacoast* (a passage not included in *Northern Windows* but central to its idea and to Ormsby's concern with regionalism):

We have heard much about regionalism, of which the chief doctrine is that only the familiar is valuable. If regionalism is to be dynamic, it would recognize, even more, the value of a trend towards the unknown, of a movement of extrication.

Regionalism, however, can be double-edged. At its most positive, it can mean a rich sifting of a local and loved locale, whether it be Hewitt's Ulster or the American South of William Faulkner or Flannery O'Connor, who had as a motto a line from Virgil's *Georgics* which suits all regionalists: *Primus meum in patriam mecum deducam musas*: I shall be the first to carry the muse to my native place.

Regionalism can provide the comfort of roots and the richness of the familiar, but at its most negative it can become provincialism and a folksy retreat from the unknown, a curtain of local piety behind which curiosity shelters. And it can also be deeply conservative, hugging an old order in literature as in politics.

In Ireland, regionalism can easily fall into this trap. In a country so taken with place and loyalty to locale, whether expressed in furious support for a parish hurling team or in biographical emphasis, there is always the danger that literature can be contained to a cosy level where place acts as a handle to hold what might otherwise be a difficult text and to stave off that shift in consciousness, that shaft of light in the mind, which art can generate.

This was brought home recently in a review published in the *Irish Literary Supplement* by J.C.C. Mays of *The Beckett Country: Samuel Beckett's Ireland*. Much of the reaction to this handsome book had an air of relief about it: old photographs showed Dublin in former times, a sepia familiarity pervaded the scenes. It was as if Beckett had become amenable at last, capable of causing a surge of comfort, like the smell of Bewley's or an old advertisement for Odearest mattresses or Lemon's sweets. Mays pointed out the dangers of such an approach:

> The impulse to recognize, to assume that all books derive their power from naming, to forge links with our familiar plot of ground and our neighbours, is only too evident in a literary culture based on place and personality. It incorporates Beckett into the tradition at the cost of what led him to detach himself from it.

Francis Stuart is another example of a writer who has detached himself from that literary culture and the early pages of *Black List, Section H*, where the young Stuart writes a letter 'from the heart of the Unionist North' to a Dublin newspaper on the subject of Home Rule, illustrate how not all those writers who have written autobiographically about the North were concerned to acquiesce in an acceptance of the familiar. It is only a short part of Stuart's book and he was not, of course, from Northern Ireland originally, but it would have been interesting to see this section included as a counterpoint in *Northern Windows*.

Regionalism has other senses. The assertion of a regional vitality can become a political statement, as it was for Hugh MacDiarmid in Scotland, say, where the choice of language itself becomes an assertion of identity. Tom Paulin, from Northern Ireland, has tried something similar, but his reasons have been less forceful and the results seem too often like ideas dipped in dictionaries of dialect rather than springing, as in MacDiarmid's first two books especially, organically from the words.

The historical plight of an oppressed people in a region can find itself expressed by writers whose work contains and enlarges upon it but who remain, disinherited and enraged, outside the parameters defined by the dominant power. There are elements of this regionalism in the work of John Montague.

For writers like MacDiarmid and, to some extent, Montague, it would not be true to say, as Edna Longley says of John Hewitt, that regionalism 'is a version of love rather than of power'. It is about love, for sure, in the spirit of Chagall's statement that 'The spirit of art resides in love'. But if it is about power, then it is power which has been denied; its very assertion in art an antidote to powerlessness.

In the foreword to his anthology of autobiographical excerpts, Ormsby tells how the origins of that book are related to his work on the poems in *A Northern Spring*. When writing these poems, most of which deal with the experiences of American GIs settled in Ulster during World War II and with ethnic groups in Belfast, Ormsby states that 'My sense of the local and its ramifications were renewed to the extent that I began thinking again about public and private, familiar and unfamiliar, individual and communal experiences as reflected in Ulster autobiography.'

In all, twenty-one writers are represented in *Northern Windows*. They include Forrest Reid, Louis MacNeice, C. S. Lewis, Sam Hanna Bell, Polly Devlin, Bernadette Devlin and Robert Greacen.

Most of the excerpts deal with childhood. For their editor, they are united by the way they preserve the singular nature of the familiar and provide access to the unfamiliar, though I imagine this would be true of a worthwhile anthology of autobiographical writing from any region. More importantly:

This selection is presented in the conviction that a region (especially one in which the urge to stereotype and polarize is so strong) should have a sense of its plurality . . . a body of autobiography is one significant expression of plurality.

Having finished reading it, though, I was left with the feeling that most of the writers wrote from within the polarities of a Catholic or Protestant background. I had little sense of plurality: rather, the first sentence of Carleton's excerpt was echoed in different ways throughout the book. This is not Ormsby's fault: it is probably the inevitable nature of such a book in Northern Ireland, no matter how the contents are juggled.

And as someone who was brought up in a Southern Catholic tradition, I found myself identifying easily and without partitionism with those who write from an Ulster Catholic background, whether to reject it or simply depict it as part of their lives, like Polly Devlin and Bernadette Devlin. I am not from the same region: yet Polly Devlin's recreation of a Catholic childhood is one I could completely and depressingly identify with, while Robert Johnstone (whose excerpt is one of the best in the book), writing about his Protestant schooling, made it sound as strange to me as a scene in a film from the last days of the Raj or the fall of Aden.

And I could identify as well with the manner and tone of the excerpt from Charles McGlinchey's *The Last of the Name*, a book full of stories that might as easily come from West Cork or Kerry. It is its *seanchaí*'s feel of closeness to the Irish language, a hidden seam of sound, which gives this book a pace and tone with which I am familiar and by which I am captivated. Again, there is no partitionism in this instance.

Yet sectarian separation surfaces throughout, often humorously, as in an excerpt from Robert Harbinson's *No Surrender*:

> Being children of the staunch Protestant quarter, to go near the Catholic idolators was more than we dared, for fear of having one of our members cut off.

Robert Johnstone tells of his own educational separateness: 'Our geography lessons preserved the medieval conceit that the sun revolved around Ulster with the rest of Ireland as remote as England or Scotland.' This educational otherness also surfaces in a piece by Michael Longley where he recalls a boy from Dublin ('A Protestant but still a focus for our suspicions') who is beaten by a teacher for saying 'Dublin, Sir' in answer to the question: 'Who owns Belfast?' Regionalism, indeed.

And yet, all this is not peculiar to Northern Ireland. Rather, it permeates the South as well, in schools at any rate, or at least it did up to recently. I can well recall, growing up in Waterford in the sixties, how my image of Protestants had to do with posh accents, girls who knew about sex at a young age, people who brought cushions to church and supported the British.

And many people in the South will identify with the fury expressed by the enraged nun in Bernadette Devlin's *The Price of My Soul*, who tore a chart of British history from the classroom wall. Patrick Pearse's speech at the grave of O'Donovan Rossa, which Devlin chose to recite for a talent competition ('The fools, the fools! They have left us our Fenian dead! While Ireland holds these graves, Ireland unfree will never be at rest') can be found in the textbook of English prose used in the South for students studying the Inter. Cert. There is no partitionism in such matters. Such attitudes are, to twist a phrase of Sebastian Barry's, part of the story of the whole island.

There are a number of sections in the book which could not have come from any other part of Ireland, or at least which could not have the same resonances for someone living in the South. Among them I would include those writers who deal with their memories of the linen industry. Of these, Florence Mary McDowell is one of the most interesting. Her picture of people working in Cogry Mill, with their bare cold feet working the spinning-frame, and some of them dividing their time between work and school, is one of hardship and poverty, and it is not one that I will forget easily.

The mills surface also in the work of Denis Ireland, who recalls the mill-girls parading on Saturday nights along North Street:

> 'You're stinkin' wi' perfume.'
> To which the crushing retort was:
> 'Holy God, sure I'd be stinkin' if I wasn't.'

Rural life is represented too, by Sam Hanna Bell's *Erin's Orange Lily* and a splendid excerpt from Patrick Kavanagh's *The Green Fool*. Again, a great deal of this could have as easily come from any other of the four provinces. To state this is not to point out a fault: rather, what appears as Ulster regionalism in fact reflects the regionalism of Ireland as a whole, and the existence of a regional slant makes no difference at all to the worth of the work. To its genesis, yes, but not to its worth.

Taken overall, Ormsby's selection backs up his intention 'to preserve the singular nature of the familiar.' None of the writers he chooses makes any pompous statement or gushes with pious blather. This faith in the worth of the everyday, and the belief that is worth writing down, is one of the book's distinguishing characteristics. I do not believe it to be a regional trait, though by its presence it helps the character of a region to shine through.

And if the poems in *A Northern Spring* prove anything, it is that the whole idea of region is even more complicated than might be thought. The last poem in the book, 'Home', expresses it well:

> Once, in the Giant's Ring, I closed my eyes
> and thought of Ireland,
> the air-wide, skin-tight, multiple meaning of here.
>
> When I opened them I was little the wiser,
> in that, perhaps, one

with the first settlers in the Lagan Valley
and the Vietnamese boat-people of Portadown.

Numerous nationalities are mentioned in the book, from the French or Russians who inhabit his grandmother's imagination, to the GIs billeted in Northern Ireland or France, or the communities of Jews or Italians, a world of dispersals and settlings, of refugees and dispossession.

The central sequence of the collection deals with American GIs based in Europe. It is written with the taut finesse which distinguished many of the poems in *A Store of Candles*. And, as well as showing the situation of these soldiers as they die among the orchards or the mud, or as they mix with locals, Ormsby creates situations which can be funny ('They called themselves the North Fermanagh Branch/of the Brotherhood of Sleeping Car Porters') or which tersely get across the immediate terror of war, and the poetry, like Wilfred Owen's, is sometimes in the pity:

If anything is left of me, it lives
in Ruth, Nevada, where my people farm
in spite of dust and drought, in spite of my death,
or a small town in Ireland where a child
carries my name, though he may never know
that I was his father.

The book is peppered with foreign phrases and also with place-names, those most distinguishing characteristics of any region, and there can be death when these are misunderstood, as in the moving, brief poem 'A Cross on a White Circle':

A cross on a white circle marked a church
and a cross on a black circle a calvary.
Reading the map too hastily we advanced
to the wrong village and so had gone too far
and were strafed by our own fighters.
In the time it takes to tell Bretteville sur Laize
from Bretteville le Rabet, twelve of us died.

In passing, it is worth mentioning that Ormsby's treatment of World War II and the way one aspect of it touched Northern Ireland reflects a moving on in history from those slightly older poets like Michael Longley for whom World War I retains a strong emotional, familial hold. World War I surfaces frequently in *Northern Windows*. It would appear less frequently in a similar book from the South.

The poems in *A Northern Spring* are every bit as well made as those in *A Store of Candles* but they have a more relaxed feel about them and there is not the same earnest desire to achieve a visual symmetry on the page. It's as if Ormsby had widened the lens. *A Store of Candles* still holds its strengths, its sifting of lives in small places and its tone that is well-controlled. Some of the poems, like 'At the Reception', have a well-made quality about them that diminishes their effect. It is when Ormsby manages to make well-managed but not over-polished poems and still sound like an ordinary man talking that his work is at its finest.

And his new book shows just how very good he can be. While it has no poem that stands out as a major piece by itself (in the way that one can isolate 'Exposure', say, or 'Immram' in collections by Heaney or Muldoon), it works as an accumulation of smaller pieces where the effect is expertly turned.

The long title sequence is of thirty-six poems. Many of them stand out, like striking photographs in an album, and, like those qualities he commends in *Northern Windows*, it is the small, the everyday and the familiar which Ormsby goes for, whether it be in a street or on a battlefield, set among nationalities. His people are not generals or public officials, but the ordinary people of farms and backstreets and ghettos:

> On the road to Pont L'Abbé we met a man
> with his wife in a wheelbarrow,
> a blanketful of belongings under her chin
> like a monstrous goitre.
> Wobbling from occupied France, their faces set
> against indignity,
> between the fires of Pont L'Abbé and the fresh ruins
> of Chef du Pont,
> they stopped at the roadside, stiff with courtesy,
> and suffered their liberation.

It is a very funny book in its wry way. With its pictures of people set in strange lands, it expands, explores and richly complicates the regionalism many of us take for granted, and it answers John Hewitt's insistence that 'Regional identity does not preclude, rather it requires, membership of a larger association.'

The gap between regionalism and provincialism can sometimes be a narrow one. Ormsby keeps it as wide as it should be and by asserting his filial loyalty to his own region, he expands the idea of region itself (a Northern Ireland with its young boy, Ho, 'In embryo the first Chinese striker in the Irish League') and makes it merge with a larger association, an association which includes the rest of us. At that point, partitionism ends.

Dennis O'Driscoll

W. S. GRAHAM: PROFESSOR OF SILENCE

W. S. Graham is among the most neglected poets of our time. It is claimed, in one anecdote I've heard, that his publisher (whom he would disparage as 'Fibber £ Fibber') assumed that he had died in the long silence that followed his collection *The Nightfishing* (1955). Graham is said to have phoned Fabers to indignantly refute their assumption. In the penultimate item of his *Collected Poems* (1979) — a book much preoccupied with communication and silence — he wrote more in irony than in anger to a dead friend:

> Speaking to you and not
> Knowing that you are there
> Is not too difficult.
> My words are used to that.

William Sydney Graham was born to his West of Ireland mother at 'five o'clock the bright nineteenth/of November nineteen-eighteen'. In 1938, some years after having served his time as an engineer, he attended Newbattle Abbey College where working people were given an opportunity to further their education. Nessie Dunsmuir, who was to become his friend, inspiration, supporter and wife, was there at the same time; and the Orcadian poets Edwin Muir and George Mackay Brown were to be associated with the college later. In order to avoid conscription, Graham spent some of the war years in Ireland, working as a docker and farm labourer.

A few years after he had left Newbattle, W. S. Graham's first collection of poems, *Cage Without Grievance* (1942), was published by his patron David Archer. It displayed some of the worst obfuscatory characteristics of his time. A Dylan Thomas accent was, no doubt, a licence to consume alcohol in the 'sodality of Soho' among painters and fellow-poets. Even the titles of Graham's poems ('As if in an Instant Parapets of Plants'; 'Say that in Lovers with Stones for Family') outdid his master's excesses. In his essay on Dylan Thomas, John Berryman listed the following as being among the features of Thomas's verse: unusual epithets, compound words, notions of dichotomy, marine imagery. Graham seemed to seize on all of them without allowing words the breathing space which Thomas did. Instead, he threatened to choke his poems with force-feeding:

Those funnels of fever (but melody to gales)
Tenant the spiral answer of a scarecrow daisy.

In Graham's first two collections — *2nd Poems* (1945) and *Cage Without Grievance* — the main interest is rhythmic rather than linguistic, and some of the poems are probably better hummed than recited. They are not representative of the kind of poetry which communicates before it is understood — the fact is that it can rarely be fully understood at all. Obscure though it is, we gain early evidence of Graham's abiding fondness for winding sentence structures:

Let nothing through love's way leave
But the ringing through hawthorn disciple's name
That ever by my bellstrong mouth I scold
On the grindwheel gale that draws me to calm.

Another justification for reading his precursory collections is the inkling they give us that he saw language from the start as a mysterious and refractory medium. He began by using (or, perhaps, abusing) language and ended by allowing himself to be used by it. To pass through the early pages of the *Collected Poems* is to make a journey through the dense smog of a city before arriving within clear view of the shimmering sea; or, to follow Graham's own biography, it is like the journey from 'Clydeside,/ Webbed in its foundries and loud blood' (p. 54) to Cornwall's 'far-off simple sea' (p. 210).

Reading Graham's verse from start to finish reminds me of a fascinating poem, 'Shaker Shaken', by his friend Edwin Morgan. Taking a Shaker sound-poem of 1847, Morgan proceeds to decode it until what seemed opaque and impervious becomes gradually coherent. The limpid later poems of Graham are like a translation of what has gone before, but the syntax and rhythm retain the stretchmarks of their struggle towards lucidity. The opening poem of *The White Threshold* (1949), his first Faber collection, depicts that struggle as a trek towards 'the word's crest' and its down-to-earth references to hobnail and rucksack come as a relief after so much that is rhetorical and recondite. But, despite successes like the confident 'Listen. Put on Morning' and partial successes like 'The Search by a Town', much of the book is still maddeningly convoluted, with poems scarcely communicating among themselves as stanza coldly snubs fellow-stanza.

Another Scottish poet, Norman MacCaig, wanted his early 'vomitorium of unrelated images' wiped away — and his first publications were excluded from his *Collected Poems*. Graham, however, was proud to display his early symptoms again and he let his work run its full course in his own *Collected Poems*. As belatedly as 1979, he was rather vaguely defending his youthful flings: 'I wouldn't like it to be easily accepted that those were boyish balloons and effervescence. No, I get a certain kick out of early poems that I don't get out of later work . . . Certain things occurred in the early poems which couldn't occur now, and make not just a random shape of ignorance but something else.' This is even less precise, and certainly less excusable, than his defence to Edwin Morgan almost forty years before: '*Cage Without Grievance* is a first book of poems. It's all right, better than most first books, because I am potentially a greater poet than most today which does not make me very great but I am . . . The chief value is the realization that my voice is heard and the involuntary responsibility which comes down on me and makes me more hard working at my poems . . .'.

Graham's hard work brought two notable advantages to *The White Threshold*. The first was an increased skill in dealing with the power, awe and mystery of the sea:

> Always the saving seadoors well
> Worth salt homecoming speaking up
> The heaving hundred weights of water,
> Save me down into a homecoming tiding
> Worth while and breath here with my smothering farers.

Equally significant were the three letters in memory of his mother, with which the collection concluded. They represented the first moves in the direction of those extraordinary poems in which Graham addresses family and friends (living and dead) and plays his own peculiar verse rhythms against the demands of colloquial language. Not that one could really describe the 'Three Letters' in *The White Threshold* as colloquial to any significant degree; but one does sense, in places at least, a loosening of the bonds of language and the resurrection of the poet's own voice. A certain grandiloquence remains, nonetheless, as in these lines to his father:

> Entirely within the fires
> And winter-harried natures
> Of your each year, the still
> Foundered man is the oracle
> Tented within his early
> Friendships . . .

That is a long way from the affecting and unbridled intimacy of his dream-encounter with his father much later:

Dad, what am I doing here?
What is it I am doing now?
Are you proud of me?
Going away, I knew
You wanted to tell me something.

The 'Seven Letters' in *The Nightfishing*, the collection which followed *The White Threshold*, are far superior to any poems previously written by Graham. For me, they mark the point at which he emerges as a thoroughly original poet. Glittering with sea imagery and flickering with puns and internal rhymes, they coil down the middle of the page in short, sinewy lines. Now, for the first (and certainly not the last) time, the reader feels drawn into the poem and spoken to directly by the poet. Some of the letters seem at once addresses to a loved-one and flirtations with the reader. The opening letter, beguiling and musical, contains the lines:

Dear you who walk
Your solitude on these
Words, walk their silence
Hearing a morning say
A welcome I have not heard
In words I have not made.

'Letter VI' is a particularly evocative love poem:

And as you lay fondly
In the crushed smell of the moor
The courageous and just sun
Opened its door.
And there we lay halfway
Your body and my body
On the high moor . . .

Elsewhere in this sequence, there are linguistically virtuosic poems in which he retraces his younger self discovering his vocation for poetry ('Then in a welding flash/He found his poetry arm/And turned the coat of his trade') and employs an embryonic imagery which will be fully developed later ('Here where I lie in language . . .'; 'I heard voices within/The empty lines and tenses'). What Edwin Morgan has termed Graham's 'obsessional preoccupation' with 'the endless dyings and metamorphoses of the self' is evident throughout

The Nightfishing. He cannot forget that we are changing and dying with each passing moment ('Only/Myself I died from into/These present words that move'; 'Now he who takes my place continually anew/Speaks me thoroughly perished into another'). The repetition at the end of 'Letter II' gives mimetic emphasis to the point:

> He dies
> Word by each word into
> Myself now at this last
> Word I die in. This last.

The title-poem of *The Nightfishing* is a long seven-part sequence rich in sea images and rhythms, though excelled in both by other poems in the collection, such as 'Letter IV'. The short poems which surround the central fishing section may seem like loose threads hanging from the mainsail of the poem, but Graham himself opined, in his interview with John Haffenden, that 'The fishing section is too long and filled with the same stuff. If it was Mozart writing that as music — and I'm not speaking of the sound of the poem — he wouldn't have gone on as long as that. It's not filled with enough invention'.

Whatever its faults, it sways with the movement of the sea, rather than with Graham's earlier word-drunkenness, though the journey he takes *is* partly a linguistic one. He refers to 'those words through which I move' and declares that 'Each word is but a longing/Set out to break from a difficult home. Yet in/Its meaning I am'. We also encounter a 'script of light', a 'book of storms'; and 'The steep bow heaves, hung on these words, towards/What words your lonely breath blows out to meet it'.

Some of the more reflective moments in 'The Nightfishing' threaten to destroy the illusion that an actual fishing trip is underway. While parts of it may seem to be the products of desk rather than deck, Graham sought and gained the approval of a fisherman for the poem, just as Richard Murphy had done in the case of 'The Cleggan Disaster'. Graham's language, despite a rhetorical cargo which makes it quite unlike Murphy's, depicts the sea with astonishing exactness. His admiration for Pound's version of 'The Seafarer' is easily deduced:

> The brute weight
> Of the living sea wrought us, yet the boat sleeked lean
> Into it, upheld by the whole sea-brunt heaved,
> And hung on the swivelling tops. The tiller raised
> The siding tide to wrench us and took a good

Ready hand to hold it. Yet we made a seaway
And minded all the gear was fast, and took
Our spell at steering. And we went keeled over
The streaming sea.

Graham's efforts to simplify his language are nowhere more evident than in
the foot-tapping ballads, 'The Broad Close' and 'Baldy Bane', with which he
concludes the collection. But even simplicity of language does not quite
guarantee clarity of purpose at this stage of Graham's career; and 'The Broad
Close', catchy and witty though it is, is a bit rambling in places. 'Baldy Bane' is
not by any means as compelling as the rest of the collection either, yet I find it
a good deal more accommodating than 'The Broad Close':

Make yourself at home here.
    My words you move within.
I made them all by hand for you
    To use as your own . . .

At the end of 'Baldy Bane', 'Silence is shouted out', and it was to be fifteen
years before Graham's next and probably finest book, *Malcolm Mooney's Land*
(1970), appeared. What he endured in material and artistic terms in the
intervening years can only be guessed at — but I am sure that it was horrific.
Malcolm Mooney's Land is the most literal manifestation imaginable of the claim
made by Joseph Brodsky in his Nobel Prize speech that literature 'addresses a
man tête-à-tête, entering with him into direct relations'. Graham, a vivid and
engaging inhabitant of these poems, fixes us with his ancient mariner's eye. His
tone is confidential but it is muffled by the barrier of art:

Meanwhile surely there must be something to say,
Maybe not suitable but at least happy
In a sense here between us two whoever
We are. Anyhow here we are and never
Before have we two faced each other who face
each other now across this abstract scene
Stretching between us. This is a public place
Achieved against subjective odds and then
Mainly an obstacle to what I mean.

In the Poetry Book Society Bulletin for spring 1970, Graham offered eight
'facts' and four 'observations' regarding *Malcolm Mooney's Land*. Among the

'observations' was the following: 'I am always very aware that my poem is not a telephone call. The poet only speaks one way. He hears nothing back. His words as he utters them are not conditioned by a real ear replying from the other side. That is why he has to make the poem stand stationary as an Art object. He never knows who will collide with it and maybe even use it as a different utensil from what he intended.' This brings us as close as is feasible to the essence of the book. Its seeds can be found in the earlier work, but nothing will have quite prepared the reader for its bountiful originality and luxuriant wit. It is among the century's outstanding collections in English. As Calvin Bedient remarked, 'The isolation almost all modern poets feel, having lost their sense of an audience, Graham has had the inspiration to theatricalize; and in so doing he has revealed more about loneliness, about the give and take of words, and about the moment, than poetry had laid bare before'.

Unlike many critics who have been crassly dismissive of Graham as a navel-gazing poet, preoccupied with nothing but his own relationship with language, Bedient identifies some of the broader implications of the poetry. Graham deals with human isolation in a profound and playful way that brings Beckett to mind. Beckett is one of the influences he has acknowledged along with Pound, Eliot, Joyce (whose fondness for puns he shares) and Marianne Moore ('her beautiful self-conscious language').

The title-poem of *Malcolm Mooney's Land* conveys a lonely journey through landscape and literature, through the 'printed' snow and the printed page. He writes of 'Footprint on foot/Print, word on word and each on a fool's errand'. From this first poem onwards, Graham recognizes the necessity and artificiality of art ('Why did you choose this place/For us to meet? Sit/With me between this word/And this . . ./Yet not mistake this/For the real thing'). He asks us to break his isolation by communicating a response ('To answer please/Tap tap quickly along the nearest/Metal'). At the close of the remarkable title-poem, we witness the triumphant metamorphosis of art into truth:

> I have made myself alone now.
> Outside the tent endless
> Drifting hummock crests.
> Words drifting on words.
> The real unabstract snow.

That creative moment is paralleled in 'The Dark Dialogues' when 'over the great/Gantries and cantilevers/Of love, a sky, real and/Particular is slowly/Startled into light'. In the beginning is the word, but the world is eventually created by Graham also.

His aspiration is to be allowed, through words, 'A place I can think in/And think anything in,/An aside from the monstrous'. Silence is never quite subjugated, however. We see a 'northern dazzle' of it, hear a 'long blast' of it, observe the 'behaviour' of it. He holds (to adopt a line from his later book) 'The Chair of Professor of Silence', fascinated and frustrated by it at once:

Having to construct the silence first
To speak out on I realize
The silence even itself floats
At my ear-side with a character
I have not met before . . .
            For some reason
It refuses to be broken now
By what I thought was worth saying.
If I wait a while, if I look out
At the heavy greedy rooks on the wall
It will disperse. Now I construct
A new silence I hope to break.

Beyond its silences, *Malcolm Mooney's Land* has something illuminating to say about love and sex, one-arm bandits and paintings. It also contains a splendidly unorthodox elegy for the painter Peter Lanyon, who was killed in a gliding accident. Having lived mainly in Cornwall from the mid-forties onwards, Graham was acquainted with many of the St Ives artists and was as much a poet among painters as were the New York school of James Schuyler, Frank O'Hara and John Ashbery. In fact, it was a painter, Nancy Wynne-Jones, who granted him the free use of the house in Madron which he and Nessie occupied. Conditions, though frugal, were quite tolerable — especially when compared to his early Cornwall phase as a caravan-dweller: 'The cottage is free. We have no telephone or car, an outside toilet with jug of flowering currant. I did get an Arts Council Grant in 1975. Also I have a Civil List Pension. That works out really at not very much. When something comes up like fixing the front door or thinking of a bathroom or buying clothes or doctoring my poor boy (I mean my cat who has gone and gone out of my poetry) we have little but I am able to put the Capitals at the beginnings of my lines and cook a good steak and kidney pie . . .' (*The Observer*, 1978).

The Peter Lanyon elegy, 'The Thermal Stair', is a far superior poem to the forceful but clotted elegy for the painter, alfred wallis, in *The White Threshold*, though 'the jasper sea' and, indeed, wallis's name occur in both. In 'The

Thermal Stair', places associated with the painter are revisited and conversations recalled. Place-names are used to great effect in the poem — the prehistoric Lanyon Quoit is delicately and appositely alluded to, while the name of a local tin-mine, Ding Dong, makes a tolling sound for the dead friend.

Graham's subsequent collection, *Implements in Their Places* (1977), included touching elegies for two further painters. The first recalled his friend, Roger Hilton, to whom the earlier 'Hilton Abstract' was also addressed. Hilton was an excellent painter whose descent into illness, self-pity and squalor will be depressingly recalled by anyone who has read his *Night Letters*, a book which ends with Graham's elegy:

> He switches the light on
> To find a cigarette
> And pours himself a Teacher's . . .
> The images of his dream
> Are still about his face
> As he spits and tries not
> To remember where he was . . .

It is appropriate that Graham should have written an elegy (or 'night letter') for Hilton, since they were both nocturnal creatures, Graham being the laureate of the 'nightshift', 'nightwalker' and 'nightfishing'. He thinks of his native Greenock 'mostly/At night', writes a beautiful love-poem 'To My Wife at Midnight', and asks in one of his letter-poems 'Are you/Awake or sound and deep/In the bolster-buried ear/Adrift?' When, in his last two books, we catch glimpses of him writing — in poems like 'Untidy Dreadful Table' and 'Yours Truly' (in which he replies to one of his own verse-letters) — it is night. The most haunting night-life occurs in 'The Beast in the Space':

> . . . on this side
> Of the words it's late. The heavy moth
> Bangs on the pane. The whole house
> Is sleeping and I remember
> I am not here, only the space
> I sent the terrible beast across.

The second of the elegies for painters in *Implements in Their Places*, 'Dear Bryan Wynter', is one which shows us Graham achieving perfect pitch in the verse-letter form. His heartbreak quality has never been more apparent and his tone (ranging between the poignant and the ironic) is deftly modulated. It is scarcely credible that twice during his lifetime the poem was belittled by an Irish critic who, in an astonishing display of tone-deafness, characterized its opening lines as a lapse 'into hilarious Thribbisms' (presumably a reference to the pseudo-poet E. J. Thribb, who appears in the philistine *Private Eye*). The style used in the poem might more profitably have been compared with the 'transparent' style favoured by certain East European poets.

Some of the poems in *Implements in Their Places* continue to deal with the conundrums of language, but he quickly sets about *using*, rather than meditating on, language. He is ready for us with all his 'language lines aboard': 'The beginning wind slaps the canvas./Are you ready? Are you ready?' The evolution of his style is complete and he can write lines as unforced and unornamented and unrestricted as these:

Ancient of runes the stone-cut voice
Stands invisible on Zennor Hill.
I climbed here in a morning of mist
Up over a fox's or badger's track
And there is no sound but myself
Breaking last year's drenched bracken.

He assumes numerous disguises in *Implements in Their Places*, 'choosing/An attitude to make a poem'. He adopts the 'attitude' of jungle-dweller, letter-writer, speech-maker and photographer, in performances that again show him to be a poet of spectacular sophistication and originality and the supreme comic poet of our time. There is a strong whiff of menace about the photography poem, however — in 'Ten Shots of Mister Simpson', sinister experiences are suggested by the references to gassings, a chimney, an inscribed number and the word 'shot'. By contrast, 'Enter a Cloud', which ends with an amusing 'Thank you' speech, is that rarity — a good poem of contentment and celebration ('I would say I was a happy man', Graham once declared).

Of the disguises adopted in the book, none is more engaging than that of the flautist and composer Johann Joachim Quantz (1697-1773). This poem, 'Johann Joachim Quantz's Five Lessons' ('a bit off my usual beat, whatever that is'), was introduced by Graham on radio as being 'inspired by the prose of Quantz, who wrote the definitive book on the transverse flute in the eighteenth century'. It is a poem about art and its creation and interpretation. 'Every poem is a different way of speaking', Graham held, and he loved to act out this very oral poem in which Quantz, in a series of atmospheric vignettes, is heard advising, chastizing and encouraging 'a young man with talent/And the rarer gift of application':

> You are getting on.
> Unswell your head. One more piece of coal.
> Go on now but remember it must be always
> Easy and flowing. Light and shadow must
> Be varied but be varied in your mind
> Before you hear the eventual return sound.

Implements in Their Places is a marvellous collection, despite the over-extended title-sequence. The uncollected poems written between that book and Graham's death on 9 January 1986 suggest that he would have followed it with an equally fine — and probably even finer — collection. He had earned the Freedom of the Language and was making endlessly inventive use of it. 'The Alligator Girls' is charming, nostalgic and sad as he remembers 'An afternoon by the river with two sisters' when he 'worked in America as a young man'. In 1947, he had won the 'Atlantic Award' for poetry, as a result of which he lectured at New York University; and one of the two published versions of 'The Alligator Girls' (*New Poetry* 5, Hutchinson, 1979) is subtitled 'Remembering Crowe Ransom'.

Inklings of approaching death can be discerned in poems such as 'Falling into the Sea', 'The Visit' and 'The Musical Farmer'. Other uncollected poems include 'I Will Lend You Malcolm' ('Mister Mooney/Will look after you wherever you wish to go') and 'Alice Where Art Thou' (in which Graham's heartbreak quality, that never succumbs to outright sentimentality, is once more in evidence as he recalls his first love). Poems like the partly autobiographical 'A Page About My Country' or this nonchalantly audacious eight-liner, entitled 'The Fifth of May', defy paraphrase:

> This morning shaving my brain to face the world
> I thought of Love and Life and Death and wee
> Meg Macintosh who sat in front of me
> In school in Greenock blushing at her desk.
> I find under the left nostril difficult,
> Those partisans of stiff hairs holding out
> In their tender glen beneath the rampart of
> The nose and my father's long upperlip.

He proved himself to be a fine occasional poet also, responding with sportive gusto to invitations to salute the sixtieth birthdays of John Heath-Stubbs and David Wright. The Wright poem is called 'An Entertainment for David Wright on his Being Sixty' — 'All good poems are entertaining',

Graham said in an interview. The entertainment in the case of this particular poem was very much 'live' — it is one of his most spontaneous works. He sustains irony, intimacy and wit with apparent effortlessness throughout 'a shapeless poem/Of 133 lines', pausing along the way to resume exploring the theme of the ever-dying self:

> You realize I am older
> By seventy-seven lines.
> I am older early
> Up this morning grazing
> Mistress Muse's pastures . . .

Among Graham's uncollected poems, one must finally mention 'A Dream of Crete', inspired I assume by his visit there in 1964. In the parts of the poem which have been published, he writes of being 'busy learning/How to translate/English into English' and of trying 'to speak what I think is/My home tongue'. It is when he finally comes to speak his own language, especially from *Malcolm Mooney's Land* onwards, that W. S. Graham speaks to all of us. He does so with an immediacy and rapport that inspire great affection among his readers, achieving what he termed 'Intellect sung in a garment of innocence'.

'It will be a pleasant thing to have people think I'm a wee bit good', he told *The Observer* as his volume of *Collected Poems* was about to appear. Ten years later, his audience remains unjustly small; but his best poems look more solid and enduring than ever.

Most of W. S. Graham's poetry is contained in his Collected Poems 1942-1977 *(Faber & Faber, 1979). Uncollected poems may be found in* Aimed At Nobody *(Faber & Faber, 1993) and* Uncollected Poems *(Greville Press, 1990). John Haffenden's interview with W. S. Graham appeared in* Poetry Review, *Vol. 76, numbers 1 and 2.*

John Arden

A POTENTIAL NATURAL CULTURAL VOICE

Kevin Rockett, Luke Gibbons and John Hill, *Cinema and Ireland*.
London: Croom Helm, 1988

There is no doubt that this book justifies its blurb: 'the first comprehensive study of the cinema in Ireland and of representations of Ireland on the cinema screen'. And as such it is informative, stimulating, and very agreeably partisan in its judgments of particular films. ('Agreeably' means I don't have to *agree with* the authors, but their point of view is always cogent and challenging.) I have one carp: there is a little too much of the post-modernist neo-druidical high-falutin about some of the language deployed. A sentence like 'Elsaesser's argument is that if we wish to understand the "affirmative" ideology of Hollywood we must also appreciate the aesthetic structure of "consequence" in which it is embedded: that of narrativity sharpened and accentuated by generic dramaturgy' could surely have been translated into English somewhere between John Hill's reading of Elsaesser and his reproduction of the latter's views on to his own printed page? It isn't all like that, thank God: but there is enough of it to limit the readership rather severely, I would guess. If no one can understand the process of film-making and film appreciation unless they have first taken a university degree, cinema as a popular art will soon go the way of the High Renaissance Senecan drama in Latin.

I am not trying to be deliberately anti-intellectual or philistine, but it is necessary to get rid of the notion that there is a marvellous mystique about the art which must inevitably keep a lot of talented people well away from it. It is a serious danger that, through over-educated phrase-fancying, the entire purpose of this otherwise vigorous book will be lost. Films, like stage-plays, used to be made by ruffians and chancers, as is well demonstrated in Kevin Rockett's chapters on the early days in Ireland. He quotes a parish priest in Killarney in 1911: 'a verbal assault on the "tramp photographers" who had invaded the peace and quiet of Beaufort . . . posturing as Irishmen, portraying the Irish as ne'er-do-wells . . . two members of the film company with painted faces making love before the camera in a churchyard . . . some local lads and lasses were, for a few paltry shillings, selling their souls to the devil by taking part in these vile activities.' The film in question was *The Colleen Bawn*, one of a series of unashamedly 'commercial' short silents expressive of the sufferings of the Irish under landlordism and British rule, made by Sidney Olcott, a Canadian Irishman, who was to find himself in trouble not only with the local clergy but, more importantly, with the authorities in Dublin Castle, who sniffed sedition. No doubt we would today think his work intolerably naïf and sentimental, as well as technically primitive, but it is clear from this book that his name ought to be listed with those of Yeats and Pearse and all the other artists who created the cultural conditions for the independence struggle. It can only be a snobbery that has hitherto kept it out. But, on the other hand, too much rarefied elitism in rehabilitating him and his colleagues would be a snobbery in reverse, and care must be taken to avoid it.

For what, after all, is cinema? Story-telling through moving photographs, that's all. It is true it can be far more expensive, in basic cash and material resources and human participation, than most of the other public arts; but all films do not have to approach the condition of *Ben Hur* or *Heaven's Gate* any more than all music must aspire to be Wagner's *Ring* or Handel's *Messiah*. And music on a scale appropriate to the national income can be sampled in certain pubs and houses in almost any town or village in Ireland. But surely film-makers have to be highly trained? In fact, of course, no more and no less than any skilled fiddler or bodhrán-player: practice and experience counts for more than all else. Combined with imagination. The country is crammed with frustrated individuals whose imaginations are unparalleled — and tragically unharnessed. Film-making should ideally be as natural to the creative mind as singing or song-making. And it holds quite as much potential for improvisation, which I take to be a notable Irish quality. Yet the general response of politicians and the like, when told that Ireland ought to be making much more cinema, is to say something evasive on the lines of: 'Ah, God, no, not an industry, we'd never compete, though maybe if we *could* get a hold on some outside investment, and see can't we con someone else from across the water into having another go at Ardmore . . .'. They are oppressed by the *mystique*, both financial and artistic. But there ought to be no mystique. If schools were doing their job, telling stories with a camera, film or video should be a part-and-parcel of all twentieth-century education from the age of — say — seven upwards.

In Galway, where for the past few years Margaretta D'Arcy was making her video equipment available to a group of children (average age, I suppose, about twelve, and living within two or three more or less working-class streets of each other), I have myself seen how they responded to the opportunity.

Once they understood the essential technical principles of the craft, they let their imaginations flow week after week. On the whole, the boys preferred to improvise stories of a melodramatic gang-structured criminal sort, derived from TV with a strong input of local juvenile street-life, while the girls preferred satirical aspects of their school-hours and a remarkable perspective of adult manners where married women entertaining neighbours intrigued and outsmarted one another with an embittered and zestful malice. Stereotyping? Sexist? Quite. But children's imaginations will not widen until they have found a means of expressing their existing cultures adequately and effectively. One ingredient of existing culture proved very appropriate to camera-expression: the comic-book. This staple of modern popular narrative immediately led them on to a keen understanding of the story-board, the idea that a film can be preconstructed on paper, saving time and trouble in laying out sequences on location.

Margaretta prepared them for work by showing them videos. The boys tended to demand sex-n-violence to begin with: and weaning them off it had its problems. A showing of *On the Waterfront*, as a violent film indeed, but one with a more complex purpose, was a bit of a fiasco. Its being in black-and-white seemed to render it totally alienating. I had not realized how incredibly old-fashioned so much exemplary 'traditional cinema' must appear to the new generation. But a few sessions of very informal 'comparative studies' began to have an effect: one did actually find the kids discussing the technical and even the emotional impact of different treatments of different stories. And their own work became gradually more complex, less brutally perfunctory, without losing its immediate freshness. In short, the vocabulary of film was soon thoroughly absorbed into their own process of thought. And this in an exceedingly ad hoc environment, a private house with no possible compulsion, either of discipline or regular attendance. A couple of days a week, with a good teacher in a good school, would have fixed it into them permanently.

Another personal recollection. In 1969 D'Arcy and I were living in Oughterard, and we had a super-8 movie-camera. We made a film of the district and its people, originally as a means of discovering for ourselves the complexion of the place. There is no better way to do this than to go from person to person with a camera and tape-recorder: if it is done properly, everyone involved begins to feel that it is their own personal film, and they will offer ideas and concepts you would never draw out in the ordinary course of conversation. In fact it *becomes* their own film: individual authorship is subsumed in the genuinely collective. The resulting picture was called *The Unfulfilled Dream* — its key image was the memorial to those who died in the

War of Independence — and not many of those who saw it were able very strongly to disagree with the interpretation. There was a great deal of social discontent in Oughterard, and a feeling that it was time for some sort of vigorous change. By 1971 there had been a change. The growth of civil rights agitation (which we had noted in the film) had become one-half of a ferocious polarization strongly affected by events in the North. In Oughterard there was now a Land League campaigning for small farmers against the grab-it-all demands of the tourist industry, arguing in favour of an agricultural co-operative in place of the new golf course, and defending the victims of a current eviction. We remade our film, incorporating these new developments. When we showed it in the local hall, it became the focus for an angry debate, where before people had nearly all come to see the earlier version in a mood of general celebration of their own topography and demography. The camera had — in a small way — become an instrument of social struggle.

In 1972 we also made a film about the rent-and-rate strike on council estates with the participation of some young men from Bohermore. Then we went to live in Corrandulla and made a film about that parish. This was less contentious, because Corrandulla was not so riven a district as Oughterard. There was one cause of dispute, the non-availability of the parish hall, owing to the conservative attitudes of an elderly priest (now deceased). For instance, he refused a request for a meeting in the hall to discuss the EEC (then up for referendum) because 'everyone in Corrandulla either knows all about it or else they don't want to know' — a sublimely democratic statement. Some neighbours asked us if cultural activities might be held in our house; plays, music, film-shows, public discussions. It was called the Corrandulla Arts and Entertainment Club.

The film grew out of it. An improvised agitprop play we had done in the house became a dramatized part of what was otherwise a documentary movie. It was shot in a style of comic surrealism and demonstrated a conflict of interest between two townlands which was then obstructing the arrival of piped water to a large number of households. Shortly after the film was shown, a compromise was reached (we like to think the film had something to do with it) and the pipes were finally laid and the water turned on to everyone's benefit.

These experiences bring me at once into contact with the main question posed by this book. Is a small country like Ireland in fact able to maintain a native film industry whose products will not only have an integrity of Irish vision but will be able to present it uncompromisingly to audiences abroad, without whom, it is assumed, the films will not be economically viable? The authors recount the sorry saga of Ardmore Studios, where every shape and

shadow of foreign fly-by-night seems to have been canvassed at one time or another to keep the cameras turning, no matter whether Irish material was being shot or Irish personnel allowed to shoot it. They sadly pin hopes (chapter 4) on the Irish Film Board, only at once to unpin them in the preface (I take it, the last part of the book to be written): 'It is all the more depressing to have to record that . . . the Film Board was being wound up as part of the government's economic austerity programme.' I suppose, cinema being, as I have implied, a potential natural cultural voice for all ages and classes, it must fall victim to the current capitalist solution to the nation's problems: export the nation itself till all that survives of it are the parasite-swarms of Dublin's forthcoming 'Finance Centre', with precious little of filmic content save the variable postures of money-changers at their tables — and even Jesus thought fit to forget non-violence in *that* company (John 2.15). And yet it is company that has to be cultivated, *if* we assume that Irish cinema must be an integral part of the pre-existing structure of the current culture of the west. But if Irish film-makers are in truth mere careerists subordinating their artistic aspirations*
to the calculations of multinational finance, nothing of interest will be produced that cannot be done as well or better elsewhere: and they would be better off doing it elsewhere.

The analyses of *Cal* and *Angel* given by John Hill in this book are a fair indication of whither such calculations lead. Both films, as he shows, offer alienating outsiders' views of the Irish, even though made by 'insiders' — 'What a fucking country' is his summing up of the theme — a falling-in to a pattern of cinema-vision already established by British or American studios to dramatize British or American preoccupations. Both films are highly professional, and their very professionalism may be said to have devoured the more complex implications, the internal contradictions, of their content. But on the other hand, what else can be done?

Hill's account of Bob Quinn's *Caoineadh Airt Uí Laoire* may suggest a few ideas; or it would, if it were entirely accurate. I am myself described by him as an 'important collaborator' on the film. Misleading. I had nothing to do with script or direction. I do remember recommending some modification in the way the British soldiers in the film handled their muskets: I fancy I was the only one on location who had actually been a (conscript) member of the Forces of the Crown. Apart from that, I simply acted my allotted role according to instructions, which is only 'collaboration' in the broadest sense.

---

* Aspirations: such a typically Irish word. As far as I know, no other English-speaking culture makes use of it quite so indiscriminately. Is it not in itself a sad symptom of 'unfulfilled dream'?

Where there *was* collaboration, it was not with me as an individual but with the Corrandulla Arts and Entertainment Club, from which some of the cast were drawn, and which provided information about locations in the area, a roof to shelter the production team during breaks in the shooting there, and — if I remember right — hot soup on a very cold day. This could not have happened if Bob Quinn had not visited our house to see films and discuss them and argue about the craft during the previous months. I may not go too far, indeed, if I say that his Cinegael project (which was to achieve much of such unique, and very Irish, quality) took on a perceptible injection from D'Arcy's work at Corrandulla.

The sponsorship of his Art O'Leary film by Official Sinn Féin was of course the crucial item that made it possible. I do not know if he secured the subsidy before or after he conceived the film, but I think afterwards; and, if so, this is important, because it shows a political party susceptible to artists' 'aspirations' rather than first taking a theoretical decision to enter the cultural field and then looking around for a useful artist to fulfil its programme.

Certainly at about the same time D'Arcy and myself gained sponsorship (practical rather than financial) from the same party for our stage-plays, *The Non-Stop Connolly Show*: and in that case they (expressly Eamonn Smullen, and Des Geraghty of the ITGWU) were happy to back up a script with the writing of which they had had no involvement — except, again, Eamonn Smullen had been to a reading of his own play *Terrorists* by the Corrandulla club.

Now Official Sinn Féin today is the Workers' Party: its current cultural voice appears to be that of Eoghan Harris, who has taken a line on the content of drama and documentary which would certainly not accommodate anything I or D'Arcy would be likely to write, and I doubt if *Caoineadh Airt Uí Laoire* would pass his muster either. His precepts seem to me to imply: (1) the fixing of Ireland firmly within multinational capitalist investment to join as closely as possible with the British, apparently because only by alliance with British socialism can Irish sectarian nationalism be defeated, and only by fetching in the big companies can Irish socialism confront its proper and legitimate enemy; and (2) the presenting of a perspective of Irish film and drama that will adopt something of the ideology of the late Oliver Cromwell, if not indeed the late Thomas Cromwell, with censorship and coercion to bring the nation kicking and screaming (and, one may fear, shooting and bombing even more than at present) into the federated Europe of the future, where all dissent, whether from left or right, will be branded and suppressed as terrorism. The associated art-works being no doubt even more 'external' in their style and sub-text than those deprecated by John Hill. Which is what I like to call the 'international jumbo-jet culture', conveying artists all over the world at great speed to supply officially non-contentious, non-subversive works to docile audiences in the interests of not-rocking-the-governments'-boats-until-the-revolutionary-parties-tell-you-the-hour-has-come. It won't do. Apart from all else, it homogenizes, like a dubious dairy-process: *Cinema and Ireland* would become a totally meaningless form of words under such conditions.

To sum up: given the appalling economic condition of the country, the bitterly divided political factions and allegiances, *and* the manifest yearning of so many of its talented inhabitants for vital artistic expression, the only hopeful future for Irish cinema will be one more and more akin to the history of Irish traditional music and song, small, intimate, personal, and related only to big-money investment or to factitious 'consensus' party-politics where there is a clear perception that the artists' creative freedom will not be thereby obstructed. Technological progress, particularly the increasing cheapness and availability of video-equipment, is marching very happily to such a conclusion. If Venezuelans, or Argentineans, can produce the sort of films we have lately been shown on RTE, under the dire conditions of *their* societies, surely the Irish can?

Tom MacIntyre

ON STATUES

Of a sudden everyone wants to become an Equestrian Statue. Some — our bravest and best — have already made the jump. Curmudgeons abound — 'Death of creativity . . . Art of the politic . . . Well-timed withdrawal . . .' — but let us consider, seriously, this translation, assumption, if you will. What, in fact, is it all about?

A brave simplicity, I suggest. The well-tended park, the plinth (Wicklow granite), your pick of postures, and — little or no delay — lick of verdigris across rump and withers, happenstance wreath to underpin the real McCoy reserved for Anniversaries and National Festivals.

Admit: it has a lot going for it.

The cost is handled by various State Agencies, aided by alert elements in the Private Sector. Further, all Equestrian Statues in the jurisdiction are, naturally, entitled to a salary appropriate to altitude, weight, patina, et cetera.

Is there a catch? The enterprise has its dangers — what enterprise of moment has not? Threat of vertigo up there? Undoubtedly. The remedy is simple. Stare straight ahead. Lockjaw? You'll have to take your chance there. (Vaccination, for multiple reasons, is not an option.) Our harsh winters? Frost and snow — were you aware? — insulate bronze. The plinths, in any case, are centrally heated.

However, an elaborate disquisition on casual hazards isn't really germane. The essential problem is: will there be sufficient room on the existing sites for all those seeking elevation? It is already clear there will not be, and 'packing them in' seems entirely inconsistent with the decorum Equestrian Statues posit, not to say decree.

Happily, a solution presents itself. *Rotate.* A few months on the desired site, a few months in some comfortable warehouse, back to the site, off to the warehouse, that amiable cycle. Tours abroad will also help to relieve pressure. Several Equestrian Statues are presently active as Ambassadors-at-Large. And the Republic of China has asked that 5,000 be sent next year for a major exhibition — *The Tenth Muse* — to be mounted in (or near) Beijing. Plinths-on-wheels (of reinforced steel) are being made available, and will shortly be standard issue.

Now: a word of caution. Once the *translation* (I prefer *translation*, although *assumption* is increasingly in vogue) has been effected, the expression — in the particular and in the general — is set. No winks, sighs, scowls, no movement of any kind (other than such as are required for the exercise of normal bodily functions) is permitted. All candidates are required to sign a statement assenting to this condition. *Fixity* is the buzz-word, and will do as well as the next.

The Central Foundry is located in the basement of the National Museum, and applications (in triplicate, and enclosing SAE) should be forwarded to The Director, Equestrian Statue Project, at the Museum. Applications will be dealt with on the usual first come, first served, basis, and canvassing will result in summary disqualification. To all interested poets, Ádh mór oraibh, 's go n-éirí go geal libh.

Desmond O'Grady

EZRA POUND AT VENICE

30 October 1885 – 31 October 1972

BIRTH

Eighteen ninety eight.
'Mrs Homer Pound and son
spend summer Europe.'

'La Venezia
struck me more agreeable
than Wyncote, PA.'

'I announced my
intention to return here.'
Your son Ezra Pound.

Nineteen hundred two.
Again saw Venice via
London's Royal Mint.

Nineteen hundred eight,
almost twenty-three years old,
Venice became life.

LIFE

Your first adult view of Venice April 1908.
European start in that room over the bakery 861 Dorsoduro
in the twenty-third year of your age.
'By the soap-smooth stone posts where San Vio
meets with il Canal Grande'
Alma Sal Veneziae & San Vio celebrate
that Venetian start & fear
in 'nothing but a small wet village.'

Wabash College never sent the money owed you.
Typically, you thought you could make yourself
a gondolier overnight & make a living.
'I could gondola for a few weeks
without any detriment to my health.'
Never got beyond getting the boat out.
Navigating a thirty-six-foot gondola with a pole
in a summer-crowded canal's no pushover.

Then the unemployment agency man understanding
why you wouldn't take a fulltime job
because of the time for poetry snapped:
'*Vous êtes jeune; vous avez des illusions.*'
So you tighten your belt. Plan a daily menu:
Breakfast bread & coffee. Lunch baked potatoes from a stall.
Dinner a bowl of *minestra d'orgo* — barley soup.
And you 'sat on the Dogana steps
for the gondolas cost too much, that year,'
watching the water change colours.
'I could, I trust, starve like a gentleman.
It's listed as part of the poetic training.'
Father Homer sent some cash.

In June the luck of rent-free rooms.
'More airy quarters overlooking 3 canals.
A fit abode for a poet.'
On the corner Fondamenta & Cal die Frati,
San Trovaso church the one side, Ognisanti the other,
facing a gondola repair-yard still there in my time.
The money saved printed your 'painted on canvas,' *A Lume Spento*.
One hundred & fifty copies at Antonini's shop Cannaregio 925.
Depressed correcting proofs
'between Salviati and the house that was Don Carlos'
you thought: 'shd/I chuck the lot into the tide-water?'
Sixty years later on that same spot with you
I asked how the view looked your own first day there.
'All sail,' your nostalgic whispered reply.

A Lume Spento your first statement. Sent to Yeats.
(As I sent you *Chords and Orchestrations* fifty years later.)
A book to show in London — your decided destination
'to sit at Yeats' feet who knew more about poetry
than anybody else, and learn what he knew.'
Then began the fifteen poems of your San Trovaso Notebook
'painted in ivory' in praise of Venice.
Printed London 1908 *A Quinzaine for this Yule*.

That Venice summer crucial.
Time to take stock of life, vocation, mission;
to print, distribute, your cut top-soil,
defeat doubt, confront London.

Taking after the O'Connell Irish side of her family
Miss Olga Rudge, concert violinist, got 252 Cal Querini, Dorsoduro
out of her father before the Great Crash.
You were at 779 on the Zattere.

A happy home, that *trinitate* 'hidden nest'.
Safe anchorage amid familiar haunts late summers, autumns.
The jewelled bird there a gift from d'Annunzio.
Two pairs of Japanese shoes.
A gray opaque of Tami Koumé on the stairs.
That big book between wooden boards was Ovid.

A marble face set in the wall by the top-floor desk
Isotta da Rimini in bas-relief.
(All still there my last stay 1987)
And your daughter Maria aged four on her first visit.
Cantos drafting by then at XXX
Nancy Cunard's Hour's Press, Paris 1930.

Dudley Fitts judged them
'the most ambitious poetic conception of our day . . .'
The challenge: a form elastic enough to hold material.
Matter: the makings of civilization, culture.
Method: free accretion of words, phrases, lines.
Dreamed from the start.

Late summer, early autumn Venice routine:
morning black malacca cane walk
to 310 San Gregario, Signora Scarpa's rented room.
Ply at Cantos on the typewriter. Answer post.
Olga practised Vivaldi violin, Cal Querini.
Maria visiting, family lunch with passion flowers in fingerbowls.

Evening stroll on the Zattere or off with Maria aged five
to Piazza Santa Steffano for 'the best ice cream in Venice'.
After dinner reading new Cantos to chosen friends
with a confusion of three pairs of rimless *pince-nez*.
Mamile Olga dressed in a Duchess of Alba pose.
Maria's long hair loose & shining after an hundred *coup de brosse*.
After Christmas 1939 George Santayana at Hotel Danieli.
'Never met anyone who seems to me to fake less,' you wrote T.S.E.
Did you really 'see eye to eye on most things'?

Health not so hearty 1962 prostrate in clinics.
End of the year back to Dorsoduro Olga for good.
'Nothing matters but the quality
of the affection —'
And back to Edwardian elegance in dress 1909:
broad-brimmed black hat, broad collars & tie,
black overcoat, malacca cane.
You cut the most numinous presence in Venice.

Grown silent you denounced the Cantos to Cory:
'a botch. That's not the way to make a work of art.' 1966.

'If a man have not order within him
he cannot spread order about him . . .'

Myself back from America I visited weekends,
told you what I'd 'seen and learned
to help kill the winter.'
You walked me in silence. I followed.
Olga cleaned house, shopped, set table.
'Nothing matters but the quality
of the affection — '
Hospitality of sacred & profane heart, home, spirit.
Walk. Stop. Observe. Walk on. In silence.
No need for talk. All was 'written down in a printed book.'
Lunch at Montin. Dinner the Cicci or home, Mamile cooking.

'I tried to make a paradiso terrestre.'
No longer a hidden nest, all came who could make it.
All talked. You listened.
And the friends dropping like rosary beads yearly.
'What's done cannot be undone —
The error is all in the not done —
I was wrong — ninety percent wrong —
I lost my head in a storm . . .'

'Let the Gods forgive what I
have made.
Let those I love try to forgive
what I have made.'

'To be men not destroyers.'

DEATH

Monday 30 October 1972
Mamile Olga planned close friends 87th birthday home.
Too weak to descend you sat up in bed. Talked Monteverdi.
Tuesday 31. Doctor decided to move you at midnight.
Ambulance boat came. You wouldn't move.
Persuaded, you walked firm erect to Calle Querini.

Restless in bed in the municipal hospital
you 'saw no reason to be there.'
Old stubbornness still young.

'Sudden blockage of the intestine.'
'You dozed off. Died.
One eye deeply, sapphirically blue, remained open.'
Halloween.
Birth and death of the poet in Venice.

Benedictine Requiem. Mass in San Giorgio Maggiore.
Coffin on the ground before the high altar.
Gondola you could afford that year to San Michele.

Small plot.
Small bay tree.
'Now he's all mine,' said Mamile
planting her foot on the sod.
'He can see the Dogana steps from here.'

'In praise for being and happening'
small stone
two words
EZRA POUND

September 1990

AN INDEX TO KRINO: ISSUES 1 – 18

Compiled by Denis O'Brien

Note

The entries are listed alphabetically under author's name.

The items in each entry are ordered as follows: (i) fiction, drama, and poetry, (ii) editorials, (iii) interviews, (iv) articles, (v) reviews, (vi) when the author is the subject of an article, review, poem or translation, the name of the second author (with an abbreviated description of the relevant work) is given at the bottom of the entry for further reference.

Individual items appearing in one of the above sections of an entry are arranged as follows: (i) 'title or description of item', (ii) abbreviation of genre, if not already stated in title, (iii) additional information about item when necessary, (iv) issue number, (v) date of publication, (vi) page numbers. For example: 'The Bright Hour' (P), with illustrations by Gerard Coughlan, 5, Spring 1988, pp.88–94.

Abbreviations: (A) Article; (D) Drama; (ed.) Editor; (F) Fiction; (I) Interview; (P) Poetry; (Photo) Photograph; (R) Review; (Tr/tr.) Translation/translator.

Sample

DAWE, Gerald

'The Bright Hour' (P), with illustrations by Gerard Coughlan, 5, Spring 1988, pp.88–94. 'A Fire in My Head' (P), 13, 1992, pp.105–7. 'Crete Summer' (P), 14, Winter 1993, p.15.

'Editorial', 1, Spring 1986. 'The Glint of de Valera's Glasses, Part 1', (Editorial), 5, Spring 1988. 'Editorial', 10, Autumn 1990.

'Aspects of Life & Language: Interview with Les A. Murray' (I), 5, Spring 1988, pp.1–8. 'Thomas Kilroy in Conversation with Gerald Dawe' (I), 13, 1992, pp.1–8.

'A Journal' (A), survey of recently published work by George Barker, W. S. Graham, Tony Harrison, Kenneth Koch, Les Murray, Frank O'Hara, Tom Paulin and others, 14, Winter 1993, pp.88–91.

Review of Henry Gifford, *Poetry in a Divided World*; Michael Hamburger, *The Truth of Poetry: Tensions in Modern Poetry*, and *A Proliferation of Prophets: Essays in German Literature*, and *After the Second Flood: Essays in Modern German Literature*, 4, Autumn 1987, pp.114–17.

See also Jill Siddall (R).

ABBEY THEATRE
'Abbey and Peacock Photographs: MacIntyre-Hickey-Mason', 5, Spring 1988, p.50.

ADAMS, Gerry
See W. J. McCormack (R).

ADCOCK, Fleur
See Bridget O'Toole (R).

AKHMATOVA, Anna
See Suzanne Krochalis (R).

ANDERSON, Barbara
See Eileen Dillon (R).

APOLLINAIRE, Guillaume
See G. L. Curtis (P).

ARDEN, John
Review of Kevin Rockett, Luke Gibbons and John Hill, *Cinema and Ireland*, 5, Spring 1988, pp.63–9.

ASTLEY, Neil
See Stephen Matterson (R).

BORGES, Jorge Luis
See Lorna Reynolds (A).

BOURKE, Angela
'Nesting' (F), 12, Winter 1991, pp.23–5.

BOURKE, Brian
'Cover Illustration', 13, 1992.

BOURKE, Eoin
'Pitfalls of the Soil: Poetry and Atavism' (A), subjects include Irish poetry, German poetry, 'national identity', 3, Spring 1987, pp.49–61. 'Two Germanys and No Germany: Poetry on Partition' (A) includes a selection of poems by former East German and West German poets, 7, 1989, pp.67–85.
Review (with Eva Bourke) of Erich Fried, *100 Poems Without a Country*, tr. Stuart Hood; Miroslav Holub, *The Fly*, tr. Jarmilla and Ian Millner et al; Marin Sorescu, *The Biggest Egg in the World*, tr. Joanna Russell-Gebbett et al; Lyubomir Levchev, *Stolen Fire*, tr. Ewald Osers, 5, Spring 1988, pp.107–21. Review of Hans Magnus Enzensberger, *Europe, Europe — Forays into a Continent*, tr. Martin Chalmers; Claudio Magris, *Danube — A Sentimental Journey from the Source to the Black Sea*, tr. Patrick Creagh, 12, Winter 1991, pp.83–9.

BOURKE, Eva
See Eoin Bourke; Sarah Kirsch (Tr).

BRETT, Heather
'Two Poems', 8/9, 1990, pp.40–41.

BROBROWSKI, Johannes
See Hugh Maxton (Tr).

BRODSKY, Joseph
See Hugh Maxton (Tr).

BROPHY, Catherine
See Eve Patten (A).

BROUSSARD, Yves
'Tending the Fire: Six Poems', translated by Roger Little, 7, 1989, pp.31–40.

BROWN, Terence
'Three Poems', 10, Autumn 1990, pp.33–5.
'Poetry and Partition: A Personal View' (A), subjects include 'Southern' and 'Northern' Irish poetry, 2, Autumn 1986, pp.17–23. 'Translating Ireland' (A), subjects include 'translation' and the poetry of Paul Durcan, Seamus Heaney, and Paul Muldoon, 7, 1989, pp.1–4.
Review of Denis Donoghue, *We Irish: The Selected Essays of Denis Donoghue, Vol. 1*; Noel Browne, *Against the Tide*, 4, Autumn 1987, pp.88–95. Review of Conor Cruise O'Brien, *Passion and Cunning and other Essays*, 6, Autumn 1988, pp.59–62. Review of Tom Paulin, *Minotaur: Poetry and the Nation State*, 13, 1992, pp.140–42. Review of Ted Hughes, *Winter Pollen: Occasional Prose*, ed. William Scammell, 18, 1995, pp.118–19.
See also W. J. McCormack (R).

BROWNE, Cornelius
'The Nature of Things' (F), 16/17, 1994, pp.41–9.

BROWNE, Noel
See Terence Brown (R).

BUCHAN, Tom
See Hayden Murphy (A).

BURKE, Raymond
Review of Humphrey Carpenter, *A Serious Character: The Life of Ezra Pound*, 6, Autumn 1988, pp.74–80.

BURNS, Elizabeth
'Three Poems', 12, Winter 1991, pp.47–8.

BURNSIDE, Sam
See Kevin Smith (R).

BURROUGHS, William
See John Minihan (photo).

BUTLIN, Ron
'Four Poems', 12, Winter 1991, pp.49–52.

BYRNE, Mairéad
'Four Poems', 8/9, 1990, pp.42–5. 'Seven Poems', 13, 1992, pp.9–16. 'Two Poems', 14, Winter 1993, p.6.
'Five Poems', 15, Spring 1994, pp.27–9.
Review of Maura Dooley, *Explaining Magnetism*; Ian Duhig, *The Bradford Count*; Michael Gorman, *Up She Flew*, 12, Winter 1991, pp.90–94.

CAESAR, Ann
See Michael Cronin (R).

CAESAR, Michael
See Michael Cronin (R).

CAFFERKY, Tony
'Mystery Dame with Red Hair' (F), 16/17, 1994, pp.79–85.

CAMPBELL, James
'The Fight Game' (F), 3, Spring 1987, pp.35–43.

CARLOS, John
'Culture of Silence: Pictures and Women' (Photo/A), 3, Spring 1987, pp.62–7. 'In Our Faces' (Photo/P/F),
8/9, 1990, pp.34–9.
Review of John Berger and Jean Mohr, *A Fortunate Man*, and *A Seventh Man*, and *Another Way of Telling*, 12, Winter 1991, pp.95–7.

CARLSON, Julia
Review of Helen Vendler, ed., *The Faber Book of Contemporary American Poetry*, 5, Spring 1988, pp.34–40.
Review of Anne Stevenson, *Bitter Fame: A Life of Sylvia Plath*; Linda W. Wagner-Martin, *Sylvia Plath: A Biography*, 8/9, 1990, pp.130–35.

CARPENTER, Humphrey
See Raymond Burke (R).

CARSON, Ciaran
See Domhnall Mitchell (A).

CASEY, Kevin
'A State of Mind' (F), 7, 1989, pp.15–19.

CASEY, Philip
'Waking' (P), 14, Winter 1993, pp.7–8.
'The State of Poetry' (A), 14, Winter 1993, p.7.

CELAN, Paul
'Seven Poems', translated by Peter Jankowsky and Brian Lynch, 8/9, 1990, pp.97–104.
See also Brian Lynch (R).

CHAR, René
See Roger Little (R).

CLIFTON, Harry
'Three Poems', 2, Autumn 1986, pp.48–50. 'The Walled Town' (P), 14, Winter 1993, pp.10–11.
'Available Air: Irish Contemporary Poetry, 1975–1985' (A), authors include Dermot Bolger, Paul Durcan,
Peter Fallon, Thomas McCarthy, Paul Muldoon and Michael O'Loughlin, 7, 1989, pp.20–30. 'The State
of Poetry' (A), 14, Winter 1993, pp.9–10.
Review of Peter Fallon, *Eye to Eye*; Dermot Healy, *The Ballyconnell Colours*, 14, Winter 1993, pp.69–72.
See also Theo Dorgan (A).

CLYDE, Tom
'An Ulster Twilight? Poetry in the North of Ireland' (A), authors include Seamus Heaney, John Hewitt,
Michael Longley, Medbh McGuckian, Derek Mahon, and John Montague, 5, Spring 1988, pp.95–102.

COADY, Michael
'Four Poems', 2, Autumn 1986, pp.24–31. 'Revolutions' (P), 14, Winter 1993, p.13.
'The State of Poetry' (A), 14, Winter 1993, pp.12–13.

COEN, John
'Bird of Eden' (Cover Illustration), 8/9, 1990. 'Poet's Head', (Photo), 13, 1992, p.107.

COFFEY, Brian
See J.C.C. Mays (A); Augustus Young (P).

COLL, John
'I Heard the Gull Skull Cry' (Four Graphics), 2, Autumn 1986, pp.32–5. 'Beckett' (Cover illustration), 5, Spring 1988.

COLLINS, Lucy
'A Wake-House' (F), 8/9, 1990, pp.14–16.

CONLON, Evelyn
See Eve Patten (A).

CONN, Stewart
See Hayden Murphy (A).

CONNOLLY, Susan
'Self-Portrait' (P), 8/9, 1990, pp.46–8.

CONNOR, Noel
'Cover Illustration', 10, Autumn 1990. 'Cover Illustration', 14, Winter 1993.

CONSTANTINE, David
See John Scattergood (R).

COOKSON, William
See Dennis O'Driscoll (R).

CORCORAN, Clodagh
See Judy Murphy (R).

CORNWELL, Neil
See Sergei Khoruzhii (Tr).

COSTELLO, Seán
'Home Time' (F), 16/17, 1994, pp.24–9.

COUGHLAN, Gerard
'Four Illustrations', with poem by Gerald Dawe, 5, Spring 1988, pp.88–94.

COUZYN, Jeni
See Bridget O'Toole (R).

CRAWFORD, Robert
'Three Poems', 12, Winter 1991, pp.52–4.
'Recent Scottish Poetry and the Scottish Tradition' (A), authors include Douglas Dunn, Ian Hamilton Finlay, W. S. Graham, Norman MacCaig, Hugh MacDiarmid, Sorley MacLean, Edwin Morgan, Iain Crichton Smith, and younger contemporaries, 3, Spring 1987, pp.18–28. 'Poetry and Politics in Scotland, 1990' (A), 10, Autumn 1990, pp.45–50.
Review of Les A. Murray, *The Daylight Moon*, 5, Spring 1988, pp.14–17. Review of 'Field Day Pamphlets 13–15: Nationalism, Colonialism, and Literature': Terry Eagleton, *Nationalism: Irony and Commitment*; Fredric Jameson, *Modernism and Imperialism*; Edward W. Said, *Yeats and Decolonization*, 7, 1989, pp.113–15.
See also Hayden Murphy (A); Andy Pollak (R).

CRONIN, Michael
'Generating Stations: New Directions in Irish Culture' (A), 12, Winter 1991, pp.1–4.
Review of Ann and Michael Caesar, eds., *The Quality of Light: Modern Italian Short Stories*, 16/17, 1994, pp.145–6.

CURTIS, G.L.
'Un Homme Détaché: *A Tribute Guillaume Apollinaire, 1880–1918*' (P), 10, Autumn 1990, pp.36–8.

DUDDY, Tom
'Old Landscape, New Figures' (F), 10, Autumn 1990, pp.71–5.

DUHIG, Ian
See Mairéad Byrne (R).

DUKES, Gerry
'Hand to Mouth: 'Translating' Beckett's Trilogy for the Stage' (A), 7, 1989, pp.90–94.

DUNMORE, Helen
See Amanda Piesse (R).

DUNN, Douglas
See Robert Crawford (A); Stephen Matterson (R); Hayden Murphy (A).

DUNNE, John
'Pictures' (F), 10, Autumn 1990, pp.9–12. 'Purtock' (F), 12, Winter 1991, pp.10–17. 'The Greatest Living Poet' (F), 16/17, 1994, pp.107–15.
'Introduction to Krino', 16/17, 1994.
'Taking the Trouble: Fiction by Sebastian Barry, Dermot Healy, and Desmond Hogan' (A), 5, Spring 1988, pp.132–9.

DUNNE, Seán
'Letter from Ireland' (P), 7, 1989, pp.5–14. 'A Shrine for Lafcadio Hearn, 1850–1904' (P), 18, 1995, pp.36–7. Review of Frank Ormsby, A Northern Spring, Northern Windows and A Store of Candles, 4, Autumn 1987, pp.96–104. Review of Medbh McGuckian, On Ballycastle Beach; Rodney Pybus, Cicadas in their Summers; Derek Walcott, The Arkansas Testament, 6, Autumn 1988, pp.81–4.

DUPIN, Jacques
See Roger Little (R).

DURCAN, Paul
See Terence Brown (A); Harry Clifton (A).

EAGLETON, Terry
See Robert Crawford (R).

EDMONDSON, Ricca
'Not on the Coast of Austria (A Western Fairytale)' (F), 8/9, 1990, pp.22–5.

ELLIOT, Alistair
See Yann Lovelock (R).

ELLIOTT, Andrew
'Four Poems', 4, Autumn 1987, pp.31–4.

ENZENSBERGER, Hans Magnus
See Eoin Bourke (R).

EUGENIDES, Jeffrey
See Mary Bergin (R).

FALLON, Brian
See Michael Mulreany (R).

FALLON, Peter
'Four Poems', 3, Spring 1987, pp.14–17. 'The Cloud Factory' (P), 14, Winter 1993, p.18.
'The State of Poetry' (A), 14, Winter 1993, pp. 16–18.
See also Harry Clifton (A) and (R); Edna Longley (R).

FALUDI, Susan
See Karlin J. Lillington (R).

FANNING, Gerard
'Eight Poems', 1, Spring 1986, pp.24–31. 'Three Poems', 6, Autumn 1988, pp.24–5. 'Seven Poems', 10, Autumn 1990, pp.67–70. 'Moving into St Vincent's Park' (P), 14, Winter 1993, p.19. 'Three Poems', 18, 1995, pp.55–6.

GRAHAM, W. S.
See Robert Crawford (A); Gerald Dawe (A); Hayden Murphy (A); Dennis O'Driscoll (A).

GRAY, Niall
Review of George O'Brien, *The Village of Longing*, and *Dance Hall Days*, 7, 1989, pp.116–18.

GREBENSCHIKOV, Boris
'Three Poems', translated by Andrei Kuznetsov, 8/9, 1990, pp.108–10.

GREIG, Andrew
See Oliver Maher (R).

GRENE, Nicholas
'John McGahern's *The Power of Darkness*' (A), 13, 1992, pp.52–60.
Review of Rory Johnston, ed., *Orders and Desecrations: The Life of the Playwright Denis Johnston*, 18, 1995, pp.101–3.

GROARKE, Vona
'Balaggan Stone Poem' (Cover Illustration), photograph by Pat Redmond, 12, Winter 1991. 'From a Disused House' (P), 14, Winter 1993, p.21.
'The State of Poetry' (A), 14, Winter 1993, pp.20–21.

HADFIELD, Charles
'Four Poems', 4, Autumn 1987, pp.16–19.

HAMBURGER, Michael
See Gerald Dawe (R); Brian Lynch (R).

HAMILL, Brendan
'The Troubles He's Seen: Fiacc and Belfast 1967' (A), 18, 1995, pp.26–35.

HAMPTON, Susan
See Bridget O'Toole (R).

HARNETT, Mireille
See Biddy Jenkinson (Tr).

HARRISON, Tony
See Gerald Dawe (A); Stephen Matterson (R).

HARTE, Liam
Review of Edna Longley, *Poetry in the Wars*; W. J. McCormack, *The Battle of the Books*, 4, Autumn 1987, pp.118–25.

HARTNETT, Michael
See Conor Kelly (R); Seán Ó Tuama (A).

HARVEY, Francis
'Voyagers' (P), 14, Winter 1993, p.23.
'The State of Poetry' (A), 14, Winter 1993, pp.22–3.

HATTENDORF, Manfred
'Journey in a Buoyant maze: Six Months in Irish Film, 1987' (A), 5, Spring 1988, pp.70–77.

HAUGHTON, Hugh
Review of J.C.C. Mays, ed., *Denis Devlin: Collected Poems*, 11, Summer 1991, pp.38–49.

HAYES, Aidan
'Five Poems', translated from Jacques Bertin, 10, Autumn 1990, pp.29–32.

HAYES, Trudy
See Judy Murphy (R).

HAYWARD, Max
See Suzanne Krochalis (R).

HEALY, Dermot
'Mayday' (F), 6, Autumn 1988, pp.6–10.
See also Harry Clifton (R); John Dunne (A).

JANKOWSKY, Peter
See Paul Celan (Tr).

JARNIEWICZ, Jerzy
'Two Essays: *The Casualties of History*, and *The Waning of Utopias*' (A), 13, 1992, pp.17–26.
Review of Anna Kamienska, *Two Darknesses*, tr. Tomasz P. Krzeszowski and Desmond Graham, 18, 1995, pp.97–100.

JENKINSON, Biddy
'Trí Dhán (Three Poems)', with French translations by Mireille Harnett, 11, Summer 1991, pp.32–7.
See also Seán Ó Tuama (A).

JOHN, Brian
Review of Thomas Kinsella, *Blood and Family*; John Montague, *Mount Eagle*, 7, 1989, pp.108–12.

JOHNSON, Linton Kwesi
See Stephen Matterson (R).

JOHNSTON, Denis
See Nicholas Grene (R).

JOHNSTON, Fred
'A Time of Honour' (F), 3, Spring 1987, pp.69–74. 'Five Poems', 12, Winter 1991, pp.74–6. 'Indian Summer' (F), 16/17, 1994, pp.30–32.

JOHNSTON, Jennifer
'Laura' (F), 10, Autumn 1990, pp.21–6. 'From Star' (F), 13, 1992, pp.101–4.

JOHNSTON, Rory
See Nicholas Grene (R).

JOHNSTONE, Robert
'Six Poems', 3, Spring 1987, pp.29–34. '*From* A Sequence in Progress: Six Poems', 13, 1992, pp.77–82.
'Postcards from Thatcherland' (A), 10, Autumn 1990, pp.76–81.
Review of Brendan Kennelly, *Cromwell*, 5, Spring 1988, pp.164–6.

JORDAN, John
'Untitled' (P), 7, 1989, p.119.
Review of Tom Paulin, ed., *The Faber Book of Political Verse*, 3, Spring 1987, pp.90–100.

JOYCE, James
See Sergei Khoruzhii (A); John Nash (R).

JOYCE, Nora
See Riana O'Dwyer (R).

KAMIENSKA, Anna
See Jerzy Jarniewicz (R).

KANTARIS, Sylvia
See Bridget O'Toole (R).

KELLY, A. A.
See Bridget O'Toole (R).

KELLY, Conor
'Four Poems', 14, Winter 1993, pp.25–7.
Review of Desmond O'Grady, *Tipperary*; Peter Sirr, *Ways of Falling*, 13, 1992, pp.135–7. Review of Greg Delanty, *Southward*; Gerard Fanning, *Easter Snow*; Michael Hartnett, *The Killing of Dreams*, 14, Winter 1993, pp.73–80.

KELLY, John
'Four Poems', 6, Autumn 1988, pp.34–6.

KELLY, Rita
'Ar M'Éirí Dom Ar Maidin (On Rising in the Morning)' (P), with English translation by Aodán Mac Póilin, 8/9, 1990, p.54.
See also Domhnall Mitchell (R).

LEONARD, Tom
See Hayden Murphy (A).

LEVCHEV, Lyubomir
See Eoin Bourke (R).

LEVERTOV, Denise
See Bridget O'Toole (R).

LIDDY, John
'The Angling Cot' (P), with illustrations by David Lilburn, 5, Spring 1988, pp.122–31.

LIGHTMAN, Alan
See Pat Boran (R).

LILBURN, David
'Five Illustrations', with poem by John Liddy, 5, Spring 1988, pp.122–31.

LILLINGTON, Karlin J.
Review of Susan Faludi, *Backlash: The Undeclared War Against Women*, 15, Spring 1994, pp.93–6.

LINDSAY, Maurice
See Hayden Murphy (A).

LITTLE, Roger
Review of Yves Bonnefoy, *On the Motion and Immobility of Douve: Du mouvement et de l'immobilité de Douve*, tr. Galway Kinnell; René Char, *The Dawn Breakers: Les Matinaux*, ed. & tr. Michael Worton; Henri Michaux, *Spaced, Displaced: Déplacements dégagements*, trs. David and Helen Constantine; Jacques Dupin, *Selected Poems*, trs. Paul Auster, Stephen Romer, and David Shapiro, 14, Winter 1993, pp.84–7.
See also Yves Broussard (Tr).

LLEWELLYN, Kate
See Bridget O'Toole (R).

LONGLEY, Edna
'Edna Longley in Conversation with Carol Rumens' (I), 15, Spring 1994, pp.1–12.
Review of Peter Fallon and Derek Mahon, eds., *The Penguin Book of Contemporary Irish Poetry*, 10, Autumn 1990, pp.95–100.
See also Liam Harte (R); Lorna Reynolds (R); David Wheatley (R).

LONGLEY, Michael
'Five Poems', 5, Spring 1988, pp.45–9. 'Perdix' (P), 14, Winter 1993, pp.33–4.
'The State of Poetry' (A), 14, Winter 1993, p.33.
See also Tom Clyde (A); Nuala Ní Dhomhnaill (Tr).

LORCA, Federico García
See Brendan Kennelly (D).

LOUGHREY, Patrick
See Andy Pollak (R).

LOVELOCK, Yann
'Granada' (P), 3, Spring 1987, pp.84–5.
Review of Pierre Reverdy, *Selected Poems*, trs. Mary Ann Caws, Patricia Terry, and John Ashbery; Alistair Elliot, tr., *French Love Poems*, 13, 1992, pp.138–9.
See also Albert Maquet (Tr); Willem M. Roggeman (Tr).

LYNCH, Brian
Review of Paul Celan, *Poems of Paul Celan*, tr. Michael Hamburger, 8/9, 1990, pp.105–7.
See also Paul Celan (Tr).

LYSAGHT, Seán
'Three Poems', 6, Autumn 1988, pp.37–9.
Review of Paul Muldoon, *Selected Poems 1968–83*; John Hughes, *The Something in Particular*; Eiléan Ní Chuilleanáin, *The Second Voyage*, 3, Spring 1987, pp.107–11.

MacINNES, Mairi
See Bridget O'Toole (R).

MacINTYRE, Tom
'Snow White: Rehearsal Script One' (D), 5, Spring 1988, pp.51–6. 'The Word for Yes' (F), 10, Autumn 1990, pp.1–3. 'Four Poems', 12, Winter 1991, pp.39–41. 'Foggy Hair and Green Eyes' (D), 13, 1992, pp.61–76. 'Artist & Model' (P), 14, Winter 1993, p.37. 'From Aisling' (P), 18, 1995, pp.20–25. 'The State of Poetry' (A), 14, Winter 1993, pp.35–6. 'An Hour with WCW (William Carlos Williams)' (A), 18, 1995, pp.16–19.
See also John Scattergood (R).

McKANE, Richard
See Suzanne Krochalis (R).

McKEOWN, Michael
See W. J. McCormack (R).

MacLEAN, Sorley
See Robert Crawford (A); Hayden Murphy (A).

MacMATHÚNA, Seán
'Leaca an Tí Mhóir (The Flags of the Big House)' (F), with English translation by author and Aodán Mac Póilin, 5, Spring 1988, pp.140–48. 'The Thief of the Winter Night' (D), translated by Aodán Mac Póilin, 11, Summer 1991, pp.80–89.

McMILLAN, Hugh
'Three Poems' (P), 12, Winter 1991, pp.60–62.

McMINN, Joe
Review of Brian P. Kennedy, *Dreams and Responsibilities: The State and the Arts in Independent Ireland*; Nina Fitzpatrick, *Fables of the Irish Intelligentsia*, 12, Winter 1991, pp.98–100.

McNAMARA, Linda
'Custodian of the Blue Hours' (F), 8/9, 1990, pp.17–21.

MacNEACAIL, Aonghas
See Hayden Murphy (A).

McNULTY, Ted
'Three Poems', 18, 1995, pp.57–8.

Mac PÓILIN, Aodán
'The Glint of de Valera's Glasses, Part II' (Editorial), 5, Spring 1988. 'Foreword', 11, Summer 1991, pp.1–4. See also Rita Kelly (Tr); Seán MacMathúna (Tr); Tomás MacSíomóin (Tr); Caitlín Maude (Tr); Róise Ní Bhaoill (Tr); Áine Ní Ghlinn (Tr); Micheál Ó Conghaile (Tr); Cathal Ó Searcaigh (Tr); Seán Ó Tuama (Tr); Alan Titley (Tr).

MacSÍOMÓIN, Tomás
'Ceithre Dhán (Four Poems)', with English translations by Aodán Mac Póilin, 5, Spring 1988, pp.57–62. 'Poetry and Science: Cooperation or Conflict' (A), translated by Aodán Mac Póilin, 11, Summer 1991, pp.90–94.

MADDOX, Brenda
See Riana O'Dwyer (R).

MAGRIS, Claudio
See Eoin Bourke (R).

MAHER, Oliver
Review of Andrew Greig, *Electric Brae*; Juan Carlos Onetti, *A Brief Life*, 16/17, 1994, pp.150–51.

MAHON, Derek
See Tom Clyde (A); Edna Longley (R).

MAHON, Joseph
'Getting Records Straight: On Poetry, Biography and Truth' (A), 4, Autumn 1987, pp.35–41.

Gabriel Rosenstock, *Portrait of the Artist as an Abominable Snowman: Selected Poems*, 11, Summer 1991, pp.104–8.

MOFFATT, Deborah
'Harlan Prior's Fortune' (F), 15, Spring 1994, pp.78–82.

MOHR, Jean
See John Carlos (R).

MOLLOY, Frances
See Eve Patten (A).

MONTAGUE, John
'Two Poems', 6, Autumn 1988, pp.63–4.
See also Tom Clyde (A); Brian John (R); Domhnall Mitchell (A).

MOONEY, Martin
'The Lost Apprentice' (P), 14, Winter 1993, p.48.
'The State of Poetry' (A), 14, Winter 1993, p.48.

MORGAN, Edwin
See Robert Crawford (A); Hayden Murphy (A).

MORRISON, Toni
See Jennifer Fitzgerald (R).

MORRISSEY, Sinéad
Review of Maria Razumovsky, *Marina Tsvetayeva*, 18, 1995, pp.115–17.

MROZEK, Slawomir
See Dusan Simko (A).

MULDOON, Paul
See Terence Brown (A); Harry Clifton (A); Seán Lysaght (R); Elizabeth Mahoney (R).

MULGREW, Geraldine
'Three Tales' (F), 4, Autumn 1987, pp.50–55. 'Evening Herald' (F), 8/9, 1990, pp.31–3. 'Door' (F), 'Coffee Beans' (F), 'Los Olvidados' (F), 15, Spring 1994, pp.13–21.

MULREANY, Michael
Review of Veronica Jane O'Meara, ed., *PS....Of Course: Patrick Swift 1927–1983*; James White, *Gerard Dillon: An Illustrated Biography*; Brian Fallon, *Irish Art 1830–1990*, 18, 1995, pp.112–14.

MURPHY, Hayden
'An Irishman Considers Scotland: Festivals and Funerals' (A), authors include Tom Leonard, Norman MacCaig, Sorley MacLean, Aonghas Macneacail, Edwin Morgan and Tom Scott, among others, 10, Autumn 1990, pp.101–9. 'Contemporary Scottish Poetry' (A), authors include David Macleod Black, Tom Buchan, Stewart Conn, Robert Crawford, Douglas Dunn, Ian Hamilton Finlay, W. S. Graham, Alan Jackson, Maurice Lindsay, George MacBeth, Hugh MacDiarmid, Walter Perrie, Alistair Reid and Kenneth White, 13, 1992, pp.108–22.

MURPHY, Judy
Review of Trudy Hayes, *The Politics of Seduction*; Ethna Viney, *Ancient Wars*; Clodagh Corcoran, *Pornography: The New Terrorism*; Ruth Riddick, *The Right to Choose*, 8/9, 1990, pp.136–8.

MURPHY, Thomas (Tom)
'Lullaby' (P), 5, Spring 1988, p.78.
See also Hugh O'Donnell (R).

MURRAY, Christopher
Review of Frank McGuinness, *Carthaginians* and *Baglady*, 7, 1989, pp.100–103.
See also Hugh O'Donnell (R).

MURRAY, Les A.
'Aspects of Language and War on the Gloucester Road' (P), 5, Spring 1988, pp.9–13.
'Aspects of Life & Language: Interview with Gerald Dawe' (I), 5, Spring 1988, pp.1–8.
'Only a Flat Earth has Margins: Footnotes on a Deadly Metaphor' (A), 18, 1995, pp.1–15.
See also Robert Crawford (R); Gerald Dawe (A).

Ó DIREÁIN, Máirtín
See Domhnall Mitchell (R); Seán Ó Tuama (A).

O'DONNELL, Hugh
Review of Thomas Murphy, *Conversations on a Homecoming,* and *Bailegangaire*; Fintan O'Toole, *The Politics of Magic: The Work and Times of Tom Murphy*; Christopher Murray, ed., *Irish University Review: Thomas Murphy Issue,* 5, Spring 1988, pp.79–87.

O'DONNELL, Mary E.
'Five Poems', 3, Spring 1987, pp.44–8.
See also Kevin Smith (R).

O'DONOGHUE, Bernard
See Stephen Matterson (R).

O'DONOGHUE, Gregory
'Two Poems', 18, 1995, pp.50–51.

O'DRISCOLL, Ciaran
'Four Poems', 10, Autumn 1990, pp.41–2.

O'DRISCOLL, Dennis
'Daydreaming at Work about the Tyrone Guthrie Centre' (P), 14, Winter 1993, p.55.
'An Interview with Miroslav Holub' (I), 10, Autumn 1990, pp.13–20.
'W.S. Graham: Professor of Silence' (A), 6, Autumn 1988, pp.48–58. 'Obiter Poetica: *From a Poetry Sketchbook*' (A), 14, Winter 1993, pp.1–5. 'Ten-point Thoughts on the State of Poetry' (A), 14, Winter 1993, pp.54–5.
Review of György Petri, *Night Song of the Personal Shadow*; Piotr Sommer, *Things to Translate,* 13, 1992, pp.131–4. Review of William Cookson, ed., *Agenda: An Anthology,* 18, 1995, pp.77–9.
See also Jill Siddall (R).

Ó DÚILL, Gréagóir
'Ceithre Dhán (Four Poems)', with English translations by author, 5, Spring 1988, pp.103–6.

O'DWYER, Riana
Review of Brenda Maddox, *Nora: A Biography of Nora Joyce,* and *Nora: The Real Life of Molly Bloom,* 8/9, 1990, pp.114–18.

O'GRADY, Desmond
'Ezra Pound at Venice: Three Poems', 10, Autumn 1990, pp.110–15.
See also Conor Kelly (R).

O'HARA, Frank
See Gerald Dawe (A).

Ó hEITHIR, Brendán
See W. J. McCormack (R).

O'LOUGHLIN, Michael
'Snapshots from Jewish Amsterdam' (P), 14, Winter 1993, pp.57–60.
'The State of Poetry' (A), 14, Winter 1993, pp.56–7.
See also Harry Clifton (A).

O'MALLEY, Des
See Thomas McCarthy (R).

O'MALLEY, Mary
'*From* The Cloven Rock' (P) 8/9, 1990, pp.71–3.

O'MEARA, Veronica Jane
See Michael Mulreany (R).

Ó MUIRTHILE, Liam
'Trí Dhán (Three Poems)', with English translations by Gabriel Rosenstock, 5, Spring 1988, pp.160–63.

O'NEILL, Karl
'Spits of Rain' (F), 16/17, 1994, pp.86–9.

PEARSE, Padraig
See Seán Ó Tuama (A).

PERRIE, Walter
See Hayden Murphy (A).

PERSSON, Åke
Review of Brendan Kennelly, *The Book of Judas*, 12, Winter 1991, pp.108–10.

PETRI, György
See Dennis O'Driscoll (R).

PIESSE, Amanda
Review of Helen Dunmore, *Recovering a Body*; Kathleen Jamie, *The Queen of Sheba*; Carol Rumens, *Thinking of Skins*, 18, 1995, pp.90–94.

PLATH, Sylvia
See Julia Carlson (R).

POLLAK, Andy
Review of Robert G. Crawford, *Loyal to King Billy: A Portrait of the Ulster Protestants*; Patrick Loughrey, ed., *The People of Ireland*, 6, Autumn 1988, pp.70–73.

POOLE, John
'The Night Burl Ives Got Lost' (F), 16/17, 1994, pp.15–23.

PORTER, Peter
See Stephen Matterson (R).

POUND, Ezra
See Raymond Burke (R); Desmond O'Grady (P).

PRICE, Dolours
'Afraid of the Dark' (F), 3, Spring 1987, pp.7–13.
Review of Claire Tomalin, *Katherine Mansfield: A Secret Life*, 5, Spring 1988, pp.41–4.

PRITCHARD, Selwyn
'Cultural Monuments: A Sequence of Six Poems', 5, Spring 1988, pp.149–54.

PROULX, E. Annie
See P. J. Tynan (R).

PYBUS, Rodney
See Seán Dunne (R).

QUINN, Niall
See Victoria White (R).

QUINN, Vincent
'Heart Like a Wheel' (F), 16/17, 1994, pp.123–31.

RAMSEY, Patrick
'Here and Now — Literature and the North' (A), 10, Autumn 1990, pp.85–9.

RAZUMOVSKY, Maria
See Sinéad Morrissey (R).

READING, Peter
See Stephen Matterson (R).

REANEY, Padraic
'The Garden' (Five Graphics), 4, Autumn 1987, pp.46–9. 'Illustration', 10, Autumn 1990. 'Cover Illustration', 11, Summer 1991.

REDMOND, Lucille
'Fish' (F), 16/17, 1994, pp.35–40.

SCHREIBMAN, Susan
'Thomas MacGreevy: Keeping the Faith' (A), 8/9, 1990, pp.86–93.

SCOTT, Malcolm
Review of Reg Hindley, *The Death of the Irish Language*; Éamon Ó Ciosáin, *Buried Alive: A Reply to 'The Death of the Irish Language'*, 11, Summer 1991, pp.109–12.

SCOTT, Tom
See Hayden Murphy (A).

SEFERIS, George
See Henry Gifford (A).

SHEERIN, Joe
'Three poems', 6, Autumn 1988, pp.41–2.

SHEPPERSON, Janet
Review of David Marcus, ed., *State of the Art: Short Stories by the New Irish Writers*, 15, Spring 1994, pp.102–4.

SHORT, Constance
'Cover Illustration'; 'Dance Sequence: Aspects of Maternity' (Six Illustrations), 15, Spring 1994, pp.60–66.

SIDDALL, Jill
'Strings of the Fathers' (F), 15, Spring 1994, pp.50–56.
Review of Gerald Dawe, ed., *The New Younger Irish Poets*, authors include Sara Berkeley, Rita Ann Higgins, Julie O'Callaghan, Dennis O'Driscoll and Kevin Smith, 12, Winter 1991, pp.111–13.

SILGARDO, Melanie
See Kathleen McCracken (R).

SIMKO, Dusan
'Slavonia on the Seine' (A), authors include Danilo Kis, Vladimir Maximov, Slawomir Mrozek, Andrei Sinyavsky and Jan Vladislav, among others; photographs by Ladislav Drezdowicz, 2, Autumn 1986, pp.51–62.

SINCLAIR, Maureen
'Two Poems', 15, Spring 1994, pp.83–5.

SINYAVSKY, Andrei
See Dusan Simko (A).

SIRR, Peter
'Three Poems', 14, Winter 1993, pp.61–3.
Review of Iain Crichton Smith, *Collected Poems*, 14, Winter 1993, pp.81–3.
See also Conor Kelly (R).

SMITH, Iain Crichton
'Six Poems', 3, Spring 1987, pp.1–5. 'Murdo Speaks' (F), 12, Winter 1991, pp.26–38.
See also Robert Crawford (A); Peter Sirr (R).

SMITH, Kevin
Review of Sam Burnside, *Walking the Marches*; Theo Dorgan, *The Ordinary House of Love*; Roy McFadden, *After Seymour's Funeral*; Mary O'Donnell, *Reading the Sunflowers in September*, 12, Winter 1991, pp.114–16.
See also Jill Siddall (R).

SMITH, Michael
See Lorna Reynolds (A).

SMYTH, Gerard
'Three Poems', 6, Autumn 1988, pp.43–4.

SOMMER, Piotr
See Dennis O'Driscoll (R).

SORESCU, Marin
See Eoin Bourke (R).

STEVENSON, Anne
See Julia Carlson (R).

WEÖRES, Sándor
See Hugh Maxton (Tr); Micheál O'Siadhail (R).

WHEATLEY, David
Review of Edna Longley, *The Living Stream*, 18, 1995, pp.108–11.

WHITE, James
See Michael Mulreany (R).

WHITE, Kenneth
See Hayden Murphy (A).

WHITE, Victoria
Review of Allan Massie, *The Novel Today: A Critical Guide to the British Novel 1970–1989*; Niall Quinn, *The Cafe Cong*, 12, Winter 1991, pp.117–19.

WILLIAMS, Raymond
See Joe Ducke (A); Stephen Matterson (A).

WILLIAMS, William Carlos
See Tom MacIntyre (A).

WILMER, Stephen
'Travesties: Ideologies and the Irish Theatre Renaissance' (A), 13, 1992, pp.83–92.

WRIGHT, James
See Patrick Meanor (A).

YOUNG, Augustus
'The Brian Coffey Cordel' (P), 13, 1992, pp.42–51. 'Four Poems', 14, Winter 1993, pp.66–8. 'Three Poems', 18, 1995, pp.52–4.
'The Love of the Drudgery' (A), on 'the state of poetry' in Ireland, 14, Winter 1993, pp.64–6.

ZELL, Ann
'Three Poems', 15, Spring 1994, pp.57–9.

ACKNOWLEDGMENTS

The Editors wish to thank all the authors for permission to use their copyright material in this anthology. Grateful acknowledgment is made to the following publishers:

The Blackstaff Press for 'Insomnia in the Afternoon' by Michael Foley.

Bloodaxe Books for 'Content and Tasteful' from *What's What* by Julia O'Callaghan (1991), and 'There Came a Pleasant Rain' by Brendan Kennelly.

Carcanet Publishers for 'Aspects of Language and War on the Gloucester Road' by Les Murray from *Collected Poems* and for 'The Woman Poet: Her Dilemma' by Eavan Boland from *Object Lessons*.

Cló-Chonnachta Teo for permission to use 'Sneachta'/'Snow', 'Muirbhé'/'Sea-woman', 'Aon Séasúr den Bhliain'/'Any Season of the Year' by Cathal Ó Searcaigh.

Dedalus Press for 'Is this a Safe Place, or What?' from *Easter Snow* by Gerard Fanning.

Faber & Faber for 'The Creamery Manager' by John McGahern from *The Collected Stories* and 'Fathers and Sons' by Brian Friel from *Fathers and Sons*.

The Gallery Press for 'Pacific Legend' and 'Up So Doun' by John Montague from *Collected Poems* (1995); 'A Northern Spring' and 'At the Jaffé Memorial Fountain, Botanic Gardens' from *A Northern Spring* (1986); 'The Walled Town' by Harry Clifton from *Night-Train through the Brenner* (1994); 'The History of Rain' by Conor O'Callaghan from *The History of Rain* (1993); 'The Bright Hour' by Gerald Dawe from *Sunday School* (1991); 'If Luck Were Corn' by Peter Fallon from *The News and Weather* (1987); 'I Thought It was Still February' by Medbh McGuckian; 'Nagasaki' and 'The Royal Asylum' by John Hughes from *Negotiations with the Chill Wind* (1991), and 'Jeremiad'; 'The Word for Yes' by Tom MacIntyre from *The Word for Yes* (1991), and '69'; 'Lullaby' by Frank McGuinness from *Booterstown* (1994) and 'Sister Anne Breslin' and 'Prisoner of War'; 'Revolutions' by Michael Coady; 'Memorials' by Eiléan Ní Chuilleanáin from *Site of Ambush* (1975), and 'A Note'; 'Night Walk' and 'Autobiography' by Paula Meehan from *Pillow Talk* (1994); 'From a Disused House' by Vona Groarke from *Shale* (1994); 'Aubade', a translation of Nuala Ní Dhomhnaill by Michael Longley from *Pharaoh's Daughter* (1990).

New Island Books for 'Bartolomé' by Sara Berkeley from *Amsterdam*; 'Snapshots from Jewish Amsterdam' by Michael O'Loughlin; 'Nesting' by Angela Bourke from *By Salt Water* (1996); 'An Díbeartach' and 'An Focal' by Michael Davitt.

Peters, Fraser & Dunlop for 'Perdix' and 'An Amish Rug' by Michael Longley from *Gorse Fires* (Secker & Warburg).

Reed Books for 'Coolgrange' by John Banville, 'Divers at the Laurentic' by Matthew Sweeney (Secker & Warburg) and 'Laura' by Jennifer Johnston (Sinclair-Stevenson).

Rogers, Coleridge & White Ltd for 'Quiet Waters: A Journey Home' by Des Hogan.

Salmon Publishing for 'Ezra Pound at Venice' by Desmond O'Grady.

The publishers have used their best efforts to trace all copyright-holders and have sought and received permission from each contributor in this anthology. However, they will make the usual and appropriate arrangements with any who may have been overlooked inadvertently and who contact them.